# LIBRARY OF HEBREW BIBLE/
# OLD TESTAMENT STUDIES

# 722

*Formerly Journal for the Study of the Old Testament Supplement Series*

*Editors*
Laura Quick, Oxford University, UK
Jacqueline Vayntrub, Yale University, USA

*Founding Editors*
David J. A. Clines, Philip R. Davies and David M. Gunn

*Editorial Board*
Sonja Ammann, Alan Cooper, Steed Davidson, Susan Gillingham,
Rachelle Gilmour, John Goldingay, Rhiannon Graybill, Anne Katrine Gudme,
Norman K. Gottwald, James E. Harding, John Jarick, Tracy Lemos,
Carol Meyers, Eva Mroczek, Daniel L. Smith-Christopher,
Francesca Stavrakopoulou, James W. Watts

# LOANWORDS IN BIBLICAL LITERATURE

## Rhetorical Studies in Esther, Daniel, Ezra and Exodus

Jonathan Thambyrajah

LONDON • NEW YORK • OXFORD • NEW DELHI • SYDNEY

**T&T CLARK**
Bloomsbury Publishing Plc
50 Bedford Square, London, WC1B 3DP, UK
1385 Broadway, New York, NY 10018, USA
29 Earlsfort Terrace, Dublin 2, Ireland

BLOOMSBURY, T&T CLARK and the T&T Clark logo
are trademarks of Bloomsbury Publishing Plc

First published in Great Britain 2023
Paperback edition published 2024

Copyright © Jonathan Thambyrajah, 2023, 2024

Jonathan Thambyrajah has asserted his right under the Copyright, Designs and Patents Act, 1988, to be identified as Author of this work.

For legal purposes the Acknowledgements on p. xiii constitute an extension of this copyright page.

All rights reserved. No part of this publication may be reproduced or transmitted in any form or by any means, electronic or mechanical, including photocopying, recording, or any information storage or retrieval system, without prior permission in writing from the publishers.

Bloomsbury Publishing Plc does not have any control over, or responsibility for, any third-party websites referred to or in this book. All internet addresses given in this book were correct at the time of going to press. The author and publisher regret any inconvenience caused if addresses have changed or sites have ceased to exist, but can accept no responsibility for any such changes.

A catalogue record for this book is available from the British Library.
Library of Congress Control Number: 2022933746

ISBN: HB: 978-0-5677-0306-4
PB: 978-0-5677-0309-5
ePDF: 978-0-5677-0307-1

Series: Library of Hebrew Bible/Old Testament Studies, volume 722
ISSN 2513-8758

Typeset by Trans.form.ed SAS

To find out more about our authors and books visit www.bloomsbury.com and sign up for our newsletters.

Χριστῷ γὰρ σωτῆρι τέ μου καὶ ἐμοῦ θεῷ εἶεν
αἰεί δόξα πολλὴ καὶ δύναμις μεγάλη.

## Contents

| | |
|---|---|
| List of Tables | xi |
| Acknowledgements | xiii |
| List of Abbreviations | xv |

**1**
**INTRODUCTION** ................................................................. 1
  1.1. Linguistics, philology and literature ............................. 1
  1.2. Existing research on loanwords in the Hebrew Bible ... 2
     1.2.1. Aramaic .................................................................. 3
     1.2.2. Akkadian and Sumerian ........................................ 6
     1.2.3. Non-Semitic languages .......................................... 7
  1.3. Linguistics and rhetoric ................................................ 10
     1.3.1. Applying linguistics to literary texts ..................... 10
     1.3.2. Variation ............................................................... 11
     1.3.3. Rhetorical approaches to the Hebrew Bible ......... 12
     1.3.4. Rhetorical approaches to narrative texts .............. 14
     1.3.5. Rhetorical figures ................................................. 15
     1.3.6. Synthesis ............................................................... 19

**2**
**THE LOANWORDS** ............................................................. 20
  2.1. Nativization of the loanwords ....................................... 20
  2.2. Identifying loanwords and the direction of borrowing .. 23
     2.2.1. Some additional observations on identifying loanwords ... 24
  2.3. The loanwords in Esther ............................................... 26
  2.4. The loanwords in Daniel ............................................... 57
  2.5. The loanwords in Ezra .................................................. 91
  2.6. The loanwords in Exodus .............................................. 109
  2.7. Language of origin ....................................................... 134
  2.8. Native synonyms .......................................................... 136
     2.8.1. The contrast between loanwords and native synonyms, implicature and creating a literary effect ... 137
     2.8.2. The semantic field of palaces in Hebrew and Aramaic ... 139
     2.8.3. Loanwords and literary effect ............................... 142

## 3
### TEXT ANALYSIS – LOANWORDS AS A MEANS FOR GROUP MAINTENANCE  143
3.1. Loanwords as a rhetorical tool for the construction of ethno-linguistic identity  143
   3.1.1. Must the loanwords have literary effect?  143
   3.1.2. How the loanwords function as a literary device  145
   3.1.3. Loanwords in literature and history  146
   3.1.4. Constructions of ethnic identity in the Hebrew Bible  146
3.2. Depicting empire, defining the other  150
   3.2.1. Loanwords: a literary tool for commenting on other nations  150
   3.2.2. Audience – Esther  150
   3.2.3. Audience – Daniel  152
   3.2.4. Loanwords in Esther and Daniel  155
3.3. Depicting empire, defining the group  186
   3.3.1. Loanwords: a literary tool for commenting on the audience's relationship to other nations  186
   3.3.2. Audience – Ezra–Nehemiah  187
   3.3.3. Ezra 1–7  189
   3.3.4. Conclusion: the loanwords create a sense of linguistic identity as a part of the group identity  205
3.4. Depicting the past, defining the group  206
   3.4.1. Loanwords: a literary tool for defining the group's shared past  206
   3.4.2. Audience – Exodus  207
   3.4.3. Exodus 25–40  208
   3.4.4. Conclusion: the loanwords highlight the group's shared history in foreign lands  228

### CONCLUSIONS  229

### APPENDIX ONE:
### ROOT CONSTRAINTS AND THE SHARED VOCABULARY OF ARAMAIC AND HEBREW  231

### APPENDIX TWO:
### LISTS AND DISTRIBUTION OF LOANWORDS AND FOREIGN NAMES IN ESTHER  234

### APPENDIX THREE:
### LISTS AND DISTRIBUTION OF LOANWORDS IN DANIEL  239

### APPENDIX FOUR:
### LISTS AND DISTRIBUTION OF LOANWORDS IN EZRA 1–7  244

APPENDIX FIVE:
LISTS AND DISTRIBUTION OF LOANWORDS IN EXODUS 25–40        247

APPENDIX SIX:
AN OUTLINE OF LINGUISTIC CHANGE IN ARAMAIC AND AKKADIAN    250

Bibliography                                                257
Index of Subjects                                           276
Index of Biblical Passages                                  279
Index of Non-Biblical Ancient Sources                       291
Index of Loanwords in Esther, Daniel, Ezra 1–7 and Exodus 25–40   293
Index of Words from Ancient Languages                       295

# TABLES

| Table 1 | The Distribution of the Loanwords in the Book of Esther | 159 |
| Table 2 | The Distribution of the Loanwords in the Book of Daniel | 165 |
| Table 3 | Lists in Daniel | 170 |
| Table 4 | Lists in Esther | 172 |
| Table 5 | The Distribution of the Loanwords in Ezra 1–7 | 190 |
| Table 6 | The Distribution of the Loanwords in Exodus 25–40 | 216 |
| Table 7 | Inherited Semitic Roots that are Distinguishable in Hebrew and Aramaic | 232 |
| Table 8 | Loanwords in Esther | 234 |
| Table 9 | Foreign Names in Esther | 235 |
| Table 10 | Loanwords in Daniel | 239 |
| Table 11 | Foreign Names in Daniel | 241 |
| Table 12 | Loanwords in Ezra 1–7 | 244 |
| Table 13 | Foreign Names in Ezra 1–7 | 245 |
| Table 14 | Loanwords in Exodus 25–40 | 247 |
| Table 15 | Northwest Semitic Consonants in Hebrew and Aramaic | 251 |

ACKNOWLEDGEMENTS

I owe gratitude to many people for their support as I wrote this book. In the first place, I give my thanks to Ian Young and Rachelle Gilmour, who, when this book was a dissertation, provided guidance and advice as my supervisors. In the same spirit, I am grateful to all those teachers (Ian included) who sparked in me a love for all ancient languages, but for Hebrew in particular.

I am also grateful to my brothers and to Dan Butler, Kat Butler, Rob Falls and Andrew Payne, without whom I would not have made it through the second year of my PhD. My family and my church, too, have helped more than I can express concisely or neatly. Among many other things, they taught me to love the Bible. More than anyone else, I am thankful to my extraordinary wife, Shell. In all things I am grateful to God, from whom every good gift comes.

# Abbreviations

| | |
|---|---|
| AB | Anchor Bible |
| *AnSt* | *Anatolian Studies* |
| AS | Assyriological Studies |
| *BASOR* | *Bulletin of the American Schools of Oriental Research* |
| *BBR* | *Bulletin for Biblical Research* |
| BDB | Brown, Francis, Samuel Driver and Charles Briggs. *A Hebrew and English Lexicon of the Old Testament*. Oxford: Clarendon, 1907. |
| *BibInt* | *Biblical Interpretation* |
| BKAT | Biblischer Kommentar, Altes Testament. Edited by Martin Noth and Hans Wolff. |
| *BO* | *Bibliotheca orientalis* |
| CAD | *The Assyrian Dictionary of the Oriental Institute of the University of Chicago*. Edited by Martha Roth, et al. 21 vols. Chicago: Oriental Institute, 1956–2010. |
| CAL | *Comprehensive Aramaic Lexicon*. Stephen Kaufman, et al. Hebrew Union College. http://cal.huc.edu. |
| *CBQ* | *Catholic Biblical Quarterly* |
| CDD | *The Demotic Dictionary of the Oriental Institute of the University of Chicago*. Edited by Janet Johnson. 30 vols. Chicago: Oriental Institute, 2001. |
| CSJH | Chicago Studies in the History of Judaism |
| DJD | Discoveries in the Judaean Desert |
| *DNWSI* | *Dictionary of the North-West Semitic Inscriptions*. Jacob Hoftijzer and Karel Jongeling. HO 21. 2 vols. Leiden: Brill, 2003. |
| FAT II | Forschungen zum Alten Testament (Series II) |
| *HALOT* | *The Hebrew and Aramaic Lexicon of the Old Testament*. Ludwig Koehler, Walter Baumgartner and Johann Stamm. Translated and edited under the supervision of Mervyn Richardson. 2 vols. Leiden: Brill, 2001. |
| HDR | Harvard Dissertations in Religion |
| HO | Handbuch der Orientalistik |
| *HS* | *Hebrew Studies* |
| HSS | Harvard Semitic Studies |
| *HTR* | *Harvard Theological Review* |
| IBC | Interpretation: A Bible Commentary for Teaching and Preaching |
| *IEJ* | *Israel Exploration Journal* |
| Int | Interpretation |

| | |
|---|---|
| *JA* | *Journal asiatique* |
| *JANESCU* | *Journal of the Ancient Near Eastern Society of Columbia University* |
| *JAOS* | *Journal of the American Oriental Society* |
| *JBL* | *Journal of Biblical Literature* |
| *JHS* | *Journal of the Hebrew Scriptures* |
| *JJS* | *Journal of Jewish Studies* |
| *JNES* | *Journal of Near Eastern Studies* |
| *JNSL* | *Journal of Northwest Semitic Languages* |
| *JQR* | *Jewish Quarterly Review* |
| *JSJ* | *Journal for the Study of Judaism in the Persian, Hellenistic, and Roman Periods* |
| *JSOT* | *Journal for the Study of the Old Testament* |
| JSOTSup | Journal for the Study of the Old Testament: Supplement Series |
| *JSS* | *Journal of Semitic Studies* |
| *JTS* | *Journal of Theological Studies* |
| *JTS (NS)* | *Journal of Theological Studies (New Series)* |
| KAT | Kommentar zum Alten Testament |
| *Leš* | *Lešonénu* |
| *MGWJ* | *Monatschrift für Geschichte und Wissenschaft des Judentums* |
| NCBC | New Century Bible Commentary |
| NICOT | New International Commentary on the Old Testament |
| OLA | Orientalia lovaniensia analecta |
| *OLZ* | *Orientalistische Literaturzeitung* |
| *Or (NS)* | *Orientalia (Nova Series)* |
| OTL | Old Testament Library |
| *OtSt* | *Oudtestamentische Studiën* |
| *RB* | *Revue biblique* |
| *REA* | *Revue des études anciennes* |
| *REJ* | *Revue des études juives* |
| *RevQ* | *Revue de Qumran* |
| SBLDS | Society of Biblical Literature Dissertation Series |
| SBLMS | Society of Biblical Literature Monograph Series |
| *SJOT* | *Scandinavian Journal of the Old Testament* |
| *SubBi* | *Subsidia biblica* |
| *VT* | *Vetus Testamentum* |
| VTSup | Supplements to Vetus Testamentum |
| WBC | Word Biblical Commentary |
| *WO* | *Welt des Orient* |
| *ZAH* | *Zeitschrift für Althebräistik* |
| *ZAW* | *Zeitschrift für die alttestamentliche Wissenschaft* |
| *ZDMG* | *Zeitschrift der deutschen morgenländischen Gesellschaft* |

1

INTRODUCTION

1.1. *Linguistics, philology and literature*

Loanwords are a contact linguistic phenomenon and a means of lexical innovation. Therefore, loanwords, in the abstract sense, are within the realm of linguistic study. Nevertheless, this is not merely an examination of Hebrew loanwords, as previous studies have been, but rather an examination of loanwords in a specific text, the Hebrew Bible. This distinction introduces literature into the discussion: because we are concerned with a text that constitutes literature, it becomes necessary to consider loanwords in the light of their literary effect.

In particular, we are using a rhetorical approach to the Bible to be able to better bridge the gap between linguistic and literary approaches to the Bible: rhetorical approaches pay attention to small details of the text and their potential to impact the audience. Because of the former, it is possible to take into account small linguistic differences. Because of the latter it is possible to take into account both sides of the 'conversation' between text and audience in the same way that certain branches of linguistics – sociolinguistics, pragmatics – take into account the recipient or audience of language.

Although there are a variety of literary purposes for which loanwords might be adapted, the one with which this study is particularly concerned is the use of loanwords as a means to express ethno-linguistic identity. As we shall see, one of the properties of loanwords is their capacity to be linked, consciously or unconsciously, to the language and culture from which they were drawn. This capacity makes loanwords an ideal tool for a text that is interested in making ethno-linguistic distinctions. Loanwords can be used to draw attention to the differences between Hebrew-speakers and foreigners, to define the audience of the text according to its multilingual capabilities and to capitalize on a group's shared identity based on stories set in the lands of people of other linguistic communities. Each of these cases is interested in constructing the boundaries of who is a part of its audience.

We shall examine four texts from the Hebrew Bible. In Daniel and Esther, the texts' use of loanwords allows their Jewish protagonists to stand apart from their setting. In the first seven chapters of Ezra, loanwords (together with the use of Aramaic) signal different contexts for language use, but also establish solidarity between the text's narrator and its audience. Finally, in Exodus, we are presented with loanwords which draw attention to the centrality of exodus motifs in the tabernacle's construction and the covenant.

### 1.2. *Existing research on loanwords in the Hebrew Bible*

Existing loanword research in the Hebrew Bible has focused almost exclusively on the lexical and linguistic aspects of the topic; aspects such as literary effect have been neglected. While there are a few, mostly recent, works which consider loanwords from all source languages, most works – especially earlier works – limited themselves to a single language. Because of this initial division of labour, the development of thought has differed somewhat between the separate discussions on the various languages. Thus, for example, it has been more characteristic of work on Aramaisms to consider the precise method which is used to identify loanwords. On the other hand, in the work on Aramaisms it has been less important to consider the historical situations that provide the opportunity for borrowing – unlike, for example, the work on Persianisms. These differences are exactly as would be expected; given how closely Aramaic- and Hebrew-speakers were located geographically, there is no need to justify the historical plausibility of borrowing. Given that Persian and Hebrew belong to different language families, argument from correspondence of form is much stronger in the case of Persianisms than in the cases of Akkadianisms and Aramaisms.

Of the existing works which cover multiple languages,[1] the following deserve particular mention: the first is Ellenbogen's *Foreign Words in*

---

1. Samuel Boyd, 'Contact and Context: Studies in Language Contact and Literary Strata in the Hebrew Bible' (PhD diss., The University of Chicago, 2014); Maximillian Ellenbogen, *Foreign Words in the Old Testament, their Origin and Etymology* (London: Lowe & Brydone, 1957); Benjamin Noonan, 'Foreign Loanwords and *Kulturwörter* in Northwest Semitic (1400–600 B.C.E.): Linguistic and Cultural Contact in Light of Terminology for Realia' (PhD diss., Hebrew Union College,

*the Old Testament*, which although old is often correct in its hypotheses. The second is Noonan's thesis, 'Foreign Loanwords and *Kulturwörter* in Northwest Semitic (1400–600 B.C.E.): Linguistic and Cultural Contact in Light of Terminology for Realia', and more recent book *Non-Semitic Loanwords in the Hebrew Bible: A Lexicon of Language Contact*. Each of Noonan's contributions is not quite comprehensive (but nevertheless important): the former does not treat non-realia, such as professions, and the latter does not treat Aramaic or Akkadian loanwords.

1.2.1. *Aramaic*
There have been very many scholars to address the Aramaisms of the Hebrew Bible.[2] One particular concern has been for the use of Aramaisms

2012); Benjamin Noonan, *Non-Semitic Loanwords in the Hebrew Bible: A Lexicon of Language Contact*, Linguistic Studies in Ancient West Semitic 14 (University Park: Eisenbrauns, 2019); Cory Peacock, 'Akkadian Loanwords in the Hebrew Bible: Social and Historical Implications' (PhD diss., New York University, 2013); Chaim Rabin, 'מלים זרות [Foreign Words],' in אנציקלופדיה מקראית [*Encyclopedia Biblica*], 9 vols (Jerusalem: Mosad Bialik, 1950–88), 4:1070–80; Robert Wilson, 'Foreign Words in the Old Testament as an Evidence of Historicity', *The Princeton Theological Review* 26 (1928): 177–247; Ian Young, Robert Rezetko and Martin Ehrensvärd, 'Aramaic', in *Linguistic Dating of Biblical Texts* (London: Equinox, 2008), 1:201–22; Young, Rezetko and Ehrensvärd, 'Loanwords', in *Linguistic Dating*, 1:280–311. Additionally, various articles in the *Encyclopedia of Hebrew Language and Linguistics* (*EHLL*): Thamar Gindin, 'Persian Loanwords', in *EHLL*, 3:66–70; Shai Heijmans, 'Greek Loanwords', in *EHLL*, 2:148–51; Dennis Kurzon, 'Indian Loanwords', in *EHLL*, 2:263–64; Paul Mankowski, 'Akkadian Loanwords', in *EHLL*, 1:82–84; Gary Rendsburg, 'Cultural Words: Biblical Hebrew', in *EHLL*, 1:640–42; Aaron Rubin, 'Egyptian Loanwords', in *EHLL*, 1:793–94; Aaron Rubin, 'Sumerian Loanwords', in *EHLL*, 3:665–66; Talya Shitrit, 'Aramaic Loanwords and Borrowing', in *EHLL*, 1:165–69.
    2. Gesenius has been credited as one of the first modern scholars to address the Aramaisms of the Hebrew Bible (Emil Kautzsch, *Die Aramaismen im Alten Testament: 1. Lexikalischer Teil* [Halle an der Saale: Max Niemeyer, 1902], 1) and Max Wagner (*Die Lexikalischen und Grammatikalischen Aramaismen im Alttestamentlichen Hebräisch* [Berlin: Töpelmann, 1966], 8) provides a summary of contributors to the topic in the nineteenth and twentieth centuries. Important modern works include: Kautzsch, *Die Aramaismen*; Theodor Nöldecke, 'Kautzsch' Aramaismen im Alten Testament', review of *Die Aramaismen im Alten Testament*, by Emil Kautzsch, *Zeitschrift der Deutschen Morgenländischen Gesellschaft* 57 (1903): 412–20; Wagner, *Die Lexikalischen*; Robert Wilson, 'Aramaisms in the Old Testament', *The Princeton Theological Review* 23, no. 2 (1925): 234–66.

in dating biblical texts.³ Driver also made a significant contribution to the topic with his article, 'Hebrew Poetic Diction', with the suggestion that Hebrew shares a poetic register with Aramaic.⁴ However, this work suffers extensively from arguments from silence.⁵

---

3. The most prominent modern proponent of Aramaisms' relevance to the dating of texts – though with several conditions imposed – is Hurvitz; see, for example, Avi Hurvitz, 'The Chronological Significance of Aramaisms in Biblical Hebrew', *IEJ* 18 (1968): 234–40, and 'Hebrew and Aramaic in the Biblical Period: The Problem of "Aramaisms" in Linguistic Research on the Hebrew Bible', in *Biblical Hebrew: Studies in Chronology and Typology*, ed. Ian Young (London: T&T Clark International, 2003), 24–37. Further, Ekshult applies this principle to loanwords in general, in Mats Ekshult, 'The Importance of Loanwords for Dating Biblical Hebrew Texts', in Young, ed., *Biblical Hebrew*, 8–23. For a convincing critique of this approach see both Robert Rezetko and Ian Young, *Historical Linguistics and Biblical Hebrew: Steps Towards an Integrated Approach*, Ancient Near Eastern Monographs 9 (Atlanta: SBL, 2014) and Young, Rezetko and Ehrensvärd, *Linguistic Dating*.

4. Godfrey Driver, 'Hebrew Poetic Diction', in *Congress Volume: Copenhagen, 1953*, VTSup 1 (Leiden: Brill, 1953), 26–39.

5. In brief, Driver relies on the non-attestation of words in poorly evidenced languages, like Ugaritic. Driver's argument is that the words that are found in the Hebrew corpus, which are shared with Aramaic *alone* ('Hebrew Poetic Diction', 35), are largely used in poetic contexts. The key issue is that it is impossible to determine whether the words that Driver considers are truly shared only with Aramaic, and not also with other languages like Phoenician or Ugaritic, since these words may not have survived in the attested material, even though they did exist. Driver counts 29 words common to only Hebrew and Aramaic among 86 pairs of poetic synonyms (33.72%) and only four words common only to Hebrew and Aramaic among 39 pairs of prose synonyms (10.26%). Thus, he concludes that poetry is more prone to Aramaism than prose (ibid.). However, this relation does not hold – rather it is reversed – when all the words he found in both Hebrew Aramaic are considered (poetic synonyms: 60/86 [69.77%]; prose synonym: 35/39 [89.74%]). For Driver's point to stand, one must accept that the poetic authors not only deliberately sought out those words shared with Aramaic but also deliberately avoided those shared with Aramaic and another language; that is, one must accept that Hebrew poetic authors preferred Aramaic words but only when they were not found in Akkadian, Arabic, Ethiopic, Ugaritic or Phoenician. Such an improbable outcome points to the problem that underlies Driver's work: at every stage it is *argumentum e silentio*. While all distributional criteria suffer in this regard, Driver's suffers particularly in that his argument relies on the non-occurrence of words in Ugaritic and Phoenician: every time he rules that a synonym is found only in Aramaic, he implicitly concludes that it was never found in Ugaritic or Phoenician or Akkadian, Arabic or Ethiopic. What Driver's data probably show is that there was likely a large degree of shared

Rendsburg has published several papers relating to the Aramaic features of the Hebrew Bible. In 'Linguistic Variation and the "Foreign" Factor in the Hebrew Bible',[6] he addresses Aramaisms across several biblical books. He explains their occurrence based on foreign setting, association with a foreign character or being addressed to foreigners. In 'Hurvitz Redux: On the Continued Scholarly Inattention to a Simple Principle of Hebrew Philology',[7] he explains Aramaisms in Ps 116, 1 Kgs 21 and Judg 5 not through foreignness but as pertaining to an Israelian dialect, that is to the Hebrew dialect spoken in the Northern Kingdom. Across several articles Rendsburg has applied this theory to a wide range of Hebrew texts.[8] Many of the passages dealt with by Rendsburg are also treated by Bompiani.[9] Key questions raised by Rendsburg's work include whether 'Aramaisms' point to Northern Hebrew rather than Aramaic influence,[10] whether Aramaisms point to Northern authorship or Southern authors

---

lexicogenesis between Hebrew and Aramaic, that was not necessarily shared with other languages, such as Akkadian. Different items of vocabulary, though shared by both languages, became prominent as the preferred term in each – possibly through deliberate attempts to distinguish (cf. Ian Young, 'The Languages of Ancient Sam'al', *Maarav* 9 [2002]: 93–103).

6. Gary Rendsburg, 'Linguistic Variation and the "Foreign" Factor in the Hebrew Bible', in *Language and Culture in the Near East*, Israel Oriental Studies 15, ed. Shlomo Izre'el and Rina Drory (Leiden: Brill, 1995), 177–90.

7. Gary Rendsburg, 'Hurvitz Redux: On the Continued Scholarly Inattention to a Simple Principle of Hebrew Philology', in Young, ed., *Biblical Hebrew*, 104–28.

8. Gary Rendsburg, 'Morphological Evidence for Regional Dialects in Ancient Hebrew', in *Linguistics and Biblical Hebrew*, ed. Walter Bodine (Winona Lake: Eisenbrauns, 1992), 65–88; Rendsburg, 'A Comprehensive Guide to Israelian Hebrew: Grammar and Lexicon', *Orient* 38 (2003): 5–35; Rendsburg, 'Aramaic-like Features in the Pentateuch', *HS* 47 (2006): 163–76; Rendsburg, 'Biblical Hebrew: Dialects and Linguistic Variation', in *EHLL*, 1:338–41; Rendsburg, 'What We Can Learn about Other Northwest Semitic Dialects from Reading the Bible?', in *Discourse, Dialogue, and Debate in the Bible: Essays in Honour of Frank H. Polak*, ed. Athalya Brenner-Iden (Sheffield: Sheffield Phoenix, 2014), 160–78; Rendsburg, 'Style-Switching in Biblical Hebrew', in *Epigraphy, Philology and the Hebrew Bible: Methodological Perspectives on Philological & Comparative Study of the Hebrew Bible in Honor of Jo-Ann Hackett*, ed. Jeremy Hutton and Aaron Rubin (Atlanta: SBL Press, 2015), 65–85 (79).

9. Brian Bompiani, 'Style-Switching: The Representation of the Speech of Foreigners in the Hebrew Bible' (PhD diss., Hebrew Union College, 2012).

10. Especially, Rendsburg, 'Aramaic-like Features in the Pentateuch'.

imitating Northern style,[11] and whether these references can provide reliable information about languages and dialects that are poorly attested or whether these unusual linguistic features are used without precision in order to create a generalized sense of foreignness.[12]

### 1.2.2. *Akkadian and Sumerian*

We are mentioning works dealing with these two languages together, because Akkadian and Sumerian stood in a close non-genetic relationship, in which the many interactions between speakers of these languages resulted in the influence of each language on the other across morphology, syntax and, most importantly for our purposes, vocabulary.[13] In general, therefore, the transmission of Sumerian loans into Hebrew is taken to be by way of Akkadian. For this reason, Akkadian and Sumerian loans are often considered in the same works.

Landesdorfer gave an early account of Sumerian loanwords in Hebrew.[14] However, the first comprehensive treatment of the topic of Akkadian loanwords was Zimmern's.[15] Nonetheless, Zimmern's work is flawed,[16] and modern scholars are better served by newer resources.[17]

Two more recent dissertations are also noteworthy in that each moves beyond purely lexical concerns, although each also only considers a subset

---

11. E.g. Rendsburg, 'What We Can Learn?', 166.

12. Cf. Ian Young, 'The "Northernisms" of the Israelite Narratives in Kings', *ZAH* 8 (1995): 65–66.

13. John Huehnergard and Christopher Woods, 'Akkadian and Eblaite', in *The Cambridge Encyclopedia of the World's Ancient Languages*, ed. Roger Woodard (Cambridge: Cambridge University Press, 2004), 218–87 (220).

14. P. Landesdorfer, *Sumerisches Sprachgut im Alten Testament: eine Biblisch-lexikalische Studie* (Leipzig: J. C. Hinrichs'sche Buchhandlung, 1916).

15. Heinrich Zimmern, *Akkadische Fremdwörter als Beweis für Babylonischen Kultureinfluß* (Leipzig: J. C. Hinrichs'sche Buchhandlung, 1917).

16. Mankowski points out that Zimmern is overgenerous in identification of loans and that many of his loan hypotheses are phonetically impossible. Kaufman also suggests that he is over-influenced by the Pan-Babylonianism movement and identifies dated lexicography as a source of problems in Zimmern's work. Stephen Kaufman, *The Akkadian Influences on Aramaic*, AS 19 (Chicago: The University of Chicago Press, 1974), 2–3; Paul Mankowski, *Akkadian Loanwords in Biblical Hebrew* (Winona Lake: Eisenbrauns, 2000), 1–2.

17. Kaufman, *The Akkadian Influences*; Édouard Lipiński, 'Emprunts Suméro-akkadiens en Hébreu Biblique', *ZAH* 1 (1988): 61–73; Mankowski, *Akkadian Loanwords*.

of the languages that loaned words to Hebrew. First is Peacock's 'Akkadian Loanwords in the Hebrew Bible: Social and Historical Implications'. Despite its title, this dissertation also examines Egyptian and Aramaic loanwords, though Peacock considers the social and historical implications of the Akkadian loans primarily. Peacock argues that the attitude of Hebrew speakers was one of purism, tending to avoid loanwords from Akkadian but apparently allowing Aramaic and Egyptian loans comparatively freely – a conclusion that is not supported by the data from the texts we have studied.[18] The second recent dissertation is Boyd's 'Contact and Context: Studies in Language Contact and Literary Strata in the Hebrew Bible'.

### 1.2.3. Non-Semitic languages

The principal non-Semitic languages from which loans are hypothesized in Hebrew are Sumerian, which we have already addressed, Persian, Egyptian and Greek. In addition to these, but less frequently, suggestions are made from Hittite, Hurrian and Indian and Dravidian languages.

The most important early work on Persian loans in Hebrew is Scheftelowitz's *Arisches im Alten Testament*,[19] which is still one of the most comprehensive works on the topic. However, there are several other significant works,[20] especially Tavernier's and Hinz's lexica of indirectly

---

18. Ibid., 384–88.

19. Isidor Scheftelowitz, *Arisches im Alten Testament: Eine sprachwissenschaftliche und kulturhistorische Untersuchung* (Berlin: S. Calvary & Co., 1901).

20. Henry Gehman, 'Notes on the Persian Words in the Book of Esther', *JBL* 43 (1924): 321–28; Isidor Scheftelowitz, 'Zur Kritik des griechischen und des massoretischen Buches Esther', *MGWJ* 47 (1903): 24–37; Scheftelowitz, 'Zur Kritik des griechischen und des massoretischen Buches Esther. (Fortsetzung)', *MGWJ* 47 (1903): 201–13; Scheftelowitz, 'Zur Kritik des griechischen und des massoretischen Buches Esther. (Schluss)', *MGWJ* 47 (1903): 110–20; Scheftelowitz, 'Zur Kritik des griechischen und des massoretischen Buches Esther. (Schluss)', *MGWJ* 47 (1903): 289–313; W. St Clair Tisdall, 'The Āryan Words in the Old Testament: I', *JQR* 1 (1911): 335–39; Tisdall, 'The Āryan Words in the Old Testament: II', *JQR* 2 (1911): 213–19; Tisdall, 'The Āryan Words in the Old Testament: III', *JQR* 2 (1912): 365–71; Tisdall, 'The Book of Daniel: Some Evidence Regarding its Date', *Journal of the Transactions of the Victoria Institute* 53 (1921): 206–55; Aren Wilson-Wright, 'From Persepolis to Jerusalem: A Reevaluation of Old Persian–Hebrew Contact in the Achaemenid Period', *VT* 65 (2015): 152–67; Young, Rezetko and Ehrensvärd, 'Loanwords', 1:280–311.

attested *iranica*, which include loanwords from Iranian into a variety of languages, including Hebrew and Aramaic.[21]

Of the works which cover Egyptian loanwords,[22] the most significant have been Lambdin,[23] Muchiki,[24] and Yahuda.[25] Recently, of especial note for our topic, Noonan has published, 'Egyptian Loanwords as Evidence for the Authenticity of the Exodus and Wilderness Traditions', in which he studies the high frequency of Egyptian loanwords in Exodus and Numbers.[26]

Greek loanwords are discussed most comprehensively by John Brown in his *Israel and Hellas*.[27] The work tackles a much broader question than loanwords, one of cultural contact between Greece and Israel. As such, while he discusses many words it is not always clear whether he is suggesting they are loanwords. This is remedied by a chapter in the second volume, 'Levels of Connection between Greek and Hebrew',[28] that clarifies his position on many of these words. Nevertheless, some of his suggestions are difficult to accept. Notably, his contention[29] that מֶלֶךְ is a loan from Greek *ϝάναξ seems implausible,[30] as West has also

---

21. Walther Hinz, *Altiranisches Sprachgut der Nebenüberlieferungen* (Wiesbaden: Otto Harrassowitz, 1975); Jan Tavernier, *Iranica in the Achaemenid Period* (Leuven: Peeters, 2007).

22. In addition to the below, J. Lieblein, 'Mots égyptiens dans la Bible', *Proceedings of the Society of Biblical Archaeology* 20 (1898): 202–10; Wilhelm Müller, 'Zwei ägyptische Wörter im Hebräischen', *OLZ* 3 (1900): 49–51.

23. Thomas Lambdin, 'Egyptian Loan Words in the Old Testament', *JAOS* 73 (1953): 145–55.

24. Yoshiyuki Muchiki, *Egyptian Proper Names and Loanwords in North-West Semitic*, SBLDS 173 (Atlanta: Scholars Press, 1999).

25. A. Yahuda, *The Language of the Pentateuch in its Relation to Egyptian* (London: Humphrey Milford, 1933); Yahuda, 'Hebrew Words of Egyptian Origin', *JBL* 66 (1947): 83–90.

26. Benjamin Noonan, 'Egyptian Loanwords as Evidence for the Authenticity of the Exodus and Wilderness Traditions', in *'Did I Not Bring Israel Out of Egypt?': Biblical, Archaeological, and Egyptological Perspectives on the Exodus Narratives*, ed. James Hoffmeier et al., BBR Supplements 13 (Winona Lake: Eisenbrauns, 2016), 49–68.

27. John Brown, *Israel and Hellas*, 3 vols. (Berlin: de Gruyter, 1995–2001).

28. John Brown, 'Levels of Connection Between Greek and Hebrew', in *Israel and Hellas*, 2:273–323.

29. Brown, *Israel and Hellas*, 1:200, 2:299.

30. As some readers may be unfamiliar, the digamma (ϝ) is a Greek consonant that disappeared before the classical period. Its approximate phonetic value is /w/.

noted.[31] An early, but extensive, work on Greek (and Latin) loanwords is Maurice Vernes' *Les emprunts de la Bible hébraïque au grec et au latin*.[32]

There has also been considerable interest in the book of Daniel specifically, from the perspective of dating the book. An earlier work dealing with the Greek loanwords in Daniel is Derenbourg's 'Les Mots grecs dans le Livre biblique de Daniel'.[33] Driver also contributed to the topic,[34] whose contributions have been reviewed recently by Young.[35] The topic is routinely discussed in commentaries on Daniel.[36]

There is likewise a degree of vocabulary shared by Greek and Hebrew that is not necessarily attributable to a loan between those two languages directly; rather, it must be attributed to a third language. Whether a single language can account for all, or even most, of the shared vocabulary is yet to be seen. In many cases, the words have been assigned the label of 'culture word'.[37] Others have gone further and suggest that the words belong to either a Mediterranean substrate,[38] or the Pre-Greek substrate, which is to say, the set of words identified in Greek that belong to the language spoken in the region prior to the arrival of the Hellenic languages.[39] Other plausible points of connection are to be found in the Anatolian languages, which has led to the suggestion that the words may

---

31. Martin West, review of *Israel and Hellas*, by John Brown, vol. 1. *Classical Review* 47 (1997): 111–12 (112).

32. Maurice Vernes, *Les emprunts de la Bible hébraïque au grec et au latin*, Bibliothèque de l'École des Hautes Études: Sciences Religieuses 29 (Paris: Ernest Leroux, 1914).

33. Hartwig Derenbourg, 'Les Mots grecs dans le Livre biblique de Daniel', in *Mélanges Graux*, ed. Ernest Thorin (Paris: E. Thorin, 1884), 235–44.

34. Samuel Driver, *An Introduction to the Literature of the Old Testament*, 9th ed. (Oxford: Clarendon, 1913), 501–508.

35. Ian Young, 'The Greek Loanwords in the Book of Daniel', in *Biblical Greek in Context: Essays in Honour of John A. L. Lee*, ed. James Aitken and Trevor Evans (Leuven: Peeters, 2015), 247–68.

36. For example, John Collins, *Daniel*, Hermeneia (Philadelphia: Fortress, 1993), 20; Louis Hartman and Alexander di Lella, *The Book of Daniel*, AB 23 (Garden City: Doubleday, 1978), 157.

37. Words which do not have a precisely recoverable origin, but seem to pass easily between languages, especially when attached to a trade good.

38. Charles Autran, 'De quelques vestiges probables, méconnus jusqu'ici, du lexique Méditerranéen dans le sémitique d'Asie Mineure, et, notamment, de Canaan', *JA* 209 (1926): 1–79.

39. Albert Cuny, 'Les Mots du Fonds Préhellénique en Grec, Latin et Sémitique Occidental', *REA* 12 (1910): 154–64.

be Hittite in origin.[40] Other words have also been investigated as Hittite loans without particular reference to Greek.[41]

### 1.3. *Linguistics and rhetoric*

Our thesis is that a particular linguistic feature (loanwords) is used by certain biblical literary texts (Esther, Daniel, Ezra 1–7 and Exod 25–40) as a rhetorical figure and, in particular, a rhetorical figure that is especially useful for commenting on topics of ethnicity. In this chapter we discuss the methodological underpinnings of this thesis and especially how linguistic theories can be applied to the literary analysis of biblical texts.

#### 1.3.1. *Applying linguistics to literary texts*

Before going further, it is worth justifying that contact linguistics *can* be applied to literary texts. As will be discussed below, in some cases like code-switching or nonce-borrowing, although the linguistic phenomenon does not occur in written texts in the strict sense, a broader sense can be applied to the written text without insuperable difficulties. What is needed, however, is a more generalized theory of written language contact.

Although the division of labour between linguistics and literary theory has left this topic in a no-man's land, recently Lars Johanson has given a brief overview of the issue and a categorization of the phenomenon, based on historical evidence:[42]

1. The low-prestige language incorporates elements of the high-prestige language into its own texts;
2. Users of the low-prestige incorporate elements of the low-prestige language into texts produced in a version of the high-prestige language;
3. The low-prestige and high-prestige languages coexist in a single text, side by side;
4. The low-prestige language is used to explain or translate content from the high-prestige language;
5. Elements of the high-prestige language are adopted to represent the low-prestige language.

---

40. Archibald Sayce, 'Hittite and Mitannian Elements in the Old Testament', *JTS* 29 (1928): 401–406.
41. Chaim Rabin, 'Hittite Words in Hebrew', *Or (NS)* 32 (1963): 113–39.
42. Lars Johanson, 'Written Language Intertwining', in *Contact Languages: A Comprehensive Guide*, ed. Peter Bakker and Yaron Matras, Language Contact and Bilingualism 6 (Berlin: de Gruyter Mouton, 2013), 273–331.

As with spoken contact situations, Johanson approaches the topic of written contact through the lens of cultural prestige; thus, when two languages are in contact it is assumed that one language will enjoy a position of cultural prestige and dominance over the other. Such cultural dominance may or may not coincide with political dominance. In the case of Hebrew and the languages from which most of its loanwords are drawn (Egyptian, Akkadian, Persian and Greek), Hebrew occupies the space of low-prestige language. In the texts studied below, situations 1 (loanwords, calques, etc.), 3 (code-switching) and possibly 4 (translation) are all encountered, putting these texts well within expectations for how written contact linguistics functions. So long as we remain cautious about the differences between written and spoken language, it is still justifiable to study the contact linguistics of the Hebrew Bible.

### 1.3.2. *Variation*

Loanwords are a linguistic phenomenon and so a linguistic approach is necessary. One of the fundamental characteristics of historical sociolinguistics is that of variation: when language differs, especially as correlated to the speaker or addressee of a conversation.[43] As we shall see below, rhetoric has a similar concept in deviation.

The pertinence of the concept of variation to our thesis is in noting that there are important ways in which loanwords vary from other words – phonologically and morphologically, syntactically, semantically and especially socio-pragmatically[44] – and that loanwords have the

---

43. Robert Bailey and Ceil Lucas, *Sociolinguistic Variation: Theories, Methods, and Applications* (Cambridge: Cambridge University Press, 2007); Rezetko and Young, *Historical Linguistics and Biblical Hebrew*, 45–49; Sali Tagliamonte, *Analysing Sociolinguistic Variation*, Key Topics in Sociolinguistics (Cambridge: Cambridge University Press, 2006), esp. 70ff.

44. A few of many references: Lyle Campbell, *Historical Linguistics*, 3rd ed. (Edinburgh: Edinburgh University Press, 2013), 56–90; Mark Donohue, 'Word Order in Austronesian from North to South and East to West', *Linguistic Typology* 11 (2007): 349–91; Jackie Hogan, 'The Social Significance of English Usage in Japan', *Japanese Studies* 23 (2003): 43–58; Stephen Keiser, 'Religious Identity and the Perception of Linguistic Difference: The Case of Pennsylvania German', *Language & Communication* 30 (2014): 1–10; Marcellinus Marcellino, 'The Forms and Functions of Western Loanwords in Selected Indonesian Print Media' (PhD diss., Georgetown, 1990); Cecilia Montes-Alcalá, 'Two Languages, One Pen: Socio-Pragmatic Functions in Written Spanish–English Code-Switching' (PhD diss., University of California, 2000); Cecilia Montes-Alcalá and Naomi Shin, 'Las Keys Versus El Key: Feminine Gender Assignment in Mixed-Language Texts', *Spanish in Context* 8 (2011): 119–43; Alexander Onysko and Esme Winter-Froemel, 'Necessary Loans – Luxury Loans?

potential to function as lexical variables, where either the loanword or native word is chosen. This is especially the case when there is a high concentration of loanwords, since it is well-known to linguists that a high concentration of loanwords can be associated with a range of stylistic effects.[45]

Literary texts, especially ancient anonymous literary texts, however, are not good candidates for sociological study: sociolinguists study vernacular, rather than literary language;[46] moreover, it is difficult to establish the relevant sociological data of anonymous authors. Therefore, literary texts present a special conundrum for the sociolinguistics of ancient languages, because literary motives have the potential to confound the data. With that in mind, our study of loanwords in the literary texts of the Hebrew Bible will need to also be a literary one: while a linguistic approach is necessary it is also not sufficient to explain the variation in the distribution of loanwords in the Hebrew Bible.

### 1.3.3. Rhetorical approaches to the Hebrew Bible

The approach taken to literary texts in this study is rhetorical. However, the term 'rhetorical' requires some definition. What we mean by rhetorical,

---

Exploring the Pragmatic Dimension of Borrowing', *Journal of Pragmatics* 43 (2011): 1550–67; Doi Schun, 'The Naturalisation Process of the Japanese Loanwords Found in the Oxford English Dictionary', *English Studies* 95 (2014): 674–99; Philip Seargent, Caroline Tagg and Wipapan Ngampramuan, 'Language Choice and Addresivity Strategies in Thai-English Social Network Interactions', *Sociolinguistics* 16 (2012): 510–31; Antje Sons, 'Aneignung des Fremden: Entlehnung aus dem Chinesischen', *Zeitschrift für Germanistische Linguistik* 26 (1998): 155–76; Rachel Varra, 'The Social Correlates of Lexical Borrowing in Spanish in New York City' (PhD diss., City University of New York, 2013).

45. For studies of similar effects in modern language contexts, see Hans Galinsky, 'Stylistic Aspects of Linguistic Borrowing: A Stylistic View of American Elements in Modern German', in *Amerikanismen der deutschen Gegenwartssprache: Entlehnungsvorgänge und ihre stilistischen Aspekte*, ed. Broder Carstensen and Hans Galinsky, 2nd ed. (Heidelberg: C. Winter, 1967), 35–72; Hogan, 'The Social Significance of English Usage in Japan'; Naoko Hosokawa, 'Nationalism and Linguistic Purism in Contemporary Japan: National Sentiment Expressed through Public Attitudes towards Foreignisms', *Studies in Ethnicity and Nationalism* 15 (2015): 48–65 (62–63); José Antonio Sánchez Fajardo, 'Anglicisms and Calques in Upper Social Class in Pre-revolutionary Cuba (1930–59): A Sociolinguistic Analysis', *International Journal of English Studies* 16 (2016): 33–56; Carolyn Stevens, 'Translations: "Internationalizing" Language and Music', in *Japanese Popular Music: Culture, Authenticity, Power* (London: Routledge, 2008), 132–55.

46. Tagliamonte, *Analysing Sociolinguistic Variation*, 8ff.

is an approach that is interested in the way the text influences its audience; that is, it is a study that is interested in the way that the text has persuasive goals that are pertinent to the situation of its audience.[47] As such, rhetorical approaches are concerned with effect on the audience rather than intent of the author.[48]

There have been many applications of rhetorical theory to the Hebrew Bible.[49] One particular tendency, however, has been especially concerned with identifying structural boundaries.[50] This has led to the transformation of the rhetorical approach into an essentially stylistic endeavour, losing its core as an attempt to understand texts as persuasive instruments.[51] Even so, there are examples of rhetorical work in the Hebrew Bible which do focus on the persuasive goals of the text.[52] It is this sort of rhetorical work that we intend in this study and as such it is important for us to establish the audience and rhetorical situation of the studied texts.

---

47. Cf. Heinrich Lausberg, *Handbook of Literary Rhetoric: A Foundation for Literary Study*, trans. Matthew Bliss, Annemiek Jansen, and David Orton, ed. David Orton and R. Dean Anderson (Leiden: Brill, 1998), 19–20.

48. Although some will be content to equate the text's effect with the author's intent, there is at least a formal distinction. The author's intent cannot be proved, as is well-known since the seminal texts of New Criticism and remains foundational to literary study. Andrew Bennett and Nicholas Royle, *An Introduction to Literature, Criticism and Theory*, 5th ed. (London: Routledge, 2018), 6, 20–26; Richard Gerrig, *Experiencing Narrative Worlds: On the Psychological Activities of Reading* (New Haven: Yale University Press, 1993), esp. 115; William Wimsatt and Monroe Beardsley, 'The Intentional Fallacy', in *The Verbal Icon: Studies in the Meaning of Poetry*, ed. William Wimsatt (Lexington: University of Kentucky Press, 1954), 3–18.

49. Among others: Alison Lo, *Job 28 as Rhetoric*, VTSup 97 (Leiden: Brill, 2003); Pieter van der Lugt, *Rhetorical Criticism and the Poetry of the Book of Job*, OtSt 32 (Leiden: Brill, 1995); Pieter van der Lugt, *Cantos and Strophes in Biblical Hebrew Poetry*, 3 vols, OtSt 53, 57, 63 (Leiden: Brill, 2005, 2010, 2013); Robert O'Connell, *The Rhetoric of the Book of Judges*, VTSup 63 (Leiden: Brill, 1996); Thomas Renz, *The Rhetorical Function of the Book of Ezekiel*, VTSup 76 (Leiden: Brill, 1999).

50. This approach was canvassed by Muilenberg, but has been replicated often. Van der Lugt's works are a particularly good example of this approach. Van der Lugt, *Rhetorical Criticism*; van der Lugt, *Cantos and Strophes*; James Muilenburg, 'Form Criticism and Beyond', *JBL* 88 (1969): 1–18.

51. This kind of approach has been strongly criticized by Joosten. Jan Joosten, 'Biblical Rhetoric as Illustrated by Judah's Speech in Genesis 44.18-34', *JSOT* 41 (2016): 15–30 (16–17).

52. For example, Lo, *Job 28 as Rhetoric*; Renz, *Rhetorical Function of Ezekiel*.

## 1.3.4. Rhetorical Approaches to Narrative Texts

All of the texts which we are studying are narrative. Therefore, some justification of the use of rhetoric to study narrative texts is required. There is, indeed, considerable scholarship that applies narratological concerns to the Hebrew Bible,[53] as well as to broader corpora.[54] Nonetheless, the combination of rhetoric and narrative as a literary approach is perhaps practised less explicitly by biblical scholars.[55] This lack, however, arises from convention rather than from any actual incompatibility. There are two avenues for combining the two methods; firstly, although narratology may be thought of as a text-based approach and rhetoric as a reader-based approach,[56] the fact that the two examine separate spheres allows them to be combined.[57] Secondly, although rhetoric does deal with the reader's response, it does so by considering the text. The two methods complement one another, rather than contradict.

Further, though there are few to have explicitly combined the two approaches in the study of the Hebrew Bible, I am also not the first to do so; one of the major premises of Sternberg's *The Poetics of Biblical Narrative* is that the biblical narrative implies ideology. He even catalogues

---

53. Foundational works include: Robert Alter, *The Art of Biblical Narrative* (New York: Basic Books, 1981); Mieke Bal, *Death and Dissymmetry*, CSJH (Chicago: Chicago University Press, 1988); Adele Berlin, *Poetics and Interpretation of Biblical Narrative* (Sheffield: Almond Press, 1983); Meir Sternberg, *The Poetics of Biblical Narrative: Ideological Literature and the Drama of Reading*, Indiana Studies in Biblical Literature (Bloomington: Indiana University Press, 1985), 375–87.

54. Some recent examples: Mieke Bal, *Narratology: Introduction to the Theory of Narrative*, 3rd ed. (Toronto, Canada: University of Toronto Press, 2009); Wolf Schmid, *Elemente der Narratologie*, 3rd ed. (Berlin: de Gruyter, 2014).

55. In some cases, while it may not be named as such, rhetorical and narrative approaches are combined, nonetheless. See, for example, Fokkelman's discussion of folk etymology in the Babel story. Jan Fokkelman, *Narrative Art in Genesis*, SSN 17 (Assen: Van Gorcum, 1975), 12–13.

56. Mark Powell, *The Bible and Modern Literary Criticism* (New York: Greenwood, 1992), 7–11.

57. See, for example, Phelan's approach of considering the implications of narrative techniques for the reader. See James Phelan, *Reading People, Reading Plots: Character, Progression, and the Interpretation of Narrative* (Chicago: The University of Chicago Press, 1989); Phelan, *Narrative as Rhetoric: Techniques, Audiences, Ethics, Ideology* (Columbus: Ohio State University Press, 1996); Phelan, *Experiencing Fiction: Judgments, Progressions, and the Rhetorical Theory of Narrative* (Columbus: Ohio State University Press, 2007).

a variety of narrative devices that have particular rhetorical force.[58] Alison Lo, likewise, applies a combination of narrative and rhetorical insights to resolve the supposed contradictions of Job 28.[59] Dinkler too supports the combination of the two approaches for the study of the New Testament, arguing that the two methods are not contradictory but rather work best when practised in conjunction:[60] her argument is that all narrative has rhetoric concerns, with the conclusion that the rhetorical aspects of narrative should be the cornerstone of combining the two approaches. In addition to rhetoric shedding light on the persuasive goals of narrative, narratology too will give context to rhetorical studies; biblical examples of rhetoric often have narrative contexts and so stand to gain from a better understanding of that context.

### 1.3.5. *Rhetorical figures*

An important feature of rhetorical analysis is its close attention to specific features of the text, or 'rhetorical figures'. In our analysis, we will be examining the effect of one particular rhetorical figure, namely the contrast between sections of the text with high and low concentrations of loanwords.

Literary rhetoric inherited the need to classify usage from its classical forbears, resulting in cumbersome lists of specialized terminology.[61] While rhetorical criticism has its roots in classical rhetoric, scholars such as Plett have attempted to modernize and systematize the field.[62] Plett's system has at its base a standard definition of what a rhetorical figure is, namely 'a deviant unit of speech'.[63] Plett is certainly not alone in this

---

58. Sternberg, *The Poetics of Biblical Narrative*, 475–81.

59. Lo, *Job 28 as Rhetoric*.

60. Michal Dinkler, 'New Testament Rhetorical Narratology: An Invitation toward Integration', *BibInt* 24 (2016): 203–28.

61. Thus, for example, the *Handbook of Literary Rhetoric* devotes over a third of its length to a glossary of Latin, Greek and French terminology. Most of the remainder of the book is likewise dedicated to explaining and exemplifying that terminology. Lausberg, *Handbook of Literary Rhetoric*.

62. Heinrich Plett, 'Figures of Speech', in *Encyclopedia of Rhetoric*, ed. Thomas Sloane (Oxford: Oxford University Press, 2001), 309–14; Plett, *Literary Rhetoric*, trans. Myra Scolz and Klaus Klein (Leiden: Brill, 2010).

63. Plett, *Literary Rhetoric*, 65. This definition is particularly compatible with the notion of M- and I-implicature described above. In this understanding, a rhetorical figure is equivalent to an M-implicature.

definition; he himself derives it from Quinn.⁶⁴ However, it goes back as far as the Classical rhetoricians.⁶⁵

Nevertheless, the definition of deviation needs to be somewhat nuanced. Gueunier, for example, notes the multiplicity of definitions of deviation and explores the problems of several.⁶⁶ In particular, her criticisms revolve around how one establishes what is deviant, the standard against which that can be measured and the fact that something might be deviant in the language as a whole, but standard for the particular text.⁶⁷ Similarly, in work on metaphor, scholars have criticized the idea that rhetorical figures, such as metaphors, can really be described as deviations from the norm, if they are a fundamental and common part of how humans communicate and think, tied closely to concepts.⁶⁸

In addition, we raise our own concerns about the criterion of deviation based around the nature of the Hebrew corpus and the problem of representativeness. The question of representativeness – even before it is applied to Hebrew – is difficult; as Kennedy points out, the only perfectly representative corpus is the one that contains the entirety of the language

---

64. Arthur Quinn, *Figures of Speech: 60 Ways to Turn a Phrase* (Davis, CA: Hermagoras, 1993); Plett, *Literary Rhetoric*, 66.

65. Quintilian, *Institutio Oratoria* IX 1.3: 'quod utraque res de recta et simplici ratione cum aliqua dicendi virtute deflectitur' (Because each case [i.e. both rhetorical tropes and rhetorical figures] is deviated from the straight, uncomplicated way of speaking with some skill of speaking, *translation mine*).

66. These are Gueurnier's definitions: 1. 'On appelle écart tout fait de parole constituant une infraction au code de la langue' (By deviation one means everything done in the performance of language [parole] that amounts to an infraction to the laws of abstract language [langue]); 2. 'On appelle écart tout fait de parole constituant une infraction par rapport à un niveau dit 'non marqué' de la parole'); By deviation one means everything done in the performance of language that amounts to an infraction when compared to an 'unmarked' register of performed language); 3. 'Tout fait de parole constituant une infraction aux lois qui régissent le fonctionnement du contexte' (Everything done in the performance of language that amounts to an infraction to the laws that govern how the context works) (translations all mine). Nicole Gueurnier, 'La Pertinence de la Notion d'Écart en Stylistique', *Langue Française* 3 (1999): 34–45 (34–40).

67. Gueurnier, 'La Pertinence de la Notion d'Écart en Stylistique', 34–40.

68. Zoltán Kövecses, *Metaphor: A Practical Introduction*, 2nd ed. (Oxford: Oxford University Press, 2010), ix–xiii; George Lakoff and Mark Johnson, *Metaphors We Live By* (Chicago: University of Chicago Press, 1980); Elena Semino and Gerard Steen, 'Metaphor in Literature', in *The Cambridge Handbook of Metaphor and Thought*, ed. Raymond Gibbs (Cambridge: Cambridge University Press, 2008), 232–46.

or dialect or variety that it claims to represent.[69] In lieu of that degree of representativeness, the primary concern is of balance: whether the corpus either balances or controls all the variables that one might expect to affect the corpus. One variable, as an example, which is commonly balanced is the genre of the written texts included, even though it has been noted that texts do not necessarily naturally cluster into genres.[70] When we do consider the particular situation of the Hebrew Bible, even if we were to use the traditional authors of the biblical texts, we would still need to balance variables like social class, gender, dialect, the age of the author at the time they wrote and the period in which each text was written.[71] All of this suggests that the Hebrew corpus may not be a representative corpus and that it is also one that is very difficult to balance. Therefore, extreme caution is required in using the concept of deviation.

However, not all of these objections hold. As Kienpointner points out,[72] Plett's development of the concept of deviation takes it beyond some of the criticisms that are levelled against this criterion: for Plett, deviation can be 'rule-strengthening' as well as 'rule-violating'.[73] Likewise, deviation is redefined as a number of potential transformations (addition, subtraction, substitution, permutation, equivalence) that operate on different domains (lexical, phonological, syntactic, etc.) rather than necessarily deviation from a particular norm.[74] In this way, Plett escapes such criticism that is based on how norms are established. Nonetheless, Kienpointner levels other criticisms: firstly, Plett's system ignores figures of thought, such as *praeteritio*; secondly, while Plett's system works well at the syntactic, morphological and phonological levels, there is less objectivity at the semantic level; and thirdly, Plett does not fully explain the communicative function of each figure.[75] In one sense, these objections are quite meaningful, because they demonstrate that Plett's system is not a panacea to the vagaries of literary interpretation: there will always be things which require subjective judgment or additional kinds of transformation

---

69. Graeme Kennedy, *An Introduction to Corpus Linguistics* (New York: Addison Wesley Longman, 1998), 62.

70. Mark Sebba and S. Fligelstone, 'Corpus Linguistics and Sociolinguistics', in *Concise Encyclopedia of Sociolinguistics*, ed. Rajend Mesthrie (Oxford: Elsevier, 2001), 767.

71. Cf. Rezetko and Young, *Historical Linguistics and Biblical Hebrew*, 21–45.

72. Manfred Kienpointner, 'Figures of Speech', in *Discursive Pragmatics*, ed. Jan Zienkowski et al. (Amsterdam: John Benjamins, 2011), 102–18.

73. Plett, *Literary Rhetoric*, 65ff.

74. Ibid.

75. Kienpointner, 'Figures of Speech', 110–11.

and domain. However, the key to Plett's kind of approach is explaining rhetorical figures in terms of transformations (deviations) and domains – a core which, if one is prepared to accept that it cannot systematically explain everything, still holds valid.

Nonetheless, given that there are such concerns when it comes to approaching rhetorical figures as deviation (or rather, 'rule-violation'), some explanation of the relevance of these issues to the question of loanwords as rhetorical figures is warranted. Therefore, we must explain what we mean, by saying that loanwords 'deviate', how that deviation can be established against a linguistic norm and show that (unlike metaphors) loanwords are in fact marked lexical choices.[76]

Having identified loanwords as a potential source of linguistic variation, one that has been extensively studied in the field of linguistics, it seems justifiable to suggest that loanwords represent a kind of rule-violation in multiple senses: loanwords themselves deviate from native words in phonological, morphological, syntactic and semantic ways. The violation of phonological, morphological and syntactic rules may be (relatively) unproblematic to establish – an example that is of frequent relevance in the study of loanwords is that of the triliteral root, since frequently loanwords are non-triliteral. Semantic norms and deviation, however, present greater challenges: it can be difficult to establish whether or not a text's lexical choice truly represents a genuine choice between a loanword and another word. However, this objection is addressed at greater length, below, in terms of neo-Gricean implicature.[77] This lexical deviation is one of two dimensions of deviation from an established norm, in which loanwords function as a rhetorical figure.

The second dimension is a type of text-level distributional transformation. Our observation in the texts we have studied is that loanwords occur in sections of very high and very low concentration, juxtaposed. For this distributional deviation, corpus and norm-defining concerns are easily addressed: the corpus is defined as the text (e.g. Esther, Daniel, etc.) and the transformation is observable between the different sections, without one needing to be defined as the norm. This proves, also, that loanwords as rhetorical features of a text, are unlike metaphors: it cannot be said that loanwords are a fundamental part of the Hebrew language if large sections of text can easily eschew them. Therefore, critiques of the idea

---

76. On this last point, see below: 2.9.1, 'The contrast between loanwords and native synonyms, implicature and creating a literary effect'.

77. See 2.8.1, 'The contrast between loanwords and native synonyms, implicature and creating a literary effect'.

that metaphors are deviation do not easily apply to the case of loanwords, since loanwords can be shown to legitimately deviate from other word choices.

Therefore, although it is not without valid points of criticism, the concept of deviation, or more accurately put, 'transformation', is still a useful tool when it comes to explaining to what effect literary texts use high concentrations of loanwords in certain sections.

### 1.3.6. *Synthesis*

We identified at the outset of this chapter that our thesis is that loanwords are used by certain biblical texts as a rhetorical figure that is especially useful for commenting on topics of ethnicity. Although the nature of the topic of loanwords demands that our discussion be informed by their linguistic properties, the literary nature of the text confounds any attempt to correlate the observed variation of loanwords with social factors. Therefore, traditional sociolinguistics is inadequate to fully account for the loanwords in the Hebrew Bible and literary concerns must be accounted for.

The key to our method, therefore, is the concept of deviation, in two dimensions – the phonological and morphological deviation of the loanwords themselves at a lexical level and the text-level distributional deviation of those loanwords. These facets of deviation are comparable to the morphological, phonological and socio-pragmatic facets of variation in the linguistic study of loanwords.

This method has consequences for the scope of our study: firstly, because our approach is rhetorical it refrains from commenting on authorial intent; in particular, it is not the goal to prove whether any particular loanword is used deliberately by an author – rather, to examine the effect of the current state of the text on its audience. Secondly, the study is limited to those texts in which there are sections of text with high concentrations of loanwords as well as sections with low concentrations. Thirdly, the study does not comment on single loanwords in the text, but rather the concentration of many loanwords in the text.

2

# The Loanwords

In this chapter we will discuss the many loan hypotheses that have been suggested for words found in Esther, Daniel, Ezra 1–7 and Exod 25–40. In order to understand the analysis, especially as it relates to our particular topic, it is necessary to first introduce the concept of nativization and then also explain the means by which the loan hypotheses are weighed. Finally, I return to the topic of how loanwords can function as a rhetorical device in preparation for the literary analysis.

## 2.1. *Nativization of the loanwords*

In the study of loanwords, there is a common distinction made between loanwords proper (*Lehnwörter*) and foreign words (*Fremdwörter*). This distinction revolves around the concept of nativization. Once a loanword has entered into a language, if it persists it is gradually conformed to the standards of that language. In the discussion of loanwords in the following chapters, the concept of nativization is highly relevant, because the ability of the word to be perceived as foreign is key to its ability to have a literary effect.

The foreign-word–loanword distinction is based on the perceived degree of nativization that a word has undergone.[1] The less nativized a word, the more salient its origin is for a reader. The more salient that origin, the greater the potential for literary exploitation is. Information on the perceptions of nativization of loans is difficult to establish. Nonetheless, it is possible to measure actual nativization to some extent: a borrowed word

---

1. Martin Haspelmath, 'Lexical Borrowing: Concepts and Issues', in *Loanwords in the World's Languages: A Comparative Handbook*, ed. Martin Haspelmath and Uri Tadmor (Berlin: de Gruyter, 2009), 35–54 (42–43).

starts with many characteristics retained from its source language.² As it becomes more and more embedded in the borrowing language, however, the phonology, orthography and morphology of the word are altered to better fit the expectations of the speakers of the borrowing language. Additionally, there may be changes in the meaning and usage of the word. A foreign word has a low degree of nativization whereas a loanword, in this sense, is fully integrated into the borrowing language.

The means of recognizing the extent of nativization in any given language varies, but in general is much simpler for modern languages than for Hebrew. The most reliable means is attested change, where both the un-nativized form and nativized form are historically attested. However, in synchronous analysis or in situations where those data are unavailable there are other criteria. Switching between scripts is sometimes used to indicate that a word is perceived as foreign or un-nativized (e.g. the practice of italicizing foreign words in English, the use of the katakana and hiragana syllabaries in Japanese, group-writing in Egyptian,³ or the practice of Thai-speakers on social media).⁴ In living languages, phonology can be a useful criterion (e.g. English: pronunciations of café).⁵ Orthography is another means (e.g. Spanish: anglicizing *crack*, as opposed to nativized *crac*).⁶ Morphological rules can distinguish the extent of nativization if the recipient language will tolerate a degree of foreign morphology and the source and recipient languages differ sufficiently in morphology (e.g. English: anime pl. anime from Japanese /anime/, as opposed to *animes;⁷ by contrast, some words undergo analogical levelling: tsunami, pl. tsunamis from Japanese, /tsunami/).⁸ Similarly, linguistic productivity, the ability of a word to produce new

---

2. Even at this point, however, the very act of borrowing requires some nativization. Thus, Yaron Matras, *Language Contact*, Cambridge Textbooks in Linguistics (Cambridge: Cambridge University Press, 2009), 172–75. Nevertheless, nativization refers also to a diachronic process; see Peter Matthews, *The Concise Oxford Dictionary of Linguistics*, 2nd ed. (Oxford: Oxford University Press, 2007), s.v. 'loan word'.

3. Alan Gardiner, *Egyptian Grammar*, 3rd ed. (Oxford: Griffith Institute, 1957), 52.

4. Seargent, Tagg and Ngampramuan, 'Language Choice and Addresivity Strategies'.

5. Pronounced /kæf/ or /ˈkæfeɪ/ and formerly /kafe/; Oxford University Press, *Oxford English Dictionary*, http://www.oed.com, s.v. 'café'.

6. Real Academia de Español, *Diccionario panhispánico de dudas*, http://www.rae.es/recursos/diccionarios/dpd, s.v. 'crac'.

7. *Oxford English Dictionary*, s.v. 'anime'.

8. *Oxford English Dictionary*, s.v. 'tsunami'.

words through derivational processes, is an indication that the word has been integrated (e.g. English: boomerang [verb] < English: boomerang [noun] < unknown aboriginal language of New South Wales).⁹ Other kinds of analogical change can also be indicators of nativization, in particular those kinds of analogical change that assume the origins of the word are native, namely folk-etymology. Folk-etymology, in the stricter sense, refers to the morphological changes due to incorrect assumptions about the origin of the word.¹⁰ Thus, Lehmann gives the example, Old English *bryd-guma* became bridegroom, where *guma* signified 'man' but became obscure at a later date and was replaced with groom.¹¹ Nevertheless, it is not just the actual morphological change that signifies a degree of nativization, but also the assumption that the word is native and must have a native etymology (e.g. Gen 11:9 derives בבל, 'Babel', from בלל, 'to confuse', except the word derives from Akkadian *bāb-ili*, 'gate of the god').¹² Another criterion for degree of nativization is semantic shift away from the word's meaning in the source language, although care must be taken to discern whether it is the source language or the recipient language that has changed (e.g. English: 'qi', meaning life force is a loan that involves semantic narrowing, borrowed from Chinese, '*qì*', meaning air, breath, life energy;¹³ in English qi, sometimes further nativized orthographically as 'chi', cannot mean air or breath). 'Listedness' or the extent to which a word is listed in native dictionaries is sometimes used as a measure of how 'entrenched' a word is in the recipient language. Similarly, the frequency of a word is cited.¹⁴

In practice, however, nativization is very difficult to measure in the case of the Biblical Hebrew corpus. The most reliable guide from the

9. *Oxford English Dictionary*, s.v. 'boomerang (n)' and 'boomerang (v)'.

10. Campbell, *Historical Linguistics*, 100: 'We might think of folk etymologies as cases where linguistic imagination finds meaningful associations in the linguistic forms which were not originally there and, on the basis of these new associations, either the original form ends up being changed somewhat or new forms based on it are created'. That is, it is not just the 'linguistic imagination' that constitutes folk-etymology but the actual morphological changes must be present too.

11. Winfred Lehmann, *Historical Linguistics: An Introduction*, 3rd ed. (London: Routledge, 1992), 226.

12. This is itself claimed to be a case of folk etymology: A. George, *Babylonian Topographical Texts*, OLA 40 (Leuven: Peeters, 1992), 253–54.

13. *Oxford English Dictionary*, s.v. 'qi'.

14. For an example of using listedness and frequency to measure nativizaztion, cf. Jonathan Stammers and Margaret Deuchar, 'Testing the Nonce Borrowing Hypothesis: Counter-evidence from English-origin Verbs in Welsh', *Bilingualism – Language and Cognition* 15 (2012): 630–43.

above methods is morphological or grammatical irregularity. The most commonly relevant measure of nativization is whether or not a word conforms to the triliteral root structure of Hebrew. However, other relevant measures include the presence of consonant clusters or combinations that are uncharacteristic of Hebrew, as well as semantic factors.

In some cases, it is possible to determine that a loanword must have entered into Hebrew (or proto-Northwest-Semitic or proto-Semitic) at a very early stage. In such cases it seems probable that the loanword is highly nativized, if there is no reason to believe otherwise.

## 2.2. *Identifying loanwords and the direction of borrowing*

Although the present study is not primarily concerned with the identification of loanwords, it is necessary to understand the methods used for that purpose in order to evaluate the loans that others have already identified. Campbell suggests the following means for identifying loans and the direction of their borrowing:[15]

Phonological clues are helpful in two senses. Firstly, non-native sounds, or native sounds used in unusual ways, can be an indicator of borrowing. The second type of phonological clue is historical. In related languages, the divergence of phonology can provide indicators of borrowing. To provide an example, Latin *sycophanta*, 'informant', is transparently a loan from Greek, συκοφάντης (*sykophantēs*) on the basis of the digraph *ph* and the vowel *y*. Further, Greek φ is a reflex of Proto-Indo-European $b^h$ or $g^{wh}$. Those sounds are mostly inherited by Latin as *f*, but in certain contexts also as *b*, *g*, *v* or *gv*.[16] *Ph* is not a regular reflex in Latin of any PIE sound. Thus, if this word was simply inherited by both languages, we should expect Greek φ to correspond to something in Latin other than *ph*.

Morphological complexity is useful for determining the direction of borrowing. Thus, because συκοφάντης is analyzable as a compound word of the morphemes, σῦκ-, 'fig', φαιν-, 'show', and the masculine first declension morpheme -ης, whereas the Latin *sycophanta* cannot be analyzed as a compound word, the Greek is likely to be the original and the Latin the borrowed form. Similarly, the presence of cognates in Greek with their absence in Latin support this direction of borrowing: σῦκον, φαίνειν, φαίνεσθαι, φάντασμα, ἱεροφάντης.

---

15. Campbell, *Historical Linguistics*, 62–66.
16. Michael Meier-Brügger, Matthias Fritz and Manfred Mayrhofer, *Indo-European Linguistics* (Berlin: de Gruyter, 2003), 129, 135–36.

Likewise, if a word has cognates in one language, or closely related languages, but lacks them in the other language, this is a possible criterion.

Finally, Campbell suggests that geographic and other semantic clues can help determine the direction of borrowing. Here, my example of *sycophanta* is not illustrative. However, to give a different example, the German 'chow-chow', denoting a specific breed of Chinese dog, is derived from the Mandarin word for any dog.[17] Both the geographical origin of the species of dog and the semantic narrowing in German suggest the Mandarin origin of the word: it is unsurprising that a Chinese dog would be named in German with a word from a Chinese language. The semantic narrowing is easier to explain if the original word is Mandarin and is subsequently borrowed by German.

In addition to Campbell's criteria, the example of *sycophanta* suggests another criterion, which is non-standard morphology. In this case, the first declension in Latin is typically feminine, whereas *sycophanta* is masculine. Other aberrant cases include Greek loans such as: *poeta, nauta, athleta, clepta, pirata*. While there are native Latin terms that also fall into this category,[18] Greek loans are over-represented.

For the sake of determining loanwords in the case of Hebrew, especially from the languages that are most closely related to it, I have included a summary of some prominent linguistic changes in the relevant languages, in an appendix.[19]

### 2.2.1. *Some additional observations on identifying loanwords*

1. Because a loanword relies on language contact, only those languages that could plausibly have been in contact with Hebrew can be considered, which impacts on the relative credibility of each of those possibilities.

2. In some cases a word can only be identified as a 'culture word'. In most cases, a word is borrowed from one (source)[20] language to one (recipient)[21] language, possibly through one or more intermediary languages. However, it is possible in some cases that there is no linear process: such words are passed between languages often and may have several entry points into any given recipient language: there is also no clear source language. Such words are termed culture words.[22] Noonan

---

17. Sons, 'Aneignung des Fremden' 168.
18. E.g. *agricola*.
19. See 'Appendix Six: An Outline of Linguistic Change in Aramaic and Akkadian'.
20. Also termed 'donor' or SL.
21. Also termed 'borrowing' or RL.
22. Thus, for example, see Mankowski, *Akkadian Loanwords*, 7–8.

cites יין as an example of a culture word: he cites Greek, οἶνος, Latin, *vinum*, Hittite, *wiyana-*, Hattic, *windu*, Akkadian, *īnu*, Phoenician, יין, Egyptian *wnš*.²³ The Greek may be reconstructed as *ϝοῖνος.²⁴

3. The limited attestation of source languages is frequently problematic. Thus, words thought to be Persian in origin might not be attested in the contemporaneous Old Persian, but only in Middle or Modern dialects of the language.

4. The phonetic equivalences can be difficult as well. For languages where a large number of relatively certain loan hypotheses exist – Persian, Egyptian and to a lesser extent Greek²⁵ – it is possible to have a greater degree of certainty over the phonetic equivalences, it is in other cases, like Hittite or Hurrian, more difficult to assess. The viability of phonetic equivalences is further complicated by the fact that the phonetics of the languages in question are not necessarily settled. Moreover, it is phonetics and not phonology that matters in linguistic transfer; because it is difficult to disprove hypothetical phonetic realizations of phonemes, it becomes necessary to allow greater latitude in considering the phonetic equivalence of a hypothetical loan and its source word. And so, whereas in the case of Aramaic and Akkadian it was possible to have relative certainty over some loan hypotheses, in the case of non-Semitic source languages there is a greater degree of doubt. Therefore, it is the general practice in more substantial works on loans from these languages to suggest loans and then after that consider what phonetic correspondences are suggested by this practice.²⁶

---

23. Noonan, 'Foreign Loanwords', 39.

24. This is based on Latin–Greek correspondences such as οἶκος and *vicus*; οἶδα and *video*. Further, the metrical effect of the digamma (ϝ) can be observed on Homeric meter: a line such as ἀνδρὶ δὲ κεκμηῶτι μένος μέγα οἶνος ἀέξει (*Iliad* VI 621: wine greatly improves the strength of a man who has been worn out) demonstrates hiatus between the fourth and fifth feet generated by a digamma. In the second foot of the line οἱ δ' ἦλθον οἴνῳ βεβαρηότες υἷες Ἀχαιῶν (*Odyssey* III 139: and the sons of the Achaeans came heady with wine) the presence of the digamma causes the omicron in ἦλθον to be scanned positionally long. Cf. Georg Autenrieth, *Homeric Lexicon* (University of Chicago), http://logeion.uchicago.edu, s.v. 'οἶνος'; Henry Liddell, Robert Scott and Henry Stuart Jones, *A Greek–English Lexicon* [hereafter cited as *Liddell, Scott and Jones*] (University of Chicago), http://logeion.uchicago.edu, s.v. 'οἶνος'.

25. Greek is a slightly more difficult case. There is a large influx of loans into Mishnaic Hebrew from Greek which can provide the basis of a phonetic equivalence. However, it is still necessary to consider the development of both languages, which reintroduces an element of doubt.

26. Thus, for example, Muchiki, *Egyptian Proper Names and Loanwords*, 313–25.

## 2.3. The loanwords in Esther

אֲבְדָן
destruction; Esth 8:6; 9:5
Native synonyms:[27] אֲבַדּוֹן; כָּלָה; חֶבֶל; מַשְׁחֵת.

It is simple to recognize אֲבְדָן as an Aramaic or Akkadian loan by its suffix that has not undergone the Canaanite shift, such that the suffix would exhibit an o-vowel rather than an a-vowel. It is recognized as an Aramaic loan by Wagner and Rabin,[28] from אַבְדָן,[29] with Kautzsch and Nöldecke offering more cautious support.[30] As a point of comparison, the native Hebrew version is attested as אֲבַדּוֹן. The form אֲבְדָן, may appear to have undergone the Canaanite shift in the first vowel, read as an o-vowel, *qāmeṣ ḥāṭûp*. However, the lack of dagesh in the *dalet* proves that the first syllable is open and that its vowel is rightly read as an a-vowel.

אִגֶּרֶת
letter; Esth 9:26, 29
(2 Chr 30:1, 6. Ezra 4:8, 11; 5:6. Neh 2:7, 8, 9; 6:5, 17, 19)
Native synonyms: מִכְתָּב.

Most scholars derive אִגֶּרֶת from Akkadian *egertu, igertu*, 'letter',[31] with some additionally suggesting transmission by Aramaic.[32] There is also a minority opinion that the word is Iranian in origin, which cites the Greek ἄγγαρος, 'Persian messenger', as indirect evidence.[33] The LSJ,

---

27. See 2.8, 'Native synonyms' for more details on what is meant by these alternatives.
28. Rabin, 'Foreign Words', 1075; Wagner, *Die Aramaismen*, 17–18.
29. Edward Cook, *Dictionary of Qumran Aramaic* (Winona Lake: Eisenbrauns, 2015), s.v. 'אבדן'; Stephen Kaufman et al., *Comprehensive Aramaic Lexicon* (Hebrew Union College), http://cal.huc.edu/, s.v. ''bdn'; Michael Sokoloff, *Dictionary of Christian Palestinian Aramaic* (Leuven: Peeters, 2014), s.v. 'ܐܒܕ'; Michael Sokoloff, *Dictionary of Jewish Palestinian Aramaic*, 2nd ed., Publications of the Comprehensive Aramaic Lexicon 2 (Ramat Gan: Bar Ilan University, 2002), s.v. 'אבדן', 'אובדן'.
30. Kautzsch, *Die Aramaismen*, 105; Nöldecke, 'Kautzsch' Aramaismen', 417.
31. Ellenbogen, *Foreign Words*, 12; Rabin, 'Foreign Words', 1073; Wilson, 'Foreign Words', 187; Zimmern, *Akkadische Fremdwörter*, 19.
32. Mankowski, *Akkadian Loanwords*, 22–25; Shitrit, 'Aramaic Loanwords and Borrowing', 166; Wagner, *Die Aramaismen*, 19.
33. Scheftelowitz, *Arisches im Alten Testament*, 37. Cf. Instituto de Lenguas y Culturas del Mediterráneo y Oriente Próximo, *Diccionario Griego-Español*, http://dge.cchs.csic.es/xdge, s.v. 'ἄγγαρος'; Liddell, Scott and Jones, s.v. 'ἄγγαρος'.

however, connects ἄγγαρος instead with Akkadian *agarru*, 'hireling'.[34] In favour of the Akkadian hypothesis, Kaufman proposes an etymology within Akkadian, albeit one that is not entirely convincing because of the debatable semantic connection between Akkadian, *egēru*, 'to be crossed, twisted', and *egirtu*, 'letter'.[35] Nonetheless, at present the Akkadian hypothesis is more convincing than the Persian, because of the lack of directly attested Iranian forms. At minimum it is beyond doubt that the word is foreign in Hebrew and likely the Akkadian hypothesis is correct.

אֲדָר
Adar; Esth 3:7, 13; 8:12; 9:1, 15, 17, 19, 21
(1 Chr 8:3. Ezra 6:15)
טֵבֵת
Tebet; Esth 2:16
נִיסָן
Nisan; Esth 3:7
(Neh 2:1)
סִיוָן
Sivan; Esth 8:9

The names of the months of the Babylonian calendar, as opposed to the native Hebrew calendar – e.g. Babylonian Nisan in place of Abib – are generally presumed to be loans into Hebrew on the strength of the semantic denotation; that is, because the month-names denote months that so obviously originate in the Akkadosphere, there is no controversy about their origin.[36]

---

34. Liddell, Scott and Jones, s.v. 'ἄγγαρος'.
35. Stephen Kaufman, 'An Assyro-Aramaic *egirtu ša šulmu*', in *Essays on the Ancient Near East in Memory of Jacob Joel Finkelstein*, ed. Maria Ellis (Hamden: Archon, 1977), 119–27 (124 n. 44). Note, however, that while Kaufman agrees with the definition found in *CAD*, some other Assyriologists gloss *egēru* differently, e.g, as 'to lie (transversely) across'. Cf. Jeremy Black, Andrew George and Nicholas Postgate, *A Concise Dictionary of Akkadian*, 2nd ed. (Wiesbaden: Harrassowitz, 2000), s.v. 'egēru(m)', and Martha Roth et al., ed., *The Assyrian Dictionary of the Oriental Institute of the University of Chicago* [*CAD*], 21 vols (Chicago: Oriental Institute, 1956–2010), vol. 4, s.v. '*egēru*'.
36. Kaufman, *The Akkadian Influences*, 114–15; Mankowski, *Akkadian Loanwords*, 9.

אֲחַשְׁדַּרְפָּן*
satrap, governor; Esth 3:12; 8:9; 9:3
(Ezra 8:36. Dan 3:2, 3, 27; 6:2, 3, 4, 5, 7, 8)
Native synonyms: מֹשֵׁל; פָּקִיד; נְצִיב; שַׂר.

The Hebrew אֲחַשְׁדַּרְפָּן – and similarly the Biblical Aramaic אֲחַשְׁדַּרְפַּן,[37] found in Daniel – derives ultimately from the Iranian languages, presumably the Old Persian, *xšaçapāvan-*, 'satrap', as a wide range of scholars agree.[38] Not only is the word's nominal form highly unusual for Hebrew, it has a good etymology in Old Persian.[39] It seems possible that the Aramaic language may have, as Wagner suggests, been an intermediary but there is no compelling evidence whether it was or not.[40] Vernes' derivation from Greek, σατράπης, 'satrap', is incorrect.[41] Due to the semantic association with Persia[42] and the convincing etymology within Persian, the Greek must also be regarded as a Persian loan. It is less clear how neatly the precise semantic referent of the word was transferred between languages; while Greek sources suggest a small number of satraps and satrapies in operation,[43] Hebrew texts routinely refer to much higher numbers.[44] The Persian evidence is somewhat ambiguous, with the lands enumerated as satrapies in the Greek sources, designated only *dahyāva-*,

---

37. Ludwig Koehler, Walter Baumgartner and Johann Stamm, *The Hebrew and Aramaic Lexicon of the Old Testament*, trans. and ed. Mervyn Richardson, 2 vols. (Leiden: Brill, 2001), s.v. 'אֲחַשְׁדַּרְפָּן'.
38. Brown, *Israel and Hellas*, 2:296–97; Ellenbogen, *Foreign Words*, 23; Gindin, 'Persian Loanwords', 3:67; John Goldingay, *Daniel*, WBC 30 (Grand Rapids: Zondervan, 1996), 5; Hartman and Di Lella, *Daniel*, 156; Robert Holmstedt and John Screnock, *Esther: A Handbook on the Hebrew Text*, Baylor Handbook on the Hebrew Bible (Waco: Baylor, 2015), 131; Klaus Koch, *Daniel 1–4*, BKAT (Neukirchen-Vluyn: Neukirchener Verlag, 2005), 245; Carol Newsom, *Daniel*, OTL (Louisville: Westminster John Knox, 2014), 104; Noonan, *Non-Semitic Loanwords*, 50; Scheftelowitz, *Arisches im Alten Testament*, 38; Scheftelowitz, 'Zur Kritik, III', 118; Wilson, 'Foreign Words', 193; Wilson-Wright, 'From Persepolis to Jerusalem', 153.
39. Roland Kent, *Old Persian: Grammar, Texts, Lexicon* (New Haven: American Oriental Society, 1950), 181.
40. Wagner, *Die Aramaismen*, 22–23.
41. Vernes, *Les Emprunts de la Bible*, 22. Cf. *Liddell, Scott and Jones*, s.v. 'σατράπης'.
42. *Liddell, Scott and Jones*, s.v. 'σατράπης'.
43. Herodotus, *Histories* III 89–94.
44. Dan 6:1, cf. Esth 8:9.

'countries'.⁴⁵ Persian references to satraps are counter-intuitively limited, only occurring twice in the Achaemenid Royal inscriptions;⁴⁶ these two references are to rulers of Bactria and Arachosia.⁴⁷ However, since these two lands are designated as *dahyāva-* in DB 1.6, it is presumed that '*dahyāva-*' denotes the land ruled by a satrap. Since the *dahyāva-* are enumerated across the inscriptions in numbers approximately equivalent to the Greek numbers,⁴⁸ it appears that the Greek sources are correct in suggesting that there was a low number of satraps. If it is correct to read the Persian evidence in this way, it appears that the Hebrew אֲחַשְׁדַּרְפָּן may designate a less specific class of governor – not necessarily just those who rule *dahyāva-*,⁴⁹ a case of semantic broadening.⁵⁰ In Dan 6, officials designated as אֲחַשְׁדַּרְפָּן are placed *under* the סָרְכִין, which may support the idea that the Hebrew word can be used for lesser officials.

אֲחַשְׁתְּרָן*
royal; Esth 8:10, 14
Native synonyms: מֶלֶךְ or מַלְכוּת in a construct chain, such as סוּס הַמֶּלֶךְ, 'the royal horse'.

It is widely agreed that אֲחַשְׁתְּרָן derives from Persian *xšaça-*,⁵¹ possibly with an Aramaic transmission.⁵² This is a plausible reconstruction, as תר is a good approximation for the Persian *ç*.⁵³ The Hebrew form exhibits a suffix in -*ān*, which Wagner suggests derives from an Aramaic adjectival

---

45. DB 1.6, DNa 15–30, XPh 14–28.

46. Kent, *Old Persian*, 181. Although Kent is old, by my count I too cannot find the word elsewhere in the Achaemenid inscriptions. Cf. Pierre Lecoq, *Les inscriptions de la Perse achéménide* (Paris: Gallimard, 1997).

47. DB 3.14, 3.56.

48. E.g. DB 1.6 lists 23 countries; Herodotus counts 20 (*Histories* III 89).

49. Ernest Lucas, *Daniel*, Apollos Old Testament Commentary 20 (Downers Grove: InterVarsity, 2002), 148.

50. There are, of course, other possible explanations, including that the counts given by Daniel and Esther are hyperbolic. However, in that case it seems surprising that the counts given by Daniel and Esther would be close. Moreover, 127 is not a very round number, as we might expect for hyperbole. Cf. Collins, *Daniel*, 264.

51. Ellenbogen, *Foreign Words*, 24; Gindin, 'Persian Loanwords', 3:67; Holmstedt and Screnock, *Esther: A Handbook*, 220; Noonan, *Non-Semitic Loanwords*, 51; Scheftelowitz, *Arisches im Alten Testament*, 39; Scheftelowitz, 'Zur Kritik, III', 118; Wilson-Wright, 'From Persepolis to Jerusalem', 155.

52. Rabin, 'Foreign Words', 1079; Wagner, *Die Aramaismen*, 23.

53. Cf. Greek, σατράπης from Persian, *xšaçapāvan-*, as discussed above.

suffix.⁵⁴ However, Persian also has nominal and adjectival suffixes in
-na-.⁵⁵ With all the correspondences being good, it is clear that this is a
loan from Persian into Hebrew, possibly through Aramaic.

אֵפֶר
dust; Esth 4:1, 3
(Gen 18:27; Num 19:9; 10; 2 Sam 13:19; 1 Kgs 20:38, 41; Job
2:8; 13:12; 30:19; 42:6; Pss 102:10; 147:16; Isa 44:20; 58:5;
61:3; Jer 6:26; Lam 3:16; Ezek 27:30; 28:18; Dan 9:3; Jon 3:6;
Mal 3:21)
Native synonyms: עָפָר; אֲדָמָה.

Zimmern derived אֵפֶר from Akkadian, *eperum*, 'earth, soil'.⁵⁶ Given
the existence of Hebrew עָפָר, 'dust',⁵⁷ Aramaic, '*pr*,⁵⁸ Akkadian, *eperum*
and other Semitic reflexes, we can safely hypothesize a Semitic * 'PR.⁵⁹
The Ge'ez, *'afar*, 'dust', is identified by Dillman as a loanword from
Amharic,⁶⁰ which lost its *ayins*.⁶¹ Similarly, Mehri, *afar*, 'cloud', is
consistent with the loss of *ayins* in that language.⁶² Therefore, all extant
lexemes can be explained as reflexes of the single Semitic root with the
exception of Hebrew אֵפֶר, unless it is borrowed from Akkadian, which

54. Wagner, *Die Aramaismen*, 23.
55. Kent, *Old Persian*, 51.
56. Zimmern, *Akkadische Fremdwörter*, 43.
57. *HALOT*, s.v. 'עָפָר'.
58. *Comprehensive Aramaic Lexicon*, s.v. ''pr'; Cook, *Dictionary of Qumran Aramaic*, s.v. 'עפר'; Jacob Hoftijzer and Karel Jongeling, *Dictionary of North West Semitic Inscriptions* [*DNWSI*], HO 21, 2 vols. (Leiden: Brill, 2003), s.v. ''pr'; Sokoloff, *DJPA*, s.v. 'עפר'; Michael Sokoloff, *Dictionary of Jewish Babylonian Aramaic of the Talmudic and Geonic Periods*, Publications of the Comprehensive Aramaic Lexicon 3 (Ramat Gan: Bar Ilan University, 2002), s.v. 'עפר'; Michael Sokoloff, *A Syriac Lexicon: A Translation from the Latin: Correction, Expansion, and Update of C. Brockelmann's Lexicon Syriacum* (Winona Lake: Eisenbrauns, 2009), s.v. 'ܥܦܪܐ'; Sokoloff, *DCPA*, s.v. 'ܥܦܪ'.
59. Cf. Leonid Kogan, *Genealogical Classification of Semitic: The Lexical Isoglosses* (Berlin: de Gruyter, 2015), 540–41.
60. Augustus Dillman, *Lexicon Linguae Aethiopicae Cum Indice Latino* (Leipzig: T. O. Weigel, 1865), 808. Cf. Wolf Leslau, *Comparative Dictionary of Ge'ez (Classical Ethiopic)* (Wiesbaden: Otto Harrassowitz, 1987), s.v. ''afar'.
61. Wolf Leslau, *Reference Grammar of Amharic* (Wiesbaden: Harrassowitz, 1995), 2.
62. Aaron Rubin, *The Mehri Language of Oman* (Leiden: Brill, 2010), 15–16.

lost its strong gutturals.⁶³ Therefore, the presence of both עָפָר and אֵפֶר in Hebrew strongly suggests that אֵפֶר is indeed a borrowing from Akkadian.

אַרְגָּמָן
purple cloth; Esth 1:6; 8:15
(Exod 25:4; 26:1, 31, 36; 27:16; 28:5, 6, 8, 15, 33; 35:6, 23, 25, 35; 36:8, 35, 37; 38:18, 23; 39:1, 2, 3, 5, 8, 24, 29; Num 4:13; Judg 8:26; 2 Chr 2:13; 3:14; Prov 31:22; Song 3:10; 7:6; Jer 10:9; Ezek 27:7, 16; Dan 5:7, 16, 29)
Native synonyms: While there are no obvious precise synonyms – without certainty over the hues meant by different colour lexemes it is hard to be sure of equivalences – the nature of the word is that it provides auxiliary information: there is no compulsion to necessarily use the word, particularly as it is almost always used in lists of colour terminology. Moreover, there is a rough equivalent in תּוֹלָע, 'crimson dye'.

The word אַרְגָּמָן is also attested in Hebrew as אַרְגְּוָן (2 Chr 2:6) and both versions are attested in other languages. In Biblical Aramaic it is attested as אַרְגְּוָן.⁶⁴ In Esther, however, only אַרְגָּמָן is attested. While it is beyond doubt that the version אַרְגְּוָן is best explained as a loan from Akkadian,⁶⁵ perhaps by way of Aramaic,⁶⁶ the status of the version אַרְגָּמָן is less certain. Zimmern and Lipiński suggested that אַרְגָּמָן was a loan from Akkadian and to be sure it corresponds in form to the Akkadian *argamannu*.⁶⁷ Nevertheless, the word is no more native to Akkadian than it is to Hebrew; Zimmern suggests its origin might be Indian;⁶⁸ Mankowski raises the

---

63. See under 'Appendix Six: An Outline of Linguistic Change in Aramaic and Akkadian'.

64. *Comprehensive Aramaic Lexicon*, s.v. ''rgwn'; Cook, *Dictionary of Qumran Aramaic*, s.v. 'ארגון'; *DNWSI*, s.v. ''rgwn'; *HALOT*, s.v. 'אַרְגְּוָן'; Sokoloff, *DJPA*, s.v. 'ארגון'; Sokoloff, *DJBA*, s.v. 'ארגון'; Sokoloff, *A Syriac Lexicon*, s.v. 'ܐܪܓܘܢ'; Sokoloff, *DCPA*, s.v. 'ܐܪܓܘܢ'.

65. Lipiński, 'Emprunts Suméro-akkadiens', 63–64; Mankowski, *Akkadian Loanwords*, 38–39; Noonan, 'Foreign Loanwords', 189–90. It is difficult to explain the shift of /m/ to /w/ without recourse to the sound changes in Middle Babylonian (see under 'Appendix Six: An Outline of Linguistic Change in Aramaic and Akkadian').

66. Cf. Kaufman, *The Akkadian Influences*, 35–36. It is perhaps no more preferable than a direct borrowing from Babylonian.

67. Lipiński, 'Emprunts Suméro-akkadiens', 63–64; Zimmern, *Akkadische Fremdwörter*, 37.

68. Ibid.

possibility that the word is derived from a culture word;[69] and similarly, Ellenbogen, Hartley and Noonan have speculated that the word may have derived from Indo-European.[70] Similarly, Hartley suggests that the word is a Hittite loan. Hartley also notes the forms from Ugaritic *'argmn*, Aramaic ארגונא, Arabic *'urgwan*, Hittite *argaman-* and Luwian *arkaman-*.[71] For additional evidence we might also consider, as Rabin has suggested, the Persian plant name, *argawān* (> Modern Persian 'purple') and Greek, ἀργεμώνιον and ἀργεμώνη, referring to a variety of purple and red flowers.[72] In addition, we also find the Latin *argemone, argemonia* and *agrimonia*, which should be considered loanwords from the Greek, based on the Greek declension of *argemone*. The Persian words may be explained as borrowed from Akkadian. However, as for the Greek words, the coincidence of form and meaning to the Akkadian are hard to ignore, given that there is no genetic relationship between Greek and Akkadian and little opportunity for borrowing between them. Nor is there any clear way to reconcile the Greek words with the suggested Indo-European roots. Nevertheless, the fact that the Greek word is restricted to botanical and medical treatises implies its foreign status. Moreover, the presence of other biological and geographical terms in Greek ending in -ωνη, may suggest a substrate word.[73]

Some of the words in this group (the Hittite, Luwian and Ugaritic) are attested with the meaning 'tribute' rather than with the meaning 'purple', indicating that a semantic shift has taken place. If we are to account for

---

69. Mankowski, *Akkadian Loanwords*, 38–39; cf. Noonan, 'Foreign Loanwords', 189–90.

70. Ellenbogen suggests that it is a word, meaning 'brightness' or similar, built on the same stem seen in Latin *argentum*, 'silver', and Greek ἀργός, 'shining', with the same suffix, *men*, seen in *lumen* and *flumen*. Noonan instead derives it from $h_ȩerk$-, 'to divide'. Ellenbogen, *Foreign Words*, 38–39; John Hartley, 'אַרְגְּמָן', in *The Semantics of Ancient Hebrew Colour Lexemes*, ed. John Hartley (Louvain, Belgium: Peeters, 2010), 198–203; Noonan, *Non-Semitic Loanwords*, 64–65. Cf. *Liddell, Scott and Jones*, s.v. 'ἀργός'.

71. Hartley, 'אַרְגְּמָן'.

72. Rabin, 'Hittite Words in Hebrew', 116–18. Rabin identifies the flowers as yellow-red. However, see the identifications of the flowers in Greek lexica, namely as *anemone coronaria, anemone hortensis* and *papaver argemone*. Cf. *Diccionario Griego-Español*, s.vv. 'ἀργεμώνιον' and 'ἀργεμώνη'; *Liddell, Scott and Jones*, s.vv. 'ἀργεμώνιον' and 'ἀργεμώνη'.

73. E.g. ἀγώνη, 'black henbane', ἐλεδώνη, 'the musky octopus', and ἐδελώνη, an unidentified flower; Βωδώνη, Δωδώνη, both city names, possibly identical, and Ἀργανθώνη, a mountain and a river.

Greek ἀργεμώνιον, it is logically simpler to derive the meaning 'tribute' from that of 'purple', rather than the other way around.[74] If the Greek words are rightly to be included in this word group, all the evidence may be accounted for if the word originates as a culture word in the Eastern Mediterranean or Aegean as a word denoting purple-red and is applied from there to the purple murex dye and 'tribute', while also being transmitted in Greek as a word for various plant species. It would most plausibly arrive in Hebrew by way of Akkadian (and probably an Anatolian language before that), both as אַרְגָּמָן and as אַרְגָּוָן. However, given the uncertainty over whether the Greek words are related, it is best to limit ourselves to stating that the while אַרְגָּוָן was transmitted to Hebrew from Akkadian, the word אַרְגָּמָן entered Akkadian (and thence Hebrew) from an Anatolian source.

בִּירָה
citadel; Esth 1:2, 5; 2:3, 5, 8; 3:15; 8:14; 9:6, 11, 12
(1 Chr 29:1, 19; 2 Chr 17:12; 27:4; Ezra 6:2; Neh 1:1; 2:8; 7:2; Dan 8:2)
Native synonyms: מִשְׂגָּב ;מָעוֹז ;מִבְצָר.

Despite Scheftelowitz's idea that the word originated in an Iranian language, there is a near consensus that בִּירָה derives from Akkadian, *birtu*, 'citadel'.[75] Most commentators also identify the vector of the loan as Aramaic, בִּירָה.[76] The consensus is based on the plural form attested in 2 Chr 17:12 and 27:4, בִּירָנִיּוֹת, which is suggestive of Aramaic

---

74. The connection between purple and tribute derives from the high value of purple dyes. If the meaning 'tribute' is the original, then the meaning 'purple' is a very severe semantic narrowing, which then underwent a very broad semantic broadening in order to be applied to other purple objects in the Greek versions of the word. If, however, the basic meaning of the word is the colour purple, all the variation in meaning is quite reasonably explained.

75. Ellenbogen, *Foreign Words*, 49; Holmstedt and Screnock, *Esther: A Handbook*, 39; Landesdorfer, *Sumerisches Sprachgut*, 65; Lipiński, 'Emprunts Suméro-akkadiens', 64–65; Mankowski, *Akkadian Loanwords*, 46–47; Wagner, *Die Aramaismen*, 34–35; Wilson, 'Foreign Words', 188; Zimmern, *Akkadische Fremdwörter*, 14.

76. Ellenbogen, *Foreign Words*, 49; Lipiński, 'Emprunts Suméro-akkadiens', 64–65; Mankowski, *Akkadian Loanwords*, 46–47, Wagner, *Die Aramaismen*, 34–35. For the Aramaic word, see *Comprehensive Aramaic Lexicon*, s.v. 'byrh'; Cook, *Dictionary of Qumran Aramaic*, s.v. 'בירה'; *DNWSI*, s.v. 'byrh'; *HALOT*, s.v. 'בִּירָה'; Sokoloff, *DJPA*, s.v. 'בירה'; Sokoloff, *DJBA*, s.v. 'בירה'; Sokoloff, *A Syriac Lexicon*, s.v. 'ܒܝܪܬܐ'.

morphology,[77] and based on the limited distribution of the word in Hebrew across only Esther, Daniel, Ezra–Nehemiah and Chronicles, compared to its frequency in Aramaic.[78] It is less clear, however, that the Aramaic word necessarily derives from Akkadian, though the possibility of an etymology *wabāru > wabru, 'settlement', and birtu, 'citadel', speaks in favour of an Akkadian origin, because there is no similarly plausibly explanation for the word's etymology in Aramaic.[79] The plural בִּירָנִיּוֹת implies that the loan is most likely from the Neo-Babylonian period, when the plural is attested as biranatu rather than birati.[80]

בִּיתָן
palace; Esth 1:5; 7:7, 8
Native synonyms: זְבֻל ;בַּיִת.

The word בִּיתָן is recognizably not of Hebrew origin, since its suffix ān has not undergone the Canaanite shift, though the word is clearly related to Hebrew בַּיִת. Rather, it is suggested that the word derives from either Akkadian[81] or possibly Aramaic.[82] It is, however, an uncommon word in Aramaic,[83] such that the Akkadian origin is more probable. Moreover, an Akkadian origin explains the vocalization, as Semitic *ay developed to Akkadian ī, where it was retained by Aramaic as ay.[84]

*גְּנֶז
treasury; Esth 3:9; 4:7
(Ezra 5:17; 6:1; 7:20; Ezek 27:24)
Native synonyms: אוֹצָר ;מַטְמֹן.

77. Kaufman, *The Akkadian Influences*, 44; Mankowski, *Akkadian Loanwords*, 46–47; Wagner, *Die Aramaismen*, 34–35.
78. Ellenbogen, *Foreign Words*, 49; Mankowski, *Akkadian Loanwords*, 47.
79. William Albright, 'The Nebuchadnezzar and Neriglissar Chronicles', *BASOR* 143 (1956): 28–33 (33 n. 22); Kaufman, *The Akkadian Influences*, 44.
80. *CAD* 2, s.v. 'birtu'.
81. Ellenbogen, *Foreign Words*, 50; Holmstedt and Screnock, *Esther: A Handbook*, 44; Mankowski, *Akkadian Loanwords*, 47–48; Wagner, *Die Aramaismen*, 35; Wilson, 'Foreign Words', 215; Zimmern, *Akkadische Fremdwörter*, 8. Mankowski and Wagner suggest an Aramaic means of transmission.
82. Kautzsch, *Die Aramaismen*, 106.
83. Indeed, it is possibly borrowed from the Hebrew. For both this possibility and the distribution, see *Comprehensive Aramaic Lexicon*, s.v. 'bytn'.
84. Édouard Lipiński, *Semitic Languages: Outline of a Comparative Grammar*, OLA 80 (Leuven: Peeters, 2001), 167–169.

There is a broad consensus that the Hebrew and Aramaic versions of גְּנַז derive from an Iranian language, hypothetically Old Persian, *ganza-*, 'treasury'.[85] Although the word is not attested in Old Persian, it is found in Farsi as *ganja*, in Pahlavi as *ganj* and in Sogdian as *γnz*.[86] It is also attested in Elamite as *hh.qa-an-za*.[87] Vernes connected the Hebrew word with Greek, γάζα, 'treasury'.[88] Since we know of the Greek, the Latin *gaza*, 'treasury', should also be brought into consideration. A final piece of evidence is the Philistine city, Gaza. The Roman geographer Mela wrote of the city: 'Next in Palestine is [a city] huge and fortified to this day, namely Gaza – that is what the Persians call a treasury [*aerarium*] and the name derives from there, because when Cambyses sought Egypt in warfare, that is where he stored the wealth and reward of the war'.[89] Though the explanation for the name of Gaza seems implausible,[90] the fact that Mela was able to give that explanation implies that he was aware of a Persian word that was at least similar enough to justify the comparison.[91] Similarly, Curtius Rufus uses *gaza* as a Persian gloss: 'the royal money,

---

85. Brown, *Israel and Hellas*, 2:296; Ellenbogen, *Foreign Words*, 57; Noonan, *Non-Semitic Loanwords*, 83; Rabin, 'Foreign Words', 1079; Scheftelowitz, *Arisches im Alten Testament*, 18; Wagner, *Die Aramaismen*, 41–42; Wilson, 'Foreign Words', 195; Wilson-Wright, 'From Persepolis to Jerusalem', 155. For the Aramaic word, see Claudia Ciancaglini, *Iranian Loanwords in Syriac*, Beiträge zur Iranistik 28 (Wiesbaden: Reichert, 2008), 142; *Comprehensive Aramaic Lexicon*, s.v. 'gnz'; *DNWSI*, s.v. 'gnz'; *HALOT*, s.v. 'גְּנַז' (Aramaic); Sokoloff, *DJBA*, s.v. 'גנז'.

86. Ellenbogen, *Foreign Words*, 57.

87. Walther Hinz and Heidemarie Koch, *Elamisches Wörterbuch*, 2 vols. (Berlin: Dietrich Reimer, 1987), s.v. 'hh.qa-an-za'.

88. Vernes, *Les Emprunts de la Bible*, 30–31. Cf. Liddell, Scott and Jones, s.v. 'γάζα'.

89. Translation mine. Mela, *De Chorographia* I 55: 'ceterum in Palaestina est ingens et munita admodum Gaza: sic Persae aerarium vocant, et inde nomen est, quod cum Cambyses armis Aegyptum peteret, huc belli et opes et pecuniam intulerat'.

90. The *ayin* in Hebrew name for the Gaza, עַזָּה, is difficult to explain if the name is based on a Persian word, not to mention chronological difficulties. The G derives from an etymological *ghayin*, but if the name were genuinely the same as the Persian word, we should nonetheless expect *gimel*.

91. Incidentally, this provides a demonstration that foreign vocabulary could be known even at the distance of centuries; the Persians were conquered by Alexander in the fourth century BCE, while Mela wrote in the first century CE. The fact that he is incorrect to identify the name of Gaza as a loanword from Persian only demonstrates that Mela's tendency was to assume that borrowing took place rather than that similarities were coincidental; it is possible that words that are not truly loanwords, but were perceived as such, could be used for the same effect.

which the Persians call *gaza*'.⁹² The word, גִּזְבָּר, attested in Hebrew and Aramaic Ezra, along with the version, גְּדָבָר, in the Aramaic of Daniel⁹³ are also recognized as loanwords from a hypothetical Persian, \**ganzabara*-, 'treasure-bearer'.⁹⁴ The word is obviously non-Semitic by its non-triliteral form. Moreover, the word has an obvious etymology in Indo-European, with the suffix *-bara-*, 'bearer', cognate with Latin *ferre*, 'to carry', and Greek, φέρειν, 'to carry'.⁹⁵ Thirdly, the suffix *-bara-* is commonly found in Persian compounds, such as *arštibara-*, 'spear-bearer', *takabara-*, 'shield-bearer', et al.⁹⁶

Between the cognate evidence and the indirect Roman evidence, it appears clear that Persian had a word at least similar to the hypothesized \**ganza-*. Furthermore, the existence of compounds of *ganza-* in Hebrew, Aramaic and Elamite with the Persian suffix *-bara-* also indicates the Persian origin of the words.⁹⁷

דַּר
pearl? Esth 1:6
Native synonyms: צְבִי.

\*ורד [reconstructed]
rose; Esth 1:6
Native synonyms: שׁוֹשָׁן.

92. Translation mine. Curtius Rufus, *Historiae Alexandri Magni* III 13.5: 'pecuniam regiam – gazam Persae vocant'.

93. Ciancaglini, *Iranian Loanwords*, 142; *Comprehensive Aramaic Lexicon*, s.vv. 'gnzwr', 'gzbr' and 'gdbr'; *DNWSI*, s.v. 'gnzwr'; *HALOT*, s.vv. 'גִּזְבָּר' and 'גְּדָבָר'; Sokoloff, *DJBA*, s.v. 'גנזור' and 'גזבר'; Sokoloff, *A Syriac Lexicon*, s.v. 'ܓܙܒܪ'.

94. Joseph Blenkinsopp, *Ezra–Nehemiah*, OTL (Philadelphia: Westminster, 1988), 78; Ellenbogen, *Foreign Words*, 54–55; F. Charles Fensham, *The Books of Ezra and Nehemiah*, NICOT (Grand Rapids: Eerdmans, 1982), 22, 46; Lisbeth Fried, *Ezra: A Commentary*, Critical Commentaries (Sheffield: Sheffield Phoenix, 2015), 70, 80; Gindin, 'Persian Loanwords', 3:67; Goldingay, *Daniel*, 65; Hartman and Di Lella, *Daniel*, 157; Koch, *Daniel*, 246; Scheftelowitz, *Arisches im Alten Testament*, 81; Noonan, *Non-Semitic Loanwords*, 80–81; Tisdall, 'The Āryan Words in the Old Testament: I', 336–39; H. G. M. Williamson, *Ezra, Nehemiah*, WBC 16 (Waco: Word, 1985), 5; Wilson, 'Foreign Words', 195.

95. Kent, *Old Persian*, 200.

96. Ibid.

97. *Comprehensive Aramaic Lexicon*, s.v. 'gzbr' and 'gzbr''; *HALOT*, s.v. 'גִּזְבָּר'; Hinz and Koch, *Elamisches Wörterbuch*, s.v. 'qa-an-za-ba-ra'.

The word דַּר is poorly defined, due to its poor attestation. Nevertheless, due to cognates in Arabic and Ethiopic and the Septuagint's translation, some lexicons gloss the word as 'pearl'.[98] Nonetheless more modern lexicons are less certain.[99] On the basis of the older view, however, Scheftelowitz likens the Hebrew, דַּר, to the Sanskrit *hāra*, 'pearl', and Farsi, *dur*, 'pearl', from which he reconstructs an Old Persian, *\*dāra-*.[100] This would imply an Indo-Iranian, *\*jʰar-*. It is possible, though quite uncertain.

However, on the basis of the Septuagint's ῥόδα, 'rose', at Esth 1:6, Brown reconstructs a Hebrew, *ורד, also 'rose', which the MT has metathesized by scribal error to וָדַר.[101]

The primary difficulty with Brown's hypothesis would be that the Septuagint supplies a word for 'pearl', πινίνου, in addition to ῥόδα, such that it appears likely that the Septuagint reads וָדַר. However, the Alpha Text contains only ῥόδα. It appears plausible, then, that a version of Hebrew Esther could have existed that read *ורד, 'rose', giving rise to the Alpha Text's ῥόδα, 'rose', instead of וָדַר, 'pearl'. On the other hand, the similarity between *resh* and *daleth* makes the metathesis likely. Moreover, whichever word is read here it is a *hapax legomenon* and so an interchange between them by a scribe is understandable.

Brown hypothesizes on the basis of his reconstruction that the word is related to Greek, ῥόδον < ϝρόδον, 'rose'.[102] To this point he also points to the Armenian *vard*, 'rose', in order to hypothesize an Iranian *\*vrda-*.[103] To this we can also add Avestan, *varəδa-*, 'rose'.[104] Nonetheless, at first appearance the word seems a poor semantic match in the context, because the context requires a flooring material. However, this difficulty is unavoidable, because the problem must be explained in the *Vorlage* of the Alpha Text, regardless of whether *ורד ever existed in the Masoretic tradition. However, the problem may be solved by understanding the word as a reference to colour rather than material. On the other hand, if

---

98. Francis Brown, Samuel Driver and Charles Briggs, *A Hebrew and English Lexicon of the Old Testament* (Oxford: Clarendon, 1907), s.v. 'דַּר'.

99. Luis Alonso Schöckel, *Diccionario Bíblico Hebreo–Español* (Madrid: Trotta, 2008), s.v. 'דַּר'; *HALOT*, s.v. 'דַּר'.

100. Scheftelowitz, *Arisches im Alten Testament*, 42.

101. Brown, *Israel and Hellas*, 1:339.

102. Ibid., 1:338–39. Cf. *Liddell, Scott and Jones*, s.v. 'ῥόδον'.

103. Ibid.

104. Christian Bartholomae, *Altiranisches Wörterbuch* (Strasbourg: Karl J. Trübner, 1904), s.v. 'varəδa-'.

we accept it, Brown's hypothesis would explain the presence of ῥόδα in the Greek versions of Esther. The Septuagint, then, has been corrected back towards the Masoretic text so that it now contains reference to pearl. If every stage of this reconstruction is correct – and it is certainly very hypothetical – then what has happened is that one Iranian word, unfamiliar to the scribe has been replaced by another. Nonetheless, both loan hypotheses are open to doubt.

דָּת

law; Esth 1:8, 13, 15, 19; 2:8, 12; 3:8, 8, 14, 15; 4:3, 8, 11, 16; 8:13, 14, 17; 9:1, 13, 14
(Deut 33:2 [?]; Ezra 7:12, 14, 21, 25, 26, 26; 8:36; Dan 2:9, 13, 15; 6:6, 9, 13, 16; 7:25)
Native synonyms: תּוֹרָה; מַאֲמַר; דָּבָר; מִצְוָה *inter alios*.

The word דָּת is a clear loanword from Persian, found in both Biblical Aramaic and Hebrew.[105] Aside from Wilson's suggestions that the word may derive from Hittite or Akkadian,[106] the best explanation is that proposed by a wide range of scholars, that the word derives from Persian's *dāta-*.[107] The Semitic versions correspond well to the Persian in form. Moreover, the Persian word has an obvious etymology as the past participle of *da-*, 'to do, make', from an Indo-European root that also yields Latin, *facere*, 'to do, make', and Greek, τίθεναι, 'to place'.[108] Thus, it is difficult to deny the Indo-European origin of the word; if the word is

---

105. *HALOT*, s.v. 'דָּת'. For other Aramaic, see *Comprehensive Aramaic Lexicon*, s.v. 'dt'; Cook, *Dictionary of Qumran Aramaic*, s.v. 'דת'; *DNWSI*, s.v. 'דת'; Noonan, *Non-Semitic Loanwords*, 89, 324; Sokoloff, *DJPA*, s.v. 'דת'; Sokoloff, *DJBA*, s.v. 'דת'; Sokoloff, *A Syriac Lexicon*, s.v. 'ܢܓܐ'.

106. Wilson, 'Foreign Words', 212.

107. Collins, *Daniel*, 157; Ellenbogen, *Foreign Words*, 61; Fensham, *Ezra and Nehemiah*, 22, 104; Gindin, 'Persian Loanwords', 3:67; Hartman and Di Lella, *Daniel*, 194; Holmstedt and Screnock, *Esther: A Handbook*, 49; Koch, *Daniel*, 90; Rabin, 'Foreign Words', 1079; Scheftelowitz, *Arisches im Alten Testament*, 43; Wagner, *Die Aramaismen*, 45; Wilson, 'Foreign Words', 195–96; Wilson-Wright, 'From Persepolis to Jerusalem', 156.

108. The root we construct would be $*d^heh_1$. Lewis and Short prefer to connect Latin *facere* with another root, related to Greek, φαίνειν. However, the roots *facere* and φαίνειν are poor matches and the root we have constructed adequately explains the data with a superior semantic cohesion between roots. Cf. Charlton Lewis and Charles Short, *A Latin Dictionary* [hereafter cited as *Lewis and Short*] (University of Chicago), http://logeion.uchicago.edu, s.v. 'facio'; Liddell, Scott and Jones, s.v. 'τίθημι'.

Indo-European, Persian offers the best candidate for the origin of the word, given that *dāta-* is attested in the Old Persian corpus. Hittite does not offer a plausible explanation, since the Hittite non-finite verbal forms do not allow for any ending that would sufficiently resemble the ת to provide a more plausible source for the Hebrew and Aramaic words.[109]

זְמָן
time; Esth 9:27, 31
(Ezra 5:3; Neh 2:6; Eccl 3:1; Dan 2:16, 21; 3:7, 8; 4:33; 6:11, 14; 7:12, 22, 25)
Native synonyms: עֵת.

Zimmern held that זְמָן derived from Akkadian, *simānu*.[110] Similarly Wagner proposed that the Akkadian loan entered Hebrew by way of Aramaic.[111] Other scholars, on the other hand, view זְמָן as an Iranian loan.[112] Scheftelowitz derives it from the Persian equivalent of Avestan *zrvan* and Pahlavi *zurwan*, 'time, Time', which was then reborrowed into the Iranian languages from a Semitic source, as attested by Pahlavi *zaman(ak)*, 'time'.[113] Gindin, on the other hand, argues that the Persian form underlying Pahlavi *zaman* is the source of the Hebrew and that *zurwan* is unrelated.[114] Indeed, the *r* of the Avestan and Pahlavi forms are unexplained.[115] Mankowski presents a hybrid view, suggesting that Akkadian *simānu*, from Akkadian *wasāmum*, resulted in Persian *\*jamāna-* – i.e. that which stands behind Pahlavi *zaman(ak)* – which resulted in Aramaic זמן and זבן,[116] which was

109. Harry Hoffner and H. Craig Melchert, *A Grammar of the Hittite Language*, Languages of the Ancient Near East 1 (Winona Lake: Eisenbrauns, 2008), 330–40.
110. Zimmern, *Akkadische Fremdwörter*, 63.
111. Wagner, *Die Aramaismen*, 49.
112. Gindin, 'Persian Loanwords', 3:67; Koch, *Daniel*, 94; Scheftelowitz, *Arisches im Alten Testament*, 45.
113. Scheftelowitz, *Arisches im Alten Testament*, 45. Cf. Bartholomae, *Altiranisches Wörterbuch*, s.v. 'zrvan-'; David Mackenzie, *A Concise Pahlavi Dictionary* (Oxford: Oxford University Press, 1971), s.v. 'zurwan'.
114. Gindin, 'Persian Loanwords', 3:67.
115. Scheftelowitz does attempt to explain it, but the parallel he makes with שֵׁבֶט and שַׁרְבִיט is unsatisfactory. See below, the explanation of שַׁרְבִיט as a loanword and the circumstances under which that alternation occurs. Scheftelowitz, *Arisches im Alten Testament*, 45.
116. *Comprehensive Aramaic Lexicon*, s.vv. 'zbn' and 'zmn'; Cook, *Dictionary of Qumran Aramaic*, s.v. 'זמן'; *DNWSI*, s.v. 'zbn' and 'zmn'; *HALOT*, s.v. 'זְמָן'; Sokoloff, *DJPA*, s.vv. 'זבן' and 'זמן'; Sokoloff, *DJBA*, s.v. 'זמן'; Sokoloff, *A Syriac Lexicon*, s.v. 'ܙܒܢ'; Sokoloff, *DCPA*, s.v. 'ܙܒ'.

the source of Hebrew זְמָן;[117] Noonan agrees that the Iranian *jamāna- was the source of the Hebrew word, by way of Aramaic, on the grounds that Akkadian *s* would not ordinarily result in *zayin*, whereas it is the regular reflex of Persian, *j*.[118] On the other hand, Noonan's theory, sees Akkadian *simanu* as unrelated, despite the similarities in form and meaning. Although it is not clear at this stage, whether or not *simanu* must also be related, it is quite sure that at the least Hebrew זְמָן is an Iranian loan (possibly through Aramaic).

חֹתָם
seal
(Gen 38:18; Exod 28:11, 21, 36; 39:6, 14, 30; 1 Kgs 21:8; 1 Chr 7:32; 11:44; Job 38:14; 41:7; Song 8:6, 6; Jer 22:24; Hag 2:23)
Also note: the denominative verb, חָתַם, 'to seal'; Esth 3:12, 8:8, 8, 10
(Lev 15:3; Deut 32:34; 1 Kgs 21:8; Neh 10:1, 2; Job 9:7; 14:14; 24:16; 33:16; 37:7; Song 4:12; Isa 8:16; 29:11, 11; Jer 32:10, 11, 14, 44; Ezek 28:12; Dan 6:18; 9:24, 24; 12:4, 9)
Native synonyms: There are no native synonyms and the word is an early borrowing into Hebrew.

The word חֹתָם is likewise uncontroversially recognized as a loan from Egyptian.[119] The Egyptian version of the word is *ḫtm*,[120] which appears to have been vocalized as *ḫātam*, on the basis of the forms found in Aramaic.[121] Therefore, the form attested in Hebrew appears to

---

117. Mankowski, *Akkadian Loanwords*, 54–55.
118. Noonan, *Non-Semitic Loanwords*, 97.
119. Brown, *Israel and Hellas*, 2:294; Ellenbogen, *Foreign Words*, 74; Lambdin, 'Egyptian Loan Words', 151; Muchiki, *Egyptian Proper Names and Loanwords*, 246–47; Noonan, *Non-Semitic Loanwords*, 108; Rabin, 'Foreign Words', 1077; Nahum Sarna, *Exodus*, JPS Torah Commentary (Philadelphia: Jewish Publication Society, 1991), 179.
120. Wolja Erichsen, *Demotisches Glossar* (Copenhagen: Ejnar Munksgrad, 1954), s.v. 'ḫtm'; Adolf Erman and Hermann Grapow, *Wörterbuch der Aegyptischen Sprache*, 6 vols (Berlin: Akademie-Verlag, 1926–61), s.v. 'ḫtm'; Janet Johnson, ed., *The Demotic Dictionary of the Oriental Institute of the University of Chicago* [*CDD*], 30 vols (Chicago: Oriental Institute, 2001), vol. 16, s.v. 'ḫtm'; Topoi Excellence Cluster (Freie Universität Berlin and Humboldt-Universität zu Berlin), *Thesaurus Linguae Aegyptiae*, http://aaew.bbaw.de/tla/, s.v. 'ḫtm'.
121. *Comprehensive Aramaic Lexicon*, s.v. 'ḫtm'; Cook, *Dictionary of Qumran Aramaic*, s.v. 'חתם'; *DNWSI*, s.v. 'ḫtm'; Sokoloff, *A Syriac Lexicon*, s.v. 'ܚܬܡܐ'.

have undergone the Canaanite shift, pointing to a borrowing prior to the fourteenth century BCE.[122] If the o-vowel in the Hebrew form were due to the vocalic shift in Egyptian at around the tenth century BCE we would expect both vowels to be affected.[123] The word's absence in Akkadian has been taken as evidence that the word is a borrowing, rather than a cognate.[124] Nevertheless, it must be admitted that the possibility that the word is Afro-Asiatic cannot be ruled out; the only evidence to speak against this is the unusual shape of the noun in Hebrew, not conforming to any of the typical noun patterns.[125] Moreover, as Orel and Stolbova note, the presence of the word in Miya, a West Chadic language, as *katam* is consistent with an Afro-Asiatic hypothesis.[126] However, it would also be plausible as a borrowing from Arabic, *ḫatm*, /xatm/.[127] Taking, then, the view that the word was borrowed, even with some caution, the directionality of the transfer still needs to be determined. Here there is little help from the form of the words or from the presence of cognates, since there are cognates on both sides. Rather, it is only the pre-eminence of Egyptian officialdom and scribal culture prior to the fourteenth century that suggest that the word should be seen to originate in Egypt and not among the Semitic languages.[128] Nevertheless, because the word has such an early entry into Hebrew, it is likely entirely nativized by the time it appears in biblical texts. Thus, it is not counted in the statistics below.

טַבַּעַת
ring; Esth 3:10, 12; 8:2, 8, 8, 10
(Gen 41:42; Exod 25–40, 41 times; Num 31:50; Isa 3:21)
Native synonyms: נֶזֶם; חָח.

---

122. See under 'Appendix Six: An Outline of Linguistic Change in Aramaic and Akkadian'; cf. Muchiki, *Egyptian Proper Names and Loanwords*, 246–47.

123. Antonio Loprieno, 'Ancient Egyptian and Coptic', in Woodard, ed., *The Cambridge Encyclopedia of the World's Ancient Languages*, 160–217 (172–73).

124. Muchiki, *Egyptian Proper Names and Loanwords*, 246–47.

125. Cf. Joshua Fox, *Semitic Noun Patterns*, HSS 52 (Winona Lake: Eisenbrauns, 2003), 287–90.

126. Vladimir Orel and Olga Stolbova, *Hamito-Semitic Etymological Dictionary* (Leiden: Brill, 1995), 434.

127. Miya has no velar fricatives and so it is reasonable that it should represent that sound with a velar stop. Russell Schuh, *A Grammar of Miya* (Berkeley: University of California Press, 1998), 12.

128. Noonan, 'Foreign Loanwords', 179–80; William Schniedewind, *A Social History of Hebrew: Its Origins through the Rabbinic Period*, ABRL (New Haven: Yale University Press, 2013), 36.

There is wide agreement that טַבַּעַת derives from Egyptian ḏbꜥ.t.¹²⁹ Not only do the two words conform closely in form, but this Hebrew word is one of a pair, אֶצְבַּע, 'finger', and טַבַּעַת, 'ring', which both apparently derive from Afro-Asiatic *ç̌ibV.¹³⁰ This leaves little room for doubt that טַבַּעַת is an Egyptian loan, since it corresponds to the Egyptian form, while אֶצְבַּע represents the native Semitic form. The fact that the /ʕ/ of the Egyptian word is maintained as ע in the Hebrew word, rather than a dental consonant, points to a time of borrowing after the period of Old Egyptian, which is to say no earlier than 2000 BCE.¹³¹ Likewise the consonant is changed to /ʔ/ or elided in the Late Period, which places the latest date for the borrowing in 700 BCE.¹³² This is likewise confirmed by the representation of Egyptian ḏ by Hebrew ט, which represents a change completed at some time between Early Egyptian and Late Egyptian.¹³³ Noonan, likewise, suggests that the presence of the *t* as ת in Hebrew points to a *terminus ante quem* for the borrowing of the Amarna period,¹³⁴ since original dentals are elided by this point.¹³⁵

יַיִן
wine; Esth 1:7, 10; 5:6; 7:2, 7, 8
(141 occurrences in Biblical Hebrew. Not in Biblical Aramaic)
Native synonyms: (Hebrew) חֶמֶר.

Brown, Noonan and Rendsburg describe יַיִן as a culture word.¹³⁶ Rabin, similarly derives it from 'non-Semitic Asian languages'.¹³⁷ Given the wide

---

129. Ellenbogen, *Foreign Words*, 75; Lambdin, 'Egyptian Loan Words', 151; Lieblein, 'Mots égyptiens', 203; Muchiki, *Egyptian Proper Names and Loanwords*, 247; Noonan, *Non-Semitic Loanwords*, 109; Rabin, 'Foreign Words', 1077; Rubin, 'Egyptian Loanwords', 794. Cf. *CDD* 25, s.v. 'ḏbꜥ'; Erichsen, *Demotisches Glossar*, s.v. 'ḏbꜥ'; Erman and Grapow, *Wörterbuch*, s.v. 'ḏbꜥ.t'; *Thesaurus Linguae Aegyptiae*, s.v. 'ḏbꜥ.t'.

130. Cf. Noonan, 'Foreign Loanwords', 181 n. 896; Orel and Stolbova, *Hamito-Semitic Etymological Dictionary*, 103. Note, of course, that any reconstruction of an Afro-Asiatic root is very hypothetical.

131. The letter transcribed in Egyptian typically as ꜥ did not come to be spoken as /ʕ/ until the New Kingdom. At earlier stages it was spoken as /d/. Loprieno, 'Ancient Egyptian', 161, 170.

132. Ibid.

133. As argued below in the case of שָׂטָה.

134. Noonan, 'Foreign Loanwords', 180–81.

135. Loprieno, 'Ancient Egyptian', 170.

136. Brown, *Israel and Hellas*, 2:304; Noonan, *Non-Semitic Loanwords*, 112–13; Rendsburg, 'Cultural Words', 1:641.

137. Translation mine, 'שפות אסיה שאין שמיות'. Rabin, 'Foreign Words', 1078.

attestation of the word,¹³⁸ the label 'culture word' is to be preferred over the earlier theory of Vernes that it was borrowed from Greek.¹³⁹ If the prototypic form begins in *w, as might suggest the Latin form *vinum*, the Greek οἶνος,¹⁴⁰ and the Hittite, *wiyana-*, the entry into Semitic languages must have been early – prior to the loss of word-initial *waw*. Because it is so early, it has not been counted in the statistics below.

כִּסֵּא
throne; Esth 1:2; 3:1; 5:1
(137 occurrences in Biblical Hebrew. Twice in Biblical Aramaic as כָּרְסֵא)
Native synonyms: מוֹשָׁב. While מוֹשָׁב has a wider semantic range than 'throne' it would suffice in the contexts here. מוֹשָׁב is used for the king's seat in 1 Sam 20:25, although it is not explicitly a throne in this case.

Several scholars derive כִּסֵּא from Sumerian ᴳᴵˢGUZA, by way of Akkadian *kussû*.¹⁴¹ Kaufman, however, outlines some of the difficulties in this hypothesis, including the dissimilarity between Akkadian *-ss-* and Sumerian *-Z-*. Noonan, however, proposes a satisfactory solution, namely that the word is an early culture word, but that the immediate point of entry for the Northwest Semitic forms is from early Akkadian – they preserve the *aleph*, which is only otherwise preserved in the Old Akkadian and Old Assyrian forms.¹⁴² In Biblical Aramaic, where the word exists as כָּרְסֵא,¹⁴³ the *-ss-* of the Akkadian has been dissimilated to a *resh*. Although we cannot rule out a third language, Noonan's solution is likely correct, that the word is an early loan from Akkadian into Northwest Semitic. Since the loan is so early in Hebrew, we cannot assume it would be genuinely felt as foreign and thus it is not counted in the statistics below. In the

---

138. See above, the discussion of the word under 1.3.4.1, 'Foreign words, culture words and loanwords'.
139. Vernes, *Les Emprunts de la Bible*, 63.
140. Liddell, Scott and Jones, s.v. 'οἶνος'.
141. Ellenbogen, *Foreign Words*, 89; Landesdorfer, *Sumerisches Sprachgut*, 45; Lipiński, 'Emprunts Suméro-akkadiens', 67; Rabin, 'Foreign Words', 1074; Alison Salvesen, 'כִּסֵּא', in *Semantics of Ancient Hebrew*, ed. Takamitsu Muraoka (Louvain: Peeters, 1998), 44–65; Zimmern, *Akkadische Fremdwörter*, 8.
142. Noonan, *Foreign Loanwords*, 50–51.
143. *Comprehensive Aramaic Lexicon*, s.v. 'kwrsy'; Cook, *Dictionary of Qumran Aramaic*, s.v. 'כרסה'; *HALOT*, s.v. 'כָּרְסֵא'; Sokoloff, *DJPA*, s.v. 'כורסי'; Sokoloff, *DJBA*, s.v. 'כורסי'; Sokoloff, *A Syriac Lexicon*, s.v. 'ܟܘܪܣܝܐ'; Sokoloff, *DCPA*, s.v. 'ܟܘܪܣܝܐ'.

case of Aramaic, although it is possible for native words to dissimilate by insertion of *resh*, it nonetheless results in a comparatively rare form, which may mark the word as not entirely nativized.[144] However, this also occurs with native forms, like דַּרְמֶשֶׂק, 'Damascus', and so the Aramaic word has also not been counted in the statistics below.

כַּרְפַּס
linen; Esth 1:6
Native synonyms: בּוּץ.[145] There is an imprecise synonym in פֵּשֶׁת, 'flax', another woven fabric of similar colouring.

There are clear affinities between Hebrew, כַּרְפַּס,[146] Aramaic, כרפס,[147] and various Indo-European forms, including Latin, *carbasus*,[148] Greek, κάρπασος,[149] Farsi, *kirpas* and Sanskrit, *kārpāsá*, 'fine fabric'.[150] These similarities have prompted a variety of hypotheses including, a Greek loan,[151] a Sanskrit loan,[152] a 'Mediterranean' word,[153] and an Iranian loan.[154] The Latin word is an apparent loan from the Greek form.[155] The Greek form itself, however, shows a high degree of variability with attested forms as κάλπασος and χάλπασος,[156] such that there is a good chance that the word is not native to Greek. It is the simplest explanation that the Indo-Iranian forms provide evidence of a Persian word, possibly the source also of the Greek and Latin words.[157]

144. See also, the Akkadian loanword, שַׁרְבִיט.
145. See Noonan, 'Foreign Loanwords', 193–94. In brief, the proposed Egyptian or Sanskrit origins to the word have poor correspondences, either phonetically or semantically.
146. *HALOT*, s.v. 'כַּרְפַּס'.
147. *Comprehensive Aramaic Lexicon*, s.v. 'krps'.
148. Lewis and Short, s.v. 'carbasus'.
149. Liddell, Scott and Jones, s.v. 'κάρπασος'.
150. Cf. Ellenbogen, *Foreign Words*, 94; Noonan, *Non-Semitic Loanwords*, 134–35.
151. Vernes, *Les Emprunts de la Bible*, 76–77.
152. Brown, *Israel and Hellas*, 2:293; Ellenbogen, *Foreign Words*, 94; Sylvia Powels, 'Indische Lehnwörter in der Bibel', *ZAH* 5 (1992): 186–200 (189–90); Rabin, 'Foreign Words', 1079; Wagner, *Die Aramaismen*, 67.
153. Cuny, 'Les Mots du Fonds Préhellénique', 161.
154. Holmstedt and Screnock, *Esther: A Handbook*, 45; Scheftelowitz, *Arisches im Alten Testament*, 47; Wilson, 'Foreign Words', 215.
155. Lewis and Short, s.v. 'carbasus'.
156. Liddell, Scott and Jones, s.vv. 'κάλπασος' and 'χάλπασος'.
157. It is simpler to explain as a Persian loan, rather than Indian because there are more obvious opportunities for contact between Hebrew and Persian than Hebrew

כֶּתֶר
diadem; Esth 1:11; 2:17; 6:8
Native synonyms: עֲטָרָה.

Parallels have been drawn to both Aramaic, כתר, a verb, 'to wear as a hat', and a noun, 'diadem'[158] and Greek, κίταρις, 'Persian head-dress'.[159] The semantic value of the Greek word, however, suggests that there is an Iranian word that underlies these reflexes. Salvesen, on the other hand, believes that the Greek derives from a Semitic original, related to the root כתר, 'to surround'.[160] Salvesen concludes that the Greek and Semitic do refer to the same garment, but that the word is Semitic in origin.[161] Indeed, as Salvesen details, the Greek word is mostly associated with the Persians and Medes.[162] The one case she notes otherwise, in Herodotus VII 90, is a textual conjecture replacing κιθῶνας, 'tunics'.[163] However, even in this case the Cypriots who wear the head-gear are part of the Persian army.

and Sanskrit. The Mediterranean hypothesis does not explain the existence of the Sanskrit, whereas an Iranian loan would suggest that the Sanskrit is simply a cognate. Noonan favours an Indian origin, on the basis of the fact that the Greek word seems to be associated with India. However, that same logic should compel the conclusion that the Hebrew is based on a Persian cognate of the Indian. More compelling would be his argument that in the Iranian languages all relevant etyma are late. Still, that is unsurprising in the case of a poorly attested language like Old Persian. Moreover, as we say, Iranian contact with Hebrew is much more plausible than Sanskrit. Noonan, *Non-Semitic Loanwords*, 134–35.

158. Kautzsch, *Die Aramaismen*, 45–46. Cf. *Comprehensive Aramaic Lexicon*, s.v. 'ktr'; Sokoloff, *DJBA*, s.v. 'כתר'; Sokoloff, *DCPA*, 'ܟܬܪ'.

159. Brown, *Israel and Hellas*, 2:296. Cf. *Liddell, Scott and Jones*, s.v. 'κίδαρις'.

160. Alison Salvesen, 'כֶּתֶר (Esth 1:11; 2:17; 6:8): "Something to Do with a Camel"?', *JSS* 44 (1999): 35–46. See also, Alison Salvesen, 'כֶּתֶר', in *Semantics of Ancient Hebrew*, ed. Takamitsu Muraoka (Louvain: Peeters, 1998), 67–73. She is correct that this root exists. Cf. Wolf Leslau, *Ethiopic and South Arabic Contributions to the Hebrew Lexicon*, University of California Publications in Semitic Philology 20 (Berkeley: University of California Press, 1958), 28; Leslau, *Comparative Dictionary*, s.v. 'katara'.

161. Salvesen, 'Something to Do with a Camel?', 45.

162. Ibid., 39ff.

163. Cf. Pierre Larcher, *Larcher's Notes on Herodotus: Historical and Critical Remarks on the Nine Books of the History of Herodotus*, 2 vols. (London: John R. Priestly, 1829), 2:383. The reason given for the emendation is that tunics do not fit as a counterpart to the μίτρα worn by the kings, understanding that as a headgear. However, the μίτρα is equally a belt.

It does not seem particularly good evidence that the Greek ever means anything other than a Persian head-dress. On the other hand, there are late references to Theophrastus' belief that the κίταρις is Cyprian, found in the Suda, Photius and a scholion on Plato.[164] However in these sources, Theophrastus' opinion is given as the opposition to the general understanding that the κίταρις is Persian.

The question, then, which Salvesen does not adequately explain is why the classical authors almost universally believe that the κίταρις is Persian, if that sense is not inherent, which she claims it is not,[165] to the Semitic word from which it was borrowed. It is of course possible for words to narrow in sense in the process of transfer. However, if a Semitic word for '(generic) headband' entered Greek as κίταρις one would expect any narrowing to be in the direction of 'Phoenician (or similar) headband', not Persian. Further still, it is puzzling that the Greeks, who had long and sustained contact with the Persians, would borrow a word for a Persian head-dress from Semitic-speakers rather from the Persians themselves. Although there is no obvious candidate for an underlying Iranian word, the Persian languages in the ancient period are poorly attested. Because of the semantic problems with the Semitic hypothesis, the likeliest explanation is that the Semitic forms were borrowed from an Iranian language and were then in turn borrowed by Greek.

סוּס

horse; Esth 6:8, 9, 9, 10, 11; 8:10
(140 occurrences in Biblical Hebrew. Not in Biblical Aramaic)
Native synonyms: רֶכֶשׁ (?). However, סוּס itself is thoroughly nativized.

Brown, Ellenbogen and Noonan note the similarity of סוּס to Indo-European forms, like Sanskrit *aśwas*.[166] In addition, Ellenbogen and Noonan

---

164. Theophrastus was a philosopher from the third century BCE. The Suda is from the tenth century and presumably reliant on Photius from the ninth, whose wording is close. Photius, *Lexicon*, s.v. 'τιάρα'; Scholion on Plato's *Republic* 553c; Suda, s.v. 'τιάρα'.

165. Salvesen, 'Something to Do with a Camel?', 45: 'כתר in Esther is best explained as referring to a headband worn widely in the Persian Empire and beyond, but with a version specific to royalty in its fabric or colour, כתר מלכות'. She also speculates (ibid., 44f.) that the word might also have been used to refer to reins or fillets worn by horses.

166. Brown, *Israel and Hellas*, 2:304–5; Ellenbogen, *Foreign Words*, 123; Noonan, *Non-Semitic Loanwords*, 159–60.

raise the following:[167] Egyptian *ssm.t*,[168] Ugaritic *ssw*,[169] and Akkadian *sīsū*, 'horse' – Old Assyrian *sisium*,[170] Aramaic סוּסִי,[171] Persian, *asas-*,[172] Cuneiform Luwian, *azzuš-*,[173] Hieroglyphic Luwian, *asus-*,[174] all 'horse'. To this we should add Median *aspas-*[175] and possibly Elamite *šiši*, 'some kind of work animal'.[176] The Canaanite word, *ss*, is attested as early as the Amarna letters.[177] Given the associations between horse domestication and Indo-European languages,[178] it is an attractive suggestion that the word for horse would spread from Indo-European. Moreover, if the Semitic and Indo-European forms are related, it must be the Indo-European forms that are primary, given the regular correspondences between Greek ἵππος, Latin, *equus* and Median, *aspas-*, suggesting PIE *$h_1ek̑wos$ or similar – if the Semitic forms were primary, then it would be impossible to explain the development of the non-sibilant Indo-European forms. Nevertheless, despite some compelling similarities, it is difficult to reconcile all aspects of the Semitic and Egyptian forms with the Indo-European.[179] Moreover, if there is a loan, it is certainly exceedingly early to allow for its presence in the Amarna letters, such that we should expect it to be fully nativized. As such, we should not treat it as capable of rhetorical effect and it is excluded from our statistics below.

167. Ellenbogen, *Foreign Words*, 123; Noonan, *Non-Semitic Loanwords*, 159.

168. New Kingdom, cf. Erman and Grapow, *Wörterbuch*, s.v. 'ssm.t'; *Thesaurus Linguae Aegyptiae*, s.v. 'ssm.t'.

169. Gregorio del Olmo Lete and Joaquín Sanmartín, *A Dictionary of the Ugaritic Language in the Alphabetic Tradition*, HO 112 (Leiden: Brill, 2015), s.v. 's/śs/św'.

170. Black, George and Postgate, *A Concise Dictionary of Akkadian*, s.v. 'sisû(m)'; *CAD* 15, s.v. '*sīsû*'.

171. *Comprehensive Aramaic Lexicon*, s.v. 'swsy'; *DNWSI*, s.v. 'sws'; Sokoloff, *DJPA*, s.v. 'סוסי'; Sokoloff, *DJBA*, s.v. 'סוסי'; Sokoloff, *A Syriac Lexicon*, s.v. 'ܣܘܣܐ'; Sokoloff, *DCPA*, s.v. 'ܣܘܣܐ'.

172. Kent, *Old Persian*, 173.

173. H. Craig Melchert, *Cuneiform Luvian Lexicon* (Chapel Hill: H. Craig Melchert, 1993), s.v. 'azzu(wa)-'.

174. Annick Payne, *Hieroglyphic Luwian: An Introduction with Original Texts* (Wiesbaden: Harrassowitz, 2010), 144.

175. Kent, *Old Persian*, 173.

176. Hinz and Koch, *Elamisches Wörterbuch*, s.v. 'ši-ši'.

177. *DNWSI*, s.v. 'ss'.

178. Cf., e.g., David Anthony, 'Horse, Wagon & Chariot: Indo-European Languages and Archaeology', *Antiquity* 69 (1995): 554–65.

179. Cf. Noonan, *Non-Semitic Loanwords*, 159–60. Noonan is correct that at the current time we cannot nominate a particular Indo-European language as the source of the Semitic words.

סֹחָרֶת

mineral used for mosaic tile; Esth 1:6
Native synonyms: The term is so specific that there are no obvious synonyms. Nonetheless, the word is used as part of an open list, such that there is no compulsion for its use.

Holmstedt and Screnock point to Arabic, *šuḥḥar*, 'blackish earth', Akkadian, *siḫru*, 'gem setting', and Egyptian *shrt*, 'mineral' (or better *śhr.t*)[180] as points of comparison, but offer no solution to their relationship.[181] Scheftelowitz, on the other hand, identifies this word as a loan from Old Persian, *θuxra-*, 'red'.[182] It is not clear how many of these roots are related to the Hebrew סֹחָרֶת. However, there is no readily constructible single point of origin to the variant sibilant consonants across the Semitic forms. If the Persian is in fact related, it is easy to explain the adoption of θ as a sibilant by Akkadian or Hebrew, given their lack of equivalent consonants. However, the reverse is not true: we would expect Persian to use its native /š/. Alternatively, we might hypothesize a Median, *suxra-* < Proto-Iranian *ćukra-*. It is plausible that the original is Egyptian, borrowed into Akkadian, which regularly treats Egyptian *h* as *ḫ*, and thence into Hebrew. However, this would leave the Persian unexplained. Therefore, although it is far from clear that all these forms must be related, we prefer the Persian hypothesis based on the current evidence.

סָרִיס

eunuch, minister;[183] Esth 1:10, 12, 15; 2:3, 14, 15, 21; 4:4, 5; 6:2, 14; 7:9
(Gen 37:36; 39:1; 40:2,7; 1 Sam 8:15; 1 Kgs 22:9; 2 Kgs 8:6; 9:32; 18:17; 20:18; 23:11; 24:12, 15, 19; 1 Chr 28:1; 2 Chr 18:8;

---

180. Erman and Grapow, *Wörterbuch*, s.v. 'śhr.t'; *Thesaurus Linguae Aegyptiae*, s.v. 'śhr.t'.
181. Holmstedt and Screnock, *Esther: A Handbook*, 47. Cf. *CAD* 15, s.v. 'siḫru'.
182. Scheftelowitz, *Arisches im Alten Testament*, 49; Scheftelowitz, 'Zur Kritik, III', 117; Kent, *Old Persian*, 188.
183. There is some disagreement on the meaning of the word. The precise meaning of the Akkadian phrase that stands behind it is still debated. See Collins, *Daniel*, 134–35; Stephanie Dalley, review of *The King's Magnates*, by R. Mattila, *BO* 58 (2001): 197–206; Goldingay, *Daniel*, 5; Koch, *Daniel*, 3; Luis Siddall, 'A Re-examination of the Title 'ša rēši' in the Neo-Assyrian Period', in *Gilgameš and the World of Assyria: Proceedings of the Conference Held at Mandelbaum House, the University of Sydney, 21–23 July, 2004*, ed. Joseph Azize and Noel Weeks (Leuven: Peeters, 2007), 225–40; A. Leo Oppenheim, 'A Note on *ša rēši*', *JANESCU* 5 (1973): 325–34.

Isa 39:7; 56:3, 4; Jer 29:2; 34:19; 38:7; 39:3, 13; 41:16; 52:25;
Dan 1:3, 7, 8, 9, 10, 11, 18)
Native synonyms: עֶבֶד.[184]

There is wide agreement that סָרִיס derives from Akkadian *ša rēši*, '(castrated?) official'.[185] The word is atypical of Hebrew, since if analyzed as a triliteral root, it would contain identical first and third consonants.[186] The Akkadian form, *ša rēši*, which is analyzable as multiple Akkadian morphemes, provides a good explanation for the form and meaning of the Hebrew word. As Mankowski notes, the equivalence of *š* to ס indicates that the word was transmitted from the Assyrian, rather than Babylonian, dialect.[187]

פּוּר
lot; Esth 3:7; 9:24, 26, 26, 28, 29, 31, 32
Native synonyms: גּוֹרָל.

The text provides an explicit gloss for פּוּר, with Hebrew גּוֹרָל, 'lot' (Esth 3:7), which in itself suggests that the word was expected to be unfamiliar to Esther's audience. Despite Scheftelowitz's contention that פּוּר derives from Avestan, *fravi-*, 'progress, fate', there is poor phonetic correspondence between the two words. Better, instead, is the suggestion of Mankowski and Rabin that it derives from Akkadian, *pūru*, 'lot'.[188] Zimmern and Landesdorfer suggest that the Akkadian itself may derive from Sumerian BUR, 'bowl', but the semantic correspondence is poor.[189] Noonan identifies the source of the Akkadian as Hittite, *pul-*, but we should be wary of the possibility that the borrowing may go the other direction.[190] Noonan is possibly correct that the occurrences in ch. 9 of

---

184. Although this is not a precise synonym, it would function appropriately in the cited locations in Esther (or perhaps as עֶבֶד הַמֶּלֶךְ).

185. Goldingay, *Daniel*, 5; Hartman and Di Lella, *Daniel*, 129; Lipiński, 'Emprunts Suméro-akkadiens', 71; Mankowski, *Akkadian Loanwords*, 123–25; Mankowski, 'Akkadian Loanwords', 84; Newsom, *Daniel*, 37; Rabin, 'Foreign Words', 1073; Wilson, 'Foreign Words', 212; Zimmern, *Akkadische Fremdwörter*, 6.

186. Cf. Joseph Greenberg, 'The Patterning of Root Morphemes in Semitic', *Word* 6 (1950): 162–81.

187. Mankowski, *Akkadian Loanwords*, 125.

188. Mankowski, *Akkadian Loanwords*, 126–27; Rabin, 'Foreign Words', 1074.

189. Landesdorfer, *Sumerisches Sprachgut*, 80–81; Zimmern, *Akkadische Fremdwörter*, 33.

190. Noonan, *Non-Semitic Loanwords*, 171.

Esther, as 'Purim', are folk-etymology.[191] However, we include these occurrences nonetheless, on the basis that the folk-etymology represents the book's view of the word's origin and, thus, is still relevant for its rhetorical effect.

פֶּחָה
governor; Esth 3:12; 8:9; 9:3
(1 Kgs 10:15; 20:24; 2 Kgs 18:24; 2 Chr 9:14; Ezra 5:3, 6, 14; 6:6, 7, 13; 8:36; Neh 2:7, 9; 3:7; 5:14, 14, 15; 12:26; Esth 3:12; 8:9; 9:3; Isa 36:9; Jer 51:23, 28, 57; Ezek 23:6, 12, 23; Dan 3:2, 3, 27; 6:8; Hag 1:1, 14; 2:2, 21; Mal 1:8)
Native synonyms: שַׂר; נְצִיב; פָּקִיד; מֹשֵׁל.

Vernes' minority view that the word is connected to Greek, ἔπαρχος, 'governor', is implausible because the phonetic correspondence of this word to פֶּחָה is weak.[192] Mankowski and several other scholars derive both Hebrew and Aramaic פֶּחָה, 'governor',[193] from Akkadian, pāḫutu, 'governor'.[194] Of these, only Mankowski provides any detailed consideration of the borrowing's mechanics, noticing, for example, that the doubling of the ḫ – necessary to explain the seghol in the Hebrew form – is typical of an Aramaic transmission.[195] Lipiński also notes that the word pāḫutu was used as an abbreviated form of the title bel pāḫiti, 'governor'.[196] This being the case, it is unlikely that the West Semitic forms and the Akkadian form developed in parallel as cognates from a proto-Semitic form; the chance of the same phrase for a governor developing independently is remote, since the derivation of pāḫutu in Akkadian does not appear to have a straightforward semantic relation to the concept of

191. Ibid., 172.
192. Vernes, *Les Emprunts de la Bible*, 125–26.
193. *Comprehensive Aramaic Lexicon*, s.v. 'pḥḥ'; *DNWSI*, s.v. 'pḥḥ'; *HALOT*, s.v. 'פֶּחָה'; Sokoloff, *DJBA*, s.v. 'פחה'.
194. Collins, *Daniel*, 182–83; Ellenbogen, *Foreign Words*, 131; Goldingay, *Daniel*, 65; Hartman and Di Lella, *Daniel*, 156; Lipiński, 'Emprunts Suméro-akkadiens', 71; Mankowski, *Akkadian Loanwords*, 128–29; Rabin, 'Foreign Words', 1074; Zimmern, *Akkadische Fremdwörter*, 6.
195. Were there no doubling in the form immediately prior to borrowing, the Biblical Hebrew form should be פֶּחַת. Mankowski, *Akkadian Loanwords*, 128–29, especially 128 n. 472.
196. Lipiński, 'Emprunts Suméro-akkadiens', 71. See also, J. Nicholas Postgate, 'The Place of the *Šaknu* in Assyrian Government', *AnSt* 30 (1980): 67–76 (68).

governorship.[197] Thus the best explanation is that פֶּחָה is a loan in Aramaic from Akkadian, whence it passed to Hebrew.

פִּלֶגֶשׁ
concubine; Esth 2:14
(Gen 22:24; 25:6; 35:22; 36:12; Judg 8:31; 19:1, 24, 25, 27, 29; 20:4, 5, 6; 2 Sam 3:7, 7; 5:13; 15:16; 16:21, 22; 19:6; 20:3; 21:11. 1 Kgs 11:3; 1 Chr 1:32; 2:46, 48; 3:9; 7:14; 2 Chr 11:21, 21; Song 6:8, 9; Ezek 23:20)
Native synonyms: שִׁפְחָה; אָמָה.

The non-triliteral form suggests a non-Semitic origin for פִּלֶגֶשׁ, as Ellenbogen and others have suggested.[198] On the basis of comparison with Greek παλλακή and παλλακίς, 'concubine', and Latin, *paelex* and *pellex*, 'concubine', Brown, Vernes, Rabin and Heijmans all suggest an Indo-European origin.[199] Cuny, on the other hand, identifies the word as 'Mediterranean' and Rendsburg and Noonan as a culture word.[200] Nevertheless, as Lewis and Short point out, the Latin and Greek are likely connected to Sanskrit *pallavaka*, as cognates, making the Mediterranean hypothesis unlikely.[201] In addition, the sibilant ending in the Indo-European forms represents a grammatical morpheme for the nominative case, rather than a part of the root – thus, it is likely that the word derives from an Indo-European language, whence it was transmitted to Hebrew with the grammatical morpheme understood as part of the lexeme. Since we have an origin point and direction of borrowing, we may rule out the culture-word hypothesis. Nonetheless, there is insufficient information to determine which of the Indo-European languages was the source of

---

197. Black, George and Postgate derive the word from Akkadian, *puḫḫu*, 'to exchange'. It seems unlikely that the same semantic leap would be made by Aramaic as well as Akkadian. Black, George and Postgate, *Concise Dictionary of Akkadian*, s.vv. 'piḫatu' and 'puḫḫu'.

198. Brown, *Israel and Hellas*, 2:298; Cuny, 'Les Mots du Fonds Préhellénique', 162; Ellenbogen, *Foreign Words*, 134; Heijmans, 'Greek Loanwords', 2:148; Rendsburg, 'Cultural Words', 1:641; Vernes, *Les Emprunts de la Bible*, 128–31.

199. Brown, *Israel and Hellas*, 2:298; Heijmans, 'Greek Loanwords', 2:148; Chaim Rabin, 'The Origin of the Hebrew Word *Pīlegeš*', *JJS* 25 (1974): 353–64; Vernes, *Les Emprunts de la Bible*, 128–31.

200. Cuny, 'Les Mots du Fonds Préhellénique', 162; Noonan, *Non-Semitic Loanwords*, 176–77; Rendsburg, 'Cultural Words', 1:641.

201. *Lewis and Short*, s.v. 'paelex'.

the loan. Given that the word is not triliteral, however, it is reasonable to assume that it would be felt as foreign.

פַּרְתְּמִים
nobles; Esth 1:3; 6:9
(Dan 1:3)
Native synonyms: חֹר; אָצִיל; אַדִּיר.

It has been long suggested that פַּרְתְּמִים derives from an Indo-European source, with comparisons being made both to Greek, πρότιμος, 'noble',[202] and Old Persian *fratama-*, 'noble'.[203] Though more recent commentators have preferred the Persian solution, it is difficult to rule the Greek option out on linguistic grounds, being an acceptable match semantically and phonetically. Nevertheless, the vocalization of the Hebrew form is closer to that of the Persian and Persian loans are more common than Greek, so that we should consider the Persian explanation more probable.

פִּתְגָם
statement, decree; Esth 1:20
(Ezra 4:17; 5:7, 11; 6:11; Eccl 8:11; Dan 3:16; 4:14)
Native synonyms: מִצְוָה; דָּבָר; מַאֲמָר.

This word is attested in both Hebrew and Aramaic.[204] Vernes believed פִּתְגָם to have derived from Greek, citing both ἐπίταγμα, 'order', and φθέγμα, 'utterance'. Both words, however, have obvious and different etymologies, connected with the verbs (ἐπί)τάσσω and φθέγγω, respectively. While it is not impossible that פִּתְגָם might still relate to one of those Greek words, there is an alternative and more widely held opinion, which is more satisfying: פִּתְגָם derives from an Iranian source, hypothetically

---

202. Derenbourg, 'Les Mots Grecs', 241; Vernes, *Les Emprunts de la Bible*, 136–37.

203. Ellenbogen, *Foreign Words*, 140; Gindin, 'Persian Loanwords', 67; Hartman and Di Lella, *Daniel*, 129; Holmstedt and Screnock, *Esther: A Handbook*, 41; Koch, *Daniel*, 3–4; Newsom, *Daniel*, 37; Noonan, *Non-Semitic Loanwords*, 185–86; Scheftelowitz, *Arisches im Alten Testament*, 51; Wilson, 'Foreign Words', 215.

204. *Comprehensive Aramaic Lexicon*, s.v. 'ptgm'; Cook, *Dictionary of Qumran Aramaic*, s.v. 'פתגם'; *DNWSI*, s.v. 'ptgm'; *HALOT*, s.v. 'פִּתְגָם'; Sokoloff, *DJPA*, s.v. 'פתגם'; Sokoloff, *DJBA*, s.v. 'פתגם'; Sokoloff, *A Syriac Lexicon*, s.v. 'ܦܬܓܡܐ'; Sokoloff, *DCPA*, s.v. 'ܦܬܓܡܐ'.

Old Persian \*patigama-, 'message, response'.²⁰⁵ While the word is not directly attested in Old Persian, it is attested in Middle Persian, Parthian, Sogdian and Armenian.²⁰⁶ The simplest explanation is that the word passed from an Iranian language into Hebrew and Aramaic.

פַּתְשֶׁגֶן
copy; Esth 3:14; 4:8; 8:13
(Ezra 4:11, 23; 5:6; 7:11)
Native synonyms: מִשְׁנֶה.

The Hebrew פַּתְשֶׁגֶן is widely agreed to derive from an Iranian language, although there is no extant Persian prototype for the loan.²⁰⁷ Nevertheless, Hebrew פַּת conforms to the well-attested Persian prefix, *pati-*, 'against, towards', such that the hypothesis is probable.²⁰⁸ Hypothesized forms include \*patičagna-,²⁰⁹ and \*patiθanhana-.²¹⁰ Given the Elamite forms cited by Tavernier, *ba-iz-[zí?]-ik-nu-iš* and *bat-ti-zí-ik-nu-še*, his reconstruction, *patičagna-*, appears best.²¹¹

---

205. Ellenbogen, *Foreign Words*, 142; Fensham, *Ezra and Nehemiah*, 22, 75; Fried, *Ezra*, 212; Gehman, 'Notes on Persian Words', 325; Gindin, 'Persian Loanwords', 3:67; Holmstedt and Screnock, *Esther: A Handbook*, 24, 69; Koch, *Daniel*, 251; Noonan, *Non-Semitic Loanwords*, 186–87; Rabin, 'Foreign Words', 1079; Scheftelowitz, *Arisches im Alten Testament*, 51–52; Scheftelowitz, 'Zur Kritik, III', 118; Wagner, *Die Aramaismen*, 96; Wilson, 'Foreign Words', 199.

206. Tavernier, *Iranica*, 410.

207. Blenkinsopp, *Ezra–Nehemiah*, 147; Ellenbogen, *Foreign Words*, 143; Gehman, 'Persian Words in Esther', 326; Gindin, 'Persian Loanwords', 67; Holmstedt and Screnock, *Esther: A Handbook*, 134; Noonan, *Non-Semitic Loanwords*, 188; Rabin, 'Foreign Words', 1079; Scheftelowitz, *Arisches im Alten Testament*, 52; Scheftelowitz, 'Zur Kritik, III', 118; Tisdall, 'The Āryan Words in the Old Testament: II', 213–14; Wagner, *Die Aramaismen*, 97; Wilson, 'Foreign Words', 199; Wilson-Wright, 'From Persepolis to Jerusalem', 156.

208. Kent, *Old Persian*, 194.

209. Gindin, 'Persian Loanwords', 67; Noonan, *Non-Semitic Loanwords*, 188; Tavernier, *Iranica*, 410. The word would relate to the root, *čag-*, 'to give', meaning 'something given back', i.e. a copy.

210. Scheftelowitz, *Arisches im Alten Testament*, 52. Scheftelowitz relates the word to a hypothetical root, *θanh-*, 'to order'.

211. Tavernier, *Iranica*, 410. Cf. Hinz and Koch, *Elamisches Wörterbuch*, s.vv. 'bat-ti-zí-ikik-nu-še' and 'ba-iz-zí-ik-nu-iš'.

רַמָּךְ\*
mare; Esth 8:10
Native synonyms: רֶכֶשׁ.

Scheftelowitz identifies רַמָּךְ as an Iranian loan.[212] Although the word is unattested in Old Persian, there does exist Pahlavi *ram(ag)*, 'herd'.[213] In addition, the ending in *-ak* is suggestive of the Persian nominal suffix.[214] However, without better attestation the loan is somewhat hypothetical.

שַׁרְבִיט
sceptre; Esth 4:11; 5:2, 2; 8:4
Native synonyms: מַקֵּל; מַטֶּה; שֵׁבֶט.

While the root of this word is Semitic, *š-b-ṭ*, the appearance of the r-consonant lacks plausible explanation within Hebrew, without recourse to other languages. Rather, the native form of the word is שֵׁבֶט. The word שַׁרְבִיט is explained by Mankowski as a loan from Akkadian, *šabbiṭu*, 'rod', likely through Aramaic:[215] the doubling of the labial consonant found in Akkadian – but in neither Hebrew nor Aramaic – has been dissimilated once the word is borrowed by Aramaic, like the dissimilation that occurs with דַּרְמֶשֶׂק, 'Damascus'.[216] Vernes' suggestion – that Greek σκῆπτρον is related[217] – is unlikely because it is phonetically too dissimilar.

שֵׁשׁ
linen; Esth 1:6, 6; 2:12, 12
(Gen 41:42; Exod 25–40, 33 occurrences; Prov 31:22; Ezek 16:10; 27:7)
Native synonyms: בּוּץ. As we have mentioned, there is also an imprecise synonym in פֵּשֶׁת.

---

212. Scheftelowitz, *Arisches im Alten Testament*, 52; so also Noonan, *Non-Semitic Loanwords*, 201.

213. Mackenzie, *Pahlavi Dictionary*, s.v. ram(ag).

214. Cf. Kent, *Old Persian*, 51.

215. Mankowski, *Akkadian Loanwords*, 147–49; cf. Rabin, 'Foreign Words', 1074; Wagner, *Die Aramaismen*, 116; Zimmern, *Akkadische Fremdwörter*, 8. For the Aramaic word, see *Comprehensive Aramaic Lexicon*, s.v. 'šrbyṭ'; Sokoloff, *DJPA*, s.v. 'שרביט'.

216. Cf. Robert Rezetko, 'The Spelling of "Damascus" and the Linguistic Dating of Biblical Texts', *SJOT* 24 (2010): 110–28 (121–24).

217. Vernes, *Les emprunts*, 166–67.

The status of שֵׁשׁ as an Egyptian loanword in Hebrew is uncontroversial in the scholarship.²¹⁸ Although some of the earlier commentary debated whether the origin of the word was from a simple form, *šś* or from the compound *šś-nšw*,²¹⁹ the simple form hypothesis has won out. Despite the concern over both sibilants being represented by שׁ, there is no need to justify it with the complex assimilations required to propose the compound form. Rather, either the two sibilants of the simple form were both heard as equivalent by Hebrew speakers or there was some form of assimilation across the vowel.

תְּכֵלֶת
dyed fabric; Esth 1:6; 8:15
(Exod 25–40, 34 occurrences; Num 4:6, 7, 9, 11, 12; 15:38; 2 Chr 2:6, 13; 3:14; Jer 10:9; Ezek 23:6; 27:7, 24)
Native synonyms: צָבוּעַ.

The word תְּכֵלֶת has analogues in Aramaic as תְּכִלְתָא, 'purple thread',²²⁰ and Akkadian as *takiltu*, 'purple wool'.²²¹ Lipiński, Propp and Zimmern consider the word a loan from Akkadian²²² and Wagner considers that while the word originated in Akkadian it entered Hebrew by way of Aramaic.²²³ The words certainly match semantically and so there is

---

218. Brevard S. Childs, *The Book of Exodus*, 1st paperback ed., OTL (Louisville: Westminster John Knox, 2004), 523; Ellenbogen, *Foreign Words*, 164; Yehoshua Grintz, '(המשך) מונחים קדומים בתורת כהנים [Archaic Terminology in the Priestly Torah (part two)]', *Leš* 39 (1975): 178–81; Holmstedt and Screnock, *Esther: A Handbook*, 46; Lambdin, 'Egyptian Loan Words', 155; Lieblein, 'Mots égyptiens', 203; Muchiki, *Egyptian Proper Names and Loanwords*, 257–58; Noonan, *Non-Semitic Loanwords*, 215; William Propp, *Exodus 19–40*, AB 2 (New York: Doubleday, 2006), 374; Rabin, 'Foreign Words', 1077; Rubin, 'Egyptian Loanwords', 794; Sarna, *Exodus*, 157.

219. In this case both ś and n must assimilate into the following š. For the Egyptian word, see *CDD* 18, s.vv. 'šs', 'šs-(n)-nsw'; Erichsen, *Demotisches Glossar*, s.vv. 'šs', 'šs-(n)-nsw'; Erman and Grapow, *Wörterbuch*, s.v. 'šs'; *Thesaurus Linguae Aegyptiae*, s.v. 'šs', and perhaps also 'sšr.w'.

220. *Comprehensive Aramaic Lexicon*, s.vv. 'tklyt'', 'tklh'; *HALOT*, s.v. 'תְּכִלְתָא' (Aramaic); Sokoloff, *DJPA*, s.v. 'תוכלה'; Sokoloff, *A Syriac Lexicon*, s.v. 'ܬܟܠܬܐ'; Sokoloff, *DCPA*, s.v. 'ܬܟܠܬ'.

221. *CAD* 18, s.v. 'takiltu'.

222. Lipiński, 'Emprunts Suméro-akkadiens', 72–73; Propp, *Exodus 19–40*, 373; Zimmern, *Akkadische Fremdwörter*, 37.

223. Wagner, *Die Aramaismen*, 118.

nothing in that respect to argue against a borrowing. The use of the word in Aramaic, however, is in Targums, Talmudic texts, the Peshitta and other texts open to influence from Hebrew,[224] so that it is more likely that the word entered Aramaic from Hebrew than the other way around. The word has no obvious etymology internal to Hebrew; on the other hand, Lipiński suggests that the Akkadian *takiltu* should be derived from *taklu*, which he glosses as 'inaltérable' (unalterable).[225] In the sense of 'indelible' the etymology is plausible for a fast dye and the form *takiltu* is identical to the feminine form of the adjective; it is not a stretch to imagine that the noun *takiltu* originated as an adjective describing a more generic noun for dye.[226] Furthermore, though there are some differences in the vocalization of the two forms, they are not so different that they cannot be explained by the processes of nativization; the *seghol* on the *lamed* can be explained by the loss of the case vowel of the Akkadian form and subsequent epenthesis to avoid the final consonant cluster. The *shewa* on the first consonant can be explained as a reduction of the vowel, due to the appearance of the epenthesized vowel.

On the other hand, the possible counter-argument to the word's status as a loanword is that it is a word inherited by each of these three languages from their common ancestor. The limitation of the Aramaic word to texts that could be influenced by Hebrew appears to argue that perhaps it was only inherited by Akkadian and Hebrew and then transferred to Aramaic. Nevertheless, possible Hebrew influence on Aramaic does not rule out the possibility that Aramaic also inherited the word from the common ancestor, which may be supported by the existence of the alternate form תוכלא in Aramaic.[227] However, that precise form is difficult to explain, whether the primary paradigm is inheritance or borrowing. Considering the unusual form of the noun, the lack of a plausible Hebrew etymology, the presence of a plausible Akkadian etymology and the fact that the formal characteristics of the Akkadian and Hebrew nouns match well, the best explanation is that the word is borrowed from Akkadian into Hebrew.

---

224. *Comprehensive Aramaic Lexicon*, s.vv. 'tklyt'', 'tklh'.

225. Lipiński, 'Emprunts Suméro-akkadiens', 73.

226. Thus, for example, in English we might refer to a daily newspaper as 'the daily'.

227. *Comprehensive Aramaic Lexicon*, s.v. 'tklh'.

## 2.4. The loanwords in Daniel

**אֲדַרְגָּזַר\***
official; Dan 3:2, 3
Native synonyms:[228] (Aramaic) פְּקִיד;[229] רַב;[230] רֵישׁ.[231]

Some have suggested that אֲדַרְגָּזַר may be connected to various Iranian lemmata,[232] including *handarža-kāra-,[233] a compound of Avestan, *aδara-*, 'within', and perhaps the root, *γžar-*, 'to flow',[234] a compound of Persian \**hadār-*, 'thousand' (cf. Median *hazār-*), and a root *gāzar-*, 'to cut', ultimately from Semitic \*GZR,[235] or from \**ādranga-āžara-*, 'announcer of financial obligation'.[236] However, *handarža-kāra-* is a difficult match because the consonants differ in order, without explanation and, as Noonan

---

228. See 2.8, 'Native synonyms' for more details on what is meant by these alternatives.

229. The root פקד is found as early as Old Aramaic (Asshur Ostracon, line 17). *Comprehensive Aramaic Lexicon*, s.v. 'pqd'; Cook, *Dictionary of Qumran Aramaic*, s.v. 'פקד'; *DNWSI*, s.v. 'pqd'; Sokoloff, *DJPA*, s.v. 'פקד'; Sokoloff, *DJBA*, s.v. 'פקד'; Sokoloff, *A Syriac Lexicon*, s.vv. 'ܦܩܕ' and 'ܦܩܝܕܐ'; Sokoloff, *DCPA*, s.v. 'ܦܩܕ'. The noun cited here is Syriac, but equally we could cite the participle of the verb.

230. This noun is attested elsewhere in Daniel (5:1) and is common in Aramaic. *Comprehensive Aramaic Lexicon*, s.v. 'rb'; *DNWSI*, s.v. 'rb'; *HALOT*, s.v. 'רַב' (Aramaic); Sokoloff, *DJPA*, s.v. 'רב'; Sokoloff, *DJBA*, s.v. 'רב'; Sokoloff, *A Syriac Lexicon*, s.v. 'ܪܒ'; Sokoloff, *DCPA*, s.v. 'ܪܒ'.

231. With the sense 'head' the noun is basic vocabulary in Aramaic, including Biblical Aramaic. The sense, 'chief', is a relatively simple development and is common to many dialects, if not attested in Biblical Aramaic. Moreover, since that development is shared by Biblical Hebrew it would be at home in Daniel. *Comprehensive Aramaic Lexicon*, s.v. 'ryš'; Cook, *Dictionary of Qumran Aramaic*, s.v. 'ריש'; *DNWSI*, s.v. 'ryš'; Sokoloff, *DJPA*, s.v. 'ריש'; Sokoloff, *DJBA*, s.v. 'ריש'; Sokoloff, *A Syriac Lexicon*, s.v. 'ܪܫܐ'; Sokoloff, *DCPA*, s.v. 'ܪܫܐ'.

232. E.g. Goldingay, *Daniel*, 65. He does not nominate an original Iranian form.

233. BDB, s.v. 'אֲדַרְגָּזַר'; Hartman and Di Lella, *Daniel*, 157; Hinz, *Altiranisches Sprachgut*, s.v. '\*handarzakara-'; Koch, *Daniel*, 246.

234. Tisdall, 'The Book of Daniel', 213.

235. Frithiof Rundgren, 'Ein iranischer Beamtenname im Aramäischen', *Orientalia Suecana* 12 (1963): 89–98 (93).

236. Benjamin Noonan, 'A (New) Old Iranian Etymology for Biblical Aramaic אֲדַרְגָּזַר', *Aramaic Studies* 16 (2018): 10–19 (15–18); Noonan, *Non-Semitic Loanwords*, 42.

points out, are a poor match in any case.²³⁷ The same poor correspondence is pointed out by Noonan in the case of *hazārgāzara-, 'chiliarch'.²³⁸ The compound of *aδara-* and *yžar-* is a speculative match semantically, comparison to English 'influence' notwithstanding.²³⁹ Noonan's suggestion of *ādranga-āžara-* is quite plausible. However, as well as *ā-dranga-* we should also consider the un-prefixed version of the root, *drang-*, 'to make firm':²⁴⁰ the א would be well-explained as a prothesis to aid with the consonant cluster. Potentially related would be the Elamite, *hh.tar-qa-sir-ma*, identified as a Median name by Hinz and Koch.²⁴¹ In either case, it seems likely that the word derives from an Iranian language even if we cannot determine the origin precisely.

אַזְדָּא
certain;²⁴² Dan 2:5, 8
Native synonyms: (Aramaic) יַצִּיב.²⁴³

Although some of the versions understand this as a participle from the verb אזד – Theodotion translates as ἀπέστη, 'it went out' – an internal Aramaic hypothesis relies on assuming an interchange between the root אזל, 'to depart', and אזד, which is otherwise unknown in this sense. As such, many scholars have suspected an Iranian loan.²⁴⁴ Scheftelowitz suggests that אַזְדָּא is an Iranian loan, meaning 'gone', constructing the hypothetical *azda-*, past passive participle of *azaiti-*, 'to go', on

---

237. Noonan, 'A (New) Old Iranian Etymology', 13–14. In particular, *h* should not be represented by א, nor *k* by ג.
238. Ibid., 15.
239. Latin: *in*, 'in', and *fluere*, 'to flow'. Cf. Tisdall, 'The Book of Daniel', 213.
240. Bartholomae, *Altiranisches Wörterbuch*, s.v. 'drang-'.
241. Hinz and Koch, *Elamisches Wörterbuch*, s.v. 'hh.tar-qa-sir-ma'.
242. The word is also glossed as 'promulgated'. The meaning 'certain' is suggested with reference to the compound form אַזְדְּכָרָא, 'herald', or 'one who makes certain/clear'. The second half of the compound is based on the Persian verbal noun *kāra*, 'one who does/makes'. Another analysis (Collins, ultimately deriving his information from Hinz) translates the word as 'verdict, decision'. Cf. Collins, *Daniel*, 148; Hinz, *Altiranisches Sprachgut*, 52.
243. Attested in Daniel 2:45. *Comprehensive Aramaic Lexicon*, s.v. 'yṣyb'; *DNWSI*, s.v. 'yṣyb'; *HALOT*, s.v. 'יַצִּיב' (Aramaic).
244. Collins, *Daniel*, 148; Hinz, *Altiranisches Sprachgut*, 52; Koch, *Daniel*, 90; Newsom, *Daniel*, 62; Frithiof Rundgren, 'Aramaica III. An Iranian Loanword in Daniel', *Orientalia Suecana* 25–26 (1976–77): 45–55; Scheftelowitz, 'Zur Kritik, IV', 310.

comparison to Sanskrit, *ajati*, 'to drive', and Greek ἄγειν, 'to drive' and based on Theodotion's translation.²⁴⁵ The word has no satisfactory etymology internal to Semitic languages, so a loan from an Iranian language is attractive. However, as Rundgren suggests,²⁴⁶ rather than Scheftelowitz's unattested source, there is a better candidate that is actually attested in Old Persian, namely *azda-*, 'known, certain'.²⁴⁷

**אֲחַשְׁדַּרְפַּן\***
satrap; Dan 3:2, 3, 27; 6:1, 2, 3, 4, 6, 7
(Ezra 8:36; Esth 3:12; 8:9; 9:3)
Native synonyms: (Aramaic) רֵישׁ ;רַב ;פְּקוֹד.²⁴⁸

See the explanation under 2.3, 'The loanwords in Esther'.

**אֵנֶב\***
fruit; Dan 4:9, 11, 18
(Job 8:12; Song 6:11)
Native synonyms: (Aramaic) פְּרִי;²⁴⁹ עִנְבָּא.²⁵⁰

The Aramaic word אֵנֶב and the related Hebrew אֵב, both 'fruit', exist in those languages alongside עֵנָב, 'fruit'.²⁵¹ The alternation between *ayin* and *aleph* points to an Akkadian loan, as Zimmern has suggested previously.²⁵² As Semitic ʿ was reflected in Hebrew and Aramaic by ע, it was reflected in Akkadian by ʾ. If so, we can suggest a Semitic word *\*ʿnb*. However, we must also account for other Semitic roots found spelt with *aleph* and no *nun*: Ugaritic *ʾib*, 'fruit, bud, flower',²⁵³ and Amharic

---

245. Scheftelowitz, 'Zur Kritik, IV', 310.
246. Rundgren, 'An Iranian Loanword in Daniel', 45–55. See also Koch, *Daniel*, 90; Noonan, *Non-Semitic Loanwords*, 47.
247. Kent, *Old Persian*, 173–74.
248. See above, under אֲדַרְגָּזֵר.
249. Found in Official Aramaic TAD D1.17. *Comprehensive Aramaic Lexicon*, s.v. 'pry'; Cook, *Dictionary of Qumran Aramaic*, s.v. 'פרי'; Sokoloff, *DJPA*, s.v. 'פרי'; Sokoloff, *A Syriac Lexicon*, s.v. 'ܦܐܪ'.
250. The word עִנְבָּא is attested in Official Aramaic (La Collection Clermont-Ganneau 42, R.8).
251. *Comprehensive Aramaic Lexicon*, s.v. 'ʿnb'; *HALOT*, s.v. 'עֵנָב' (Aramaic); Sokoloff, *DJPA*, s.v. 'ענבה'; Sokoloff, *DJBA*, s.v. 'ענבה'; Sokoloff, *A Syriac Lexicon*, s.v. 'ܥܢܒܐ'; Sokoloff, *DCPA*, s.v. 'ܥܢܒ'.
252. Zimmern, *Akkadische Fremdwörter*, 55.
253. *DULAT*, s.v. 'ib'.

*abbäbä*, 'flower'.²⁵⁴ These lexemes might imply that the Aramaic is based on the root אבב and that the nun is the result of dissimilation. However, as Kaufman argues, *'nb* always means fruit not blossom and dissimilation of *bb* to *nb* is unknown in Imperial Aramaic. Therefore, the root אבב is separate. Thus, the Akkadian *inbu*, 'grape', is the source of this Aramaic word.

אַפֶּדֶן*
palace; Dan 11:45
Native synonyms: (Hebrew) בַּיִת; זְבֻל.

There is a near consensus that the *hapax legomenon* אַפֶּדֶן derives from Old Persian, *apadāna-*, 'palace'.²⁵⁵ Not only is the word attested in Persian, but it also has plausible etymologies in Persian.²⁵⁶ Likewise, it only appears here in Daniel, where Persianisms are relatively common.

אֵפֶר
dust; Dan 9:3
(Gen 18:27; Num 19:9, 10; 2 Sam 13:19; 1 Kgs 20:38, 41; Esth 4:1, 3; Job 2:8; 13:12; 30:19; 42:6; Pss 102:10; 147:16; Isa 44:20; 58:5; 61:3; Jer 6:26; Lam 3:16; Ezek 27:30; 28:18; Jon 3:6; Mal 3:21)
Native synonyms: (Hebrew) עָפָר; אֲדָמָה.

See the explanation under 2.3, 'The loanwords in Esther'.

אַרְגְּוָן
purple; Dan 5:7, 16, 29
(Exod 25:4; 26:1, 31, 36; 27:16; 28:5, 6, 8, 15, 33; 35:6, 23, 25, 35; 36:8, 35, 37; 38:18, 23; 39:1, 2, 3, 5, 8, 24, 29; Num 4:13;

---

254. Leslau, *Contributions to the Hebrew Lexicon*, 9. However, note that the forms Leslau cites from Tigre, *'ambäba* and Tigrinya, *'ambäbä*, demonstrate that the original Ethiosemitic is more likely spelt with *ayin*.

255. Ellenbogen, *Foreign Words*, 35; Noonan, *Non-Semitic Loanwords*, 59; Rabin, 'Foreign Words', 1079; Scheftelowitz, 'Zur Kritik, IV', 310; Tisdall, 'Āryan Words III', 370–71; Wagner, *Die Aramaismen*, 28; Wilson, 'Foreign Words', 214; Wilson-Wright, 'From Persepolis to Jerusalem', 155. Only Derenbourg suggests otherwise, citing Greek πέδον. Derenbourg, 'Les Mots Grecs', 242.

256. E.g. *apa + dā*. See Kent, *Old Persian*, 128. See also Rüdiger Schmitt, 'Apadāna i. Term', in *Encyclopaedia Iranica*, ed. Eshan Yarshater (New York: Bibliotheca Persica, 1987), 2:145–46.

Judg 8:26; 2 Chr 2:13; 3:14; Esth 1:6; 8:15; Prov 31:22; Song 3:10; 7:6; Jer 10:9; Ezek 27:7, 16)
Native synonyms: (Aramaic) There are no obvious, precise synonyms, although rough synonyms may exist: סָמְקָא.[257] However, the word is used as a part of the list of items, which would not be substantially changed were it missing.

See the explanation under 2.3, 'The loanwords in Esther'.

**אַשָּׁף\***
exorcist; Dan 1:20; 2:2, 10, 27; 4:4; 5:7, 11, 15
Native synonyms: (Aramaic) חָרָשׁ.[258]

The word אַשָּׁף derives from Akkadian *(w)āšipu*, 'exorcist'.[259] Landesdorfer and Ellenbogen also suggest that the word arrived in Akkadian from Sumerian, *išib*.[260] However, as Mankowski shows, the word has a good Semitic etymology. Moreover, he continues, the word must be borrowed from Akkadian – rather than inherited from proto-Semitic or borrowed in the other direction – since the Akkadian points to a Semitic root, *\*wšp*, which would have a reflex *\*ישׁף* in Hebrew.[261]

**בִּירָה**
citadel; Dan 8:2
(1 Chr 29:1, 19; 2 Chr 17:12; 27:4; Ezra 6:2; Neh 1:1; 2:8; 7:2; Esth 1:2, 5; 2:3, 5, 8; 3:15; 8:14; 9:6, 11, 12)
Native synonyms: (Hebrew) מִבְצָר; מָעוֹז; מִשְׂגָּב.

See the explanation under 2.3, 'The loanwords in Esther'.

257. *Comprehensive Aramaic Lexicon*, s.v. 'smqh'.
258. Although this word is not found in Official or Biblical Aramaic, it is found at Qumran (e.g. 4QEn[b] 1.3.2) and other Aramaic dialects. *Comprehensive Aramaic Lexicon*, s.v. 'ḥrš'; Cook, *Dictionary of Qumran Aramaic*, s.v. 'חרש'; Sokoloff, *DJPA*, s.v. 'חרש'; Sokoloff, *DJBA*, s.v. 'חרש'; Sokoloff, *A Syriac Lexicon*, s.v. 'ܚܪܫܐ'; Sokoloff, *DCPA*, s.v. 'ܚܪܫ'.
259. Collins, *Daniel*, 129, 138; Hartman and Di Lella, *Daniel*, 131; Lipiński, 'Emprunts suméro-akkadiens', 64; Mankowski, *Akkadian Loanwords*, 43–44; Mankowski, 'Akkadian Loanwords', 84; Newsom, *Daniel*, 38; Noonan, *Non-Semitic Loanwords*, 325; Rabin, 'Foreign Words', 1074; Wagner, *Die Aramaismen*, 31; Wilson, 'Foreign Words', 214; Zimmern, *Akkadische Fremdwörter*, 67.
260. Ellenbogen, *Foreign Words*, 43; Landesdorfer, *Sumerisches Sprachgut*, 39–40.
261. Mankowski, *Akkadian Loanwords*, 43–44.

גְּדָבַר*
treasurer; Dan 3:2, 3
(Ezra 1:8; 7:21)
Native synonyms: (Aramaic) חָשְׁבָּן.[262]

See the explanation of גְּנַז under 2.3, 'The loanwords in Esther'.

דָּת
law; Dan 2:9, 13, 15; 6:6, 9, 13, 16; 7:25
(Deut 33:2 (?); Ezra 7:12, 14, 21, 25, 26, 26; 8:36; Esth 1:8, 13, 15, 19; 2:8, 12; 3:8, 8, 14, 15; 4:3, 8, 11, 16; 8:13, 14, 17; 9:1, 13, 14)
Native synonyms: (Aramaic) פְּקוּד.[263]
Native synonyms: (Hebrew) תּוֹרָה; מַאֲמַר; דָּבָר; מִצְוָה; *inter alios*.

דְּתָבַר*
judge; Dan 3:2, 3
Native synonyms: (Aramaic) שְׁפֵט;[264] דִּין.[265]

For דָּת, see the explanation under 2.3, 'The loanwords in Esther'. It is uncontroversial that דְּתָבַר is a Persianism.[266] Just as גְּדָבַר reflects a Persian compound built on גְּנַז and בַּר, the Biblical Aramaic דְּתָבַר reflects a compound built from דָּת, 'law', and בַּר, 'bearer'. Although the compound form is not attested in Persian, Ellenbogen outlines a variety of cognate evidence in favour of its existence.[267]

---

262. While the noun is not attested outside Hatran Aramaic, the verb on which it is based is common in Aramaic, including Biblical Aramaic (Dan 4:32). *Comprehensive Aramaic Lexicon*, s.v. 'ḥšbn', 'ḥšb'; Cook, *Dictionary of Qumran Aramaic*, s.v. 'חשב'; *DNWSI*, s.v. 'חשבן'; *HALOT*, s.v. 'חשב'; Sokoloff, *DJPA*, s.v. 'חשב'; Sokoloff, *DJBA*, s.v. 'חשב'; Sokoloff, *A Syriac Lexicon*, s.v. 'ܚܫܒ'; Sokoloff, *DCPA*, s.v. 'ܚܫܒ'.

263. As we have noted above, the root פקד is found even in Old Aramaic (Asshur Ostracon, line 17) and in a wide array of Aramaic dialects.

264. Cf. Ezra 7:25. *Comprehensive Aramaic Lexicon*, s.v. 'špṭ'; *HALOT*, s.v. 'שְׁפֵט'; Sokoloff, *A Syriac Lexicon*, s.v. 'ܫܦܛ'.

265. Cf. Ezra 7:25. *Comprehensive Aramaic Lexicon*, s.v. 'dyn'; Cook, *Dictionary of Qumran Aramaic*, s.v. 'dyn'; *DNWSI*, s.v. 'dyn'; *HALOT*, s.v. דִּין; Sokoloff, *DJPA*, s.v. 'דין'; Sokoloff, *DJBA*, s.v. 'דין'; Sokoloff, *A Syriac Lexicon*, s.v. 'ܕܝܢܐ'; Sokoloff, *DCPA*, s.v. 'ܕܝܢ' (s.v. 'ܕܘܢ').

266. Ellenbogen, *Foreign Words*, 62; Hartman and Di Lella, *Daniel*, 157; Noonan, *Non-Semitic Loanwords*, 89.

267. Ellenbogen, *Foreign Words*, 62.

## 2. The Loanwords

**הַדָּבָר\***
royal official; Dan 3:24, 27; 4:33; 6:8
Native synonyms: (Aramaic) רֵישׁ; רַב; פְּקוֹד.[268]

Despite Wilson's connection between הַדָּבָר and Babylonian *itbaru*, 'friend', the phonetic correspondence is poor.[269] Rather, as several scholars suggest, the word הַדָּבָר appears to be a compound based on the morpheme בַּר, 'bearer' likewise attested in גְּדָבַר and דְּתָבַר.[270] For the other component, Noonan suggests Old Persian *hadā-*, also pointing out Manichaean Parthian, *'dy'wr*, 'friend'.[271] Babylonian *itbaru* (< *ibru*)[272] seems to be unrelated.

**הַדָּם\***
member; Dan 2:5; 3:29
Native synonyms: (Aramaic) אֲבַר.[273]

Scholars have identified הַדָּם as a loanword from an Iranian source on the basis of Avestan *handāman-*, 'bodily member', and Pahlavi *handām*, 'member, limb'.[274] The nasal has been assimilated, as readily happens in Aramaic. הַדָּם is widely attested in Aramaic, but not before the Persian period, such that the loan hypothesis should cause no controversy on that count. Moreover, the word is isolated in Semitic languages, with no plausible etymology.[275] A loan from an Iranian language is the most plausible explanation.

---

268. See above, under אֲדַרְגָּזֵר.
269. Wilson, 'Foreign Words', 196.
270. Ellenbogen, *Foreign Words*, 64; Hartman and Di Lella, *Daniel*, 158; Koch, *Daniel*, 254; Tisdall, 'The Āryan Words in the Old Testament I', 339.
271. Noonan, *Non-Semitic Loanwords*, 91–92.
272. *CAD* 7, s.v. 'ibru'.
273. Attested earliest at Qumran (4Q561 1.4) and a variety of other kinds of Aramaic. *Comprehensive Aramaic Lexicon*, s.v. ''br'; Cook, *Dictionary of Qumran Aramaic*, s.v. 'אבר'; *DNWSI*, s.v. ''br'; Sokoloff, *DJPA*, s.v. 'אבר'; Sokoloff, *DJBA*, s.v. 'אבר'; Sokoloff, *A Syriac Lexicon*, s.v. 'ܐܒܪ'; Sokoloff, *DCPA*, s.v. 'ܐܒܪ'.
274. Ellenbogen, *Foreign Words*, 65; Noonan, *Non-Semitic Loanwords*, 92; Scheftelowitz, 'Zur Kritik, IV', 310; Wilson, 'Foreign Words', 196. So also, Collins, *Daniel*, 148.
275. See Ellenbogen for a discussion of the verb הדם. Ellenbogen, *Foreign Words*, 65.

הֵיכָל

temple, palace; Dan 1:4; 4:1, 26; 5:2, 3, 5; 6:19
(80 occurrences in Biblical Hebrew. 13 occurrences in Biblical Aramaic)
Native synonyms: (Hebrew) בֵּית מִקְדָּשׁ (temple); זְבֻל ;בַּיִת (palace).
Native synonyms: (Aramaic) בֵּית אֱלָהָא (temple); בֵּית מַלְכּוּ (palace).

This word is attested not only in Aramaic, but in Hebrew and Ugaritic. A wide range of scholars recognize this word as deriving from Sumerian, é.gal, 'palace, temple',[276] generally by way of Akkadian *ekallu*, 'palace, temple'.[277] Mankowski offers an explanation of the apparent phonetic discrepancies between the Akkadian and Northwest Semitic versions of the word; he suggests that the *h* represents a pharyngeal onset to the sound represented by É in the cuneiform.[278] Recently, Rubio has cast doubt on the reality of the existence of this consonantal onset in Sumerian itself, because of the rarity of supposed cases of this phoneme.[279] However, though it would be strengthened by the presence of the Sumerian phoneme, Mankowski's argument actually lies in the presence of this pharyngeal onset – which need not necessarily have had phonemic status or orthographic representation – in Akkadian not Sumerian. Thus, it remains possible to explain the word as a Sumerian loan into Akkadian and thence into other Semitic languages. On the basis of the etymology as 'great house' in Sumerian (É + GAL) and the lack of etymology elsewhere, it is still the likeliest explanation.

Nonetheless, the word appears to have spread to Northwest Semitic very early. Because of this and because of its wide attestation, it appears unlikely to be a word readily recognizable as a loanword from a particular source, though Hebrew and Aramaic readers may have been aware of its counterparts in other languages. Thus, we have not counted it in the below analysis.

276. Pennsylvania Museum of Anthropology and Archaeology, *Electronic Pennsylvania Sumerian Dictionary* [*ePSD*], http://psd.museum.upenn.edu/, s.v. 'é.gal'.
277. *CAD* 4, s.v. 'ekallu'; Ellenbogen, *Foreign Words*, 67; Landesdorfer, *Sumerisches Sprachgut*, 42; Lipiński, 'Emprunts suméro-akkadiens', 65; Mankowski, *Akkadian Loanwords*, 51–52; Noonan, *Non-Semitic Loanwords*, 94–95; Rabin, 'Foreign Words', 1072; Rubin, 'Egyptian Loanwords', 794; Wilson, 'Foreign Words', 188; Zimmern, *Akkadische Fremdwörter*, 8, 68.
278. Mankowski, *Akkadian Loanwords*, 51–52.
279. Gonzalo Rubio, 'Sumerian Temples and Arabian Horses: On Sumerian e2-gal', in *The First Ninety Years: A Sumerian Celebration in Honor of Miguel Civil*, ed. Lluís Feliu et al. (Berlin: de Gruyter, 2017), 284–99, especially 286.

הַמְנִיךְ*

necklace; Dan 5:7, 16, 29
Native synonyms: (Aramaic) כְּבֵל.[280]

This word has *qere* and *kethiv* variants, הַמְנִיכָא and המונכא. As regards the *qere* form, Ellenbogen and Scheftelowitz, derive הַמְנִיךְ from Persian, *\*hamyanak-*, on the basis of the Farsi *hamyan*, 'girdle'.[281] Ellenbogen also suggests that the Greek, μανιάκης, 'necklace', was in fact derived from the Aramaic[282] – Derenbourg and Vernes suggest the opposite.[283] Ellenbogen, in his suggestion that the Greek μανιάκης is derived from Aramaic, presumably because the *he* of the Aramaic has been misinterpreted as an article, is likely correct because Aramaic מניך is also attested, showing that the confusion was present among Aramaic speakers.[284] As for the Persian origin of הַמְנִיךְ, it is the most likely scenario, since it is difficult to otherwise explain the ending in *kaph*, indicating the common Persian nominal suffix *-ak-*.[285] The *kethiv* form is in some respects closer to the Persian prototype, if we imagine some sort of interchange between *waw* and *yodh*. Nonetheless, it is also difficult to rule out that the *kethiv* might represent an entirely different lexeme.

זָכוּ

innocence; Dan 6:23
Native synonyms: (Aramaic) The root דכי represents the form of this Semitic root that is native to Aramaic. It is attested in Imperial Aramaic.[286]

Hartman and Di Lella suggest that זָכוּ derives from the Akkadian, *zākûtu*, 'cleanliness', based on comparison to the native Aramaic root,

---

280. Attested in Official Aramaic (e.g. Clermont-Ganneau, Elephantine Ostracon 175, 16 recto 2). *Comprehensive Aramaic Lexicon*, s.v. 'kbl'; Sokoloff, *DJBA*, s.v. 'כבל'; Sokoloff, *A Syriac Lexicon*, s.v. 'ܟܒܠ'.
281. Ellenbogen, *Foreign Words*, 70; Scheftelowitz, 'Zur Kritik, IV', 312. Similarly, Collins, *Daniel*, 247; Hartman and Di Lella, *Daniel*, 184.
282. Ellenbogen, *Foreign Words*, 70.
283. Derenbourg, 'Les Mots Grecs', 240; Vernes, *Les emprunts*, 37.
284. Ellenbogen, *Foreign Words*, 70; contra Noonan, *Non-Semitic Loanwords*, 96; see also *Comprehensive Aramaic Lexicon*, s.v. 'mnyk'.
285. Cf. Kent, *Old Persian*, 51.
286. TAD A4.1, recto, line 5. *Comprehensive Aramaic Lexicon*, s.v. 'dky'; Cook, *Dictionary of Qumran Aramaic*, s.v. 'dky'; Sokoloff, *DJPA*, s.v. 'דכי'; Sokoloff, *DJBA*, s.v. 'דכי'; Sokoloff, *A Syriac Lexicon*, s.v. 'ܕܟܐ'; Sokoloff, *DCPA*, s.v. 'ܕܟܐ'.

דכי.²⁸⁷ The *daleth* of דכי represents the normal reflex of Semitic *ḏ* in Aramaic, which implies זכו derives from a language that has /z/ as a reflex for *ḏ*. We can also bring Hebrew זָכָה, 'to be innocent', as a point of comparison. Landesdorfer also compares Sumerian A.ZAG.²⁸⁸ However, in light of the cognates in Hebrew and Akkadian, it seems likely that the word is native to the Semitic languages. Kaufman believes the word is more likely to derive from a Canaanite source, like Hebrew, because he finds the development from the sense of the Akkadian word 'to be clear', 'to be free of claims', to the sense of the Aramaic word, 'to be innocent', 'to be victorious', unlikely.²⁸⁹ Nevertheless the Akkadian word can be used in the sense of 'to become clean or pure'.²⁹⁰ The connection with innocence seems straightforward.

זְמָן
time; Dan 2:16, 21; 3:7, 8; 4:33; 6:11, 14; 7:12, 22, 25
(Ezra 5:3; Neh 2:6; Esth 9:27, 31; Eccl 3:1)
Native synonyms: (Aramaic) עִדָּן;²⁹¹ עֵת.²⁹²

See the explanation under 2.3, 'The loanwords in Esther'.

זַן
kind; Dan 3:5, 7, 10, 15
(2 Chr 16:14; Pss 144:13, 13)
Native synonyms: (Aramaic) In the above instances it is used in the phrase, וְכֹל זְנֵי זְמָרָא, 'all sorts of music'. For such purposes, כֹּל alone would be sufficient.²⁹³

Notwithstanding Vernes' suggestion that זַן derives from Greek, γένος, 'kind', a poor phonetic match,²⁹⁴ there is a good case that this word derives

---

287. Hartman and Di Lella, *Daniel*, 196.
288. Landesdorfer, *Sumerisches Sprachgut*, 90.
289. Kaufman, *The Akkadian Influences*, 112.
290. *CAD* 21, s.v. 'zakû'.
291. Attested in Official Aramaic (e.g. TAD B2.11, recto 13). *Comprehensive Aramaic Lexicon*, s.v. "dn"; Cook, *Dictionary of Qumran Aramaic*, s.v. "dn"; *DNWSI*, s.v. "dn"; Sokoloff, *DJPA*, s.v. 'עדן'; Sokoloff, *DJBA*, s.v. 'עדן'; Sokoloff, *A Syriac Lexicon*, s.v. 'ܥܕܢܐ'.
292. Attested in Official Aramaic (La Collection Clermont-Ganneau 229, V.2).
293. *Comprehensive Aramaic Lexicon*, s.v. 'kl'.
294. Vernes, *Les Emprunts de la Bible*, 41–42.

instead from the Iranian, *-zana-, as a variety of scholars claim.[295] While *-zana- is not directly attested, it is found in the compounds *paruzana-*, 'many kinds of men', *Varkazana-*, a month name, and *vispazana-*, 'all kinds of men'.[296] From these words it has been supposed by Kent that the word means 'man'.[297] However, it is clear that the meaning of 'kind' accords just as completely with the evidence. Moreover, the Greek, γένος, and likewise the Latin, *genus*, 'kind',[298] offer good evidence to construct an Indo-European stem, *$\hat{g}en$-, with the meaning, 'kind'. Thus, the best explanation is that זַן is an Iranian loanword. As Noonan points out, the word must be originally Median rather than Persian,[299] since we should expect the result to be *-dana- in Old Persian. However, in Median, the word would be *-zana-. The compound, *vispazana*, must also derive from Median – in Persian, *vispa-* is instead *visa-*. Thus, זַן has every indication of being a Median loanword, presumably through Old Persian.

חוֹתָם
seal
(Gen 38:18; Exod 28:11, 21, 36; 39:6, 14, 30; 1 Kgs 21:8; 1 Chr 7:32; 11:44; Job 38:14; 41:7; Song 8:6, 6; Jer 22:24; Hag 2:23)
Also note: the denominative verb, חָתַם, 'to seal'; Dan 6:18; 9:24, 24; 12:4, 9
(Lev 15:3; Deut 32:34; 1 Kgs 21:8; Neh 10:1, 2; Esth 3:12; 8:8, 8, 10; Job 9:7; 14:14; 24:16; 33:16; 37:7; Song 4:12; Isa 8:16; 29:11, 11; Jer 32:10, 11, 14, 44; Ezek 28:12)
Native synonyms: There are no native synonyms and the word is an early borrowing into Hebrew.

See the explanation under 2.3, 'The loanwords in Esther'. Note that since the borrowing is so early, this word has not been counted in the statistics below.

---

295. Collins, *Daniel*, 184; Ellenbogen, *Foreign Words*, 71–72; Koch, *Daniel*, 248; Noonan, *Non-Semitic Loanwords*, 97–98; Scheftelowitz, 'Zur Kritik, IV', 312; Wagner, *Die Aramaismen*, 49; Wilson-Wright, 'From Persepolis to Jerusalem', 156.
296. Kent, *Old Persian*, 196, 208.
297. Kent, *Old Persian*, 211.
298. *Lewis and Short*, s.v. 'genus'.
299. Noonan, *Non-Semitic Loanwords*, 98.

חַרְטֹם

magician; Dan 1:20; 2:2, 10, 27; 4:4, 6; 5:11; Dan 5:7 (4QDan$^a$)
(Gen 41:8, 24; Exod 7:11, 22; 8:3, 14, 15; 9:11, 11)
Native synonyms: (Hebrew) כַּשָּׁף;[300] יִדְּעֹנִי.
Native synonyms: (Aramaic) חָרָשׁ.[301]

This word is applied to both the Egyptian magicians of Pharaoh's court but also here in Daniel to the magicians of the Babylonian Empire. There are two suggestions for the origin of this word, that it derives from Sumerian[302] or, more commonly, that it derives from Egyptian.[303] While Landesdorfer's Sumerian solution is interesting, it suffers from the fact that the word is only attested in its component parts in Sumerian. The Egyptian word, ḥr-tp, on the other hand, is known from the pyramid texts.[304] While there are certain phonetic difficulties, Muchiki explains and accounts for them: the Egyptian prototype, ḥr-tp, 'chief', is at first glance difficult because of the equivalence of $p$ with ב and $t$ with ט. Muchiki explains the first change through the development of $p > b$, which he claims is similar enough to ב, with the support of the Greek versions of the Egyptian name Chnum, χνουμις and χνουβις.[305] The latter change is explained as assimilation of the $t$ towards the $ḥ$.[306] On the basis of the present evidence, the Egyptian explanation is the best. For the precise meaning of the word, Holm argues that both the Egyptian, ḥr-tp, and the Hebrew, חַרְטֹם, were court officials, capable of magic, especially dream interpretation.[307]

---

300. Mankowski, *Akkadian Loanwords*, 74–75.
301. See above, under אַשָּׁף.
302. Landesdorfer, *Sumerisches Sprachgut*, 43.
303. Collins, *Daniel*, 128, 138; Hartman and Di Lella, *Daniel*, 131; Tawny Holm, *Of Courtiers and Kings: The Biblical Daniel Narratives and Ancient Story-Collections*, Explorations in Ancient Near Eastern Civilizations 1 (Winona Lake: Eisenbrauns, 2013), 104–10; Koch, *Daniel*, 10; Lambdin, 'Egyptian Loan Words', 150–51; Muchiki, *Egyptian Proper Names and Loanwords*, 245; Newsom, *Daniel*, 37; Noonan, *Non-Semitic Loanwords*, 102–103; Wilson, 'Foreign Words', 211; Yahuda, *The Language of the Pentateuch*, 93–94.
304. *CDD* 15, s.v. 'ḥr-tb'; Erichsen, *Demotisches Glossar*, s.v. 'ḥr-tp (ḥr-tb)'; Erman and Grapow, *Wörterbuch*, s.v. 'ḥr-tp'; *Thesaurus Linguae Aegyptiae*, s.v. 'ḥr-tp'.
305. Cf. Guy Wagner, *Elephantine XIII: Les papyrus et les ostraca grecs d'Elephantine*, Deutsches Archäologisches Institut Kairo 70 (Mainz: Philipp von Zaber, 1998), ostracon 39.2, and *Berlin Griechische Urkunden (BGU)* 1, 6.3, 15, 20.
306. Muchiki, *Egyptian Proper Names and Loanwords*, 245.
307. Holm, *Of Courtiers and Kings*, 98–99, 104–14.

## 2. The Loanwords

יַיִן
wine; Dan 1:5, 8, 16; 10:3
(141 occurrences in Biblical Hebrew. Not in Biblical Aramaic)
Native synonyms: (Hebrew) חֶמֶר.

See explanation under, 2.3, 'The loanwords in Esther'. Note that since it is such an early loan, it has not been counted in the statistics below.

כָּרוֹז
herald; Dan 3:4
Native synonyms: (Aramaic) שְׁלוּחַ.[308]
*כְּרַז
to announce; Dan 5:29
Native synonyms: (Aramaic) חַוֵּה.[309]

The word is unattested in Hebrew or Akkadian, but in Babylonian Aramaic the alternative form כלוז is also found.[310] Several scholars identify similarities between Aramaic כָּרוֹז and Greek, κῆρυξ, 'herald' as grounds for a loan from Greek.[311] The Greek word is associated with the verb κηρύσσειν, 'to herald', thus pointing to a stem, κηρυχ-. Noonan suggests that the *zayin* is the simplification of the word-final consonant cluster, based on the claim that Biblical Aramaic does not tolerate such clusters.[312] However, such consonants are permissible in foreign lexemes, as in אֲרְתַּחְשַׁשְׂתְּא (Ezra 4:11, et passim). Wilson, on the other hand, derives it from 'Mittano-Aryan' on the basis of Armenian, *karoz*, 'herald'.[313] Together, the Greek and Armenian forms suggest an Indo-European root, *$keh_2rug^h$-. The simplest explanation is a loan from an Indo-European language into Aramaic.[314] Moreover, the reflex required of Indo-European

---

308. While this form is only attested in later Aramaic, the relation to the common Aramaic verb שלח (e.g. Dan 6:23) is transparent. *Comprehensive Aramaic Lexicon*, s.v. 'šlwḥ'; Sokoloff, *DJBA*, s.v. 'שלוח'.
309. Attested in Biblical Aramaic: Dan 2:4, etc. *HALOT*, s.v. 'חוה'.
310. *Comprehensive Aramaic Lexicon*, s.v. 'krwz'.
311. Derenbourg, 'Les Mots Grecs', 239; Noonan, *Non-Semitic Loanwords*, 131; Scheftelowitz, 'Zur Kritik, IV', 310; Vernes, *Les Emprunts de la Bible*, 76.
312. Benjamin Noonan, 'Daniel's Greek Loanwords in Dialectal Perspective', *BBR* 28 (2018): 575–603 (591–93).
313. Wilson, 'Foreign Words', 197–98.
314. Shaffer noted a word, *kirezzi*, that he attributed to Hurrian in the Akkadian legal texts from Nuzi, presuming it to come from a Hurrian substrate. However, as Noonan argues, it is now clear that Hurrian *kirezzi* means 'release', as it is used in parallel to the Hittite *pāra tarnumar* (see von Dassow). Eva von Dassow, 'Freedom in Ancient Near Eastern Societies', in *The Oxford Handbook of Cuneiform Culture*, ed.

ǵʰ, a reflex that could explain Aramaic *zayin* necessitates that the word derive from a *satem* language: Armenian, Balto-Slavic or Indo-Iranian. Of these options Iranian is the most probable explanation, by geographic proximity, despite a lack of direct evidence for the word. Some have suggested \*xrausa-.³¹⁵ However, the constructed Indo-European root implies an Iranian, \*kārūj-. The verb כְּרַז should be explained as denominative.

כַּרְבֵּל\*
head clothing; Dan 3:21
(1 Chr 15:27)
Native synonyms: (Aramaic) There are some more precise synonyms from later Aramaic, like מַצְנְפָא, 'turban'.³¹⁶ However, the word is used in a list and could easily be omitted. Alternatively, a generic word for garment could be used.

Kaufman derives this word from Akkadian, *karballatu*, 'cap', which he also identifies as a loanword in Akkadian.³¹⁷ The Akkadian designates a military garment, worn by the Cimmerians.³¹⁸ If Kaufman is right that the word is a loan in Akkadian – and the use of pseudo-logograms to spell the word does suggest that the word is unlikely to be native³¹⁹ – it is probable that the word is also a loan in Aramaic. Koch suggests that possibly the Akkadian is itself an Iranian loan, from \*karbatla-.³²⁰ However, in the absence of more definite proof, we shall treat it as an Akkadian loan.

Karen Radner and Eleanor Robson (Oxford: Oxford University, 2011), 205–28 (219, 221); Noonan, 'Daniel's Greek Loanwords', 590–91; Aaron Shaffer, 'Hurrian *kirezzi*, West-Semitic krz', *Or(NS)* 34 (1965): 32–34.

315. Hartman and Di Lella, *Daniel*, 157; Koch, *Daniel*, 247. Goldingay also suggests this possible form, but stops short of affirming the word's status as a loanword. Goldingay, *Daniel*, 65.

316. E.g. Tg. Onq. Exod 28:39 or the Peshitta of Lev 8:9. Cf. *Comprehensive Aramaic Lexicon*, s.v. 'mṣnph'; Sokoloff, *DJPA*, s.v. 'מצנפה'; Sokoloff, *A Syriac Lexicon*, s.v. 'ܡܨܢܦܬܐ' listed as if under 'ܢܦ'.

317. Kaufman, *The Akkadian Influences*, 63.

318. *CAD* 8, s.v. 'karballatu'.

319. Ibid. The word is written either syllabically, e.g. *kar-ba-al-la-tu* or with the pseudo-logograms KAR.BAL and KAR.ZI (on the basis, ZI=balātu). These logographic spellings are termed 'pseudo-logographic' because they are essentially syllabic readings. If the word is genuinely Akkadian, then its logographic reading should relate to a genuine Sumerian word, rather than a syllabic reading. Alternatively, if the logograms do in fact point to an actual Sumerian word KAR.BAL, that also suggests a foreign origin for *karballatu*.

320. Koch, *Daniel*, 253.

כָּרְסֵא\*
throne; Dan 5:20; 7:9, 9
(137 occurrences in Biblical Hebrew. Twice in Biblical Aramaic as כָּרְסֵא)
Native synonyms: (Aramaic) מוֹתָב.[321]

See the explanation of כִּסֵּא under 2.3, 'The loanwords in Esther'. Note that since the borrowing is so early, this word has not been counted in the statistics below.

לְחֵנָה
concubine; Dan 5:2, 3, 23
Native synonyms: (Aramaic) Although I can find no obvious synonyms, the word is used exclusively as a part of a list.

Kaufman, Newsom, Mankowski and Landsberger suggest that לְחֵנָה derives from the Akkadian, *laḫḫinu, alaḫḫinatu* or similar.[322] The correspondence of form and meaning are good. Moreover, the word is well-attested in Akkadian, as far back as Old Akkadian, whereas it is rare in Aramaic and only attested late.[323] Therefore, an Akkadian loan is likely.

לַפִּיד
torch; Dan 10:6
(Gen 15:17; Exod 20:18; Judg 7:16, 20; 15:4, 4, 5; Job 41:11; Isa 62:11; Ezek 1:13; Nah 2:5; Zech 12:6)
Native synonyms: (Hebrew) זִיקוֹת, if understood as firebrand.[324]
Loosely, אֵשׁ might also be used by itself to satisfy the meaning as it is used in Dan 10:6.

---

321. Attested in Official Aramaic, for example, TAD D23.1, panel 5A, 1, line 9. *Comprehensive Aramaic Lexicon*, s.v. 'mwtb'; Cook, *Dictionary of Qumran Aramaic*, s.v. 'mwtb'; *DNWSI*, s.v. 'mwtb'; Sokoloff, *DJPA*, s.v. 'מותב'; Sokoloff, *DJBA*, s.v. 'מותב'; Sokoloff, *A Syriac Lexicon*, s.v. 'ܡܘܬܒܐ' (s.v. 'ܝܬܒ').

322. Kaufman, *The Akkadian Influences*, 66; Benno Landsberger, 'Akkadisch-hebräische Wortgleichungen', in *Hebräische Wortforschung: Festschrift zum 80. Geburtstag von W. Baumgartner*, ed. Benedikt Hartman et al., VTSup 16 (Leiden: Brill, 1967), 176–204 (198–204); Mankowski, *Akkadian Loanwords*, 80–82; Newsom, *Daniel*, 167.

323. *CAD* 1, s.v. 'alaḫḫinu'; *Comprehensive Aramaic Lexicon*, s.vv. 'lḥnh', 'lḥn'.

324. E.g. Isa 50:11, NRSV.

Noonan (in his dissertation) suggested this word – attested in Aramaic also³²⁵ – was Greek in origin, citing along with Vernes, Greek λάμπας (stem, λάμπαδ-), 'lantern'.³²⁶ Brown and Rabin, on the other hand, suggested an Anatolian origin, such as Hittite, *lappiya-*, 'kindling', or 'fever'.³²⁷ The presence of the μ in λάμπας can be interpreted in two ways: either it is a dissimilation of a geminated labial or the geminated labials found in the other forms are the result of assimilating the nasal. It does not provide us, then, with a useful criterion for deciding the relationship between these lemmata. However, the Hebrew form contains a *daleth* which is absent from the Hittite form. Rabin attempts to solve this problem by suggesting that the word was borrowed from the Hittite instrumental case, which terminates in a dental consonant. He suggests that this is analogous to the Greek solution, which he characterizes as borrowing from the accusative case or genitive.³²⁸ However, these situations are not similar. In the case of the Greek, the word's stem contains the dental, not a grammatical morpheme as in the case of Hittite. The Greek, therefore, offers a better model than the Hittite. Moreover, the Greek has the etymologically related verb, λάμπω, 'to shine'. The Hittite, then, might be explained as cognate to the Greek.

More recently, however, Noonan has updated his position, nominating an alternative solution in the hypothetical Luwian form, \**lappit-*.³²⁹ Certainly, not all of the data can be sufficiently explained with just the Greek and Hebrew: the unexplained difference in vocalization between Greek and Hebrew is difficult to account for. However, without attestation of the form in Luwian, the Greek solution is superior.

מַדָּע
knowledge; Dan 1:4, 1:17
(2 Chr 1:10, 11, 12; Eccl 10:20)
Native synonyms: (Hebrew) דֵּעָה; דַּעַת.

---

325. *Comprehensive Aramaic Lexicon*, s.v. 'lpyd', 'lmpd'; Cook, *Dictionary of Qumran Aramaic*, s.v. 'lpyd'; Sokoloff, *DJPA*, s.v. 'למפד'; Sokoloff, *A Syriac Lexicon*, s.v. 'ܠܡܦܕܐ, ܠܡܦܐܕܐ, ܠܡܦܐܕܐ'; Sokoloff, *DCPA*, s.v. 'ܠܡܦܕ'.
326. Noonan, 'Foreign Loanwords', 222; Vernes, *Les Emprunts de la Bible*, 81–82. Note also Rendsburg, 'Cultural Words', 1:641, who likewise cites the Greek, but in favour of the label 'culture word'.
327. Brown, *Israel and Hellas*, 2:298; Rabin, 'Hittite Words in Hebrew', 128–29.
328. Rabin, 'Hittite Words in Hebrew', 128–29.
329. Noonan, *Non-Semitic Loanwords*, 141.

Collins, Kautzsch and Wagner rightly suggest that מַדָּע is an Aramaism.³³⁰ This is largely because of the presence of the *dagesh* in the *daleth*, understood as an assimilation of the *yodh* of the root ידע, 'to know'. In addition, were the root native to Hebrew we should expect some remnant of the *yodh*, either as a *mater lectionis* or in the colouring of the vowel.³³¹

מְחִיר
hire; Dan 11:39
(Deut 23:19; 2 Sam 24:24; 1 Kgs 10:28; 21:2; 1 Chr 4:11; 2 Chr 1:16; Job 28:15; Ps 44:13; Prov 17:16; 27:26; Isa 45:13; 55:1; Jer 15:13; Lam 5:4; Mic 3:11)
Native synonyms: (Hebrew) שָׂכָר.

Most scholars derive this word from Akkadian, *maḫīru*, 'price'.³³² Wagner also argues that the vocalization of the loan points to Aramaic transmission, since the reduction of the a-vowel of the Akkadian prototype would be atypical of Hebrew. Since the vowel-pattern is unusual for Hebrew, it is plausible that the word is a loan. However, such patterns cannot provide us with certainty. Although the word is probably an Akkadianism, it is still a possibility that the word derives from a common Semitic root.

מֶלְצַר
sentry; Dan 1:11, 16
Native synonyms: (Hebrew) שׁוֹמֵר; נוֹצֵר.

Also attested as מִנְזָר, the Hebrew מֶלְצַר is derived from Akkadian *maṣṣaru*, 'sentry'.³³³ The *nun* and *lamedh* may be explained as dissimilatory effects, which Mankowski attributes to Aramaic transmission.³³⁴

---

330. Collins, *Daniel*, 127; Kautzsch, *Die Aramaismen*, 51; Wagner, *Die Lexikalischen und Grammatikalischen Aramäismen*, 72–73.
331. See Paul Joüon and Takamitsu Muraoka, *A Grammar of Biblical Hebrew*, 2nd ed., SubBi 27 (Rome: Editrice Pontificio Istituto Biblico, 2006), 236.
332. Mankowski, *Akkadian Loanwords*, 92; Mankowski, 'Akkadian Loanwords', 83; Rabin, 'Foreign Words', 1073; Wagner, *Die Aramaismen*, 75; Zimmern, *Akkadische Fremdwörter*, 18.
333. Goldingay, *Daniel*, 5; Hartman and Di Lella, *Daniel*, 130; Mankowski, *Akkadian Loanwords*, 95–97; Newsom, *Daniel*, 37; Rabin, 'Foreign Words', 1073; Zimmern, *Akkadische Fremdwörter*, 7.
334. Cf. Mankowski, *Akkadian Loanwords*, 95–97.

Greek, Μολοσσός, 'Molossian', and Latin, *minister*, 'servant', offer poor correspondence in sense and in form and are best considered unrelated.[335]

נְבִזְבָּה
coin, money; Dan 2:6; 5:17
Native synonyms: (Aramaic) כְּסֶף.[336]

The Biblical Aramaic word נְבִזְבָּה is difficult to reconcile with a Semitic origin. Akkadian, *nibzu*, 'tablet', which Noonan and *HALOT* suggest as a possible cognate, does not provide a satisfactory explanation for the second ב.[337] Some have suggested an Iranian origin,[338] including Tisdall's suggestion of an Iranian loan based on Avestan *nivāzan-*, 'attractive', is interesting, even if it requires an emendation of נְבִזְבָּה to *נִבְזָנָה.[339] Alternatively Tisdall suggests that the root may be *nibāzan-*, with the same emendation.[340] However, it is impossible in either case to then account for the extra-biblical appearances of the word in Aramaic.[341] Scheftelowitz also suggests an Iranian loan based on the Modern Persian, *nävaxtä*, implying a Pahlavi *nibazw*, but basing the loan on a lemma found only in Modern Persian is speculative.[342] Vernes and Derenbourg suggest that the word derives from Greek, νομίσμα.[343] The Greek νομίσμα, 'coin', has an appropriate semantic match with נְבִזְבָּה – or, to be more precise, the sense of 'coin', or 'money' would fit all the known Hebrew cases.[344]

335. Cf. Derenbourg, 'Les Mots Grecs', 242–43; Vernes, *Les Emprunts de la Bible*, 90–91.
336. כְּסֶף is known in this sense as early as Old Aramaic, e.g. Tell Shioukh Fawqani 95 F 204 I/3 line 5. The word is common in Biblical Aramaic and used in this sense in Ezra 7:17ff.
337. *HALOT*, s.v. נְבִזְבָּה; Noonan, *Non-Semitic Loanwords*, 339.
338. Collins, *Daniel*, 148; Koch, *Daniel*, 90; Newsom *Daniel*, 62.
339. Tisdall, 'The Āryan Words, III', 369.
340. Ibid., 368–69.
341. Cf. *Comprehensive Aramaic Lexicon*, s.v. 'nbzbh'.
342. Scheftelowitz, 'Zur Kritik, IV', 311.
343. Derenbourg, 'Les Mots Grecs', 241; Vernes, *Les Emprunts de la Bible*, 97.
344. It also fits all known Aramaic uses of the word, where it is used in the Targums (translations mine):
Tg. J. Jer 40:5: 'The Chief executioner gave him a gift and a *gift/money* (נבזבה) and sent him away'. In this case, the meaning 'money' avoids the redundancy of the meaning 'gift'.
Tg. Esth II 5.1-03.2: 'In the third year of the kingship of Ahasuerus a town by name Hendika rebelled against him and the king gathered many armies to subdue it and he dispatched them quickly against it and he appointed over them, Mordecai over

Moreover, it has a clear etymology internal to Greek, based on the verb νομίζειν and the nominalizing suffix -μα.[345] The correspondence between Greek σμ and Aramaic זב is unusual, but explicable as assimilation (the *sigma* assimilates to the voiced quality of the *mu*; the *mu* assimilates to the oral [i.e. non-nasal] quality of the *sigma*). The correspondence of the first μ to ב is more difficult; it is possible, however, that it was a change conditioned by the assimilation of σμ to זב. Moreover, it is unlikely that נְבִזְבָּה has a Semitic origin. Therefore, the Greek hypothesis is best, based on the present evidence.

נֶבְרְשָׁה*
torch, lampstand; Dan 5:5
Native synonyms: (Aramaic) דְּלִיק;[346] נְהוֹר.[347]

Several scholars derive נֶבְרְשָׁה from Old Persian *\*nibrāza-*, on the basis of Avestan *brāz-*, 'to shine', combined with the prefex *ni-*.[348] The

---

half of them and Haman over half of them and he gave them provisions and all of their *supplies/money* (נבזבה) equally, enough for 3 years'. Again, the meaning 'money' avoids redundancy, while still fitting the context.

Tg. Ps.-J. Deut 23:24: 'The promised offering that exits your lips, you must actually bring to stand. You should obey the precepts of what is right, but what is not right, you should certainly not do. Just as you have vowed, you should also pay: sin offerings and guilt offerings, burnt offerings and the consecrated victims you will offer before the Lord, your God. And you should bring the slaughter victims and you should give the *gifts/money* (נבזבה) for the sanctuary, of which you have spoken, and the alms for the poor, whatever you have said with your mouth'. Either 'gifts' or 'money' would be appropriate in this case.

345. *Liddell, Scott and Jones*, s.v. 'νόμισμα'.
346. While דְּלִיק is only attested late, the verbal root is attested in Biblical Aramaic (Dan 7:9). *Comprehensive Aramaic Lexicon*, s.vv. 'dlyq', 'dlq'; Cook, *Dictionary of Qumran Aramaic*, s.v. 'dlq'; *HALOT*, s.v. 'דלק' (Aramaic); Sokoloff, *DJPA*, s.v. 'דלק'; Sokoloff, *DJBA*, s.v. 'דלק'; Sokoloff, *A Syriac Lexicon*, s.v. 'ܕܠܩܐ', 'ܕܠܡܐ' (s.v. 'ܕܠܡ'); Sokoloff, *DCPA*, s.v. 'ܕܠܡ'.
347. Found in Biblical Aramaic (Dan 2:22), with the meaning 'light'. *Comprehensive Aramaic Lexicon*, s.v. 'nhwr'; Cook, *Dictionary of Qumran Aramaic*, s.v. 'nhwr'; *HALOT*, s.v. 'נְהוֹר' (Aramaic); Sokoloff, *DJPA*, s.v. 'נהור'; Sokoloff, *DJBA*, s.v. 'נהור'; Sokoloff, *A Syriac Lexicon*, s.v. 'ܢܗܘܪܐ' (s.v. 'ܢܗܘܪ'); Sokoloff, *DCPA*, s.v. 'ܢܗܘܪ' (s.v. 'ܢܗܘܪ').
348. Ellenbogen, *Foreign Words*, 110; Noonan, *Non-Semitic Loanwords*, 150; Scheftelowitz, 'Zur Kritik, IV', 310; Tisdall, 'Āryan Words III', 366–67. Similarly, Collins, *Daniel*, 246; Hartman and Di Lella, *Daniel*, 184.

root is attested in Parthian and Manichaean Middle Persian as *brāz*,[349] both meaning 'to shine'. On the basis of these, the reconstruction in Old Persian is quite plausible.

Wilson, on the other hand, derives the word from Akkadian *nabur šeti*, 'top of the wall', in comparison to the emphatic form, נֶבְרַשְׁתָּא.[350] Wilson's explanation is unsatisfactory, however, because it does not account for the word's meaning in Syriac, 'light, fire'.[351] Rather, if we seek an Akkadian origin, we should consider Millard's more plausible option from Akkadian, *barāru*, 'to shine, flicker'.[352] A nominal prefix in *m-* would dissimilate to *n-* according to Barth's law of dissimilation. From Late Babylonian on, *\*rt* often becomes *\*št*.[353] Thus a feminine noun would be *\*mabrartu > \*nabraštu*. However, as Millard recognizes, this all depends on a reappraisal of what the Akkadian word, *barāru*, means, which is used to refer to a disease of the eyes.[354] Millard is right that some related words, such as *birbirrū*, 'light of the gods', appear to indicate that the root refers to luminosity, such that it would plausibly produce a noun that meant 'lampstand'.

Both the Persian and Millard's Akkadian suggestions have merit, although both are hypothetical: the only obvious point of discrimination between the two hypotheses is the semantic fit, but since both hypotheses rely on unattested forms any semantic observations are speculative. If only because the meaning of the Iranian root is more secure, the Persian hypothesis is marginally to be preferred.

שַׂבְּכָא; סַבְּכָא
musical instrument; Dan 3:5, 7, 10, 15
סוּמְפּוֹנְיָה; סִיפֹנְיָה
musical instrument; Dan 3:5, 10, 15

---

349. Desmond Durkin-Meisterernst, *Dictionary of Manichaean Middle Persian and Parthian*, Corpus Fontium Manichaeorum: Subsidia (Turnhout, Belgium: Brepols, 2004), s.v. 'br'z'.

350. Wilson, 'Foreign Words', 198.

351. Cf. *Comprehensive Aramaic Lexicon*, s.v. 'nbršh'; Robert Payne-Smith, *A Compendious Syriac Dictionary*, rev. Jessie Payne-Smith (Oxford: Clarendon, 1903), s.v. 'ܢܒܪܫܬܐ'.

352. Alan Millard, 'The Etymology of Nebrašta', Daniel 5:5', *Maarav* 4 (1987): 87–92.

353. Huehnergard and Woods, 'Akkadian and Eblaite', 239.

354. Millard, 'The Etymology of Nebrašta'', 91–92. Cf. *CAD* 2, s.v. 'barāru'. Millard argues for a meaning of a reddish glow.

Native synonyms: (Aramaic) (for blown instruments) קֶרֶן.³⁵⁵ There are also later synonyms, like חֲצֹצְרָה.³⁵⁶ Both for the blown instruments and the stringed instruments, it should be noted that these words are used as parts of lists and so are not used by compulsion.

פְּסַנְתֵּרִין; פְּסַנְטֵרִין
musical instrument; Dan 3:5, 7, 10, 15
קַתְרוֹס (*qere*); קיתרוס (*kethiv*, perhaps intending קִיתָרוֹס)
musical instrument; Dan 3:5, 7, 10, 15
Native synonyms: (Aramaic) (for stringed instruments) כִּנָּר.³⁵⁷

The words קַתְרוֹס, פְּסַנְתֵּרִין and סוּמְפֹּנְיָה are routinely identified as Greek in origin, based on comparison with κίθαρις,³⁵⁸ ψαλτήριον,³⁵⁹ and συμφωνία.³⁶⁰ In addition the form סִיפֹנְיָה has been likened to the Greek

---

355. Although קֶרֶן is likely an Indo-European loanword it is so nativized that it is acceptable as a native synonym here. See the discussion on קֶרֶן below. It is attested in Biblical Aramaic (Dan 3:5).

356. *Comprehensive Aramaic Lexicon*, s.v. 'ḥṣwṣrh'; Sokoloff, *DJPA*, s.v. 'חצוצרה'; Sokoloff, *DJBA*, s.v. 'חצוצרה'.

357. Although not found in Biblical Aramaic, it is found in both Old Aramaic (Sefire Treaty Text 1, 222 a29) and later dialects (e.g. Tg. Onq. Gen 4:21 or Syriac, Aphrahat, *Dem* 9.184:11). *Comprehensive Aramaic Lexicon*, s.v. 'knr'; *DNWSI*, s.v. 'knr'; Sokoloff, *DJPA*, s.v. 'כינר'; Sokoloff, *DJBA*, s.v. 'כנר'; Sokoloff, *A Syriac Lexicon*, s.v. 'ܟܢܪ'; Sokoloff, *DCPA*, s.v. 'ܟܢܪ'.

358. Collins, *Daniel*, 184; Derenbourg, 'Les Mots Grecs', 238; Ellenbogen, *Foreign Words*, 148; Hartman and Di Lella, *Daniel*, 157; Heijmans, 'Greek Loanwords', 2:148; Koch, *Daniel*, 248; Noonan, *Non-Semitic Loanwords*, 191–92; Scheftelowitz, 'Zur Kritik, IV', 310; Vernes, *Les Emprunts de la Bible*, 151. Goldingay makes the same comparison but is unsure of the direction of borrowing; see Goldingay, *Daniel*, 65.

359. Collins, *Daniel*, 184; Derenbourg, 'Les Mots Grecs', 239; Ellenbogen, *Foreign Words*, 135; Goldingay, *Daniel*, 65; Hartman and Di Lella, *Daniel*, 157; Heijmans, 'Greek Loanwords', 2:148; Koch, *Daniel*, 248; Noonan, *Non-Semitic Loanwords*, 179–80; Rabin, 'Foreign Words', 1078; Scheftelowitz, 'Zur Kritik, IV', 310; Vernes, *Les Emprunts de la Bible*, 132–33.

360. Derenbourg, 'Les Mots Grecs', 239; Ellenbogen, *Foreign Words*, 122; Goldingay, *Daniel*, 65; Hartman and Di Lella, *Daniel*, 157; Heijmans, 'Greek Loanwords', 2:148; Koch, *Daniel*, 248; Noonan, *Non-Semitic Loanwords*, 158; Rabin, 'Foreign Words', 1078; Scheftelowitz, 'Zur Kritik, IV', 310; Vernes, *Les Emprunts de la Bible*, 101–102.

σίφων, 'tube, pipe'.³⁶¹ Wilson's explanation of פְּסַנְטֵרִין deriving from *pisannu* offers a poor phonetic match.³⁶² Nevertheless, while these Aramaic words are plainly non-Semitic in their non-triliteral form, it is unclear that they necessarily derive from Greek originally. Beekes identifies several of these words – κίθαρις, σίφων and ἰαμβύκη (see below) – as deriving from the Pre-Greek substrate.³⁶³ In addition, while ψαλτήριον itself appears to be a word formed within Greek, it is based on a pre-Greek root.³⁶⁴ Nevertheless, it remains probable that the vector of these words into Aramaic was through Greek, rather than a loan directly from the substrate. In the case of סוּמְפּוֹנְיָה and פְּסַנְטֵרִין, however, it is clear that the point of origin is Greek, since the words have clear etymologies within the Greek language: συμφωνία is composed of the Greek prefix συν and the root φων-; ψαλτήριον is as we have mentioned related to the root ψάλλειν.³⁶⁵

סַבְּכָא is also identified in connection with Greek σαμβύκη, σάμβυξ, ζαμβύκη and ἰαμβύκη³⁶⁶ – though Goldingay considers the word Semitic.³⁶⁷ To this we should add Latin, *sambuca*, 'instrument', and *sambucus*, 'sambuca-player' or 'elder tree'.³⁶⁸ Against the idea that the word is Semitic, it is hard to explain correspondences to the Greek *iota*, from a Semitic sibilant. On the other hand, such interchanges are typical of pre-Greek vocabulary. In addition to the multiple forms, the Greek word gives every indication that it is a loan from the pre-Greek substrate, by the consonant cluster μβ-, typical of pre-Greek words.³⁶⁹ Thus the word is likely pre-Greek, subsequently transmitted from Greek into Latin and the Semitic languages.

361. Heijmans, 'Greek Loanwords', 2:148; Wilson, 'Foreign Words', 198. However, others treat it as an alternative form of or error for סוּמְפּוֹנְיָה and thus still related to συμφωνία; see, e.g., Noonan, *Non-Semitic Loanwords*, 158.

362. Wilson, 'Foreign Words', 199.

363. Robert Beekes, *Etymological Dictionary of Greek*, 2 vols (Leiden: Brill, 2010), s.vv. 'ἴαμβος', 'κίθαρις', and 'σίφων'.

364. Beekes, *Etymological Dictionary*, s.v. 'ψάλλειν'.

365. Liddell, Scott and Jones, s.vv. 'ψάλλω', 'συμφωνέω'.

366. Derenbourg, 'Les Mots Grecs', 238–39; Scheftelowitz, 'Zur Kritik, IV', 310.

367. Goldingay, *Daniel*, 65.

368. *Lewis and Short*, s.v. 'sambuca' and 'sambucus'. Although it is tempting to make a connection between the elder tree and a (wooden) musical instrument, it seems unlikely that an elder tree could generate enough timber to be used successfully for that purpose.

369. Beekes in fact considers the word a loan from Semitic. Nonetheless, there is no reason to consider the Aramaic form native to Semitic and the prenasalization and multiple forms are common features of Pre-Greek words; see Beekes, *Etymological Dictionary*, 1:xxiv and 2:1304–5.

Noonan suggests that these words entered the Semitic languages from non-Attic dialects, based on a variety of dialectal features.³⁷⁰ In the case of סִיפֹנְיָה, קַתְרֹס and סַבְּכָא, we should exercise caution: given the variability of words of pre-Greek origin, it may be that Attic or other dialects of Greek may have contained multiple forms of the same lexeme.

סְגַן*
official; Dan 2:48; 3:2, 3, 27; 6:8
(Ezra 9:2; Neh 2:16, 16; 4:8, 13; 5:7, 17; 7:5; 12:40; 13:11; Isa 41:25; Jer 51:23, 28, 57; Ezek 23:6, 12, 23)
Native synonyms: (Aramaic) רֵישׁ ;רַב ;פְּקוֹד.³⁷¹

It is widely agreed that סְגַן derives from Akkadian, *šaknu*.³⁷² As Mankowski and Ellenbogen point out, the word must be an Assyrian loan rather than Babylonian to explain the correspondence of *š* to ס.³⁷³ Lipiński explains the correspondence of *k* to ג by proposing that the word was borrowed from the construct form, such that the *k* was intervocalic.³⁷⁴

סַרְבַּל*
garment, likely a head garment; Dan 3:21, 27
Native synonyms: (Aramaic) As with כַּרְבֵּל, above, the word is used in a list and could easily be omitted. Alternatively, a generic word for garment could be used.

Montgomery considered this word to be native to Aramaic, derived from the root סבל, 'to carry'.³⁷⁵ However, other scholars have not been convinced. Vernes identified סַרְבַּל as derived from Greek, σαράβαρα,³⁷⁶

---

370. Noonan, *Non-Semitic Loanwords*, 203; Noonan, 'Daniel's Greek Loanwords'.
371. See above, under אֲדַרְגָּזַר.
372. Collins, *Daniel*, 172; Ellenbogen, *Foreign Words*, 120; Goldingay, *Daniel*, 65; Hartman and Di Lella, *Daniel*, 156; Lipiński, 'Emprunts suméro-akkadiens', 70; Mankowski, *Akkadian Loanwords*, 106–7; Mankowski, 'Akkadian Loanwords', 83; Rabin, 'Foreign Words', 1073; Wilson, 'Foreign Words', 189; Zimmern, *Akkadische Fremdwörter*, 6.
373. Ellenbogen, *Foreign Words*, 120; Mankowski, *Akkadian Loanwords*, 106.
374. Lipiński, 'Emprunts suméro-akkadiens', 70. See also, Kaufman, *The Akkadian Influences*, 139. Correspondences between *k* and ג are also found in Akkadian names in the Hebrew Bible, like תִּגְלַת פִּלְאֶסֶר (2 Kgs 15:29), based on *tukultī-apil-ešarra* or סַרְגוֹן (Isa 20:1), based on *šarru-kīn*.
375. James Montgomery, *A Critical and Exegetical Commentary on the Book of Daniel* (Oxford: Clarendon, 1927), 211–12.
376. Vernes, *Les Emprunts de la Bible*, 106–7.

'Scythian trousers',[377] and Wilson, as derived from Akkadian *sarbillu*, *šarbillu*.[378] This is unlikely, however, because the word is normally glossed as 'storm'.[379] Also of relevance as Wilson notes, may be the Modern Persian, *šalwar*, 'trousers'.[380] So also is Pahlavi, *šalwar*.[381]

Several scholars, therefore, suggest an Iranian origin.[382] An Iranian origin is likely, although the correspondence of *š* to Aramaic ס still would require explanation. Instead, if the Modern Persian and Pahlavi forms were unrelated, it would be possible that this word would derive from a cognate of Avestan *sāra-vāra-*, 'helmet', built from *sāra-*, 'head', and *vāra-*, 'defence'[383] (cf. MMP and Parthian, *s'rw'r*, 'helmet'),[384] despite Wilson's (unfounded) claims that the word does not exist.[385]

The semantic match initially seems poor; however, this is only due to the identification of Greek σαράβαρα as 'trousers'. Liddell, Scott and Jones do so based on 'Persian shalvâr or shulvâr (braccae)'.[386] However, the word is poorly attested in Greek – in Antiphanes, cited by Liddell, Scott and Jones, it is unclear what the nature of the garment is and the Byzantine lexicographer Photius glossed the word only as ἐσθὴς Περσική, 'Persian raiment', though recognizing a minority opinion that the word means trousers.[387] Theodoretus defines the word as Περσικῶν περιβολαίων εἴδη, 'a kind of Persian covering'.[388] Little weight should be given, then, to the identification of the Greek word as trousers.

It may be that this word should be identified as 'trousers'. The likeliest scenario, however, in our view is that the Pahlavi and Modern Persian words are unrelated and that the Greek and Aramaic should instead be connected with the Iranian 'helmet' words. In either case, this is a loan from the Iranian languages.

377. Liddell, Scott and Jones, s.v. 'σαράβαρα'.
378. Wilson, 'Foreign Words', 190.
379. *CAD* 17, s.v. 'šarbillu'.
380. Wilson, 'Foreign Words', 190.
381. Noonan, *Non-Semitic Loanwords*, 165.
382. Brown, *Israel and Hellas*, 2:296; Collins, *Daniel*, 188; Koch, *Daniel*, 253; Noonan, *Non-Semitic Loanwords*, 165; Scheftelowitz, 'Zur Kritik, IV', 311.
383. Bartholomae, *Altiranisches Wörterbuch*, s.vv. 'sāra-', 'vāra-', 'sāra-vāra-'.
384. Durkin-Meisterernst, *Dictionary of Manichaean Middle Persian and Parthian*, s.v. 's'rw'r'.
385. Wilson, 'Foreign Words', 190.
386. Liddell, Scott and Jones, s.v. 'σαράβαρα'.
387. Antiphanes, *Fragments* 201; Photius, *Lexicon*, s.v. 'σαράβαρα'.
388. Theodoretus, *Interpretatio in Danielem* 81.1324.17.

סָרִיס
eunuch; Dan 1:3, 7, 8, 9, 10, 11, 18
(Gen 37:36; 39:1; 40:2, 7; 1 Sam 8:15; 1 Kgs 22:9; 2 Kgs 8:6;
9:32; 18:17; 20:18; 23:11; 24:12, 15, 19; 1 Chr 28:1; 2 Chr 18:8;
Esth 1:10, 12, 15; 2:3, 14, 15, 21; 4:4, 5; 6:2, 14; 7:9; Isa 39:7;
56:3, 4; Jer 29:2; 34:19; 38:7; 39:3, 13; 41:16; 52:25)
Native synonyms: (Hebrew) עֶבֶד. Although this is not a precise synonym, it would function appropriately in the cited locations in Daniel (or perhaps as עֶבֶד הַמֶּלֶךְ).

See the explanation under 2.3, 'The loanwords in Esther'.

סָרֵךְ*
official; Dan 6:3, 4, 5, 7, 8
Native synonyms: (Aramaic) רֵישׁ; רַב; פְּקוֹד.[389]

Despite Vernes' and Derenbourg's suggestion, Greek ἄρχων provides a poor match for סָרֵךְ.[390] Much better is Scheftelowitz's identification of סָרֵךְ with Old Persian *sāra-ka-*, 'overseer', on the evidence of Avestan *sāra-*, 'head',[391] and the Pahlavi proper noun, *Sarakos*.[392]

פֶּחָה
governor; Dan 3:2, 3, 27; 6:8
(1 Kgs 10:15; 20:24; 2 Kgs 18:24; 2 Chr 9:14; Ezra 5:3, 6, 14;
6:6, 7, 13; 8:36; Neh 2:7, 9; 3:7; 5:14, 15; 12:26; Esth 3:12;
8:9; 9:3; Isa 36:9; Jer 51:23, 28, 57; Ezek 23:6, 12, 23; Hag 1:1,
14; 2:2, 21; Mal 1:8)
Native synonyms: (Aramaic) מְדַבְּרָן;[393] שִׁלְטוֹן.[394]

389. See above, under אֲדַרְגָּזֵר.
390. Derenbourg, 'Les Mots Grecs', 240; Vernes, *Les Emprunts de la Bible*, 107.
391. Bartholomae, *Altiranisches Wörterbuch*, s.v. 'sāra-'.
392. Scheftelowitz, *Arisches im Alten Testament*, 76; Scheftelowitz, 'Zur Kritik, IV', 312. So also, Hartman and Di Lella, *Daniel*, 194; Noonan, *Non-Semitic Loanwords*, 166; for the suffix *-ka-* see Kent, *Old Persian*, 51.
393. D participle, of common Aramaic verb, דבר, which is attested, in Imperial Aramaic, for example, in TAD D7.29.7. *Comprehensive Aramaic Lexicon*, s.v. 'dbr'; Cook, *Dictionary of Qumran Aramaic*, s.v. 'dbr'; *DNWSI*, s.v. 'dbr'; *HALOT*, s.v. 'דבר'; Sokoloff, *DJPA*, s.v. 'דבר'; Sokoloff, *DJBA*, s.v. 'דבר'; Sokoloff, *A Syriac Lexicon*, s.v. 'ܕܒܪ'; Sokoloff, *DCPA*, s.v. 'ܕܒܪ'.
394. Attested in Dan 3:2. *Comprehensive Aramaic Lexicon*, s.v. 'šlṭwn'; Cook, *Dictionary of Qumran Aramaic*, s.v. 'šlṭwn'; *HALOT*, s.v. 'שִׁלְטוֹן'; Sokoloff, *DJPA*, s.v. 'שלטון'; Sokoloff, *DJBA*, s.v. 'שלטון'.

See the explanation under 2.3, 'The loanwords in Esther'.

פַּרְזֶל
iron; Dan 2:33, 33, 34, 35, 40, 40, 40, 41, 41, 41, 42, 43, 43, 45; 4:12, 20; 5:4, 23; 7:7, 19
(76 occurrences in Biblical Hebrew. Only in Daniel in Biblical Aramaic)
Native synonyms: (Aramaic) There are no obvious synonyms for 'iron'.

While the earlier loan hypothesis was that Aramaic פַּרְזֶל and Hebrew בַּרְזֶל derived from the Akkadian *parzillu*, 'iron',[395] more recently it has been considered a loan in that language also. Rendsburg and Mankowski consider this a culture word, citing in addition Ugaritic *brḏl*, 'iron', Phoenician *brzl*, 'iron', Arabic *firzil*, 'fetter', and Old South Arabian *frzn*, 'iron'.[396] Rendsburg also cites a number of Ethiopic forms,[397] which lack the final *l*-consonant, Egyptian *bj3*, 'copper', and various Sumerian compounds ending in BAR that refer to metals.[398] Nevertheless he does not explain the process by which the extra consonants are added. Noonan, on the other hand, hypothesizes a Luwian origin, where the word is attested as *parzašša-* < *\*parza-* and in the compound *parzagulliya-*; the loaned forms would indicate that the Luwian word also existed in a suffixed form, *\*parzilli-*.[399] In addition we note Latin, *ferrum* < *\*fersum*, 'iron'. It is possible, then, that the Luwian and Latin forms point to an Indo-European word, *\*bʰers-*, so that the case for a Luwian or Hittite origin is greatly strengthened. However, in light of the Ethiopic forms, the preferable explanation – although we cannot explain every detail of the word's propagation through all of these languages – is that the forms which do contain the *l*-consonant derive from the Luwian form, since there is a plausible explanation for its generation in that language. While it is possible that Aramaic פַּרְזֶל derives proximately from Akkadian *parzillu* or one of the other similar forms, the simpler explanation is that it derives from Luwian directly.

---

395. Ellenbogen, *Foreign Words*, 52–53; Zimmern, *Akkadische Fremdwörter*, 59.
396. Mankowski, *Akkadian Loanwords*, 49–50; Rendsburg, 'Culture Words', 1:640–41.
397. Cf. Leslau, *Comparative Dictionary*, s.v. 'bᵊrat'.
398. Rendsburg, 'Culture Words', 1:640–41. For the Egyptian: *CDD* 6, s.v. 'bj3'; Erman and Grapow, *Wörterbuch*, s.v. 'bj3'; *Thesaurus Linguae Aegyptiae*, s.v. 'bj3'.
399. Noonan, 'Foreign Loanwords', 56–58; Noonan, *Non-Semitic Loanwords*, 78–79.

פַּרְתְּמִים
nobles; Dan 1:3
(Esth 1:3; 6:9)
Native synonyms: (Hebrew) אַדִּיר; אָצִיל; חֹר.

See the explanation under 2.3, 'The loanwords in Esther'.

פַּת־בַּג
royal food; Dan 1:5, 8, 13, 15, 16; 11:26[400]
Native synonyms: (Hebrew) אֹכֶל; מַאֲכָל, provided such words are further qualified, perhaps in construct with מֶלֶךְ.

Despite Vernes' attempt to construct a Greek source for this word,[401] and Wilson's Armenian hypothesis,[402] the consensus is that פַּת־בַּג derives from Old Persian, *patibaga-.[403] There is no morphological reason to suggest an Aramaic transmission, though it cannot be ruled out.[404] According to Scheftelowitz,[405] the Persian form is a hypothetical construction of the known Persian elements, *pati-*, 'thereto, against',[406] and *baga-*, 'god, provider'.[407] Wagner, less plausibly relates the first element to what he cites as *pitav-*, 'food'.[408]

In Parthian, there exists *ptbg*, 'splendour, radiance'.[409] Although semantically dissimilar, the similarity of form is striking. As such, it may still be related in some capacity. In Greek we find ποτιβάζις in a fragment of the fourth-century BCE Greek historian of the Persian court, Dinon, in Athenaeus' *Deipnosophists*, which is glossed as a bread of barley and

---

400. Apparently missing in the Greek versions. Cf. Collins, *Daniel*, 366.
401. Vernes, *Les Emprunts de la Bible*, 136.
402. Wilson, 'Foreign Words', 214.
403. Collins, *Daniel*, 127, 139; Ellenbogen, *Foreign Words*, 141; Gindin, 'Persian Loanwords', 3:67; Goldingay, *Daniel*, 5; Hartman and Di Lella, *Daniel*, 130; Koch, *Daniel*, 5; Newsom, *Daniel*, 37; Noonan, *Non-Semitic Loanwords*, 185–86; Rabin, 'Foreign Words', 1079; Scheftelowitz, 'Zur Kritik, IV', 311; Wagner, *Die Aramaismen*, 96; Wilson-Wright, 'From Persepolis to Jerusalem', 156.
404. Wagner, *Die Aramaismen*, 96.
405. Scheftelowitz, 'Zur Kritik, IV', 311.
406. Kent, *Old Persian*, 194.
407. Ibid., 199.
408. Wagner, *Die Aramaismen*, 96.
409. Durkin-Meisterernst, *Dictionary of Manichaean Middle Persian and Parthian*, s.v. 'ptbg'.

wheat.⁴¹⁰ So although direct evidence for the existence of the Persian compound is lacking, the existence of the Greek supports this hypothesis.

The Hebrew word seems to have undergone some level of nativization, by which it has been re-analyzed for the first half to be written as the more widely attested word פַּת, 'fragment, piece', associated with the root פתת.⁴¹¹ The fact that the first half has been mistaken for a native word does not, however, mean that the compound itself would be stripped of its foreign association; despite the prevalence of פַּת, the morpheme *בַּג is not attested except as a part of this compound. Moreover, if an ancient audience lacked knowledge of the phylogeny that makes Persian and Hebrew so obviously different to us, there is no reason for such an audience to assume that the (false) equivalence of פַּת־בַּג and פַּת would rule out the foreign origin of פַּת־בַּג.

פִּתְגָם
statement, decree; Dan 3:16; 4:14
(Ezra 4:17; 5:7, 11; 6:11; Esth 1:20; Eccl 8:11)
Native synonyms: (Aramaic) מִלָּה;⁴¹² פְּקוּד.⁴¹³

See the explanation under 2.3, 'The loanwords in Esther'.

צִי
ship; Dan 11:30
(Num 24:24; Pss 72:9; 74:14; Isa 13:21; 23:13; 33:21; 34:14; Jer 50:39; Ezek 30:9)
Native synonyms: (Hebrew) אֳנִיָּה.

The word צִי is thought to be a loan from Egyptian *ḏ(ꜣ)j*, 'river-boat'.⁴¹⁴ The phonetic equivalence, moreover, is good and the semantic

---

410. Athenaeus, *Deipnosophists* 11.110.
411. Cf. Koch, *Daniel*, 5; Lucas, *Daniel*, 47; *Comprehensive Aramaic Lexicon*, s.v. 'פתת'.
412. Attested in Biblical Aramaic (e.g. Dan 2:9). *HALOT*, s.v. 'מִלָּה'. See also *Comprehensive Aramaic Lexicon*, s.v. 'mlh'; Cook, *Dictionary of Qumran Aramaic*, s.v. 'mlh'; *DNWSI*, s.v. 'mlh'; Sokoloff, *DJPA*, s.v. 'מילה'; Sokoloff, *A Syriac Lexicon*, s.v. 'ܡܠܬܐ'; Sokoloff, *DCPA*, s.v. 'ܡܠܐ'.
413. As discussed above, the root פקד is found even in Old Aramaic (Asshur Ostracon, line 17). If not this noun form, there is no barrier to forming a similar one.
414. Ellenbogen, *Foreign Words*, 145; Lambdin, 'Egyptian Loan Words', 153–54; Muchiki, *Egyptian Proper Names and Loanwords*, 253–54; Noonan, *Non-Semitic Loanwords*, 189; Rabin, 'Foreign Words', 1077; Rubin, 'Egyptian Loanwords', 794.

equivalence is acceptable. Distribution too favours a loan, as the word is without Semitic cognate.[415]

קֶרֶן
horn; Dan 3:5, 7, 10, 15; 7:7, 8, 8, 8, 8, 11, 20, 20, 21, 24; 8:3, 3, 5, 6, 7, 8, 9, 20, 21
(79 occurrences in Biblical Hebrew. Only in Daniel in Biblical Aramaic)
Native synonyms: (Aramaic) As I suggest below, this word is thoroughly nativized. There are no obvious synonyms.

Vernes thought that קֶרֶן derived from Latin *cornu*,[416] whereas Derenbourg likened it to Greek κέρας.[417] Noonan argues, moreover, that the word – despite the prevalence of versions of this word across Semitic languages – must derive from an Indo-European prototype, since the word has an etymology in Indo-European, where it lacks one in Semitic: it derives from the Indo-European word for 'top, head'.[418] The word is, however, completely regular across all the Semitic languages in which it is attested, conforming to the common *qatl* pattern.[419] Nor does it appear that there is anything particularly uncommon in the combination of root letters involved.[420] If it is in fact a loan, which is at least plausible, it is almost completely nativized and thus has not been counted in the statistics below.

רָז
secret; Dan 2:18, 19, 27, 28, 29, 30, 47, 47; 4:6
(Also in Biblical Hebrew: Isa 24:16?; Sir 8:18)
Native synonyms: (Aramaic) אֲחִידָה.[421]

It is not controversial to many that the Biblical Aramaic word רָז – or the Hebrew word attested in Isaiah and Sirach – derives from an

---

Cf. *CDD* 24, s.v. 'ḏj'; Erichsen, *Demotisches Glossar*, s.v. 'ḏj'; Erman and Grapow, *Wörterbuch*, s.v. 'ḏ3j'.

415. Muchiki, *Egyptian Proper Names and Loanwords*, 253–54.
416. Vernes, *Les Emprunts de la Bible*, 154–55.
417. Derenbourg, 'Les Mots Grecs', 237–38.
418. Noonan, 'Foreign Loanwords', 115–16.
419. Fox, *Semitic Noun Patterns*, 135–38.
420. Words beginning in קר are common, including קְרָא, קְרָב and several others. Likewise, words ending in רן are not uncommon: אָרָן, תְּרָן.
421. Cf. Dan 5:12. *HALOT*, s.v. 'אֲחִידָה'.

Iranian source, perhaps Old Persian, *rāz-.[422] The indirect evidence for the word's existence in Persian is found in Pahlavi, rāz, 'secret',[423] Manichaean Middle Persian r'z, 'secret, mystery',[424] Soghdian rāz, 'mystery',[425] Avestan razah-, 'solitude, remoteness',[426] Sanskrit rahas, 'solitariness, secret',[427] and Modern Persian rāz-, 'secret'.[428]

The word is also widely attested in Aramaic, where it is highly productive – the *Comprehensive Aramaic Lexicon* lists fifteen derivatives[429] – such that it is plausible that Aramaic transmitted the word from Persian into Hebrew, where it is attested in Sir 8:18 and Isa 24:16 and prominently in scrolls from Qumran. Establishing the direction of this borrowing is, however, not so straightforward as assumed. The main evidence in favour of the direction Persian > Aramaic is the Avestan, razah- and Sanskrit, rahas, which bolsters the sense that the word has a good distribution in Indo-Iranian languages; however, the Avestan and Sanskrit forms point to an Indo-Iranian root, *raĵʰas-, which would require Old Persian *radah-, which is a poor model for the Aramaic רז. Rather, if we are to maintain that the word was loaned from an Iranian language into Aramaic, it must have been from an Eastern Iranian language or perhaps from Median. This is not without problems: the Semitic languages and the Middle Iranian languages universally point to a form like *rāz, not *razah-, as would be the Median form. However, without more evidence forthcoming, we tentatively accept the Median hypothesis.

שֵׁגָל*

queen; Dan 5:2, 3, 23

(Deut 28:30 [*kethiv*]; Neh 2:6; Ps 45:10; Isa 13:16 [*kethiv*]; Jer 3:2 [*kethiv*]; Zech 14:2 [*kethiv*])

---

422. Ellenbogen, *Foreign Words*, 153; Hartman and Di Lella, *Daniel*, 139; Koch, *Daniel*, 94; Noonan, *Non-Semitic Loanwords*, 198–200; Scheftelowitz, 'Zur Kritik, IV', 311–12; Wagner, *Die Lexikalischen und Grammatikalischen Aramaismen*, 106; Wilson, 'Foreign Words', 200.

423. Mackenzie, *Pahlavi Dictionary*, s.v. 'rāz'.

424. Durkin-Meisterernst, *Dictionary of Manichaean Middle Persian and Parthian*, s.v. 'r'z-'.

425. Badr-uz-zaman Gharib, *Sogdian Dictionary* (Tehran: Farhangan, 1995), s.v. 'r'z' and 'r'zh'.

426. Bartholomae, *Altiranisches Wörterbuch*, s.v. 'razah-'.

427. Monier Monier-Williams, *A Sanskrit–English Dictionary* (Oxford: Oxford University Press, 1899), s.v. 'rahas'.

428. Cf. Hinz, *Altiranisches Sprachgut*, s.v. 'rāz'.

429. Cf. *Comprehensive Aramaic Lexicon*, s.v. 'rz', 'rz''.

Native synonyms: (Aramaic) In Dan 5:2, מַלְכָּה which would otherwise be a potential synonym, appears to be used as a distinct entity to the שֵׁגָל. Nonetheless, a circumlocution would be possible, such as אִנְתָּה דִּי מַלְכָּא. Alternatively, the word could be omitted from the lists it occurs in without changing much of the overall sense.

Several scholars derive this word from Akkadian.[430] However, they base their arguments on a variety of Akkadian prototypes. Wilson cites *šigirtu*, 'lady of the harem', Kaufman, Newsom and Zimmern, *ša ekalli*, '[she] of the palace', and Mankowski and Lipiński, *issi ekalli* > *\*sekalli*, 'woman of the palace'. Wilson's Akkadian word I cannot find in standard lexica.[431] Both other explanations are possible and we must also consider the possibility that the word is native to Hebrew, given the existence of the verbal root, שָׁגַל, 'to rape' (Deut 28:30 and others). Mankowski's contention that 'the semantic connection [of the verb] is tenuous' is not obvious[432] – the connection between coarse words for sex and the king's consort is clear enough.[433] Kaufman's explanation that the Hebrew verb is denominative is superior.[434] Moreover, since the Akkadian is attested (as a Sumerogram, SAL.É.GAL, 'woman of the palace'),[435] and with a clear etymology, as a calque from Sumerian, it is clear that whether the prototype of the word is *ša ekalli* or *issi ekalli*, the best explanation is that this word derives from Akkadian and the associated verb is denominative.

תּוֹר
bull; Dan 4:22, 29, 30; 5:21
(Not in Biblical Hebrew, except as שׁוֹר [58 times]. 7 occurrences in Biblical Aramaic)

---

430. Kaufman, *The Akkadian Influences*, 97; Landesdorfer, *Sumerisches Sprachgut*, 42; Lipiński, 'Emprunts suméro-akkadiens', 72; Mankowski, *Akkadian Loanwords*, 137–38; Newsom, *Daniel*, 167; Wilson, 'Foreign Words', 191; Zimmern, *Akkadische Fremdwörter*, 7.

431. I have checked the *Chicago Akkadian Dictionary*; Black, George, Postgate, *A Concise Dictionary of Akkadian*; and Wolfram von Soden, *Akkadisches Handwörterbuch*, 3 vols (Wiesbaden: Harrassowitz, 1972–85).

432. Mankowski, *Akkadian Loanwords*, 138 n. 514.

433. Cf., for example, the etymology of English, 'concubine', which is derived from words for sex. See *Oxford English Dictionary*, s.v. 'concubine'.

434. Kaufman, *The Akkadian Influences*, 97 n. 335.

435. *CAD* 4, s.v. 'ekallu' in '\*ša ekalli'.

Native synonyms: בָּקָר.[436] However, תּוֹר itself is very early and quite nativized.

Vernes linked the Hebrew version of this word, שׁוֹר, with Greek, ταῦρος, 'bull'.[437] Cuny put it, rather, in the pre-Greek substrate.[438] Brown treats it as a very early culture word.[439] The word is attested in Indo-European at least by Greek, ταῦρος, 'bull', and several related forms and Latin, *taurus*, 'bull'. However, the possibility exists that we should connect with these words the Sanskrit, *sthūrus*, and Germanic forms, like German, *Stier*.[440] If this is the case, then the word is difficult to explain as a loan from Semitic into Indo-European. However, the word is likewise well-attested in Semitic languages: as well as Hebrew שׁוֹר, we find Aramaic תּוֹר,[441] Ugaritic, *ṯr*,[442] and Akkadian, *šūru*,[443] all with the meaning 'bull', giving every appearance of deriving from a Proto-Semitic *\*ṯawr*. If there is a loan from Indo-European to Semitic, it is certainly an early one and thoroughly nativized in the Hebrew Bible. A third unknown source for the words in both language families also remains a possibility. Nonetheless, since this word is borrowed very early, it has not been counted in the statistics below.

תִּפְתָּיֵ\*
official; Dan 3:2, 3
Native synonyms: (Aramaic) רֵישׁ; רַב; פָּקוֹד.[444]

Because there are identical consonants in the first and third positions of the root, we might initially suspect a loan.[445] Rosenthal suggests

---

436. Although it is not attested in Biblical or Official Aramaic, the word appears to be a genuine Northwest Semitic word (cf. Hebrew בָּקָר). Nonetheless, even if it is borrowed from Hebrew, or in both Hebrew and Aramaic from a third source, תּוֹר is, as we say very early and quite nativized – not to be counted in our statistics. *Comprehensive Aramaic Lexicon*, s.v. 'bqr'; *HALOT*, s.v. 'בָּקָר'; Sokoloff, *DJPA*, s.v. 'בקר'; Sokoloff, *DJBA*, s.v. 'בקר'; Sokoloff, *A Syriac Lexicon*, s.v. 'ܒܩܪܐ'.
437. Vernes, *Les Emprunts de la Bible*, 163.
438. Cuny, 'Les Mots du Fonds Préhellénique', 162.
439. Brown, *Israel and Hellas*, 2:304.
440. Cf. *Lewis and Short*, s.v. 'taurus'.
441. *Comprehensive Aramaic Lexicon*, s.v. 'twr''.
442. *DULAT*, s.v. 'ṯr'.
443. *CAD* 17, s.v. 'šūru B'.
444. See above, under אֲדַרְגָּזַר.
445. Cf. Greenberg, 'The Patterning of Root Morphemes in Semitic', 162–81.

an etymology in Persian as a hypothetical compound, *tāyu-pātā-*.[446] Similarly, Koch suggests another hypothetical compound between the verb *tai-*, 'to see', and *pati-*, 'leader, chief', together meaning 'police officer'.[447] However, a non-hypothetical candidate is attested in the Elamite, *teipti*, 'lord'.[448] If this is the origin of the word, we must explain its transmission from Elamite to Aramaic and not just into Aramaic but into a dialect of Aramaic used by the biblical authors. It is not impossible that the word should enter Biblical Aramaic directly. However, it is more probable that the word arrived in Aramaic from Elamite through the intermediary of Persian.

תַּרְשִׁישׁ

gemstone, traditionally 'topaz'; Dan 10:6
(Exod 28:20; 39:13; Song 5:14; Ezek 1:16; 10:9; 28:13)
Native synonyms: (Hebrew) There are rough synonyms for the general class of noun, jewel or ornament: חֵפֶץ; עֲדִי; אֶקְדָּה. If it is necessary for the text to refer to topaz, specifically, the options of which we are aware are limited to תַּרְשִׁישׁ and פִּטְדָה, both loanwords.[449] However, it is not obvious that תַּרְשִׁישׁ is necessarily topaz, the gemstone being difficult to identify.[450] There is evidence that the gemstone is yellow-green in colour, because of how it is treated by the versions.[451] It may be that the colour

---

446. Franz Rosenthal, *A Grammar of Biblical Aramaic*, 6th rev. ed. (Wiesbaden: Harrassowitz, 1995), 62.
447. Koch, *Daniel*, 246. The forms are cited by Koch as *tai/i-* and *pati(s)-*. Bartholomae cites them as *dā(y)-*, 'sehen', and *patay-*, 'Herr'. Bartholomae, *Altiranisches Wörterbuch*, s.vv. 'dā(y)-' and 'patay-'.
448. Hinz and Koch, *Elamisches Wörterbuch*, s.v. 'te-ip-ti'.
449. For פִּטְדָה, see below, under 2.6, 'The loanwords in Exodus 25–40'.
450. For possibilities see David Baker, 'Tarshish (place)', *ABD* 6:331–33.
451. See Noonan, 'Foreign Loanwords', 108–109. Most often the versions understand the stone as chrysolite. In Exodus, the Septuagint translates χρυσόλιθος 'chrysolite', or literally 'golden stone' (Exod 28:20; 39:13). The Vulgate generally prefers *chrysolithus* (Exod 28:20; 39:13; Ezek 10:9; 28:13; Dan 10:6). Josephus (*Antiquities* 3.168; *War* 5.234) uses χρυσόλιθος to describe the high priest's breastplate, but is presumably deriving this from the Septuagint. The Peshitta is unhelpful; in Exod 28:20; 39:13; and Ezek 1:16; 10:9 it uses ܒܪܘܠܐ and in Song 5:14 it paraphrases with ܟܐܦܐ. In the other cases there is no clear correspondence at the level of individual words. However, the versions do not present a singular picture. In Song 5:14, the Vulgate chooses *hyacinthus*, 'jacinth', and in Ezek 1:16, *mar*, 'the sea', perhaps implying a blue colour. In the Septuagint there is also some degree of uncertainty. Often the

of the stone is particularly in view or the precise identity of the stone, in which case it would seem that the choice of the word is compulsory, but there is no clear means of evaluation – at least without a more secure identification of the gemstone in question.

The word for the gemstone, תַּרְשִׁישׁ, coincides with the place name, תַּרְשִׁישׁ, possibly identical to Greek Ταρτησσός. Both, however, are difficult to identify. Nonetheless, the coincidence of the two names implies that the gemstone is related to the location. Therefore, Noonan suggests that the word תַּרְשִׁישׁ is 'Tartessian',[452] while Vernes suggests it derives from Greek, citing the location name, Ταρτησσός.[453] These analyses are based on the equivalence of Greek Tartessus with biblical Tarshish. Although this equivalence is not certain, it is certainly very plausible. López Ruiz demonstrates both the phonetic equivalence – assuming an interdental sibilant underlying the Greek *tau* and Hebrew *shin* – how the epigraphic evidence points to a location in the Mediterranean and how earlier knowledge of this equivalence might have been lost by the Hellenistic period.[454] Albright, on the other hand, suggested that תַּרְשִׁישׁ is a Phoenician *tarf'il* noun – presumably based on the root, רשש, 'to crush' – which he suggests means 'a mine'.[455] If this is the case, the location name תַּרְשִׁישׁ is likely unrelated to Greek, Ταρτησσός: while it is plausible that

---

Septuagint simply transliterates, θαρσις in Dan 10:6, Song 5:14 and Ezek 1:16. However, Ezek 10:9 translates as ἄνθραξ, 'carbuncle', implying a red colour. Possibly we should also include Ezek 28:13 with Ezek 10:9, although the correlation between the Greek and Hebrew lists of gemstones in this verse do not appear to be straightforward. Contrary to Noonan, the Targumim do not necessarily support a yellow-green colour. Tg. Onq. Exod 28:20, 39:13, understands תַּרְשִׁישׁ as כְּרוֹם יָמָא, 'gemstone (lit: colour) of the sea'. So also, in Tg. J. Ezek 28:13. On the other hand, colour terminology as applied to the sea is not always straightforward (see Cyrus Gordon, 'The Wine-Dark Sea', *JNES* 37 [1978]: 51–52.) Nonetheless, chrysolite seems to be the most common understanding of the versions.

452. Noonan, 'Foreign Loanwords', 106–109; Noonan, *Non-Semitic Loanwords*, 228–29.

453. Vernes, *Les Emprunts de la Bible*, 173–74.

454. Carolina López Ruiz, 'Tarshish and Tartessos Revisited: Textual Problems and Historical Implications', in *Colonial Encounters in Ancient Iberia: Phoenician, Greek, and Indigenous Relations*, ed. Michael Dietler and Carolina López Ruiz (Chicago: The University of Chicago Press, 2009), 255–80.

455. William Albright, 'New Light on the Early History of Phoenician Colonization', *BASOR* 83 (1941): 14–22 (21–22).

both could have derived from a third name, the relationship between the consonants is difficult to explain if one is borrowed directly from the other – and here we also rule out Vernes' proposal. Gordon suggested that the word, rather, was a native Hebrew word, meaning 'the sea', a *qaṭlîl* noun based on the same root as תִּירוֹשׁ, 'new wine', observing the ancient Greek tradition of referring to the sea as οἶνοψ, 'wine-dark'.[456] However, it is clear from the Syriac ܡܐܪܝܬܐ, 'new wine, must', that the root of תִּירוֹשׁ is ירשׁ < *wrṯ*, as Gordon concedes.[457] This makes the explanation of תַּרְשִׁישׁ as a *qaṭlîl* untenable.

However, without sufficient evidence from the Iberian languages it is hard to decide between the remaining options. Nonetheless, in either Phoenician or Tartessian explanations, the name of the gemstone would derive from the location: Albright's etymology works for a place but not a gemstone and Noonan assumes the place name is anterior. Thus, whether from Phoenician or from 'Tartessian', the word for the gemstone is likely a loanword, based on the name of its place of origin.

### 2.5. *The loanwords in Ezra*

אֲגַרְטָל\*
leather bag; Ezra 1:9, 9
Native synonyms:[458] (Hebrew) חָרִיט; כִּיס.

There are parallels for Hebrew אֲגַרְטָל in Aramaic, קַרְטָלָא, Hittite, *kurtal-*, Greek, κάρταλλος and Modern Persian, *gartāl*.[459] Landesdorfer suggests it may derive from Sumerian A, 'water', GAR, 'to close off', and TAL, 'to be broad, ample'.[460] Nonetheless, no such compound is

---

456. Gordon, 'Wine-Dark Sea', 51–52.
457. Ibid., 52. Possibly also, the Hittite *tuwarša* provides indirect evidence for this root, if it is a Semitic loanword, as Aartun thinks. Rabin, however, thinks the Hebrew is borrowed from the Hittite, in which case the word cannot be evidence of a Semitic root behind תַּרְשִׁישׁ. Kjell Aartun, 'Neue Beiträge zum Ugaritischen Lexikon', in *Ugarit-Forschungen 16*, ed. Kurt Bergerhof et al. (Kevelaer: Butzon & Bercker, 1984), 1–52 (35); Rabin, 'Hittite Words', 137–38.
458. See 2.8, 'Native synonyms' for more details on what is meant by these alternatives.
459. Rabin, 'Hittite Words', 126–28; Scheftelowitz, *Arisches im Alten Testament*, 68; Vernes, 'Les Emprunts de la Bible', 20–21; Wagner, *Die Aramaismen*, 18–19; Wilson, 'Foreign Words', 215.
460. Landesdorfer, *Sumerisches Sprachgut*, 59.

attested and there is no obvious evidence that it would have existed. Fried offers the Persian, *bātugara-*, 'drinking cups', as a possible source.[461] While the semantic equivalence is quite good, the form requires some gymnastics: Fried suggests that the form originally began with ב, but that was confused with the preposition and that there was metathesis between the *g* and *t* and confusion between *r* and *l* (באטגרא?).[462] Not only is the solution convoluted, but it fails to explain the apparently related forms in Aramaic, Greek and Hittite.

Because there are more than three consonants, we assume that the origin is likelier to be among the Indo-European languages than the Semitic languages.[463] Moreover, although it is possible that the words come from Hittite or Greek, such an origin would provide only poor explanation for the א of the Hebrew word. Therefore, we suggest that an Iranian language is the likeliest origin, although Ellenbogen and Wilson-Wright argue otherwise.[464]

Wilson-Wright objects that an Iranian loan in this period could not contain the consonant *l*.[465] While it is true that no attested Iranian languages in the time-period have a consonant *l* in their regular orthography, the ל could be explained as dissimilation from the ר. Alternatively, with a word that is so poorly attested in Hebrew, we cannot rule out a problem with the transmission of the text.[466] Ellenbogen's objections are met by considering the Hittite and Persian forms of which he was unaware.

Therefore, based on the cognate evidence, if there were a cognate Iranian form *\*krtar-*, the resolution of the syllabic consonant would explain both the vocalization of *k* to *g* and the א as a prothetic aid to pronunciation. Thus, an Iranian loan is the one that best explains the data.

461. Fried, *Ezra*, 71.
462. Ibid.
463. Cf. Noonan, *Non-Semitic Loanwords*, 40–41.
464. Blenkinsopp, Noonan and Williamson also consider Persian a possibility, though uncertain. Ellenbogen objects because of the use of a Greek word by the author of Ezra. Wilson-Wright objects because of the *lamed*. Blenkinsopp, *Ezra–Nehemiah*, 79; Ellenbogen, *Foreign Words*, 9–11; Noonan, *Non-Semitic Loanwords*, 40–41; Williamson, *Ezra, Nehemiah*, 5; Wilson-Wright, 'From Persepolis to Jerusalem', 154.
465. Wilson-Wright, 'From Persepolis to Jerusalem', 154.
466. Cf. the discussion of רן in Ian Young, 'Late Biblical Hebrew and the Qumran Pesher Habakkuk', *JHS* 8 (2008): 1–38 (18–21); Young, Rezetko and Ehrensvärd, 'Loanwords', 1:306–7, 310.

אִגְּרָה\*

letter; Ezra 4:8, 11; 5:6
(2 Chr 30:1, 6; Neh 2:7, 8, 9; 6:5, 17, 19; Esth 9:26, 29)
Native synonyms: (Aramaic) מִכְתָּב.[467]

See the explanation under אִגֶּרֶת, under 2.3, 'The loanwords in Esther'.

אַדְרַזְדָּא

devoutly?; Ezra 7:23
Native synonyms: (Aramaic) We offer for the sense 'devoutly' the synonym בְּהֵימָנוּ.[468] Because of the hypothetical nature of the gloss of this word we can only have relative certainty about possible synonyms. If, however, אַדְרַזְדָּא should be glossed as 'strong' or 'complete', there are other obvious synonyms: שְׁלִים, 'complete',[469] or תַּמִּים, 'perfect, complete',[470] and חַסִּין, 'strong'.[471]

Ellenbogen, Fensham, Hinz, Scheftelowitz and Williamson identify אַדְרַזְדָּא as a loanword from Persian, though any Old Persian prototype for the word remains hypothetical.[472] Scheftelowitz suggests \*drazhda-,

---

467. Although מִכְתָּב is only attested late, it has an obvious relation to the common verbal root כתב. *Comprehensive Aramaic Lexicon*, s.v. 'ktb'; Cook, *Dictionary of Qumran Aramaic*, s.v. 'ktb'; *DNWSI*, s.v. 'ktb'; *HALOT*, s.v. 'כתב'; Sokoloff, *DJPA*, s.v. 'כתב'; Sokoloff, *DJBA*, s.v. 'כתב'; Sokoloff, *A Syriac Lexicon*, s.v. 'ܟܬܒ'; Sokoloff, *DCPA*, s.v. 'ܟܬܒ'.

468. The word הֵימָנוּ is attested in Ahiqar, line 132 (TAD C1.1). See also *Comprehensive Aramaic Lexicon*, s.v. 'hymnw'; Cook, *Dictionary of Qumran Aramaic*, s.v. 'hymnw'; Sokoloff, *DJPA*, s.v. 'הימנו'; Sokoloff, *DJBA*, s.v. 'הימנו'; Sokoloff, *A Syriac Lexicon*, s.v. 'ܗܝܡܢܘܬܐ'; Sokoloff, *DCPA*, s.v. 'ܗܝܡܢ'.

469. Based on the common root שלם. *Comprehensive Aramaic Lexicon*, s.v. 'šlm'; Cook, *Dictionary of Qumran Aramaic*, s.v. 'šlm'; *DNWSI*, s.v. 'šlm'; *HALOT*, s.v. 'שלם'; Sokoloff, *DJPA*, s.v. 'שלם'; Sokoloff, *DJBA*, s.v. 'שלם'; Sokoloff, *A Syriac Lexicon*, s.v. 'ܫܠܡ'; Sokoloff, *DCPA*, s.v. 'ܫܠܡ'.

470. Based on the common root תמם. Attested in Official Aramaic, e.g. TAD D1.16 R.2. See also *Comprehensive Aramaic Lexicon*, s.v. 'tmym'; *DNWSI*, s.v. 'tmym'; Sokoloff, *DJPA*, s.v. 'תמים'; Sokoloff, *A Syriac Lexicon*, s.v. 'ܬܡܝܡ'; Sokoloff, *DCPA*, s.v. 'ܬܡܝܡ'.

471. Attested in Official Aramaic: e.g. TAD A6.10 4. See also: *Comprehensive Aramaic Lexicon*, s.v. 'ḥsyn'; *DNWSI*, s.v. 'ḥsyn'; Sokoloff, *DJBA*, s.v. 'חסין'; Sokoloff, *A Syriac Lexicon*, s.v. 'ܚܣܝܢ'.

472. Ellenbogen, *Foreign Words*, 16; Fensham, *Ezra and Nehemiah*, 22, 107; Hinz, *Altiranisches Sprachgut*, 92–93; Scheftelowitz, *Arisches im Alten Testament*, 68–69; Williamson, *Ezra, Nehemiah*, 97.

'complete' based on Avestan *děrěšta-*, 'strong', and Modern Persian, *durust*, 'complete'.⁴⁷³ Instead, Hinz and Noonan suggest that it derives from Old Persian, \*drazdā-, on the basis of Avestan, *zrazda-*, 'devout'.⁴⁷⁴ This offers a satisfying solution, based on the coincidence of form.

אָסְפַּרְנָא
completely; Ezra 5:8; 6:8, 12, 13; 7:17, 21, 26
Native synonyms: (Aramaic) תַּמִּים;⁴⁷⁵ שְׁלִים.⁴⁷⁶

Scheftelowitz, Ellenbogen and Fensham agree that אָסְפַּרְנָא derives from the Iranian languages but disagree on the specifics of the borrowing.⁴⁷⁷ Fensham nominates Persian \*usprna-, 'energetically'.⁴⁷⁸ While Scheftelowitz derives the word from an 'Old Bactrian' word *asa-perena-*, 'voll Schnelligkeit' (full speed),⁴⁷⁹ Ellenbogen fails to find that word in existence and so opts for a hypothetical \*asprna-, 'completely'. Noonan, Tavernier and Williamson also nominate a similar origin.⁴⁸⁰ Ellenbogen's suggested word finds the best cognate evidence of the options, since it is attested in Armenian, Avestan, Sogdhian and Pahlavi.⁴⁸¹ Hinz also points to Elamite *áš-bar-na*, 'complete', as evidence of the word's existence in Persian.⁴⁸² Although \*asprna- is never directly attested, the cognate evidence is sufficient to suppose that the word, or something similar, could have existed in Old Persian or some similar contemporaneous Iranian dialect. While the hypothetical nature of the word detracts from our certainty about the origin of אָסְפַּרְנָא, the loan hypothesis is preferable to trying to explain the word on the basis of Semitic roots alone. While non-nominal borrowings are rarer than their nominal counterparts, they

473. Scheftelowitz, *Arisches im Alten Testament*, 68–69.
474. Hinz, *Altiransiches Sprachgut*, 92–93; Noonan, *Non-Semitic Loanwords*, 43.
475. Attested in Official Aramaic (e.g. TAD D1.16 R.2). See also, the notes on the synonyms for אֲדַרְזְדָא, above.
476. The verbal root of this adjective is attested in Ezra 5:16. See also, the notes on the synonyms for אֲדַרְזְדָא, above.
477. Ellenbogen, *Foreign Words*, 33–34; Fensham, *Ezra and Nehemiah*, 82; Scheftelowitz, *Arisches im Alten Testament*, 73–74. Fried also attributes the word to Persian but does not nominate a Persian word. Fried, *Ezra*, 249.
478. Fensham, *Ezra and Nehemiah*, 82.
479. Scheftelowitz, *Arisches im Alten Testament*, 74. By Old Bactrian he apparently means Avestan, which was once falsely presumed to be the ancestor of Bactrian.
480. Noonan, *Non-Semitic Loanwords*, 57–58; Tavernier, *Iranica*, 406–407; Williamson, *Ezra, Nehemiah*, 71.
481. Ellenbogen, *Foreign Words*, 33–34.
482. Hinz, *Altiranisches Sprachgut*, s.v. '\*asprna-'.

are nevertheless quite possible; in English, for example, there is the loan from Latin, *in toto*, 'completely', which matches the present example well.

אֲפַרְסַתְכָי*
a type of official; Ezra 4:9

אֲפַרְסְכָי*
a type of official; Ezra 5:6; 6:6
Native synonyms: (Aramaic) פְּקוֹד;[483] רַב;[484] רֵישׁ.[485]

Scheftelowitz identified both these words (אֲפַרְסַתְכָיָא and אֲפַרְסְכָיָא) as loans from the Iranian language family, hypothesizing an Old Iranian *\*apara-saraka-*.[486] There is some disadvantage to this suggestion in that neither the whole word, nor *\*saraka-*, are directly attested in Old Persian. Nevertheless, there are good grounds based on cognates to assume the presence of *\*saraka-*. Others prefer to treat the two words separately.[487] To do so is preferable since Scheftelowitz gives no good grounds for the presence of the ת in the long version.

For אֲפַרְסְכָיָא, Eiler identifies *\*frasaka-* as the underlying Iranian word.[488] For this same hypothesis, Hinz brings the evidence of Elamite, *pír-ra-iš-šá-ik-qa*, and Akkadian, *iprasakku*, names of Persian officials.[489] For אֲפַרְסַתְכָיָא, Hinz offers the etymology internal to Persian, built as a

---

483. The root פקד is found as early as Old Aramaic (Asshur Ostracon, line 17). The noun cited here is Syriac, but equally we could cite the participle of the verb. For the relevant lexica for these synonyms see under אֲדַרְגָּזֵר, in 2.4, 'The loanwords in Daniel'.

484. This noun is attested elsewhere in Biblical Aramaic, Dan 5:1.

485. With the sense 'head' the noun is basic vocabulary in Aramaic, including Biblical Aramaic. The sense 'chief' is a relatively simple development and is common to many dialects, if not attested in Biblical Hebrew. Moreover, since that development is shared by Biblical Hebrew it would be at home in Daniel.

486. Scheftelowitz, *Arisches im Alten Testament*, 75–77. Thus also, Fensham, *Ezra and Nehemiah*, 22, 72–73.

487. Blenkinsopp, *Ezra–Nehemiah*, 113, 121; Wilhelm Eilers, *Iranische Beamtennamen in der keilschriftlichen* Überlieferung, Abhandlungen für die Kunde des Morgenlandes 25 (Leipzig: Deutsche Morgenländische Gesellschaft, 1940), 5–43; Hinz, *Altiranisches Sprachgut*; Williamson, *Ezra, Nehemiah*, 54; Noonan, *Non-Semitic Loanwords*, 61–62.

488. Eilers, *Iranische Beamtennamen*, 5–43, especially 10 and 30ff.

489. Hinz, *Altiranisches Sprachgut*, s.v. '*\*frasaka-*'. So also Blenkinsopp, *Ezra–Nehemiah*, 121; Williamson, *Ezra, Nehemiah*, 54.

compound of *fra-*, 'above', *stā-*, 'to stand' and the nominal suffix, *-ka-*, giving rise to hypothetical Persian prototype, *\*frastāka-*.[490] While Eilers offers an alternative etymology in *\*fraištaka-*,[491] Hinz's suggestion is closer phonetically. Therefore, despite some doubts about the precise forms, the non-triliteral nature of these two words suggest strongly that the word has non-Semitic origins. Furthermore, the ending in *-k* is characteristic of a noun from an Iranian language and Hinz's etymology of אֲפַרְסַתְכָיֵא and Elamite evidence for אֲפַרְסְכָיֵא are convincing.

אֲפְּתֹם
treasury? progeny? suddenly?; Ezra 4:13
Native synonyms: (Aramaic) אוֹצָר.[492]

There are a wide range of opinions on this word and none entirely satisfactory. Scheftelowitz, Ellenbogen and Fensham agree in deriving this word from an Iranian source, noting Avestan *paθma-*, 'treasury'.[493] However, this word is typically 'path' not 'treasury'.[494] Tisdall, on the other hand, rejects that particular hypothesis, in favour of Old Persian *\*apa-tauma-*, 'progeny'.[495] Noonan too derives the word in this way, but argues that it refers to some kind of income, based on comparison to Akkadian *aptumu*.[496] Tisdall and Noonan's suggestion is superior, because it offers a Persian precedent rather than Avestan and because it corresponds more closely to the form of the Hebrew word. On the other hand, it relies on an unattested compound, which is likewise unattested in the daughter languages.

Hinz, on the other hand, points to Pahlavi *abdom*, 'finally', with a hypothetical forerunner in Old Iranian of *\*apatama(m)-*.[497] Wilson, while he considers the Iranian origin a possibility, prefers the idea that the

---

490. Hinz, *Altiranisches Sprachgut*, s.v. '*frastāka-*'. So also Blenkinsopp, *Ezra–Nehemiah*, 113; Williamson, *Ezra, Nehemiah*, 54.
491. Eilers, *Iranische Beamtennamen*, 40.
492. Attested in Official Aramaic (e.g. TAD B4.2 R.6). See also *Comprehensive Aramaic Lexicon*, s.v. ''wṣr'; *DNWSI*, s.v. ''wṣr'; Sokoloff, *DJPA*, s.v. 'אוצר'; Sokoloff, *A Syriac Lexicon*, s.v. 'ܐܘܨܪ'; Sokoloff, *DCPA*, s.v. 'ܐܘܨܪ'.
493. Ellenbogen, *Foreign Words*, 36–37; Fensham, *Ezra and Nehemiah*, 74; Scheftelowitz, *Arisches im Alten Testament*, 78–79.
494. Bartholomae, *Altiranisches Wörterbuch*, s.v. 'paθman-'.
495. Tisdall, 'The Āryan Words, III', 369–70.
496. Noonan, *Non-Semitic Loanwords*, 62–63.
497. Hinz, *Altiranisches Sprachgut*, s.v. '*apatama-*'. Williamson also considers this a possibility. Williamson, *Ezra, Nehemiah*, 56.

word derives from Akkadian *appittima*, which he glosses as 'suddenly'.[498] Similarly, Vogt suggests the same Akkadian word with the gloss, 'so, in this way'.[499] Zadok and Tadmor suggest, however, that the context requires a noun, rather than an adverb.[500] Certainly an adverb would require us to explain why מַלְכִים, 'kings', is plural – there is only one king obviously affected. However, it is not impossible and the reading מַלְכִים is also suspect, due to the apparently Hebrew inflexion. Rather, we should also consider another possibility, that the word is Semitic and that the ending in *ōm* reflects the adverbial ending (old locative, *ū*) found in several Semitic languages, including in later Aramaic – e.g. Syriac, ܒܟܠܐܒ, 'always'.[501] If this is the case, it is reasonably probable that the word is simply native to Aramaic. However, there is no obvious candidate for an etymology. One possibility is that it would be cognate with Hebrew פִּתְאֹם, 'suddenly', with a prosthetic *aleph*. However, we would still need to explain the *dagesh* in the *pe*. All of these options are unsatisfactory in some respect, but the explanation that at present has the fewest problems is Noonan's, that it is derived from Persian \*aptauma-, 'tribute'.

אֻשַּׁרְנָא\*
furnishing; Ezra 5:3, 9
Native synonyms: (Aramaic) There are no obvious precise synonyms for this word. However, we note in context that the word is used in a phrase that is redundant: in both cases it is used in conjunction with a semantically equivalent phrase: בַּיְתָא דְנָה לִבְּנֵא.

Zimmern suggested that אֻשַּׁרְנָא derives from the Akkadian, *šurinnu*, 'emblem, divine symbol'.[502] Scheftelowitz, on the other hand, suggests it

---

498. Wilson, 'Foreign Words', 194. Williamson also considers this a possibility. Williamson, *Ezra, Nehemiah*, 56.

499. Ernst Vogt, *A Lexicon of Biblical Aramaic: Clarified by Ancient Documents*, trans. J. Fitzmyer, SubBi 42 (Rome: Gregorian & Biblical Press, 2011), 48f.

500. The context is וְאַפְּתֹם מַלְכִים תְּהַנְזִק. Either it is to be translated as a noun, 'and you will damage the kings' treasury/progeny/etc.' or as an adverb, 'and thus/suddenly/etc. you will damage the kings'. Chaim Tadmor, '"אַפְּתֹם" in Ezra 4:13', in *Michael: Historical, Epigraphical and Biblical Studies in Honor of Prof. Michael Heltzer*, ed. Yitzhak Avishur and Robert Deutsch (Tel Aviv: Archeological Center Publications, 1999), 143\*–45\*; Ran Zadok, 'Two Terms in Ezra', *Aramaic Studies* 5 (2007): 260–61. So also Fried, *Ezra*, 212.

501. Burkhart Kienast, *Historische Semitische Sprachwissenschaft* (Wiesbaden: Harrassowitz, 2001), 172–73.

502. Zimmern, *Akkadische Fremdwörter*, 68.

derives from Old Persian and Avestan, *visarna-*, 'break'.⁵⁰³ Nevertheless, neither is a good semantic match for the Aramaic, which means 'furnishings' or 'carpentry equipment', and is found among other places in texts from Elephantine.⁵⁰⁴ Hinz and Williamson suggest a hypothetical *\*āčarna-*, based on the appearance of versions of this word not only in Aramaic, but also in Elamite, *ha-za-ir-na*, 'furniture'.⁵⁰⁵ Similarly, Hinz points to *ha-za-ir-na-qa-ra*, 'furniture-maker', as the result of a hypothetical *\*āčarnakara-*.⁵⁰⁶ Since the *qa-ra* of the Elamite form corresponds obviously to the Persian verb, *kar-*, 'to do, make', and the common Persian suffix, *kara-*, 'maker', the suggestion that both words have some Iranian origin is likely.

בִּירָה
citadel; Ezra 6:2
(1 Chr 29:1, 19; 2 Chr 17:12; 27:4; Neh 1:1; 2:8; 7:2; Esth 1:2, 5; 2:3, 5, 8; 3:15; 8:14; 9:6, 11, 12; Dan 8:2)
Native synonyms: (Aramaic) כְּרָךְ.⁵⁰⁷

See the explanation under 2.3, 'The loanwords in Esther'.

*גְּנַז
treasury; Ezra 5:17; 6:1; 7:20
(Esth 3:9; 4:7; Ezek 27:24)
Native synonyms: (Aramaic) אוֹצָר.⁵⁰⁸

*גִּזְבָּר
treasurer; Ezra 1:8; 7:21
(Dan 3:2, 3)

---

503. Scheftelowitz, *Arisches im Alten Testament*, 79–80.
504. The context in both Ezra 5:3 and 5:9 is the following question: מַן־שָׂם לְכֹם טְעֵם בַּיְתָא דְנָה לִבְּנֵא וְאֻשַּׁרְנָא דְנָה לְשַׁכְלָלָה, 'Who gave you a decree to build this house and to finish this *structure*?' (NRSV). As mentioned it is found elsewhere, often in lists of supplies used for construction or repairs. See *Comprehensive Aramaic Lexicon*, s.v. ''šrn'; *DNWSI*, s.v. ''šrn'.
505. Hinz, *Altiranisches Sprachgut*, s.v. '\*āčarna-'; Williamson, *Ezra, Nehemiah*, 70.
506. Hinz, *Altiranisches Sprachgut*, s.v. '\*āčarnakara-'; similarly, Noonan, *Non-Semitic Loanwords*, 70–71.
507. Attested as Official Aramaic, indirectly as a Pahlavi ideogram. *Comprehensive Aramaic Lexicon*, s.v. 'krk'; *DNWSI*, s.v. 'krk'; Sokoloff, *DJPA*, s.v. 'כרך'; Sokoloff, *DJBA*, s.v. 'כרך'.
508. See above, under the entry for אַפֶּתֹם.

Native synonyms: (Hebrew) Although there is no single word equivalent, it is simple to imagine a noun phrase, such as נְצִיב שִׂימָה, 'officer of the treasury', which would have an equivalent meaning.
Native synonyms: (Aramaic) חָשְׁבָּן.[509]

See the explanation under 2.3, 'The loanwords in Esther'.

דַּרְכְּמוֹנִים
coins; Ezra 2:69
(Neh 7:69, 70, 71)
Native synonyms: (Hebrew) שֶׁקֶל; בֶּקַע; גֵּרָה. While these synonyms denote different values to the *drachma*, they are readily convertible, one to the other.

The words דַּרְכְּמוֹנִים and אֲדַרְכֹּן (Ezra 8:27; 1 Chr 29:7), both words for coins, are sometimes considered by-forms of the same word and sometimes considered distinct.[510] In one version of reading them as the same, Albright suggested that אֲדַרְכֹּן might be a corruption of דַּרְכּוֹן, itself a version of דַּרְכְּמוֹנִים – incorrectly claiming that אֲדַרְכֹּן only occurs once.[511] The argument is less convincing, since the word in fact occurs twice. Given no clear evidence that the words are the same and no clear explanation of the absence of the *mem* in one form, each word should be considered individually. דַּרְכְּמוֹנִים is thought by other scholars to have been borrowed from Greek, δραχμή, 'drachma, coin', or perhaps, δραχμίον, the diminutive of the same.[512] While the word has no good

---

509. While the noun is not attested outside Hatran Aramaic, the verb on which it is based is common in Aramaic, including Biblical Aramaic (Dan 4:32). *Comprehensive Aramaic Lexicon*, s.v. 'ḥšbn', 'ḥšb'; Cook, *Dictionary of Qumran Aramaic*, s.v. 'ḥšb'; *DNWSI*, s.v. 'ḥšbn'; *HALOT*, s.v. 'חשב'; Sokoloff, *DJPA*, s.v. 'חשב'; Sokoloff, *DJBA*, s.v. 'חשב'; Sokoloff, *A Syriac Lexicon*, s.v. 'ܚܫܒ'; Sokoloff, *DCPA*, s.v. 'ܚܫܒ'.

510. While Blenkinsopp and Clines do not address the question directly, both words are translated as 'darics'. Fensham and Williamson, on the other hand, distinguish 'darics' in 8:27 from 'drachmas' in 2:69. Blenkinsopp, *Ezra–Nehemiah*, 94, 167; David Clines, *Ezra, Nehemiah, Esther*, NCBC (Grand Rapids: Eerdmans, 1984), 61, 113; Fensham, *Ezra and Nehemiah*, 57, 117; Williamson, *Ezra, Nehemiah*, 28, 114.

511. William Albright, review of *Introduction a la Bible, Tome I*, by André Robert and André Feuillet, *BO* 17 (1960): 241–42 (242).

512. Noonan, *Non-Semitic Loanwords*, 87–88; Vernes, 'Les Emprunts de la Bible', 51; Wagner, *Die Aramaismen*, 44. So also H. G. M. Williamson, 'Eschatology in Chronicles', *Tyndale Bulletin* 28 (1977): 123–26.

explanation internal to the Semitic languages, the word has a plausible etymology in Greek, deriving from the verb δράσσομαι, 'to take in the hand'.[513] Moreover, the semantic and phonetic match is good, such that the Greek solution is plausible. Scheftelowitz, on the other hand, suggests that the Greek derives from the Semitic, which in turn derives from an unknown Iranian donor word.[514] There are some grounds to this case, given the presence of variable dialectal forms in Greek (δαρχμά, δαρχμά, δαρκνά)[515] and Pahlavi *drahm*, 'drachma'.[516] However, since there is only late evidence for the existence of a Persian prototype and because there is no plausible etymology, at present the best explanation is that Greek, δραχμή, is the original form.

דָּת

law; Ezra 7:12, 14, 21, 25, 26, 26
(Deut 33:2 [?]; Ezra 8:36; Esth 1:8, 13, 15, 19; 2:8, 12; 3:8, 8, 14, 15; 4:3, 8, 11, 16; 8:13, 14, 17; 9:1, 13, 14; Dan 2:9, 13, 15; 6:6, 9, 13, 16; 7:25)
Native synonyms: (Aramaic) פְּקוּד.[517]

See the explanation under 2.3, 'The loanwords in Esther'.

הֵיכָל

temple; Ezra 3:6, 10; 4:1, 14; 5:14, 14, 14, 15; 6:5, 5
(80 occurrences in Biblical Hebrew. 13 occurrences in Biblical Aramaic)
Native synonyms: (Hebrew) מִקְדָּשׁ; בַּיִת.
Native synonyms: (Aramaic) בֵּית אֱלָהָא.

See the explanation under 2.4, 'The loanwords in Daniel'. Note that since the word is borrowed early and is highly nativized, it has not been counted in the statistics below.

---

513. *Diccionario Griego-Español*, s.vv. 'δραχμή', 'δραχμίον', 'δράσσομαι'.
514. Scheftelowitz, *Arisches im Alten Testament*, 71–72.
515. *Diccionario Griego-Español*, s.v. 'δραχμή'.
516. Henrik Nyberg, *A Manual of Pahlavi*, 2 vols (Wiesbaden: Harrassowitz, 1974), 2:179, s.v. 'drahm'.
517. The root פקד is found even in Old Aramaic (Asshur Ostracon, line 17). See also: *Comprehensive Aramaic Lexicon*, s.v. 'pqd'; Cook, *Dictionary of Qumran Aramaic*, s.v. 'פקד'; *DNWSI*, s.v. 'pqd'; Sokoloff, *DJPA*, s.v. 'פקד'; Sokoloff, *DJBA*, s.v. 'פקד'; Sokoloff, *A Syriac Lexicon*, s.v. 'ܦܩܕ'; Sokoloff, *DCPA*, s.v. 'ܦܩܕ'.

זְמָן
time; Ezra 5:3
(Neh 2:6; Esth 9:27, 31; Eccl 3:1; Dan 2:16, 21; 3:7, 8; 4:33; 6:11, 14; 7:12, 22, 25)
Native synonyms: (Aramaic) עִדָּן;[518] עֵת.[519]

See the explanation under 2.3, 'The loanwords in Esther'.

כֻּתֹּנֶת
tunic; Ezra 2:69
(Gen 3:21; 37:3, 23, 23, 31, 31, 32, 32, 33; Exod 28:4, 39, 40; 29:5, 8; 39:27; 40:14; Lev 8:7, 13; 10:5; 16:4; 2 Sam 13:18, 19; 15:32; Neh 7:69, 71; Job 30:18; Song 5:3; Isa 22:21)
Native synonyms: בֶּגֶד; סָדִין.

There are several competing etymologies for the word כֻּתֹּנֶת. The first option is that the word derives from an Indo-European source, whether from Greek χιτών, *khitōn*, Latin, *tunica* < *ctunica*, or some ancestor of the two; this hypothesis is supported by Vernes on the basis of the similarity of the words.[520] Cuny offers a variation on the first option which is that the word is also a loan in Greek and Latin from the pre-Greek substrate language – an unknown language spoken in Greece or Anatolia prior to the arrival of Greek-speakers – and that it is from this language that Hebrew borrowed the word.[521] A third hypothesis, given by many scholars is that the word derives from Sumerian, *gada*, by way of Akkadian *kitu* and *kitinnu*.[522] The fourth explanation offered, by Noonan and Rendsburg, is that the word is a culture word.[523] As Noonan notes, the word exists in both a western n-form *ktn* and an eastern plain form *kt*.[524]

---

518. Attested in Official Aramaic (e.g. TAD B2.11, R.13). *Comprehensive Aramaic Lexicon*, s.v. "dn'; Cook, *Dictionary of Qumran Aramaic*, s.v. "dn'; *DNWSI*, s.v. "dn'; Sokoloff, *DJPA*, s.v. 'עדן'; Sokoloff, *DJBA*, s.v. 'עדן'; Sokoloff, *A Syriac Lexicon*, s.v. 'ܥܕܢ'.

519. Attested in Official Aramaic (La Collection Clermont-Ganneau 229, V.2).

520. Vernes, *Les Emprunts de la Bible*, 77.

521. Cuny, 'Les Mots du Fonds Préhellénique', 161.

522. Brown, *Israel and Hellas*, 1:205; Ellenbogen, *Foreign Words*, 96; Landesdorfer, *Sumerisches Sprachgut*, 47; Propp, *Exodus 19–40*, 433; Rabin, 'Foreign Words', 1073; Zimmern, *Akkadische Fremdwörter*, 37.

523. Noonan, *Non-Semitic Loanwords*, 87–88; Rendsburg, 'Cultural Words', 1:641.

524. Noonan, 'Foreign Loanwords', 199–201; Noonan, *Non-Semitic Loanwords*, 87–88. For the *ktn* form he cites Akkadian, *kitinnu*, *kidinnu*, and Old Akkadian and

There are multiple ways of explaining this: it is possible that the development in Akkadian from the plain form in Old Akkadian to the n-form in Assyrian is the origin of all the n-forms. If this were the case, it would stand to reason that the Sumerian form were the original and that the word diffused westwards through Akkadian. However, it is also possible that n-form in Assyrian was borrowed from the west. If this is the case, the connection between the n-form and plain form must lie in an unattested language or unattested in a known language. A third possibility is that the n-forms arose multiple times, independently. As the evidence stands, the explanation to be preferred provisionally is the Sumerian hypothesis, since it adequately explains the evidence and does not require any more evidence than what is already attested.

מִדָּה
מִנְדָּה
tribute; Ezra 4:13, 20; 6:8; 7:24
(Neh 5:4)
Native synonyms: (Aramaic) הֲלָךְ; בְּלוֹ. In Ezra these two words (each signifying different forms of tribute or tax) are frequently used in a list together with מִדָּה (4:13, 20; 7:24). Thus, מִדָּה could easily be omitted. Neither בְּלוֹ nor הֲלָךְ should be thought of as loans in the traditional sense.[525] It does seem at least plausible that the technical sense of 'tribute' is derived from Akkadian, rather than from a parallel semantic development in Aramaic.[526] However, the forms of these words do not correspond easily to the Akkadian. The -t- of *biltu* is missing, when compared to the Aramaic, בְּלוֹ.[527] Similarly, while the Akkadian *ilku* would have had an etymological *h, corresponding to the Aramaic ה in הֲלָךְ, that guttural has been long absent by the time of Ezra–Nehemiah.

Mari, *kutanu*, Aramaic forms starting in the Imperial period as כתן, Arabic *kattān*, Ethiopic, *ketān*, Linear B, *ki-to*, Greek, χιτών, *khitōn*, and Latin, *tunica*. For the *kt* form he cites Old Akkadian, *kitû*, and Sumerian, *gada*.

525. *Contra* Ellenbogen, *Foreign Words*, 51, 69; Fensham, *Ezra and Nehemiah*, 74; Kaufman, *The Akkadian Influences*, 44, 58; Zimmern, *Akkadische Fremdwörter*, 10.

526. Kaufman, *The Akkadian Influences*, 44, 58. Kaufman also notes that *biltu* and *maddattu* often occur together. Cf. *CAD* 2, s.v. 'biltu'.

527. Even in the emphatic form, the form is בְּלוֹא. Cf. Idumean Ostracon 2.81.2. Thus, the noun in Aramaic appears to be masculine, such that the lack of a ת representing the Akkadian -t- is difficult.

Any loan would have to be very old. Moreover, there are common roots יבל, 'to bring', and הלך, 'to go', in Aramaic which act as the source for the morphemes בְּלוֹ and הֲלָךְ.⁵²⁸ Therefore, if there is any lexical transfer in these cases it is that the semantics of *biltu* and *ilku* are applied to the native morphemes, בְּלוֹ and הֲלָךְ, formed from the verbal roots יבל and הלך. Since these words use native morphemes, it is unlikely they would have the same force as full loanwords.

While בְּלוֹ and הֲלָךְ are calques, מִדָּה and its byform מִנְדָּה must be derived from Akkadian, *maddattu*, 'tribute'. Many scholars argue for this loan hypothesis, since the verbal root on which it is based – *nadānu*, 'to give' – has the form נתן in Aramaic and Hebrew.⁵²⁹ Therefore, an origin in Aramaic or Hebrew is unlikely. The *-tt-* of *maddattu* is somewhat difficult. However, as Mankowski proposes, a development, *maddattu* > \**maddātu* would allow for the Aramaic to reinterpret the single *-t-* as the feminine construct form, מִדַּת, implying an absolute form, מִדָּה.⁵³⁰

נִדְבָּךְ\*
layer; Ezra 6:4, 4
Native synonyms: (Aramaic) מַשְׁטוּחַ.⁵³¹

Ellenbogen and Kaufman identify this word as a loan in Aramaic, from Akkadian, *natbākum*, 'layer (of bricks)'.⁵³² The word is also attested in Akkadian as *nadabākum*, which explains the Aramaic *daleth*, but derives from the Akkadian verb *tabākum*, 'to make layers'.⁵³³ The prefix 'na-' is

---

528. *Comprehensive Aramaic Lexicon*, s.vv. 'blw', 'hlk', 'ybl'.
529. Ellenbogen, *Foreign Words*, 98; Fensham, *Ezra and Nehemiah*, 74; Fried, *Ezra*, 214; Kaufman, *The Akkadian Influences*, 67; Lipiński, 'Emprunts Suméro-akkadiens', 68; Mankowski, *Akkadian Loanwords*, 111–12; Zimmern, *Akkadische Fremdwörter*, 9.
530. Mankowski, *Akkadian Loanwords*, 111–12.
531. Although this form of the noun is Palestinian Targumic Aramaic, the verb on which it is based is common in most dialects of Aramaic. *Comprehensive Aramaic Lexicon*, s.v. 'šṭḥ'; Sokoloff, *DJPA*, s.v. 'שטח'; Sokoloff, *DJBA*, s.v. 'שטח'; Sokoloff, *A Syriac Lexicon*, s.v. 'ܫܛܚ'; Sokoloff, *DCPA*, s.v. 'ܫܛܚ'. There is also a Hebrew root: *HALOT*, s.v. שטח.
532. Ellenbogen, *Foreign Words*, 111; Kaufman, *The Akkadian Influences on Aramaic*, 76.
533. *CAD* 11, 18, s.vv., 'natbāku', 'tabāku'.

easily explained in Akkadian as an assimilatory effect, due to the dental.[534] Because of the etymology in Akkadian, it is best explained as a loan from there.

נְכַס*
property; Ezra 6:8; 7:26
(Josh 22:8; 2 Chr 1:11, 12; Eccl 5:18; 6:2)
Native synonyms: (Aramaic) קִנְיָן.[535]

The word נְכַס finds a parallel in Sumerian, $nig_2.ka_9$, 'accounting', which then appears to have been loaned into Akkadian as *nikkassu*, 'account, property'. If the direction of this borrowing is correct, then there is no reason to doubt that the Aramaic נְכַס and Hebrew נְכֶס are loans from Sumerian by way of Akkadian. The Sumerian word appears to be based on *nig*, 'property, thing'. Many scholars agree on the Sumerian origin.[536] Given the workable etymology in Sumerian, a loan from Sumerian into Akkadian is the best explanation; from there the word spread to Aramaic and Hebrew.[537]

נִשְׁתְּוָן*
command; Ezra 4:7, 18, 23; 5:5; 7:11
Native synonyms: (Aramaic) פְּקוּד.[538]
Native synonyms: (Hebrew) מַאֲמַר; דָּבָר; מִצְוָה.

Aside from Vernes' suggestion that נִשְׁתְּוָן derives from Greek, ἐπιστολή, 'letter',[539] there is a consensus that the word is derived from

---

534. In brief, in presence of a dental the labial nasal *m* assimilates to the place of articulation, producing the dental nasal *n*. For details, see under 'Appendix Six: An Outline of Linguistic Change in Aramaic and Akkadian'.

535. Attested in Official Aramaic (e.g. TAD B2.6 206, R.19). See also: *Comprehensive Aramaic Lexicon*, s.v. 'qnyn'; *DNWSI*, s.v. 'qnyn'; Sokoloff, *DJPA*, s.v. 'קִנְיָן'; Sokoloff, *DJBA*, s.v. 'קנין'; Sokoloff, *A Syriac Lexicon*, s.v. 'ܩܢܝܢ'; Sokoloff, *DCPA*, s.v. 'ܩܢܝܢܐ'.

536. Landesdorfer, *Sumerisches Sprachgut*, 76–77; Lipiński, 'Emprunts Suméro-akkadiens', 69–70; Mankowski, *Akkadian Loanwords*, 103; Noonan, *Non-Semitic Loanwords*, 152–53; Rubin, 'Sumerian Loanwords', 665; Wagner, *Die Aramaismen*, 84; Zimmern, *Akkadische Fremdwörter*, 20.

537. Cf. Wagner, *Die Aramaismen*, 191.

538. See under the entry for דָּת.

539. Vernes, *Les Emprunts de la Bible*, 98.

Old Persian;⁵⁴⁰ Scheftelowitz suggests a derivation from a hypothetical pronunciation \*niwišθwa of the attested Old Persian word, nipištam-, 'letter'.⁵⁴¹ Tisdall and other scholars, on the other hand, prefer to derive it from the verbal stem nišadaya-/ništaya-, 'to enjoin'.⁵⁴² Similarly, Ellenbogen points to Avestan ništa-, 'to order', and Pahlavi ništavanak, 'something authoritative'.⁵⁴³ While Scheftelowitz's explanation has the advantage of relying on an attested nominal form, Tisdall's explanation has a better phonetic match and the weakness of relying on a hypothetical noun is mitigated by the attestation of the verbal root. Thus, Tisdall's explanation is preferable.

סוּס
horse; Ezra 2:66
(140 occurrences in Biblical Hebrew. Not in Biblical Aramaic)
Native synonyms: רֶכֶשׁ (?). However, סוּס itself is thoroughly nativized.

See the explanation under 2.3, 'The loanwords in Esther'. Note that due to its early entry into Hebrew and high degree of nativization, this word has not been counted in the statistics below.

פֶּחָה
official; Ezra 2:6; 5:3, 6, 14; 6:6, 7, 13
(1 Kgs 10:15; 20:24; 2 Kgs 18:24; 2 Chr 9:14; Ezra 8:36; Neh 2:7, 9; 3:7; 5:14, 14, 15; 12:26; Esth 3:12; 8:9; 9:3; Isa 36:9; Jer 51:23, 28, 57; Ezek 23:6, 12, 23; Dan 3:2, 3, 27; 6:8; Hag 1:1, 14; 2:2, 21; Mal 1:8)
Native synonyms: (Aramaic) פְּקוֹד; רַב; רֵישׁ.⁵⁴⁴
Native synonyms: (Hebrew) מֹשֵׁל; נְצִיב; פָּקִיד.

See the explanation under 2.3, 'The loanwords in Esther'.

---

540. Blenkinsopp, *Ezra–Nehemiah*, 147; Ellenbogen, *Foreign Words*, 116; Fensham, *Ezra and Nehemiah*, 22, 75; Fried, *Ezra*, 201, 204; Rabin, 'Foreign Words', 1079; Scheftelowitz, *Arisches im Alten Testament*, 89–90; Tisdall, 'The Āryan Words, III', 365–66; Wagner, *Die Aramaismen*, 85; Wilson, 'Foreign Words', 215.
541. Scheftelowitz, *Arisches im Alten Testament*, 89–90.
542. Hinz, *Altiranisches Sprachgut*, s.v. 'ništa-vana-'; Noonan, *Non-Semitic Loanwords*, 156; Tisdall, 'The Āryan Words, III', 365–66. Cf. Kent, *Old Persian*, 212.
543. Ellenbogen, *Foreign Words*, 116.
544. See above, under אֲפַרְסַתְכָיֵא.

פַּרְשֶׁגֶן
copy; Ezra 4:11, 23; 5:6; 7:11
(Esth 3:14; 4:8; 8:13)
Native synonyms: (Aramaic) The verbal root, אעף, 'to double', could supply a derivative noun.⁵⁴⁵
Native synonyms: (Hebrew) מִשְׁנֶה.

See the explanation under פִּתְשֶׁגֶן in 2.3, 'The loanwords in Esther'. The difference in form might be explained as assimilation of the ת followed by dissimilation with ר. However, generally it is explained as a slightly different, but closely related, source word, using a Persian prefix such as *fra-* or *pari-*, rather than *pati-*.⁵⁴⁶

פִּתְגָם
decree; Ezra 4:17; 5:7, 11; 6:11
(Esth 1:20; Eccl 8:11; Dan 3:16; 4:14)
Native synonyms: (Aramaic) פִּקּוּד.⁵⁴⁷

See the explanation under 2.3, 'The loanwords in Esther'.

שְׁרֹשִׁי
corporal punishment; Ezra 7:26
Native synonyms: (Aramaic) potential synonyms (e.g. עֲנָשׁ) are generic.⁵⁴⁸ Nonetheless, this word is used as part of a list and could easily be omitted.

Following Rundgren, several scholars have suggested that שְׁרֹשִׁי derives from Persian, based on the Avestan form, *sraošyā-*, 'punishment'.⁵⁴⁹ The form, while not attested in Old Persian, is known in Pahlavi as *srōš*.⁵⁵⁰ Rundgren proposes that the word שְׁרֹשִׁי – also, שְׁרֹשִׁי in the *kethiv* – is

---

545. In Official Aramaic it is spelt as עקף. Cf. TAD B4.2 R.8.
546. Cf. Scheftelowitz, *Arisches im Alten Testament*, 52; Tisdall, 'The Āryan Words II', 213–14.
547. See under the entry for דָּת.
548. We can see this from the same verse, Ezra 7:26, where עֲנָשׁ must be used in construct with נִכְסִין, to specify the king of punishment.
549. Blenkinsopp, *Ezra–Nehemiah*, 152; Fensham, *Ezra and Nehemiah*, 22, 108; Noonan, *Non-Semitic Loanwords*, 214–15; Frithiof Rundgren, 'Zur Bedeutung von ŠRŠW – Esra VII 26', *VT* 7 (1957): 400–404. Cf. Bartholomae, *Altiranisches Wörterbuch*, s.v. 'sraošyā'.
550. Nyberg, *A Manual of Pahlavi*, 2:179, s.v. 'srōš'.

another version of the Aramaic, סְרוֹשִׁיתָא, 'corporal punishment', known from Imperial Aramaic.⁵⁵¹ The correspondence between סְרוֹשִׁיתָא and *srauš̌yā-* is acceptable, if we accept Rundgren's suggestion that the ending in יְתָא represents a degree of nativization, by comparison to Aramaic, אֲחְשָׁמִיתָא, 'dinner', with Middle Iranian, *xšam*.⁵⁵² The correspondence between סְרוֹשִׁיתָא, *srauš̌yā-* and שְׁרֹשׁוּ is acceptable. Therefore, tentatively, this solution seems correct.

תּוֹר
bull; Ezra 6:9, 17; 7:17
(Not in Biblical Hebrew, except as שׁוֹר [58 times]. 7 occurrences in Biblical Aramaic)
Native synonyms: בָּקָר.⁵⁵³ However, תּוֹר itself is very early and quite nativized.

See the explanation under 2.4, 'The loanwords in Daniel'. Note that because it is so early and nativized, it is not counted in the statistics below.

תִּרְגֵּם
to translate; Ezra 4:7
Native synonyms: there are no obvious synonyms.

Given that the root רגם is unknown in Hebrew or Aramaic, but common in Akkadian, Rabin and Zimmern have suggested that the verb תִּרְגֵּם derives from the Akkadian noun, *targumannu*, 'interpreter, dragoman', which itself would be built from the Akkadian verb, *ragāmu*, 'to call out, prophesy, summon, bring a legal complaint, etc.'.⁵⁵⁴ Elsewhere, however, others have also pointed to the Hittite, *tarkummāi*, 'to announce, explain translate',⁵⁵⁵ or a hypothetical Luwian noun, based on the Indo-European roots *tr̥g, 'to speak', and *ǵʰeu̯, 'to pour forth'.⁵⁵⁶ We can determine that

---

551. Rundgren 'ŠRŠW', 402.
552. Ibid., 403.
553. See the comments under 2.4, 'The loanwords in Daniel'.
554. Rabin, 'Foreign Words', 1074; Zimmern, *Akkadische Fremdwörter*, 7.
555. Rabin, 'Hittite Words', 134–36; Noonan, *Non-Semitic Loanwords*, 226–27; Frank Starke, 'Zur Herkunft von akkad. *ta/urgumannu(m)* "Dolmetscher"', *WO* 24 (1993): 20–38.
556. Jose Virgilio Garcia Trabazo, 'Hethitisch *tarkummae-*: ein etymologischer Vorschlag', in *Proceedings of the Eighth International Congress of Hittitology, Warsaw, 5–9 September 2011*, ed. Piotr Taracha (Warsaw: Agade, 2014), 296–307.

there appears to be a genuinely Semitic root, *RGM, because – although not known in Hebrew or Aramaic – it is found in Ugaritic, meaning 'to say',[557] and so there would be a possibility that *targumannu*, 'interpreter', might derive from this Semitic root. However, as von Soden pointed out, there is a difficulty in that the suffix *-annu*, rather than *-ānu*, is typical of loanwords in Akkadian.[558] Therefore, those who point to Luwian and Hittite source words to the Akkadian word are probably correct to do so. Nonetheless, the Hebrew is closer in form to the Akkadian word than the Anatolian versions and it is likely that the Hebrew word borrowed the Akkadian (perhaps with the involvement of Aramaic), which in turn borrowed the Anatolian.[559]

תִּרְשָׁתָא
governor; Ezra 2:63
(Neh 7:65, 69; 8:9; 10:2)
Native synonyms: מֹשֵׁל; פָּקִיד; נְצִיב; שַׂר.

Although there is no clear original form attested in Old Persian, it is generally agreed that תִּרְשָׁתָא derives from an Iranian source.[560] The main argument in favour of this hypothesis is the semantic content of the Hebrew word, that it refers to an official in the Persian hierarchy – or perhaps a religious official[561] – and the Avestan, *taršta-*, 'feared', pointing to Indo-Iranian *tr̥šta-*.[562] Therefore the best explanation of the word is that it derives from an Iranian language, likely Persian.

557. *DULAT*, s.v. 'rgm'; cf. Jesús Luis Cunchillos, Juan Pablo Vita, José Angel Zamora and Raquel Cervigón, *A Concordance of Ugaritic Words* (Piscataway: Gorgias, 2003), s.v. 'CUW-6181 trgm'. Each of the seven occurrences is a form of the verb *rgm*.
558. Wolfram von Soden, 'Dolmetscher und Dolmetschen im Alten Orient', in *Aus Sprache, Geschichte und Religion Babyloniens*, ed. Luigi Cagni and Hans-Peter Müller (Naples: Istituto Universitario Orientale, 1989), 351–57 (355).
559. *HALOT*, s.v. 'תרגם'; Itamar Singer, 'The Hittites and the Bible Revisited', in *'I Will Speak the Riddles of Ancient Times': Archaeological and Historical Studies in Honor of Amihai Mazar on the Occasion of His Sixtieth Birthday*, ed. Aren Maeir and Pierre de Miroschedji, 2 vols (Winona Lake: Eisenbrauns, 2006), 2:723–56 (746).
560. Blenkinsopp, *Ezra–Nehemiah*, 92; Fensham, *Ezra and Nehemiah*, 22, 56; Fried, *Ezra*, 131; Noonan, *Non-Semitic Loanwords*, 229–30; Rabin, 'Foreign Words', 1079; Scheftelowitz, *Arisches im Alten Testament*, 93–94; Tisdall, 'The Āryan Words, II', 218–19; Wagner, *Die Aramaismen*, 120–21.
561. Noonan, *Non-Semitic Loanwords*, 229.
562. Bartholomae, *Altiranisches Wörterbuch*, s.vv. 'taršta-', 'θrah-'.

## 2.6. The loanwords in Exodus

אַבְנֵט
sash, girdle; Exod 28:4, 39, 40; 29:9; 39:29
(Lev 8:7, 13; 16:4; Isa 22:21)
Native synonyms:[563] קֶשֶׁר; אֵזוֹר; מֵזַח.

The Egyptian origin of this word is uncontroversial.[564] The Egyptian word is found as both a noun, *bndw*, 'sash', and a verb, *bnd*, 'to wrap'.[565] The prothetic *aleph* of אַבְנֵט implies that the Hebrew word could be a loan, since the function of prothesis is to aid with a pronunciation that is otherwise difficult. There is a complicating factor in that the words are found in Egyptian in group writing, suggesting that they have a foreign origin.[566] Nevertheless, given that the word's only attested Semitic version is the Hebrew אַבְנֵט, and given the prothetic *aleph* as well as the presence of a plausible etymology in Egyptian, it is a simpler explanation that the word originated in Egyptian or at least that Egyptian was the language from which the word entered into Hebrew.

אַחְלָמָה
gemstone, traditionally 'amethyst'; Exod 28:19; 39:12
Native synonyms: as with תַּרְשִׁישׁ, which we have discussed above,[567] and other gemstones which are found in the tabernacle accounts here in Exodus, there are difficulties in identifying the precise nature of the gemstones. Nonetheless, there are alternatives for the general class of noun, jewel or ornament: אֶקְדָּח עֲדִי חֵפֶץ. Moreover, it would be easy for the text to omit this list of gemstones entirely.

---

563. See 2.8, 'Native synonyms' for more details on what is meant by these alternatives.
564. Ellenbogen, *Foreign Words*, 2; Yehoshua Grintz, 'מונחים קדומים בתורת כהנים' [Archaic Terminology in the Priestly Torah], *Leš* 39 (1975): 5–20 (7); Lambdin, 'Egyptian Loan Words', 146; Noonan, 'Foreign Loanwords', 182–83; Noonan, *Non-Semitic Loanwords*, 35–36; Propp, *Exodus 19–40*, 434; Rabin, 'Foreign Words', 1077.
565. *Thesaurus Linguae Aegyptiae*, s.vv. 'bnd', 'bnd.w'.
566. See above, under 1.3.4.1, 'Foreign words, culture words and loanwords'.
567. See 2.4, 'The loanwords in Daniel'.

This word is uncontroversially a loan from Egyptian *ḫnmt*.[568] The prosthetic *aleph* is evidence that the Hebrew form is secondary and the Egyptian is the primary form. While the correspondence of *n* and ל is atypical, it is not so difficult that we should reject a borrowing.

אֵפֹד

אֲפֻדָּה

אָפַד

ephod; Exod 25:7; 28:4, 6, 8, 12, 15, 25, 26, 27, 27, 28, 28, 28, 31; 29:5, 5, 5, 5; 35:9, 27; 39:2, 5, 7, 8, 18, 19, 20, 20, 21, 21, 21, 22 (52 occurrences in Biblical Hebrew. Not in Biblical Aramaic) Native synonyms: סָדִין; בֶּגֶד; קַשְׂקֶשֶׂת. While חֹשֶׁן and צִיץ are roughly equivalent in the type of garment, they are used within the context of the tabernacle accounts in opposition to אֵפֹד. It is not plausible that they could have been used in its place.

Noonan initially argued that the Hebrew and Ugaritic nouns, אֵפֹד and *'ipd*, are both derived from the Egyptian *ifd*,[569] on the basis of the relative scarcity of the forms of this noun in all languages except Egyptian[570] – he also cites versions of the word in Akkadian, *epattu* < *\*epadtu*, Hittite, *ipantu*-, Eblaite, *'ipdum* and Syriac, *'āpūdā* and *pedtā* – and on the basis of the presence of an etymology in Egyptian (the verb, *ifd*, 'to quadruple'). While the relative frequencies of the word are not necessarily convincing, the presence of a plausible etymology in Egyptian is persuasive. Noonan also notes that the verb, אָפַד, must therefore be denominative, deriving from the Egyptian loanword.[571] Likewise, the noun, אֲפֻדָּה, should be regarded as ultimately deriving from the Egyptian *ifd*.

However, in Noonan's more recent work he has instead designated this word as a culture word and suggests that the Hittite form is the origin of the Semitic forms, which have assimilated the *n*.[572] However, the direc-

---

568. Ellenbogen, *Foreign Words*, 22; Grintz, 'Archaic Terminology', 8; Lambdin, 'Egyptian Loan Words', 147; Muchiki, *Egyptian Proper Names and Loanwords*, 238–39; Noonan, *Non-Semitic Loanwords*, 49–50; Propp, *Exodus 19–40*, 440; Rabin, 'Foreign Words', 1077; Rubin, 'Egyptian Loanwords', 794. For the Egyptian word, see Erman and Grapow, *Wörterbuch*, s.v. 'ḫnm.t'; *Thesaurus Linguae Aegyptiae*, s.v. 'ḫnm.t'.

569. Erman and Grapow, *Wörterbuch*, s.v. 'ifd'; *Thesaurus Linguae Aegyptiae*, s.v. 'ifd'.

570. Noonan, 'Foreign Loanwords', 186–89.

571. Ibid.

572. Noonan, *Non-Semitic Loanwords*, 58–59.

tionality of any loan hypothesis involving this *dis legomenon* Hittite word, first noted by Hoffner,[573] is more likely to go the other way: geminated dentals in Akkadian readily dissimilate to nasal and dental, a process attested even in Old Akkadian.[574] Thus, Noonan's earlier explanation, that the word is Egyptian in origin, is best due to the etymology available within Egyptian. From Egyptian it spread to the Semitic languages, including to Akkadian at an early date: Egyptian *ifd* > Akkadian, *epattu*, pl. *epadātu* > \**epantu* > Hittite, *ipantu-*. The Hebrew best represents the Egyptian form and likely derives thence directly.

אַרְגָּמָן
purple cloth; Exod 25:4; 26:1, 31, 36; 27:16; 28:5, 6, 8, 15, 33; 35:6, 23, 25, 35; 36:8, 35, 37; 38:18, 23; 39:1, 2, 3, 5, 8, 24, 29 (Num 4:13; Judg 8:26; 2 Chr 2:13; 3:14; Esth 1:6; 8:15; Prov 31:22; Song 3:10; 7:6; Jer 10:9; Ezek 27:7, 16; Dan 5:7, 16, 29)
Native synonyms: There is a rough equivalent in תּוֹלָע. See the discussion under 2.3, 'The loanwords in Esther'.

See the explanation under 2.3, 'The loanwords in Esther'.

\*בַּד
pole; Exod 25:13, 14, 15, 27, 28; 27:6, 6, 7; 30:4, 5; 37:4, 5, 14, 15, 27, 28; 38:5, 6, 7; 40:20
Native synonyms: בּוּץ; פֵּשֶׁת.

Noonan has identified the word בַּד as a loan from Egyptian *bd3*, 'masthead'.[575] Noonan's grounds for identifying the loan are the word's lack of etymology in the Semitic languages and the lack of Semitic cognates.[576] Gordon, however, does propose a Semitic etymology by linking this Hebrew word to the Ugaritic *bd*, a compound of the preposition *b-* and *d*, a uniconsonantal version of *'id*, 'hand'.[577] However, the meaning of this compound, 'in/from the hands of', is quite distinct from the proposed

---

573. Harry Hoffner, 'Hittite Equivalents of Old Assyrian *kumrum* and *epattum*', *Wiener Zeitschrift für die Kunde des Morgenlandes* 86 (1996): 151–56 (154–56).

574. Huehnergard and Woods, 'Akkadian and Eblaite', 238.

575. Noonan, 'Foreign Loanwords', 109–10; Noonan, *Non-Semitic Loanwords*, 71–72. For the Egyptian word, see Erman and Grapow, *Wörterbuch*, s.v. 'bd3'; *Thesaurus Linguae Aegyptiae*, s.v. 'bd3'.

576. Noonan, 'Foreign Loanwords', 110, especially n. 468.

577. Cyrus Gordon, *Ugaritic Textbook*, rev. ed. (Rome: Editrice Pontificio Istituto Biblico, 1998), 57.

meaning of the noun, 'handles'. Although there is insufficient information to conclude that Hebrew בַּד and Egyptian *bḏ3 must* represent a borrowing, to suppose otherwise seems less probable. If, however, we accept that there is a borrowing, it is clear that the borrowing must have been from Egyptian into Hebrew. The Egyptian is written as *bḏ3*, with *ḏ* rather than *d*; therefore – if this word were to be borrowed into Egyptian from Hebrew – any loan must have taken place no earlier than the late second millennium BCE, to account for the equivalence between Egyptian *ḏ* and Hebrew ד.[578] The word is, however, attested in Egyptian in the second intermediate period, prior to that.[579] Thus, the word cannot have been borrowed into Egyptian from Hebrew or another Semitic source, else we should expect it to be spelt in Egyptian as *bd3*. Thus, בַּד is to be considered a loan in Hebrew from Egyptian.

בָּרֶקֶת
gemstone, traditionally 'emerald'; Exod 28:17; 39:10
(Ezek 28:13)
Native synonyms: for the general class of noun, jewel or ornament:
חֵפֶץ; עֲדִי; אֶקְדָּח. See also under אַחְלָמָה.

The gemstone בָּרֶקֶת is paralleled by Neo-Babylonian *barraqtu*,[580] and Aramaic, ברקתא or ברקא, which is found in the translations of Exod 28 and 39.[581] There is a possibility that the word should be connected with the Semitic root for lightning, *brq*, attested in Hebrew, Akkadian and Aramaic, as a genuine Semitic root, as Noonan suggests,[582] or by folk-etymology, as Brown suggests.[583] In addition to these Semitic attestations, a version of the word is found in Egyptian, in the Sehel Famine inscription, as *brg.t*,[584] which could be plausibly explained as borrowed from Semitic, as it is by Harris[585] – although it is not written in group writing. It is also

---

578. Loprieno, 'Ancient Egyptian', 170.
579. Noonan argues that a homonymous word is to be found also in the Edwin Smith Surgical Papyrus, although the determinative used differs. Cf. Noonan, 'Foreign Loanwords', 192.
580. *CAD* 2, s.v. 'barraqtu'.
581. *Comprehensive Aramaic Lexicon*, s.v. 'brq', 'brqt', 'brqh'; Sokoloff, *DJBA*, s.v. 'ברקת'; Sokoloff, *DJPA*, s.v. 'ברקה'; Sokoloff, *Syriac Lexicon*, s.v. 'ܒܪܩ'.
582. Noonan, *Non-Semitic Loanwords*, 327–28.
583. Brown, *Israel and Hellas*, 1:332–33.
584. Sehel Famine Inscription, IV.16.
585. John Harris, *Lexicographical Studies in Ancient Egyptian Minerals* (Berlin: Akademie-Verlag, 1961), 105.

found in several Indo-European languages: Latin, *smaragdus*, *zmaragdus* and *maragdus*,[586] Sanskrit, *marakata*,[587] and Greek σμάραγδος, ζμάραγδος and μάραγδος.[588] In addition, then, there are first-century BCE Greek references to an Egyptian mine named Σμάραγδος, also Ζμάραγδος and Ζμάρακτος, modern Gebel Zabarah,[589] as the source of the gemstone.[590] It is plausible that the origin of the word is that place name, just as Byblos (Gubla) is suggested to be the source of Greek βυβλίον/βιβλίον, 'book', because of its trade in papyrus.[591] However, it is equally plausible that the mine was named for the gemstone. Another point of connection is that just as the Semitic forms have been associated with the root for lightning, the Greek forms might be associated with the verb, σμαραγέω, 'to thunder'.[592]

The Latin forms *smaragdus* and *zmaragdus* are likely loaned from the Greek: although the *sm–m* variation between the Greek and Sanskrit forms might indicate the s-mobile phenomenon in Indo-European languages[593] – a phenomenon operative on the earliest stages of that language family[594] – or it might be that sm-form is native to Greek, while the m-form is native to Latin and that the two borrowed from one another,

---

586. *Lewis and Short*, s.vv. 'maragdus', 'smaragdus', 'zmaragdus'. For the identification of the precise stone, see at n. 670, the discussion of Greek, σμάραγδος.

587. Monier-Williams, *A Sanskrit–English Dictionary*, s.v. 'marakata'.

588. *Liddell, Scott and Jones*, s.vv. 'σμάραγδος', 'μάραγδος'. From Theophrastus, *de Lapidibus*, 23–27 (third century BCE), we can conclude that this stone was green and rare (unlike malachite) and distinct from jasper and that it comes in a 'true' form as well as a 'false' form that could be sourced from Cyprus. For this description, emerald probably fits best. Non-emerald beryl, green quartz (chalcedony or jasper) or perhaps malachite, would best describe the false *smaragdus*, although the opaque malachite is not likely to have been confused with the true *smaragdus*, which was transparent.

589. Trismegistos Online Publications, *Trismegistos*, http://www.trismegistos. org, s.v. 'Smaragdus Mons'; Herbert Verreth, *A Survey of Toponyms in Egypt in the Graeco-Roman Period*, Trismegistos Online Publications 2 (Leuven: Trismegistos Online Publications).

590. *Liddell, Scott and Jones*, s.v. 'Σμάραγδος'.

591. *Diccionario Griego-Español*, s.v. 'βύβλος'.

592. *Liddell, Scott and Jones*, s.v. 'σμαραγέω'.

593. S-mobile refers to a feature of Indo-European languages, where the same root is attested in multiple branches of the family with word-initial *s* in some lemmata, but absent in others. The distribution of the s across languages is unpredictable.

594. Cf. Calvert Walkins, 'Proto-Indo-European: Comparison and Reconstruction', in *The Indo-European Languages*, ed. Anna Giacalone Ramat and Paolo Ramat (London: Routledge, 1998), 25–73 (53): 'In all cases [of reconstructed morphemes] C1 may be preceded by an *s*, with no discernible semantic content ('s-mobile')'.

a third more plausible possibility is that it should be explained as the same variation that is found between μίκρος and σμίκρος or μύραινα and σμύραινα.⁵⁹⁵ This third option would also explain the variants in *zm*, since the *sm–zm* variation is likewise attested elsewhere in Greek, as in σμύρνα and ζμύρνα, deriving from a prototype *μύρνα.⁵⁹⁶ So also in our case it is likely that the earliest Greek form is μάραγδος, from which the others developed within Greek. Therefore, it is only the relationship between the m-form and the b-form that needs to be explained. As noted above, the word can be found in Egyptian as *brg.t*. There are cases, however, of words in Egyptian with both *br-* and *mr-* variants,⁵⁹⁷ which may explain that variation, whereas /bVr/ alternating with /mVr/ would be unusual in both Hebrew and Akkadian.⁵⁹⁸ Therefore, it is likeliest that the m-forms are developed in Egyptian, whence they pass to Greek. This, however, must have taken place prior to its Greek attestations in the fifth century BCE,⁵⁹⁹ implying that Egyptian *brg.t* existed much earlier than its first attestation.

We must still, however, decide between a Semitic origin and an Egyptian origin: the t-suffix is plausible with either a Semitic or Egyptian origin; while there might be an etymology in Semitic *brq*, 'to flash [of lightning]', the exact relationship of that to an emerald is not entirely clear; on the other hand, the well-known presence of emeralds in Egypt, as well as their absence in the Levant and Mesopotamia, speak in favour of an Egyptian origin.⁶⁰⁰ An Egyptian origin to the word is the most plausible option.

---

595. It is more plausible in that it requires fewer and simpler borrowings. Instead of Greek and Latin borrowing terms from one another, Latin borrowed all its versions of the word from Greek.

596. *Liddell, Scott, and Jones*, s.v. 'σμύρνα'.

597. Compare, for example, *mrrj* and *brr.y*, 'wood used for wagons', and *mrk* and *brk*, 'gift'. *Thesaurus Linguae Aegyptiae*, s.vv. 'mrrj', 'mrk'.

598. In Hebrew we have minimal pairs: מרר, 'to be bitter', and ברר, 'to examine'; מרא, 'to beat', and ברא, 'to create'; מרד, 'to rebel', and ברד, 'to hail'. In Akkadian, it is true that in Neo-Assyrian where *m* represents etymological *w*, that may be replaced by orthographic *b*. However, an etymological *w* would not work for this word and even where it is written *m*, transcriptional evidence suggests that it was not pronounced thus. See below, under 'Appendix Six: An Outline of Linguistic Change in Aramaic and Akkadian'.

599. E.g. Herodotus, *Histories* II 44; III 41.

600. It is true that the earliest concrete evidence of large-scale emerald-mining in Egypt only comes from the Ptolemaic era. However, there is no connection whatsoever between Semitic speakers and emerald mines. Moreover, other known sources of emeralds do not seem to have been mined early enough (Austria, India, the

גָּבִיעַ
goblet, goblet-shaped candleholder; 25:31, 33, 33, 34; 37:17, 19, 19, 20
(Gen 44:2, 2; 44:12, 16, 17; Jer 35:5)
Native synonyms: כּוֹס; גֻּלָּ.

Noonan follows Koehler and Baumgartner in designating גָּבִיעַ, 'goblet, goblet-shaped candleholder', a loan from Egyptian *qbḥ.w* or *qbḥy.t*.[601] It is also necessary to account for the Hebrew word קְבַעַת, Phoenician, *qbʿ*, Aramaic, קוּבַּע,[602] and Akkadian, *qabûtu*, pl. *qabuāti*,[603] all with the meaning, 'goblet' or 'vessel for liquids'. Thus, in addition to the g-form considered here, there is also a q-form; all the q-forms can be traced back through the normal rules to a proto-Semitic *\*qbʿ*.[604] The goal, therefore, is to explain the relationship of the g-form lemma, the q-form lemmata and the Egyptian lemma. There is a possibility that the Egyptian might also be related, genetically, so that we might hypothesize a proto-Afro-Asiatic ancestor; if this were the case, we would suggest that the q-form and Egyptian are ordinary cognates, while the g-form is a loan from Egyptian. However, the correspondence of Semitic ʿ to Egyptian *ḥ* would be irregular,[605] and so it is necessary to consider the possibility that either the q-form is borrowed from Egyptian or the Egyptian is borrowed from the q-form.

---

Urals) or were inaccessible (Colombia, Brazil). Therefore, even if large-scale mining were not underway, Egypt is still the most likely source of ancient emeralds. James Harrell, 'Archeological Geography of the World's First Emerald Mine', *Geoscience Canada* 31 (2004): 69–76; Ian Shaw and Judith Bunbury, 'A Petrological Study of the Emerald Mines in the Egyptian Eastern Desert', in *Lithics at the Millennium*, ed. Norah Moloney and Michael Shott (London: Archaeopress, 2003), 203–13.

601. *HALOT*, s.v. 'גָּבִיעַ'; Noonan, *Non-Semitic Loanwords*, 79–80. So also, Sarna, *Exodus*, 155. For the Egyptian word, see *CDD* 19, s.v. 'qbḥ.t'; Erichsen, *Demotisches Glossar*, s.v. 'ḳbḥ'; Erman and Grapow, *Wörterbuch*, s.vv. 'ḳbḥ.w', 'ḳbḥj.t'; *Thesaurus Linguae Aegyptiae*, s.vv. 'ḳbḥ', 'ḳbḥ.w', 'ḳbḥ.jt'.

602. This should be distinguished from the homophone, קוֹבַּע, also found in Hebrew, which is a loan from Hurrian, meaning 'helmet'. *Comprehensive Aramaic Lexicon*, s.v. 'qwbʿ'; Sokoloff, *A Syriac Lexicon*, s.v. 'ܩܘܒܥܐ'.

603. *CAD* 13, s.v. 'qabûtu'.

604. Although it is somewhat unusual that the Akkadian form's *a* would not have been coloured to *e*, it does happen with other nouns, like *etūdum*, which is also attested as *atūdum*. *CAD* 1, s.v. 'atūdum'. Cf., *HALOT*, s.v. 'עָתוּד'.

605. Orel and Stolbova, *Hamito-Semitic Etymological Dictionary*, xviii–xx.

The early attestation of the Egyptian lemma from the Old Kingdom onwards[606] is more in favour of an Egyptian origin, since the q-form Semitic word is apparently first attested in Standard Babylonian. Nevertheless, that conclusion would rely on our assumption that the word did not exist before that point in time in Semitic.

The word does, however, display some degree of semantic range in Egyptian that does not appear in the Semitic forms, with possible meanings of 'libation water' attested from the Old Kingdom and 'watery region' attested from the Second Intermediate Period.[607] It is, perhaps, simpler to explain the situation as semantic narrowing, as only a single meaning is borrowed by the Semitic languages. It cannot be ruled out, however, that Egyptian, after borrowing the word from Semitic, might have developed the semantic range independently.

Conversely, if the Egyptian form was the source of the q-forms it is difficult to explain why the West Semitic q-forms should use ע rather than ח. If, however, the q-form was borrowed by Egyptian while graphemic ʿ was still pronounced /d/, which is to say prior to Middle Egyptian, the correspondence is adequate as Egyptian would have no other pharyngeal consonant.[608] Therefore, the q-form in Hebrew should be regarded as the native form; the presence of both q-form and g-form in Hebrew, however, speaks in favour of the g-form being a loan from the Egyptian form.

As for the correspondence ג–q, it seems difficult to justify at the stage when Egyptian q represented an uvular, but an acceptable correspondence once the uvulars have merged with the velars during the first millennium BCE,[609] providing a *terminus post quem* for the borrowing. However, because the correspondence ע–ḫ requires the pharyngeal–glottal opposition to still operate on the fricatives, else we should expect the ḫ to correspond to ה or א. Therefore, the end of the first millennium BCE is the *terminus ante quem*.[610]

Thus, in the second millennium BCE Egyptian borrowed the q-form from a Semitic language that maintained its guttural consonants and, in the first millennium BCE, the word was borrowed back from Egyptian into Hebrew and Phoenician. The Aramaic form, though attested as early as Official Aramaic,[611] must be borrowed from one of the Canaanite dialects to account for the vocalization.

606. *Thesaurus Linguae Aegyptiae*, s.v. 'ḳbḥ.w'.
607. *Ibid.*, s.v. 'ḳbḥ', 'ḳbḥ.w', 'ḳbḥ.jt'.
608. Loprieno, 'Ancient Egyptian', 170.
609. Ibid.
610. Ibid., 171.
611. *Comprehensive Aramaic Lexicon*, s.v. 'qwbʿ'.

הִין
a measurement of volume; Exod 29:40, 40; 30:24
(Lev 19:36; 23:13; Num 15:4, 5, 6, 7, 9, 10; 28:5, 7, 14, 14, 14;
Ezek 4:11; 45:24; 46:5, 7, 11, 14)
Native synonyms: לֹג; בַּת. While these synonyms denote different volumes to the *hin*, they are readily convertible, one to the other. Nonetheless, the *hin* would be the simplest measurement to use, most appropriate to the size.

Another loan that is undisputed is הִין, from Egyptian *hn.w*.[612] Although there is a discrepancy in the size between the Hebrew *hin* and the Egyptian,[613] the words are similar enough that a loan is probable.

זֶרֶת
a measurement of distance; Exod 28:16, 16; 39:9, 9
(1 Sam 17:4; Isa 40:12; Ezek 43:13)
Native synonyms: אַמָּה. As with the *hin*, above, the cubit, אַמָּה, differs in magnitude to the span, זֶרֶת. However, whereas in that case it would be relatively simple to express the quantities in synonymous terms, to do so here would require fractions.

It is proposed that the word may be borrowed from Egyptian *ḏr.t*.[614] As Lambdin pointed out,[615] any borrowing must be early, to account for the

---

612. Ellenbogen, *Foreign Words*, 68; Grintz, 'Archaic Terminology', 15–17; Lambdin, 'Egyptian Loan Words', 149; Muchiki, *Egyptian Proper Names and Loanwords*, 243; Noonan, *Non-Semitic Loanwords*, 95; Propp, *Exodus 19–40*, 471; Rabin, 'Foreign Words', 1077; Rubin, 'Egyptian Loanwords', 794; Sarna, *Exodus*, 192. For the Egyptian word, see *CDD* 13, s.v. 'hn'; Erman and Grapow, *Wörterbuch*, s.v. 'hnw'.

613. Ellenbogen explains the differences in size: the Egyptian *hin* is approximately .45 litres and the Hebrew, 6. As for the fact that there is a discrepancy, the situation is comparable to several modern situations where names for measures are similar but sizes differ. Thus, for example, Australian and American 'cup' measures differ. Ellenbogen, *Foreign Words*, 68.

614. Grintz, 'Archaic Terminology', 18; Lambdin, 'Egyptian Loan Words', 149–50; Nöldecke, 'Kautzsch' Aramaismen', 417; Noonan, *Non-Semitic Loanwords*, 99–100; Rabin, 'Foreign Words', 1077; Rubin, 'Egyptian Loanwords', 794; Sarna, *Exodus*, 180; Wilson, 'Foreign Words', 211. Muchiki also considers it a possibility. Muchiki, *Egyptian Proper Names and Loanwords*, 244. For the Egyptian word, see Erichsen, *Demotisches Glossar*, s.v. 'tr.t'; Erman and Grapow, *Wörterbuch*, s.v. 'ḏrt'; *CDD* 24, s.v. 'ḏr(.t)'; *Thesaurus Linguae Aegyptiae*, s.v. 'ḏr.t'.

615. Lambdin, 'Egyptian Loan Words', 149–50.

presence of the *t* in the Hebrew version. Likewise, an early borrowing would be necessary for there to be a palatal realization of Egyptian *ḏ*. The etymology of the word in Egyptian as 'hand', as well as a measurement,[616] is at least, preferable to the lack of a convincing etymology in Semitic. Therefore, a borrowing from Egyptian is currently the best explanation.

חֶלְבְּנָה
galbanum; Exod 30:34
Native synonyms: There may be a rough synonym in לֹט, 'myrrh'. However, the specific species of resin may be different. חֶלְבְּנָה is found in Exodus within a list of similar substances, like, נָטָף, 'stacte'. It is not immediately clear whether the list in Exod 30:34 is a closed list or open. However, given the warnings about the (mis)use of the incense, it seems best to understand it as a formula for a specific incense.[617] Thus, there are no obvious native synonyms.

Cuny suggests that חֶלְבְּנָה is a Mediterranean substrate word, citing Greek χαλβάνη, *chalbanē*, and Latin *galbanum*.[618] Landesdorfer points to Sumerian *ḫalub*[619] and Akkadian *ḫuluppu*, suggesting a Sumerian origin.[620] However, a more plausible Akkadian source-word would be *ḫilbanītu*, the resin of the *ḫilabāna* plant.[621] The *-an-* infix in the Greek and Latin forms is typical of Northwest Semitic languages, but indicative of a non-Canaanite source.[622] It is possible to account for the Greek as a loan from Aramaic. The correspondence between Greek χ and Latin *g* would, however, be atypical of a loan from Greek to Latin. Similarly, while the Akkadian could plausibly be the donor term for the Greek and Hebrew forms, the correspondence of *ḫ* to *g* would be unusual. Therefore, it seems

---

616. *Thesaurus Linguae Aegyptiae*, s.v. 'ḏr.t'.
617. Cf. Thomas Dozeman, *Exodus*, Eerdmans Critical Commentary (Grand Rapids: Eerdmans, 2009), 672; John Durham, *Exodus*, WBC 3 (Nashville: Thomas Nelson, 1987), 407–408; Victor Hamilton, *Exodus: An Exegetical Commentary* (Grand Rapids: Baker Academic, 2011), 517–18.
618. Cuny, 'Les Mots du Fonds Préhellénique', 162. Propp also notes these as possible cognates. Propp, *Exodus 19–40*, 485.
619. Landesdorfer cites the word as *ǧalub*. The *Pennsylvania Sumerian Dictionary*, however, cites it as *ḫalub*. *ePSD*, s.v. 'ḫalub'.
620. Landesdorfer, *Sumerisches Sprachgut*, 70.
621. *CAD* 6, s.v. 'ḫalbanītu'.
622. See under 'Appendix Six: An Outline of Linguistic Change in Aramaic and Akkadian'.

best to agree with Cuny that an unknown language is at work. It is difficult to say, however, whether that language is the source of the word or simply one of the intermediaries. Thus 'culture word' is the most appropriate designation in this case.

חָרוּת
engraved; Exod 32:16
Native synonyms: חָרוּשׁ.

The only loanword in ch. 32 is an Aramaism, which is clear, as Wagner points out,[623] from comparison[624] between the two versions of the verb חרת and חרשׁ, both meaning 'to engrave'.

חֹתָם
seal; Exod 28:11, 21, 36; 39:6, 14, 30
(Gen 38:18; 1 Kgs 21:8; 1 Chr 7:32; 11:44; Job 38:14; 41:7; Song 8:6, 6; Jer 22:24; Hag 2:23)
Also, note the denominative verb, חָתַם, 'to seal'.
(Lev 15:3; Deut 32:34; 1 Kgs 21:8; Neh 10:1, 2; Esth 3:12, 8:8, 8, 10; Job 9:7; 14:14; 24:16; 33:16; 37:7; Song 4:12; Isa 8:16; 29:11, 11; Jer 32:10, 11, 14, 44; Ezek 28:12; Dan 6:18; 9:24, 24; 12:4, 9)
Native synonyms: There are no native synonyms and the word is an early borrowing into Hebrew.

See the explanation under 2.3, 'The loanwords in Esther'. Note that, due to its age, this loan has not been counted in the statistics below.

טַבַּעַת
ring; Exod 25:12, 12, 12, 14, 15, 26, 26, 27; 26:24, 29; 27:4, 7; 28:23, 23, 24, 26, 27, 28, 28; 30:4; 35:22; 36:29, 34; 37:3, 3, 3, 5, 13, 13, 14, 27; 38:5, 7; 39:16, 16, 17, 19, 20, 21, 21
(Gen 41:42; Num 31:50; Esth 3:10, 12; 8:2, 8, 8, 10; Isa 3:21)
Native synonyms: נֶזֶם; חָח. In addition, although not originally native, we can include the nativized חֹתָם.

See the explanation under 2.3, 'The loanwords in Esther'.

---

623. Wagner, *Die Aramaismen*, 59. Also Sarna, *Exodus*, 206.
624. See under 'Appendix Six: An Outline of Linguistic Change in Aramaic and Akkadian'.

יַיִן
wine; Exod 29:40
(141 occurrences in Biblical Hebrew. Not in Biblical Aramaic)
Native synonyms: חֶמֶר.

See the explanation under 2.3, 'The loanwords in Esther'. Note that due to its age and nativization, this word has not been counted in the statistics below.

\*יָע
basins; Exod 27:3; 38:3
(Num 4:14; 1 Kgs 7:40, 45; 2 Kgs 25:14; 2 Chr 4:11, 16; Jer 52:18)
Native synonyms: סֵפֶל.

The Egyptian word *i'*, 'washbasin', is nominated by Yahuda and Grintz as a prototype for the Hebrew word.[625] The Egyptian noun is related to the verb *i'y*, 'to wash', and other similar nouns, *i'-w*, 'washing', attested as early as the Old Kingdom.[626] As Yahuda notes, the meanings of the Hebrew and Egyptian words are apparently dissimilar: the Hebrew is ordinarily translated as 'shovel',[627] whereas the Egyptian is a washbasin.[628] In addition to the two instances in Exodus, the noun also appears in Num 4:14; 1 Kgs 7:40, 45; 2 Kgs 25:14; 2 Chr 4:11, 16 and Jer 52:18. In each case, the noun appears in a list of other utensils for use at the altar. Within the list it is grouped with two other words for basins.[629] There is also a related verb in Isa 28:17, typically translated as 'to sweep away'.[630] In this case the verb's subject is hail and in the parallel line, waters wash away (מַיִם יִשְׁטְפוּ). The word is also attested in Targumic translations of Exod 27:3.[631]

---

625. Grintz, 'Archaic Terminology', 19; Yahuda, 'Hebrew Words of Egyptian Origin', 83–84.
626. *Thesaurus Linguae Aegyptiae*, s.vv. 'i'', 'i'j', 'i'.w'. Cf. Erman and Grapow, *Wörterbuch*, s.v. 'i''.
627. *HALOT*, s.v. 'יָע'. Cf. NRSV, ESV, JPS, 'shovels'.
628. *Thesaurus Linguae Aegyptiae*, s.vv. 'i'', 'i'j'.
629. Thus, for example, 1 Kgs 7:40: 'And Hiram made the lavers, and the shovels, and the basins' (NRSV).
630. *HALOT*, s.v. 'יָעָה'. Cf. NRSV, ESV, JPS, 'sweep away'.
631. Frg. Tg. V, Exod 27:3. Cf. *Comprehensive Aramaic Lexicon*, s.v. 'y'y'; Marcus Jastrow, *Dictionary of Targumim, Talmud and Midrashic Literature* (Peabody: Hendrickson, 2006), s.v. 'יָעָה'; Sokoloff, *DJPA*, s.v. 'יעי'.

Koehler and Baumgartner also notice the potentially related Arabic verb *waʿāy*, 'to collect, hold', Old South Arabian, *yʿy*, 'to snatch away', and the Arabic noun, *wiʿāʾ*, 'vessel'. Thus, as Yahuda points out the meaning 'shovel' has no satisfactory etymology within the Semitic languages.[632] If in fact the word is genuinely Semitic, the Arabic glosses would support the meaning of 'washbasin' more than 'shovel'.

Moreover, the meaning 'washbasin' fits the biblical context well – in the lists it is not disruptive to replace one implement with another and it is straightforward to understand the verb of 28:17 as 'washing away'.

If all this is the case, we must take seriously the idea that this is a native Semitic word. However, the similarity of the Hebrew and Egyptian forms is striking. Therefore, we might also consider the possibility of a word going back to Afro-Asiatic. However, an original Semitic *w – as indicated by the Arabic *w* – ought to correspond to an Egyptian *w*, not *i*.[633] Moreover, the word is early in Egyptian and has a clear etymology in the verb *iʿy*, 'to wash', so that it is unlikely that Egyptian borrowed from the Semitic languages. Therefore, the best explanation is that the Hebrew is borrowed from Egyptian, that the Aramaic of the Targums to Exod 27:3 is based on the Hebrew of that verse and that the Arabic is unrelated.

יָשְׁפֵה

gemstone, traditionally 'jasper'; Exod 28:20; 39:13
(1 Chr 8:16; Ezek 28:13)
Native synonyms: for the general class of noun, jewel or ornament:
חֵפֶץ; עֲדִי; אֶקְדָּח. See also under אַחְלָמָה.

The word יָשְׁפֵה has been derived from a number of languages, including Iranian,[634] Hurrian,[635] Greek,[636] and 'non-Semitic Asian languages'.[637] Explanations of the word need to account for its wide attestation, as noted by Noonan:[638] Akkadian, *(y)ašpu*, Aramaic, יָשְׁפֵה,[639] Arabic, *yašb*

---

632. Yahuda, 'Hebrew Words of Egyptian Origin', 83–84.
633. Orel and Stolbova, *Hamito-Semitic Etymological Dictionary*, xx.
634. E.g. BDB, s.v. 'יָשְׁפֵה'. Cf. Young, Rezetko and Ehrensvärd, 'Loanwords', 1:304.
635. Brown, *Israel and Hellas*, 1:87; Ellenbogen, *Foreign Words*, 81; Noonan, 'Foreign Loanwords', 88–89.
636. Vernes, *Les Emprunts de la Bible*, 65.
637. My translation of שפות אסיה שאין שמיות; Rabin, 'Foreign Words', 1078.
638. Noonan, 'Foreign Loanwords', 88–89.
639. *Comprehensive Aramaic Lexicon*, s.v. 'yšph'; Sokoloff, *A Syriac Lexicon*, s.v. 'ܝܫܦܐ'.

and *yašm*,[640] Neo-Persian, *yašm* and Sogdian, *'yšph*, Greek, ἴασπις, *iaspis*, Hebrew, יָשְׁפֵה, and Latin, *iaspis*. To Noonan's list we should also add Elamite, *ya-aš-pu*.[641] More conjecturally, it may also be necessary to consider Egyptian *nšm.t*[642] and Hebrew לֶשֶׁם. The Egyptian stone, *nšm.t*, was likely green feldspar, 'Amazonite',[643] which was found in Egypt,[644] but the Akkadian word seems to refer to green jasper; nevertheless, the similarities between the stones are sufficient that it is reasonable to make a connection. It is necessary to note that Egyptian *nšm.t* and Hebrew לֶשֶׁם have been explained otherwise: many scholars agree that the word לֶשֶׁם is borrowed from *nšm.t*, 'green feldspar'.[645] The discrepancy between *n* and ל, as Muchiki points out, is not necessarily a barrier to the loan hypothesis because Egyptian *n* shifted to *l* at word onset.[646] Nevertheless, the simpler explanation is that the word is cognate between the languages, deriving from a Proto-Afro-Asiatic *lĉm* or similar. It is reasonable, then, that some dialect of Egyptian might have inherited the word as *išm.t*.[647] Thus, we would need to contend with four forms: the l-form, the n-form, the *yšm*-form and the *yšp*-form. The l-form would be explained as native to Semitic, the n-form and *yšm*-form as native to Egyptian.[648] The *yšp*-form

---

640. The form *yašb* should not be linked to the *yšp*-forms by inheritance, since if it were inherited from the same root as the other Semitic examples, we should expect *yašf*. Cf. Kienast, *Historische Semitische Sprachwissenschaft*, 29.

641. Hinz and Koch, *Elamisches Wörterbuch*, s.v. 'ya-aš-pu'.

642. Erman and Grapow, *Wörterbuch*, s.v. 'nšm.t'; *Thesaurus Linguae Aegyptiae*, s.v. '*nšm.t*'.

643. Ibid.

644. Peter Moorey, *Ancient Mesopotamian Materials and Industries: The Archaeological Evidence* (Winona Lake: Eisenbrauns, 1999), 82.

645. Ellenbogen, *Foreign Words*, 97; Grintz, 'Archaic Terminology', 8; Lambdin, 'Egyptian Loan Words', 152; Muchiki, *Egyptian Proper Names and Loanwords*, 248; Noonan, 'Foreign Loanwords', 89–90; Rubin, 'Egyptian Loanwords', 794.

646. Muchiki, *Egyptian Proper Names and Loanwords*, 248.

647. Cf., for example, Loprieno's use of dialects to explain the re-emergence of the phoneme *l in the New Kingdom. If there is dialectal variance in the unpredictable correspondences of Proto-Afro-Asiatic *l to *i*, *r* and *n* as attested in the written forms, it would be entirely unsurprising for a single Afro-Asiatic lemma to have multiple reflexes across dialects. Antonio Loprieno, *Ancient Egyptian: A Linguistic Introduction* (Cambridge: Cambridge University Press, 1995), 31. Similarly, cf. the pairs, *iš*, 'ein Lebensmittel', and *nš*, 'Korn'; *nš*, 'Speichel', and *iš.w*, 'Speichel'. *Thesaurus Linguae Aegyptiae*, s.vv. 'iš', 'iš.w', 'nš'.

648. The Arabic *yšm*-form was either borrowed indirectly from the Egyptian form or developed independently from *yašb*. The Neo-Persian form, then, might be a loan from Arabic.

could easily be explained as a development from the *yšm*-form by an assimilatory effect, as the *m* was devoiced and denasalized in contact with the *š*. The *yšp*-form then could have passed to Akkadian, Sogdian, Elamite, Hurrian and Hittite. If the Neo-Persian form *yašm* is not taken from Arabic, it might be borrowed from the Elamite because of the interchange between *m* and *p* in that language.[649] Nevertheless, the connection between *nšm.t* and יָשְׁפֶה is only speculative. Whether or not we accept that connection, however, Noonan is likely right that the proximate entry of יָשְׁפֶה into Hebrew and West Semitic was from Hurrian,[650] as that explains the Hebrew word's vocalization.[651] Likewise Noonan is right that it is likely that Greek and Latin derived the word from West Semitic.[652] Since יָשְׁפֶה arrives from Hurrian, it is likely that Exodus refers to green jasper, rather than green feldspar. It is unlikely, then, that the Hebrew word carries any particular association with Egypt, even if its early origins might be Egyptian.

כִּיּוֹר

washbasin; Exod 30:18, 28; 31:9; 35:16; 38:8; 39:39; 40:7, 11, 30 (Lev 8:11; 11:35 [?]; 1 Sam 2:14; 1 Kgs 7:30, 38, 38, 38, 38, 40, 43; 2 Kgs 16:17; 2 Chr 4:6, 14; 6:13; Zech 12:6)
Native synonyms: סֵפֶל.

It is uncontroversial that the word כִּיּוֹר entered Hebrew from Akkadian, *kiūru*.[653] What is less clear, however, is its origin beyond Akkadian, with Landesdorfer and Albright suggesting Sumerian and Noonan and Mankowski suggesting Urartian, *kiri*. More recently, Noonan suggests that a hypothetical Hurrian form, *\*kiuri*, cognate to Urartian, *kiri*, might be the source of the Akkadian and of the Hebrew directly.[654] This is

---

649. Françoise Grillot-Susini, *Éléments de Grammaire Élamite, Études Élamites* (Paris: Editions Recherche sur les Civilisations, 1987), 10.
650. Noonan, 'Foreign Loanwords', 90; cf. Noonan, *Non-Semitic Loanwords*, 114.
651. The lack of the dagesh in the פ is difficult to explain if the word is native. However, if the word is transferred from Akkadian, it is equally difficult to explain why Akkadian *pû* would be reflected as Hebrew פֶה.
652. Noonan, 'Foreign Loanwords', 89.
653. William Albright, *Archeology and the Religion of Israel*, 5th ed. (BaltiB more: The Johns Hopkins University Press, 1968), 217; Landesdorfer, *Sumerisches Sprachgut*, 72; Mankowski, *Akkadian Loanwords*, 65–66; Noonan, 'Foreign Loanwords', 243–44; Rubin, 'Sumerian Loanwords', 665.
654. Noonan, *Non-Semitic Loanwords*, 120–21.

possible, but without an actual attestation of this word it remains preferable locate the source of the Hebrew word in Akkadian, *kiūru*, in order to explain the Hebrew vocalization.

כְּתֹנֶת
tunic; Exod 28:4, 39, 40; 29:5, 8; 39:27; 40:14
(Gen 3:21; 37:3, 23, 23, 31, 31, 32, 32, 33; Lev 8:7, 13; 10:5; 16:4; 2 Sam 13:18, 19; 15:32; Ezra 2:69; Neh 7:69, 71; Job 30:18; Song 5:3; Isa 22:21)
Native synonyms: בֶּגֶד; סָדִין.

See the explanation under 2.5, 'The loanwords in Ezra 1–7'.

נֹפֶךְ
gemstone, traditionally 'garnet'; Exod 28:18; 39:11
(Ezek 27:16; 28:13)
Native synonyms: for the general class of noun, jewel or ornament:
חֵפֶץ; עֲדִי; אֶקְדָּח. See also under אַחְלָמָה.

Many scholars list נֹפֶךְ as borrowed from Egyptian *mfk3t*, 'turquoise', or in its later form *mfkt*.[655] It is unproblematic that the *m* should be realized as נ: as Noonan notes, the representation of Egyptian *m* as Akkadian *n* is attested in the Neo-Assyrian version of an Egyptian place name, *pr-ḥtḥr-mfk3t – piḫattiḫurunpiki*.[656] It is no surprise, therefore, that Egyptian *m* should also appear as נ in Hebrew. Whether the variation is due to the Egyptian realization of the consonant or due to a dissimilatory effect, such that מפ* > נפ is still unclear.

סמ*
herbs; Exod 25:6; 30:7, 34, 34; 31:11; 35:8, 15, 28; 37:29; 39:38; 40:27
(Lev 4:7; 16:12; Num 4:16; 2 Chr 2:3; 13:11)
Native synonyms: מִרְקַחַת; עֵשֶׂב; דֶּשֶׁא.

---

655. Grintz, 'Archaic Terminology', 8; Lambdin, 'Egyptian Loan Words', 152; Muchiki, *Egyptian Proper Names and Loanwords*, 251; Noonan, *Non-Semitic Loanwords*, 153–54; Rabin, 'Foreign Words', 1077; Rubin, 'Egyptian Loanwords', 794. For the Egyptian word, see *CDD* 9, s.v. 'mfkj'; Erichsen, *Demotisches Glossar*, s.v. 'mfkj'; Erman and Grapow, *Wörterbuch*, s.v. 'mfk3.t'; *Thesaurus Linguae Aegyptiae*, s.v. 'mfk3.t'.

656. Noonan, *Non-Semitic Loanwords*, 153.

Vernes' suggestion that the word סַם is derived from Greek ὀσμή, 'scent',[657] is implausible, since although the consonants of the Hebrew and Greek words are similar, the vowels and syllabification differ significantly. More plausibly Landesdorfer suggested that the origin of this word was Sumerian *šim*, entering into Hebrew by way of Akkadian, *šammu*.[658] Mankowski suggests that the word was borrowed into Hebrew and Aramaic from Assyrian.[659] Kaufman, on the other hand, thinks the Hebrew is native, but with an Aramaized spelling.[660] He points to the following attestations: in Aramaic as סמם, in Arabic as *samm* and in Akkadian as *šammu*.[661] It is also necessary to account for not only the Sumerian, *šim*,[662] but also Egyptian *sm.w*.[663] The Semitic roots taken in isolation might point to a Proto-Semitic *\*śmm*. As Mankowski points out, however, one would expect in that case that the Hebrew word would retain the *ś* as שׂ.[664] The Hebrew form at least, then, would have to be borrowed from either Aramaic or Assyrian Akkadian, which pronounced the *š* as /s/.[665] The question, then, is how to account for the Sumerian and Egyptian forms. The Sumerian form is easily explained as a loanword from Akkadian. Orel and Stolbova trace the Egyptian word to an Afro-Asiatic *\*cim*, which ought to correspond to Proto-Semitic *\*sim*.[666] If that reconstruction is right, the best solution will be that the Egyptian is unrelated to the Semitic forms. Otherwise, if Orel and Stolbova have incorrectly connected the Egyptian word to the Chadic and Rift forms, it might go back to an Afro-Asiatic *\*sVm*, corresponding to a Proto-Semitic *\*šVm*. In either case, the best explanation for the Hebrew word is that it was borrowed from either Aramaic or Assyrian. In deciding between the two options Mankowski is right that the simpler explanation is that the

657. Vernes, *Les Emprunts de la Bible*, 103.
658. Landesdorfer, *Sumerisches Sprachgut*, 50–51.
659. Mankowski, *Akkadian Loanwords*, 118–20.
660. Kaufman, *The Akkadian Influences*, 100. Noonan follows this opinion; Noonan, *Non-Semitic Loanwords*, 345.
661. Kaufman, *The Akkadian Influences*, 118.
662. *ePSD*, s.v. 'šim'.
663. *CDD* 17, s.v. 'sm'; Erichsen, *Demotisches Glossar*, s.v. 'sm'; Erman and Grapow, *Wörterbuch*, s.v. 'smw'; *Thesaurus Linguae Aegyptiae*, s.v. 'sm.w'.
664. Kaufman, *The Akkadian Influences*, 120.
665. See under 'Appendix Six: An Outline of Linguistic Change in Aramaic and Akkadian'. This explains the presence of both *s* and *š* such that we need not treat these as two separate words. Cf. Propp, *Exodus 19–40*, 375.
666. Orel and Stolbova, *Hamito-Semitic Etymological Dictionary*, 95.

Hebrew form was borrowed from Assyrian rather than Aramaic because it does not require us to hypothesize meanings for the Aramaic word that are otherwise unattested.

סַפִּיר
gemstone, traditionally 'sapphire'; Exod 24:10; 28:18; 39:11 (Job 28:6, 16; Song 5:14; Isa 54:11; Lam 4:7; Ezek 1:26; 10:1; 28:13)
Native synonyms: for the general class of noun, jewel or ornament: חֵפֶץ; עֲדִי; אֶקְדָּח. See also under אַחְלָמָה.

Although several scholars propose that this word may derive from the Sanskrit, *śanipriya*, 'emerald or sapphire',[667] Powels suggests that the given etymology for the word ('one whom Saturn loves' > 'emerald, sapphire') is probably folk etymology for a word that is not native to Sanskrit.[668] Grintz, Noonan and Propp suggest that the word is based on a Semitic root related to Arabic, *safara*, 'to remove, clean, shine, be white',[669] Hebrew, שפר, 'to please, to clean', and Aramaic, שפר, 'to please'.[670] Noonan also makes note of the Amorite names, *Sapirum* and *Baḫlisapar*.[671] On the basis of the comparison, the proto-Semitic root would be ŠPR. Therefore, if the word is Semitic it must derive from some unknown Semitic language which inherited Š as /s/ and retained P as /p/ or Akkadian, which pronounced š as /s/ in the Neo-Assyrian dialect.[672] Nonetheless, without an obvious candidate for a loan from Akkadian, we are limited to saying that the word is likely Semitic in origin, but unlikely to have originated in Hebrew itself.

---

667. Brown, *Israel and Hellas*, 2:193; Ellenbogen, *Foreign Words*, 125; Rabin, 'Foreign Words', 1079.

668. Powels, 'Indische Lehnwörter', 198.

669. Edward Lane, *An Arabic–English Lexicon* (London: Williams & Norgate, 1863), s.v. 'safara'.

670. Grintz, 'Archaic Terminology', 9; Noonan, *Non-Semitic Loanwords*, 347; Propp, *Exodus 19–40*, 440. Hebrew and Aramaic glosses from *HALOT*, s.vv. 'שפר' and 'שפר (Aramaic)'. For the Aramaic, see also: *Comprehensive Aramaic Lexicon*, s.v. 'špr'; Cook, *Dictionary of Qumran Aramaic*, s.v. 'špr'; Sokoloff, *DJPA*, s.v. 'שפר'; Sokoloff, *DJBA*, s.v. 'שפר'; Sokoloff, *A Syriac Lexicon*, s.v. 'ܫܦܪ'.

671. Noonan, 'Foreign Loanwords', 95.

672. See under 'Appendix Six: An Outline of Linguistic Change in Aramaic and Akkadian'.

פְּאֵר
turban; Exod 39:28
(Isa 3:20; 61:3, 10; Ezek 24:17, 23; 44:18)
Native synonyms: מִצְנֶפֶת; טָבוּל.

Rabin and Noonan derive פְּאֵר from Egyptian *pry, pyr*.[673] Zimmern, on the other hand, suggests the possible origin in Akkadian, *apāru*.[674] The Akkadian, however, is not a good match without further explanation – we would expect some representation of the vocalic first syllable – whereas the Egyptian offers a fair approximation. Noonan suggests the Hebrew word's atypical morphology – presumably he means either the unusual vocalization or the apparently feminine form of the plural – is evidence that it was borrowed.[675] The word could plausibly be borrowed from Egyptian, but it is not certain.

*פַּח
metal plate; Exod 39:3
Native synonyms: רָקִיעַ.
(Num 17:3)

Despite the suggestion of Vernes that פַּח derives from Greek, παγίς[676] – the correspondence is quite poor if the Greek term is to be the original – and despite the suggestion of Zimmern that it derives from Akkadian *paḫu*, 'sleeve'[677] – which would be a very poor match semantically – there is no doubt among scholars that the word derives from Egyptian *pḫ3*, 'plating',[678] which offers a superior match in sense and form.[679]

---

673. Noonan, *Non-Semitic Loanwords*, 169–70; Rabin, 'Foreign Words', 1077. Cf. *CDD* 7, s.v. 'pyr'; Erman and Grapow, *Wörterbuch*, s.v. 'prj', 'pjr'; *Thesaurus Linguae Aegyptiae*, s.v. 'prj', 'pjr'.
674. Zimmern, *Akkadische Fremdwörter*, 15.
675. Noonan, 'Foreign Loanwords', 207.
676. Vernes, *Les Emprunts de la Bible*, 124–25.
677. Zimmern, *Akkadische Fremdwörter*, 15.
678. *CDD* 7, s.v. 'pḫ'; Erichsen, *Demotisches Glossar*, s.v. 'pḫ'; Erman and Grapow, *Wörterbuch*, s.v. 'pḫ3'; *Thesaurus Linguae Aegyptiae*, s.v. 'pḫ3'.
679. Ellenbogen, *Foreign Words*, 130; Lambdin, 'Egyptian Loan Words', 153; Muchiki, *Egyptian Proper Names and Loanwords*, 253; Noonan, *Non-Semitic Loanwords*, 173; Rabin, 'Foreign Words', 1077; Rubin, 'Egyptian Loanwords', 794.

פִּטְדָה
gemstone, traditionally 'topaz'; Exod 28:17; 39:10
(Job 28:19; Ezek 28:13)
Native synonyms: for the general class of noun, jewel or ornament:
חֵפֶץ; עֲדִי; אֶקְדָּח. See also under אַחְלָמָה.

That the word פִּטְדָה is a borrowing should at least be suspected on the basis of the sequence טד which occurs only rarely in Hebrew and never without a full vowel intervening.[680] Some scholars have suggested that the word is derived from Sanskrit, *pīta*, 'yellow'.[681] This is unconvincing, because it is difficult to explain why Sanskrit *t* would produce Hebrew טד. Instead, Propp and Grintz suggest that the word derives from a hypothetical Egyptian *\*pdd.t* on the basis that topaz was thought to come from Egypt or Cush.[682] Although Noonan originally associated the word with a 'Nubian' language (via Egyptian) on the basis of the Cushite origin,[683] more recently he simply claims an Egyptian origin.[684] Nevertheless, so far, there is no convincing explanation of the word's original form or source.

קֶרֶן
horn; Exod 27:2, 2; 29:12; 30:2, 3, 10; 37:25, 26; 38:2, 2
(79 occurrences in Biblical Hebrew. Only in Daniel in Biblical Aramaic)
Native synonyms: As I suggest in the discussion under 2.4, 'The loanwords in Daniel', this word is thoroughly nativized. There are no obvious synonyms.

See the explanation under 2.4, 'The loanwords in Daniel'. Note that due to its age and nativized status, this word has not been counted in the statistics below.

רִמּוֹן
pomegranate; Exod 28:33, 34, 34; 39:24, 25, 25, 26, 26
(47 occurrences in Biblical Hebrew. Not in Biblical Aramaic)

---

680. Noonan, *Non-Semitic Loanwords*, 174.
681. Ellenbogen, *Foreign Words*, 133; Powels, 'Indische Lehnwörter', 197–98.
682. Grintz, 'Archaic Terminology', 8–9; Propp, *Exodus 19–40*, 439. Cf. Job 28:19; Strabo, *Geography* XVI 4.6.
683. Noonan, 'Foreign Loanwords', 98.
684. Noonan, *Non-Semitic Loanwords*, 174–75.

Native synonyms: there are no direct synonyms for 'pomegranate'. In Exod 28 and 39, the word, however, is used metonymically for its shape. With that in mind, there are possibilities, such as: צָנֵפָה; דּוּר.

Zimmern suggested that the word was borrowed from Akkadian, *armannu*.[685] Noonan rather suggested that the word is a culture word, citing reflexes not only in Akkadian, *nurmû* and *lurmû* among many others, but also Sumerian, *nurma*, Ethiopic, *rōmān*, Hittite, *nurati-*, Hurrian, *nuranti*, several forms of Aramaic, including רמן in Imperial Aramaic and Arabic *rummān*.[686] The degree of variance in the Akkadian forms suggests that the word is not likely original to Akkadian, so that Zimmern's position is to be rejected. To minimize hypothetical developments, one assumes that the forms in *nu-* form a genetic group and likewise the forms without. However, the precise connections between the words is difficult to establish, such that Noonan's label of culture word is appropriate. In addition, the word is likely early in Semitic, given that apparently רִמּוֹן has undergone the Canaanite shift, if we compare it to the Arabic form, *rummān*. Therefore, we have not counted it in the statistics below.

שְׁבוֹ
gemstone, traditionally 'agate'; Exod 28:19; 39:12
Native synonyms: for the general class of noun, jewel or ornament: חֵפֶץ; עֲדִי; אֶקְדָּח. See also under אַחְלָמָה.

This word is uncontroversially a loan from Akkadian, *šubû*.[687] In Akkadian it is recognized as a loan from Sumerian, *šuba*,[688] and thus its presence in Hebrew is best explained as a loan from Akkadian.

שׁוֹר
bull; Exod 34:19
(58 times in Biblical Hebrew. Not in Biblical Aramaic, except as תּוֹר [7 times])
Native synonyms: בָּקָר.

---

685. Zimmern, *Akkadische Fremdwörter*, 54.
686. Noonan, *Non-Semitic Loanwords*, 200–201.
687. Ellenbogen, *Foreign Words*, 155; Landesdorfer, *Sumerisches Sprachgut*, 55; Mankowski, *Akkadian Loanwords*, 136–37; Noonan, *Non-Semitic Loanwords*, 206; Propp, *Exodus 19–40*, 440; Rubin, 'Sumerian Loanwords', 665.
688. *ePSD*, s.v. 'šuba'; Propp, *Exodus 19–40*, 440.

See the explanation under תּוֹר, under 2.4, 'The loanwords in Daniel'. Note however, that this word is early and highly nativized. Therefore, it has not been counted in the statistics below.

שִׁטָּה
acacia; Exod 25:5, 10, 13, 23, 28; 26:15, 26, 32, 37; 27:1, 6; 30:1, 5; 35:7, 24; 36:20, 31, 36; 37:1, 4, 10, 15, 25, 28; 38:1, 6
(Deut 10:3; Num 25:1; Josh 2:1; 3:1; Isa 41:19; Joel 4:18; Mic 6:5)
Native synonyms: there is a rough synonym to be found in עֵץ.

The acacia, שִׁטָּה, is a loanword from Egyptian šnḏ or šnḏ.t and is treated as such by many scholars.[689] The word is loaned also to Akkadian as šamṭu and samṭu.[690] It also appears in Jewish Aramaic, under the influence of Hebrew. The use of ṭ in Akkadian and ט in Hebrew suggests that šnḏ.t underwent the same change as ṯḥs (ṯ > t),[691] resulting in a form *šnḏ.t, as Egyptian g and d are regularly represented by the emphatic series in Hebrew and Aramaic.[692] That Egyptian n is represented by m in the Akkadian forms remains puzzling: not only is it unlikely for the n to be represented by m, but the development in Akkadian is generally from n to m, rather than the other way around.[693] Nevertheless, there are possible explanations for the discrepancy, including hypercorrection or the existence of some intermediary between the Egyptian and Akkadian forms.

Although the word's singular form appears feminine, its plural is the form typical of the masculine plural: שִׁטִּים. The attested cases of the word do not make it clear whether it is in fact masculine or feminine. The Akkadian is masculine in form, while the Egyptian has both masculine (šnḏ) and feminine (šnḏ.t) forms. Although in some cases native Hebrew

---

689. Ellenbogen, *Foreign Words*, 160; Lambdin, 'Egyptian Loan Words', 154–55; Muchiki, *Egyptian Proper Names and Loanwords*, 256; Noonan, *Non-Semitic Loanwords*, 208–9; Propp, *Exodus 19–40*, 375; Rabin, 'Foreign Words', 1077; Rubin, 'Egyptian Loanwords', 794; Sarna, *Exodus*, 157; Wilson, 'Foreign Words', 211. Cf. *CDD*, s.v. 'šnt'; Erichsen, *Demotisches Glossar*, s.v. 'šnt.t'; Erman and Grapow, *Wörterbuch*, s.v. 'šnḏ'; *Thesaurus Linguae Aegyptiae*, s.vv. 'šnḏ', 'šnḏ.t'.

690. *CAD* 15, 17, s.vv. 'šamṭu', 'samṭu'.

691. As argued below in the case of תַּחַשׁ.

692. Muchiki, *Egyptian Proper Names and Loanwords*, 264, 308.

693. See under 'Appendix Six: An Outline of Linguistic Change in Aramaic and Akkadian'.

words do have unusual pluralizations, it is likely that, in this case, the atypical morphology is because of the word's foreign origin.

שֵׁשׁ
linen; Exod 25:4; 26:1, 31, 36; 27:9, 16, 18; 28:5, 6, 8, 15, 39, 39; 35:6, 23, 25, 35; 36:8, 35, 37; 38:9, 16, 18, 23; 39:2, 3, 5, 8, 27, 28, 28, 28, 29
(Gen 41:42; Esth 1:6, 6; 2:12, 12; Prov 31:22; Ezek 16:10; 27:7)
Native synonyms: בּוּץ; פֵּשֶׁת.

See the explanation under 2.3, 'The loanwords in Esther'.

תַּחְרָא
garment; Exod 28:32; 39:23
Native synonyms: סָדִין; בֶּגֶד.

While Lambdin doubted[694] and Muchiki denied[695] that תַּחְרָא was borrowed from Egyptian *dḥr*, 'leather',[696] Yahuda and more recently Noonan have affirmed its status as a loanword.[697] Lambdin's doubt was based firstly on the typical correspondence Egyptian *d* with Hebrew ט rather than ת and secondly on the ā'-termination of the Hebrew word.[698] Noonan and Yahuda, however, are right to accept the loan; as Noonan points out, Muchiki himself notes that Egyptian loans in Aramaic use this correspondence.[699] It is therefore unsurprising that the same should be the case in Hebrew.

תַּחַשׁ
leather; Exod 25:5; 26:14; 35:7, 23; 36:19; 39:34
(Num 4:6, 8, 10, 11, 12, 14, 25; Ezek 16:10)
Native synonyms: עוֹר.

---

694. Lambdin, 'Egyptian Loan Words', 155.
695. Muchiki, *Egyptian Proper Names and Loanwords*, 258.
696. Erman and Grapow, *Wörterbuch*, s.vv. 'dḥr', 'dḫ''; *Thesaurus Linguae Aegyptiae*, s.vv. 'dḥr', 'dḫ''.
697. Noonan, *Non-Semitic Loanwords*, 218; Yahuda, 'Hebrew Words of Egyptian Origin', 84–85.
698. Lambdin, 'Egyptian Loan Words', 155.
699. E.g. פתשת, derived from *p(3)-(n-)t(3)-šd.t*. Muchiki, *Egyptian Proper Names and Loanwords*, 186; Noonan, 'Foreign Loanwords', 213 n. 1091.

There are three main options canvassed for the origin of the word תַּחַשׁ: native (cognate with Arabic),[700] Hurrian,[701] and Egyptian.[702] These three opinions offer three different translations, 'beadwork', 'dugong hide', and 'tanned hide', respectively.

Cross' Arabic suggestion is based on comparison to the Arabic *tuḫas* or *duḫas*, 'dugong'.[703] The Hurrian proposal is based on comparison with Akkadian, *duḫšu*, or *dušû*, 'gemstone', 'tanned leather', 'goat skin', a colour term.[704] This term, along with Sumerian DUḪ.ŠI.A, in turn, are derived by Dalley from Hurrian *tuḫšiwe*.[705] The Hebrew, then, would be borrowed from Akkadian, *duḫšu*. Finally, Noonan argues for a connection between תַּחַשׁ and Egyptian *ṯḥs*, 'to stretch (leather)'.[706] The term in Egyptian is very old.[707] However, the formal equivalence of the two nouns relies on a merger during the New Kingdom of *ṯ* with t.[708] Therefore, a loan into Hebrew would be from the New Kingdom at the earliest. The equivalence of Egyptian s with Hebrew שׁ is attested elsewhere,[709] and may be due to the Egyptian consonant having a palatalized trait.[710]

700. Frank Cross, 'The Priestly Tabernacle in the Light of Recent Research', in *The Temple in Antiquity: Ancient Records and Modern Perspectives, Based on a Symposium Held at Brigham Young University in March 1981*, ed. Truman Madsen (Provo: Brigham Young University, 1984), 91–105 (95–96, 104).

701. Stephanie Dalley, 'Hebrew *Taḥaš*, Akkadian *Duḫšu*, Faience and Beadwork', *JSS* 45 (2000): 1–19; Propp, *Exodus 19–40*, 375.

702. Noonan, 'Foreign Loanwords', 214–16; Benjamin Noonan, 'Hide or Hue? Defining Hebrew תַּחַשׁ', *Biblica* 93 (2012): 580–89.

703. Cross, 'The Priestly Tabernacle', 95.

704. *CAD* 3, s.v. 'dušû'.

705. Dalley, 'Hebrew *Taḥaš*', 8–9.

706. Noonan, *Non-Semitic Loanwords*, 218–19. Cf. Erman and Grapow, *Wörterbuch*, s.v. 'ṯḥs'; *Thesaurus Linguae Aegyptiae*, s.v. 'ṯḥs'. Mastnjak rejects Noonan's hypothesis, because he finds the connection between 'leather' and 'stretching' too dubious. However, the attested uses of the word as cited in the lexica point universally to the association of this word with leather. Nathan Mastjnak, 'Hebrew taḥaš and the West Semitic Tent Tradition', *VT* 67 (2017): 204–12 (208).

707. The word is attested in the Old Kingdom's sixth dynasty, i.e. twenty-fourth century. E.g. from the Necropolis of Sakkara, in the Grave of Tjy, sixth dynasty. Cf. *Thesaurus Linguae Aegyptiae*, s.v. 'ṯḥs'.

708. Loprieno, *Ancient Egyptian*, 38; incidentally, this makes the *terminus post quem* for the borrowing into Hebrew 1550 BCE.

709. Muchiki, *Egyptian Proper Names and Loanwords*, 264.

710. Loprieno, *Ancient Egyptian*, 34.

Noonan points out that the Arabic and Hebrew forms are inconsistent with a common source word.⁷¹¹ He also discredits links between imagery of marine mammals and the tabernacle, which could bolster the appropriateness of dugong skin in this context and rejects the plausibility of the Israelites' access to this product.⁷¹² Therefore, we are left to decide between the Hurrian and the Egyptian origins. Admittedly, both options are plausible. However, because Hurrian and Egyptian are unrelated languages and because the forms and meanings coincide between these words, at least insofar as they are both used to describe leather, it seems likely that this is a case of lexical transfer: either the word originated in twenty-fourth-century Egyptian and passed into Hurrian, Sumerian, Akkadian and Hebrew or it originated in Hurrian and passed into Egyptian, Sumerian and Akkadian and from there into Hebrew. While we cannot rule either possibility out, as Noonan suggests, the use of this word alongside many other Egyptianisms in the tabernacle narrative does bolster the case that the word entered Hebrew directly from Egyptian, whatever its earlier history.⁷¹³

תְּכֵלֶת
dyed fabric; Exod 25:4; 26:1, 4, 31, 36; 27:16; 28:5, 6, 8, 15, 28, 31, 33, 37; 35:6, 23, 25, 35; 36:8, 11, 35, 37; 38:18, 23; 39:1, 2, 3, 5, 8, 21, 22, 24, 29, 31
(Num 4:6, 7, 9, 11, 12; 15:38; 2 Chr 2:6, 13; 3:14; Esth 1:6; 8:15; Jer 10:9; Ezek 23:6; 27:7, 24)
Native synonyms: צָבוּעַ.

See the explanation under 2.3, 'The loanwords in Esther'.

תַּרְשִׁישׁ
gemstone, traditionally 'topaz'; Exod 28:20; 39:13
(Song 5:14; Ezek 1:16; 10:9; 28:3; Dan 10:6)
Native synonyms: אֶקְדָּח; עֲדִי; חֵפֶץ. See the discussion under, 2.4, 'The loanwords in Daniel'.

See the explanation under 2.4, 'The loanwords in Daniel'.

---

711. Noonan, 'Hide or Hue?', 583.
712. Ibid., 583.
713. Ibid., 587–88.

## 2.7. Language of origin

The majority of the loanwords that have been identified in the past chapters derive from Akkadian, Greek or an Iranian language (in Daniel, Esther and Ezra) or from Egyptian (mostly in Exodus), with the possibility of the involvement of Aramaic. We have already indicated that in general, Hebrew occupies a place of low cultural or political prestige relative to these languages.[714]

Egypt was a culturally and politically dominant force in both the Bronze and Iron Ages,[715] even to the point that Egyptian became the language of the ruling class of Canaanite city states in the Late Bronze.[716] However, it would soon be eclipsed by Akkadian as the dominant language of international affairs, even within Egypt's cultural sphere. Nonetheless, Egypt remained an important source of cultural influence in the Levant and beyond, even into the Persian period.[717]

Akkadian played the role of a diplomatic *lingua franca* in the late Bronze Age and had enduring influence in both the Assyrian and Babylonian empires.[718] Even after it began to be displaced by Aramaic, it remained relevant, both as the native language of the ruling Assyrians and Babylonians, but also as an important literary language. Nevertheless, Aramaic became and remained the language of Assyrian, Babylonian and later Persian officialdom and diplomacy.[719] Even as Persian, and later Greek, became the language of the ruling class, Aramaic persisted as an important international language, even to the point of displacing local vernaculars.[720]

---

714. See 1.3.1, 'Applying Linguistics to Literary Texts'.

715. Gregory Mumford, 'Egypt and the Levant', in *The Oxford Handbook of the Archaeology of the Levant: c. 8000–332 BCE*, ed. Margreet Steiner and Ann Killebrew (Oxford: Oxford University Press, 2014), 72–85.

716. Ibid., 77.

717. Ibid., 78–85.

718. Wilfred van Soldt, 'Akkadian as a Diplomatic Language', in *Semitic Languages: An International Handbook*, ed. Stefan Weninger et al. (Berlin: de Gruyter, 2011), 405–15; Juan Pablo Vita Barra, 'Akkadian as a *Lingua Franca*', in *A Companion to Ancient Near Eastern Languages*, ed. Rebecca Hasselbach-Andee (Hoboken: John Wiley, 2020), 357–72.

719. Margaretha Folmer, 'Imperial Aramaic as an Administrative Language of the Achaemenid Period', in Weninger et al., eds., *Semitic Languages*, 587–97; Folmer, 'Aramaic as a *Lingua Franca*', in Hasselbach-Andee, ed., *A Companion to Ancient Near Eastern Languages*, 373–400; Seiro Haruta, 'Aramaic, Parthian, and Middle Persian', in *The Oxford Handbook of Ancient Iran*, ed. Daniel Potts (Oxford: Oxford University Press, 2013), 779–94 (780–81).

720. Folmer, 'Aramaic as a *Lingua Franca*', 385, 390.

Persian, the most prominent Iranian language in the written record, became a language of international importance with the rise of the Achaemenid Persian empire. However, while Persian was the language of the ruling dynasty, it never became the language of official imperial business – a role played by Aramaic,[721] and to a lesser extent Elamite or Babylonian, should kings wish to place themselves in an Elamite or Mesopotamian cultural context.[722]

The Achaemenid period, however, was one characterized by linguistic diversity. In Egypt, although Aramaic was the administrative language, Egyptian and a number of other vernaculars persist.[723] In fact, very many languages (such as Hebrew) are attested within the borders of the Persian empire in this period, but used as local vernaculars rather than for official Imperial communication.[724] This also includes Greek, since Greeks were present in Persian cities as mercenaries and as deportees, gathered in *poleis* of Hellenic culture.[725] Nonetheless, it is not until the Hellenistic period that Greek truly rose to prominence in the ancient Near East. Although it would eventually overtake Aramaic as the most important international language in this region, Aramaic was nevertheless prominent, even in the Hellenistic period, especially in the Seleucid empire.[726]

This brief overview of each of these languages describes their sociolinguistic status at a societal level. However, we are approaching loanwords from the perspective of individual texts; we cannot assume that the authors and editors of specific biblical texts *necessarily* viewed these languages and their speakers in these ways. Despite the high prestige (at a societal level) of Akkadian, for example, it would not be all that surprising if it turned out that a biblical text were to treat Akkadian loanwords (and speakers of Akkadian) as undesirable. Similarly, although Hebrew is the low-prestige language, from an international perspective, we would again

---

721. Folmer, 'Imperial Aramaic as an Administrative Language', 587–97; Haruta, 'Aramaic, Parthian, and Middle Persian', 780–81.

722. Katrien de Graef, 'The Use of Akkadian in Iran', in Potts, ed., *The Oxford Handbook of Ancient Iran*, 263–82 (263, 279); Folmer, 'Imperial Aramaic as an Administrative Language', 592–93.

723. Dorothy Thompson, 'The Multilingual Environment of Persian and Ptolemaic Egypt: Egyptian, Aramaic, and Greek Documentation', in *The Oxford Handbook of Papyrology*, ed. Roger Bagnall (Oxford: Oxford University, 2011), 395–417 (397–99).

724. Folmer, 'Imperial Aramaic as an Administrative Language', 591.

725. Georges Rougement, 'The Use of Greek in Pre-Sasanian Iran', in Potts, ed., *The Oxford Handbook of Ancient Iran*, 795–801 (769, 798).

726. Folmer, 'Aramaic as a *Lingua Franca*', 390–91; Haruta, 'Aramaic, Parthian, and Middle Persian', 781.

be unsurprised were a biblical text to treat Hebrew with greater respect. Thus, at the level of individual literary texts, we cannot allow our assumptions about the relative status of Ancient Near Eastern languages to drive our conclusions about what the texts mean, literarily. Rather, we must allow each text to be evidence of its own beliefs and assumptions about the relative status of these different languages.

### 2.8. *Native synonyms*

Throughout the analysis above, there are potential synonyms listed for each of the loanwords in question. In part, this is because we wish to address the objection that a particular loanword is only used because the text had no other choice. In addition, it will have relevance to the concept of implicature, discussed below. Nonetheless, identifying native alternatives comes with certain challenges and provisos.

The first challenge is this: the claim that a word had no native synonyms is by nature *argumentum e silentio*. It is often simple to prove that a word had a native synonym, but it is impossible to prove that it did not. Likewise, in cases where we have suggested synonyms, it is very possible that there were further synonyms, which have not survived in the canon. For our purposes, however, this impossibility is not a great challenge, because we are more interested in cases where native synonyms exist, than where they do not.

The second challenge is defining what we mean by synonym. Although it would be possible to define 'synonym' as referring to words that denote the exact same object, this is not what is relevant for our purposes. Since we are interested in literary texts, greater flexibility is required: even if there is no exact synonym, it is still possible in many cases for Hebrew (or Aramaic, where appropriate[727]) to express itself by other means: either by use of a partial synonym, a category – e.g. 'musical instrument' instead of 'flute' – by periphrasis or by rephrasing the text more extensively – e.g. when the word is a part of a list of elements or is in some other sense redundant, there is no barrier to the text expressing itself without

---

727. Aramaic, it should be noted, offers additional challenges because the dialect of Aramaic needs to be considered. In the case of Aramaic synonyms, I have tried to use synonyms that are attested in Biblical or Imperial Aramaic, because that is the preferable situation. However, that is often not possible. Where it is not possible, I have chosen synonyms that are attested in a wide range of Aramaic dialects or that are plainly related to verbal roots that are well-attested either in Biblical or Imperial Aramaic or a large number of other Aramaic dialects.

using the loanword. It is best when there is an exact synonym, because that allows for the clearest contrast. However, even in other cases, the opposition does not necessarily need to be between two single words, but rather between two means of expressing the same thing. Therefore, the synonyms or alternatives offered are not intended to work in all occurrences of the loanword, only in the specific situation of the literary texts being analyzed.

Nevertheless, the analysis does not rise or fall on the plausibility of any single native alternative, because the texts discussed have been selected on two criteria: (a) the high proportion of loanwords and (b) the uneven distribution of loanwords in the book. Even in cases where a single loanword may have been used because the text had no alternative, it is unlikely to be significant to the overall conclusions, which are based on the concentration and distribution of many loanwords.

### 2.8.1. *The contrast between loanwords and native synonyms, implicature and creating a literary effect*

A common distinction between luxury and necessity loans[728] is based on whether the recipient language 'needed' to borrow a word or not.[729] A luxury loan in this scheme is a loan that denotes the same thing as an existing word in the recipient language. A necessity loan is a loan that denotes something previously inexpressible in the language. It is sometimes suggested that necessity loans are more common than luxury loans.[730] Thus, 'sashimi' in English would be a necessity loan from Japanese whereas 'seppuku' would be a luxury loan.

However, the necessity–luxury distinction is a deficient way of thinking about loanwords: it is not true in the strictest sense, for example, that 'seppuku' is truly equivalent to the pre-existing 'suicide' or even 'ritual suicide'. Nor is it true that English 'needed' to borrow 'sashimi' to express 'raw fish'. Instead, there are a wide range of motivations that may or may not favour borrowing as opposed to language-internal means of lexical creation (onomatopoeia, portmanteau, derivation, etc.).

---

728. Also termed 'core' and 'cultural' loans.

729. Thus, for example, this distinction is made in Martin Haspelmath, 'Lexical Borrowing', 46–50.

730. E.g. Terry Crowley and Claire Bowen, *An Introduction to Historical Linguistics*, 4th ed. (Oxford: Oxford University Press, 2010), 206: 'Languages are more likely to copy words from other languages in the area of cultural vocabulary than in core vocabulary'.

In order to address this deficiency, the luxury–necessity distinction was developed further by Onysko and Winter-Froemel into a distinction between 'catachrestic' and 'non-catachrestic' loans.[731] The terminology is based on the classical rhetorical term *catachresis*, the use of a word in its improper context or the use of a word that does not strictly apply because an appropriate word does not exist in the language.[732] It is the latter definition that Onysko and Winter-Froemel employ; a catachrestic loan is that which is borrowed because the options found in the recipient language are somehow deficient. The difference between the catachrestic–non-catachrestic categorization and the luxury–necessity categorization is the recognition that connotation as well as denotation is relevant. That is, although '*seppuku*' and 'suicide' denote the same act, '*seppuku*' connotes a foreign setting and a particular method and so is a catachrestic loan but not a 'necessary' one. Non-catachrestic loans do likewise connote; the distinction is that non-catachrestic loans both connote and denote meanings already available in the recipient language's lexicon.

In providing native alternatives to the loanwords, above, we are attempting to demonstrate that these words are generally catachrestic loans, whether or not they are luxury or necessity.

Onysko and Winter-Froemel also develop their idea by relating the catachrestic–non-catachrestic distinction to Levinson's theory of I-implicature and M-implicature.[733] The principle of I- and M-implicature is that atypical language is used to describe something atypical; that is, an unmarked form will be used to convey a regular set of assumptions whereas a marked form will be used to convey a complementary set of assumptions. This set of complementary assumptions relies on the existence of the unmarked form.

Levinson provides as an example the difference between 'Sue smiled' and 'The corners of Sue's lips turned slightly upwards'.[734] The first case I-implicates that Sue's smile was an ordinary smile. The second case implicates that Sue's smile is somehow abnormal, namely that it is a smirk or grimace. The logic of the first case is that the speaker has not chosen to make a particular point of any single characteristic and so it would be unreasonable to assume that such a characteristic was intended. The logic of the second case is that if the speaker had wanted to convey

---

731. Onysko and Winter-Froemel, 'Necessary Loans – Luxury Loans?'
732. Richard Nate, 'Catachrēsis', in Sloane, ed., *Encyclopedia of Rhetoric*, 88–89.
733. A concept described in Stephen Levinson, *Presumptive Meanings* (Cambridge: MIT, 2000), 135–53.
734. Ibid., 138.

a typical smile (s)he would have avoided the connotations built into this description of a smile. The second case – M-implicature – thus depends on the contrast with the unmarked form.

In the case of catachrestic loans, we are dealing with M-implicature. The potential (in the mind of the reader/addressee) for the sentence to be expressed in a way without the loanword (whether or not the text actually would have done so) implicates that what makes the loanword unique, its foreign association, is relevant for some connotative reason. It is important to note that this process of implicature is based in the potential contrast in the mind of the reader/addressee, rather than in the intention of the author/speaker/text. While it is true that a skilled communicator will attempt to utilize the effect of this implicature, its function is independent of the intention of the author. Therefore, when it comes to catachrestic loanwords, the fact that these loanwords have a *potential* for contrast is all that is needed to activate their set of connotations, rather than an author or speaker necessarily making a deliberate, conscious decision between a native word and a loanword. The presence of catachrestic loanwords in the text creates implicature in the minds of the recipients of the text, regardless of the conscious intent of the author.[735] The fact that these loanwords occur in high concentrations juxtaposed with low concentrations, however, implies that there is at least subconscious intent.

### 2.8.2. *The semantic field of palaces in Hebrew and Aramaic*

An example can be illustrative. Among the loanwords discussed, there are several words which refer to palaces, אַפֶּדֶן and בִּיתָן, or a citadel, בִּירָה. Now, each of these words does have a particular nuance: these words are not entirely equivalent. The Persian donor term for אַפֶּדֶן, *apadāna-*, is used for a stone-columned hall,[736] but in Dan 11:45, the context suggests instead tents that are of a palatial nature. The Akkadian donor term for בִּיתָן appears to refer to the inner part of the palace,[737] which provides a slight

---

735. Note also that since we are studying the texts from a rhetorical standpoint, authorial intention is outside of the view of study. See 1.3.3 'Rhetorical Approaches to the Hebrew Bible', and 1.3.6, 'Synthesis'.

736. The columns are identified as features of the palace by D²Sa 1 and A²Hb 1. One might have argued that D²Sa and A²Hb were clarifying that the examples of *apadāna-* in question have stone columns, but the word itself does not necessarily refer to a columned palace, except that the other occurrences of this word (A²Sa 3–4 and A²Ha 5) do not mention stone columns and yet are inscribed on the stone columns of the palace that has been mentioned. Kent, *Old Persian*, 113–14, 154–55, 168.

737. *CAD* 2, s.v. bītānu; *HALOT*, s.v. בִּיתָן.

contrast to the way it is used in Esth 1:5 and 7:7–8, where it specifies the location of a royal garden, but one that is large enough to accommodate all of the people of Susa (Esth 1:5). The Akkadian donor term for the word בִּירָה refers to a citadel or by metonymy a city.[738] This term has undergone significant broadening in Hebrew, such that it might also refer to a temple,[739] perhaps by analogy with בַּיִת.[740] In Esther and Daniel, however, it is exclusively used as the epithet of Susa. In Esth 3:15, שׁוּשַׁן הַבִּירָה is contrasted with הָעִיר שׁוּשָׁן, such that it is clear that הַבִּירָה technically refers to a specific part of the city. However, in other situations, such as 9:6, it seems likely that שׁוּשַׁן הַבִּירָה refers to the city in general, since the book does not give the sense that there are many Jews operating within the citadel proper. In this way the Hebrew word's use is consistent with the equivalent word in Akkadian.

These words are used in ways where they could easily be dispensed with, with limited effect; the main thing that changes due to their inclusion is that greater specificity is given and that a loanword is introduced to the text.

Esther 1:5 is indicative of how בִּירָה and בִּיתָן are used in the texts we have studied – they are used in the same construct phrases in Esth 1:5; 2:3, 5, 8; 3:15; 7:7–8; 8:14; 9:6, 11, 12 and Dan 8:2; בִּירָה is used in an equivalent phrase for Ecbatana in Ezra 6:2.

Esther 1:5.

וּבִמְלוֹאת הַיָּמִים הָאֵלֶּה עָשָׂה הַמֶּלֶךְ לְכָל־הָעָם הַנִּמְצְאִים בְּשׁוּשַׁן הַבִּירָה
לְמִגָּדוֹל וְעַד־קָטָן מִשְׁתֶּה שִׁבְעַת יָמִים בַּחֲצַר גִּנַּת בִּיתַן הַמֶּלֶךְ:

In both cases the loanword is used to give greater specificity. If we wish to consider alternative ways that this text could have been written, we might try substitution for native alternatives:

וּבִמְלוֹאת הַיָּמִים הָאֵלֶּה עָשָׂה הַמֶּלֶךְ לְכָל־הָעָם הַנִּמְצְאִים בְּשׁוּשַׁן הָעִיר
לְמִגָּדוֹל וְעַד־קָטָן מִשְׁתֶּה שִׁבְעַת יָמִים בַּחֲצַר גִּנַּת בֵּית הַמֶּלֶךְ:

Another option is to consider subtraction of the loanwords:

וּבִמְלוֹאת הַיָּמִים הָאֵלֶּה עָשָׂה הַמֶּלֶךְ לְכָל־הָעָם הַנִּמְצְאִים בְּשׁוּשַׁן לְמִגָּדוֹל
וְעַד־קָטָן מִשְׁתֶּה שִׁבְעַת יָמִים בַּחֲצַר גִּנַּת הַמֶּלֶךְ:

---

738. *CAD* 2, s.v. birtu; *HALOT*, s.v. בִּירָה.
739. E.g. 1 Chr 29:1, 19; possibly also, Neh 2:8.
740. *HALOT*, s.vv. בַּיִת and הֵיכָל.

This would not change the denotative force of the sentence: all of the noun phrases still refer to the same thing. It only impacts the connotative force of the sentence.

The use of אַפֶּדֶן in Dan 11:45 is similar.

וְיִטַּע אָהֳלֵי אַפַּדְנוֹ בֵּין יַמִּים לְהַר־צְבִי־קֹדֶשׁ וּבָא עַד־קִצּוֹ וְאֵין עוֹזֵר לוֹ:

In the same way as the above examples, the loanword only gives greater specificity to the construct phrase. We could consider a version with a synonym from a highly nativized word:

וְיִטַּע אָהֳלֵי הֵיכָלוֹ בֵּין יַמִּים לְהַר־צְבִי־קֹדֶשׁ וּבָא עַד־קִצּוֹ וְאֵין עוֹזֵר לוֹ:

Or, we could simply subtract the loanword:

וְיִטַּע אֹהָלָיו בֵּין יַמִּים לְהַר־צְבִי־קֹדֶשׁ וּבָא עַד־קִצּוֹ וְאֵין עוֹזֵר לוֹ:

Again, this would not change the denotative force of the sentence: only connotative force of the sentence is affected.

Each of these words has a slight nuance, such that it is not a precise synonym for any Hebrew word. There are rough native synonyms: 'palace' might be expressed as בַּיִת, as it is for example in Esth 2:9, as well as many other places;[741] 'citadel' might equally be expressed as מִבְצָר, as for example, in 2 Chr 17:19.[742] However, these words are not precise synonyms. This suggests that we are dealing with catachrestic loans: loanwords where there are possible ways to express the same thing in native terminology, but the borrowed word is adopted with further nuances and connotations.

Thus, in the semantic field of palaces and citadels, we have a variety of native options, but then we also have a selection of loanwords which M-implicate; that is, the choice of these loanwords, over native, more generic options, implies that a particular connotation of these loanwords is intended. As we have seen, these words do have a variety of nuances, which at times may be relevant. However, one particular nuance is that these loanwords refer to foreign objects, rather than native ones.

When these words occur in isolation, for example, אַפֶּדֶן in Dan 11:45, we cannot be sure that the 'foreign' nuance is likely to have had much of an impact on the readers of the text. However, in other cases, such as בִּיתָן

---

741. *HALOT*, s.vv. בַּיִת.

742. For other synonyms, see the lists of synonyms in the discussion of the loanwords.

in Esth 1, where there are very many loanwords used, it is far more likely that this nuance would be the salient feature of all of these loanwords – that what is implicated by these words is that they are different to other words because they connote a foreign connection.

We have outlined how this might be applied to the semantic field of palaces and citadels. With reference to the lists of synonyms in the discussion of loanwords, above, it is possible to construct similar arguments for the rest of the semantic fields with which we are dealing (officials, precious goods, administration, etc.). However, the more pertinent factor to consider is that we should only use this type of analysis for those texts which contain a high proportion of loanwords (such as Esther, Daniel, Ezra and Exodus). In cases where loanwords are used in isolation or in low concentrations, it is probable that the foreign factor is not relevant. However, in cases where the loanwords are used in great concentration that is a much smaller risk.

As an additional precaution, we have limited ourselves to texts where there are sections that have high concentrations and sections that have low concentrations, which do not correspond neatly to redactional theories of the text, so that we can avoid the possibility that the loanwords only appear in high concentration as a function of the text's idiolect.

### 2.8.3. *Loanwords and literary effect*

Understanding that catachrestic loanwords implicate explains one part of how the loanwords function as a rhetorical figure. However, to return to our original explanation, there are other factors too. The loanwords also deviate phonetically, morphologically and distributionally. We have often noticed in the above analysis of loanword hypotheses the phonetic and morphological differences, because they are core to how we identify loanwords in the first place. There may be other loanwords that have been so nativized that we cannot recognize them, but they equally have little literary import, because they do not deviate. In the literary analysis that follows we will look at the distribution of the loanwords. However, it is the combination of all three factors (pragmatics/implicature, phonetics and morphology and distribution) that allow the loanwords to function as a rhetorical figure.

3

# Text Analysis – Loanwords as a Means for Group Maintenance

## 3.1. *Loanwords as a rhetorical tool for the construction of ethno-linguistic identity*

Before we begin analyzing particular texts, we return to our main thesis: loanwords can be used for literary purposes, namely to generate ethno-linguistic distinctions. However, there are several points we must clarify here. Firstly, we need to discuss what it means for the loanwords to be used for literary purposes: whether their purpose must be literary and how they function as a literary device. Secondly, we must clarify what is meant by 'ethno-linguistic' distinctions.

### 3.1.1. *Must the loanwords have literary effect?*
As we have noted above, the scholarly interest in loanwords has mostly been interested in their identification and also their use for so-called linguistic dating. As such, some justification of the relevance of a literary approach to what has traditionally been a purely linguistic topic is necessary. A question, as we have already touched on, that may be of especial interest to some scholars is that of intentionality, whether loanwords could have been deliberately used for rhetorical purposes by biblical authors.

As an initial response to this question, we must first make a distinction between the intent of an author and the effect of the text. Insofar as the loanwords appear in the text and influence its readers, it is necessary to give a literary account of them regardless of the intent of any author. Additionally, we should recognize that authorial intent is impossible to prove.[1]

---

1. See 1.3.3, 'Rhetorical Approaches to the Hebrew Bible', and 1.3.6, 'Synthesis'.

From our methodological perspective, there is no need – nor is it possible – to demonstrate authorial intent. However, this approach may leave some unsatisfied and so I propose two modified questions, where we are on more solid ground than speculating as to authorial intent: firstly, whether it is plausible that biblical authors could use loanwords for literary effect expecting that their audience would be aware of that effect; and secondly, whether, given the uneven distribution of the loanwords, it is plausible that the loanwords are not used with a literary effect.

To the question of plausibility, there are several analogies we could make. To begin with, we could compare another ancient literature, that of the Greeks, where it is clear that Greek writers were capable of recognizing borrowing from other languages and even other dialects of Greek. For example, Pseudo-Xenophon writes, 'Moreover, hearing every kind of speech, they [i.e. the Athenians] chose this from the one and that from the other. While other Greeks use their own kind of speech and custom and dress, the Athenians use one cobbled together from all the Greeks and the barbarians.'[2] The so-called Old Oligarch was familiar with the concept that languages borrowed words from one another and believed himself, and one assumes his reader, able to identify these words. Bonner gives a catalogue of instances where Greeks are conscious of and are able to imitate the differences in Greek dialects.[3] We can find a more dramatic example in the case of Plautus' *Poenulus*, where he makes use of an entire speech in Punic language for the sake of portraying his Phoenician character more realistically.[4]

However, we do not need to look as far as the Classical world to find parallels. We have already discussed the use of style-switching for literary purposes as applied to Aramaic and closely related dialects of Hebrew. This provides us with a suitable framework for understanding how loanwords may be used for literary purposes. Just as high concentrations of dialectal syntax or vocabulary can be used to portray particular characters or settings, so, we suggest, it is plausible that a biblical text would use loanwords in high concentration to achieve similar effects. Another common feature of Hebrew narrative is etymological or pseudo-etymological

---

2. Pseudo-Xenophon (the Old Oligarch), *On the Constitution* 2.8: ἔπειτα φωνὴν πᾶσαν ἀκούοντες ἐξελέξαντο τοῦτο μὲν ἐκ τῆς, τοῦτο δὲ ἐκ τῆς· καὶ οἱ μὲν Ἕλληνες ἰδίᾳ μᾶλλον καὶ φωνῇ καὶ διαίτῃ καὶ σχήματι χρῶνται, Ἀθηναῖοι δὲ κεκραμένῃ ἐξ ἁπάντων τῶν Ἑλλήνων καὶ βαρβάρων (translation mine).

3. Robert Bonner, 'The Mutual Intelligibility of Greek Dialects', *The Classical Journal* 4 (1909): 356–63.

4. Plautus, *Poenulus* 1.5.

wordplay.[5] If biblical authors are interested in the origins of names for non-linguistic purposes, it is plausible that they would be interested in exploiting the origin of unfamiliar words.

All of this combines to suggest that it is highly plausible that an author could use loanwords for literary effect expecting that their audience would be aware of that effect.

To the second question, as we will see in the analysis below, the distribution of loanwords is highly uneven across biblical texts, even within single books. One might attempt to explain this unevenness by redactional layers, dialect or other such factors, though no one factor would be able to explain the whole distribution. However, when it comes to the final form of the text, we must still account for every literary effect of the final text, whether it traces back to an author or editor. Moreover, each reader will ascribe that literary effect to the implied author of the text. With the kind of variation in distribution of loanwords that is found in the biblical texts we are studying, it seems implausible that it is entirely random. It is not always clear who created the literary effect of the loanwords, but it is clear that whatever process of authorship stands behind these texts, it has produced a final form, where the loanwords seem distributed, as if by an intentional process.

In summary, it is difficult to explain the current distribution of loanwords in biblical texts based on non-literary factors alone. In addition, comparative evidence suggests that it is highly plausible that biblical authors would have used loanwords in this way, for literary effect, and expected their audience to notice. Although we suggest that it is methodologically incorrect to seek to prove authorial intention behind literary features of a text, we do view it as the more plausible explanation for the distribution of loanwords in these texts. On this basis, we explore what the literary effect of those loanwords is in the following sections.

### 3.1.2. *How the loanwords function as a literary device*

We saw, in our discussion of native synonyms, that loanwords have a pragmatic effect.[6] When there is an alternative to the loanword, the contrast between the native word and the loanword generates a difference in the meaning of the two words. In rhetorical terms, the loanword deviates from the native vocabulary. Especially since such words are borrowed from other languages and cultures, the loanword carries with it reference to

---

5. E.g. Gen 30:24. Cf. Herbert Marks, 'Biblical Naming and Poetic Etymology', *JBL* 114 (1995): 21–42.

6. See above, 2.8, 'Native synonyms'.

those other languages and cultures. In addition, we have seen that linguists have observed that loanwords are deployed for a wide range of desired effects. In particular, however, this study is focused on one effect: the use of loanwords to generate a foreign atmosphere.[7] The distinction that is generated between the native and foreign words, especially when these foreign words are used in high concentrations, puts the reader in mind of foreign culture and foreign environments. Again, this effect can be used for a variety of purposes, but we will focus on the ways in which it can serve as a tool for constructing identity.

### 3.1.3. *Loanwords in literature and history*

In studying loanwords as a feature of literature, it is not intended, however, that their status as a feature of linguistic contact in a particular historical context should be disregarded. As Mankowski notes, 'to identify a word as a loanword is to make a specific historical claim'.[8] In particular, to identify loanwords that are contained within Hebrew from another culture is to suggest a high level of cultural contact between those two cultures. In identifying the precise time periods and dialects involved in the lexical transfer, it is possible to achieve a greater understanding of the relationship between the two cultures.[9] Nonetheless, it would also be incorrect to ignore the literary context in which we access these linguistic data. In literary texts, there are literary consequences for word choices, including when the vocabulary is foreign. Whereas focusing on the linguistics and history of a particular loan leads to studying the moment of lexical transfer, focusing on literature leads to studying the ongoing life of the word in the language, after the initial moment of lexical transfer.

### 3.1.4. *Constructions of ethnic identity in the Hebrew Bible*

Ethnicity or ethnic identity exists when a group holds several related features in common, including among others, (a belief in) a common origin, shared historical narratives and cultural identifiers, such as dress, religion or language.[10] Chandra provides a more minimal definition, that

---

7. See above, 1.3.2, 'Variation'.

8. Mankowski, *Akkadian Loanwords*, 4.

9. For this approach, refer to Noonan, *Non-Semitic Loanwords*, especially Chapter 7.

10. John Hutchinson and Anthony Smith, 'Introduction', in *Ethnicity*, ed. John Hutchinson and Anthony Smith (Oxford: Oxford University Press, 1996), 1–14 (6–7); Manning Nash, *The Cauldron of Ethnicity in the Modern World* (Chicago: University of Chicago Press, 1989), 10–15.

'Ethnic identities ... are *a subset of categories in which descent-based attributes are necessary for membership*'.[11] Some of these features or attributes are susceptible to analysis through archaeology,[12] but literary texts offer another window onto the situation.

Often biblical scholars approach ethnicity according to constructivist principles: ethnic groups are defined by constructed boundaries that may be crossed, under certain circumstances. So, for example, Miller suggests that Israelite identity in the Hebrew Bible is based on the belief of a common heritage, rather than necessarily based on actual common ancestry.[13] In addition, he suggests that ethnicity is social (rather than onto-logical – it is the *belief* in common origin that matters) and constructed around aggregative and oppositional forces: aggregative forces unite the members of the group, while oppositional forces make distinctions between those inside the group and those outside.[14]

One logical consequence of constructivist approaches is the possibility of the co-existence of multiple ethnic identities, where, for example, an individual might have multiple ancestries or the features of multiple different ethnic identities. This is particularly of relevance to texts from or set in multi-ethnic contexts, such as Persian Yehud or among Judaeans in the Persian Court.

---

11. Kanchan Chandra, 'What is Ethnic Identity? A Minimalist Definition', in *Constructivist Theories of Ethnic Politics*, ed. Kanchan Chandra (Oxford: Oxford University Press, 2012), 51–96 (51). Emphasis original.

12. The bibliography on this is extensive. Among many others: Elizabeth Bloch-Smith, 'Israelite Ethnicity in Iron I: Archaeology Preserves What is Remembered and What is Forgotten in Israel's History', *JBL* 122 (2003): 401–25; Izak Cornelius, '"A Tale of Two Cities": The Visual Imagery of Yehud and Samaria, and Identity/Self-Understanding in Persian-Period Palestine', in *Texts, Contexts and Readings in Postexilic Literature Explorations into Historiography and Identity Negotiation in Hebrew Bible and Related Texts*, ed. Louis Jonker, FAT II 53 (Tübingen: Mohr-Siebeck, 2011), 213–37; Diana Edelman, 'Ethnicity and Early Israel', in *Ethnicity and the Bible*, ed. Mark Brett (Leiden: Brill, 1996), 25–55; Ingo Kottsieper, '"And They Did Not Care to Speak Yehudit": On Linguistic Change in Judah during the Late Persian Era', in *Judah and the Judeans in the Fourth Century B.C.E.*, ed. Oded Lipschits et al. (Winona Lake: Eisenbrauns, 2007), 95–124; Neil Silberman and David Small, eds., *The Archaeology of Israel: Constructing the Past, Interpreting the Present*, JSOTSup 137 (Sheffield: Sheffield Academic Press, 1997).

13. James Miller, 'Ethnicity and the Hebrew Bible: Problems and Prospects', *Currents in Biblical Research* 6 (2008): 170–213 (175).

14. Ibid., 172–74.

More recently, however, scholars have tried to grapple with the fact that 'ethnic actors' and texts often act on primordialist assumptions, that is, that a person is born into a particular ethnicity and may not be able to cross ethnic boundaries.[15] Therefore, we must remain sensitive to the possibility that the texts we are dealing with might not assume that it is possible for a character to change their ethnicity.

In addition, we must take account of Brubaker's convincing arguments that ethnicity is a category, rather than a group: people may be placed into ethnic categories by other ethnic actors, but these 'groups' have no basis in real traits;[16] that is, ethnicity is a rhetorical tool. Building on Brubaker's understanding, Chandra suggests that ethnicity should be discussed in terms of 'categories' and the 'attributes' that are necessary to be placed in those categories.[17]

Therefore, we should be cautious to pay attention to how texts/ethnic actors categorize people into groups, based on attributes, such as language use, ancestry, and so on, while still recognizing that we are viewing ethnic boundaries through the eyes of a literary text, which has its own rhetorical goals and may champion a particular view of ethnic identity – whether or not that view was consistent with how the society at large viewed ethnicity. When, below, we speak of ethnic groups, it is only in reference to the 'group' as portrayed by the text/ethnic actor for its own rhetorical purposes.

In discussing Israelite ethnicity a variety of approaches have been taken, including attempts to identify these aggregative and oppositional social forces: shared memory of the exile;[18] or a combination of ethnicity,

---

15. Francisco Gil-White, 'How Thick is Blood? The Plot Thickens…: If Ethnic Actors are Primordialists, What Remains of the Circumstantialist/Primordialist Controversy?', *Ethnic and Racial Studies* 22 (1999): 789–820; Dermot Nestor, 'We Are Family: Deuteronomy 14 and the Boundaries of an Israelite Identity', *The Bible and Critical Theory* 9 (2013): 38–53.

16. Rogers Brubaker, 'Ethnicity without Groups', *European Journal of Sociology* 43 (2002): 163–89; Brubaker, *Ethnicity without Groups* (Cambridge, MA: Harvard University Press, 2004).

17. Kanchan Chandra, 'Attributes and Categories: A New Conceptual Vocabulary for Thinking about Ethnic Identity', in Chandra, ed., *Constructivist Theories of Ethnic Politics*, 97–131.

18. Ehud Ben Zvi, 'Inclusion in and Exclusion from Israel as Conveyed by the Use of the Term "Israel" in Postmonarchic Biblical Texts', in *The Pitcher is Broken: Memorial Essays for Gösta W. Ahlström*, ed. Steven Holloway and Lowell Handy, LHBOTS 190 (Sheffield: JSOT Press, 1995), 95–149; Ehud Ben Zvi, 'On Social

nationality, role, religion.[19] Religious or theological ideas are also identified as key elements of the construction of Israelite identity.[20] There have also been approaches that focus primarily on the biblical texts: Wetter takes Ruth as a case study for crossing ethnic boundaries, suggesting that even the apparently central requirement of shared ancestry is malleable.[21] In her work on Esther, Wetter points to the overlap of religious and ethnic identity.[22] Eskenazi examines the construction of Jewish identity through opposition to others in Ezra–Nehemiah.[23] Similarly, Southwood focuses on the intermarriage crisis in Ezra–Nehemiah.[24] Sparks, too, uses several biblical texts as a starting point for his discussion of ethnicity throughout Israelite history.[25]

So far, however, there has been a lack of attention given to the stylistic means employed by these texts to engage with ideas about foreigners. While it is commonplace to engage with biblical texts as a source for understanding ethnicity at a variety of stages of Israelite history, there has been little attempt to understand the literary means at the disposal of these texts to depict ethnic others. Loanwords, as we have suggested, are a particularly apt method for texts to do this, because of their capacity to make distinctions between different linguistic cultures.

---

Memory and Identity Formation in Late Persian Yehud: A Historian's Viewpoint with a Focus on Prophetic Literature, Chronicles and the Dtr. Historical Collection', in Jonker, ed., *Texts, Contexts and Readings in Postexilic Literature*, 95–148.

19. Jon Berquist, 'Constructions of Identity in Postcolonial Yehud', in *Judah and the Judeans in the Persian Period*, ed. Oded Lipschitz and Manfred Oeming (Winona Lake: Eisenbrauns, 2006), 53–66.

20. Diana Edelman, 'YHWH's Othering of Israel', in *Imagining the Other and Constructing Israelite Identity in the Early Second Temple Period*, ed. Ehud Ben Zvi and Diana Edelman (London: Bloomsbury, 2014), 41–69.

21. Anne-Mareike Wetter, 'Ruth: A Born-Again Israelite?', in Ben Zvi and Edelman, eds., *Imagining the Other*, 144–62.

22. Anne-Mareike Wetter, 'How Jewish is Esther? Or: How is Esther Jewish? Tracing Ethnic and Religious Identity in a Diaspora Narrative', *ZAW* 123 (2011): 596–603.

23. Tamara Eskenazi, 'Imagining the Other in the Construction of Jewish Identity in Ezra–Nehemiah', in Ben Zvi and Edelman, eds., *Imagining the Other*, 230–56.

24. Katherine Southwood, *Ethnicity and the Mixed Marriage Crisis in Ezra 9–10: An Anthropological Approach*, Oxford Theological Monographs (Oxford: Oxford University Press, 2012).

25. Kenton Sparks, *Ethnicity and Identity in Ancient Israel: Prolegomena to the Study of Ethnic Sentiments and Their Expression in the Hebrew Bible* (Winona Lake: Eisenbrauns, 1998).

There are some limits for this text-centred approach. As Edelman notes, texts are unable to tell us much with certainty about the early stages of Israelite ethnicity.[26] This is a subset of a larger issue, which is that it is difficult to generalize from the extant texts to more widely held beliefs about ethnicity: the texts that have been preserved, mostly through canonization, may not have (always) represented the majority view. Nor is it necessarily true that texts within what has been preserved must agree with one another. Further, we must recognize that the difficulties associated with dating texts likewise make it difficult to date the views on ethnicity that we find in those texts. Instead, what a text-centred approach reveals, is what the texts themselves either assume or want to show about ethnicities.

In summary, what we intend to discuss in the analysis below is how these four texts represent ethnicity and ethnic boundaries: rather than an exercise in recovering what Israelite ethnicity *was*, we have a slightly different goal. We are studying the rhetoric of how ethnicity is presented by these four literary texts.

### 3.2. *Depicting empire, defining the other*

#### 3.2.1. *Loanwords: a literary tool for commenting on other nations*

Over the following sections I present the effect of loanwords in a variety of biblical texts that depict foreign empires. In addition to depicting the setting, loanwords in Esther and Daniel also act as a means of setting up an opposition between the Jewish protagonists and their foreign rulers. This ethnic distinction, created by the loanwords, has consequences for the characterization of Daniel and Esther and for how the text presents ethnicity to its audience.

#### 3.2.2. *Audience – Esther*

As is consistent with both our rhetorical and sociolinguistic methodology, we begin each section with a discussion of the audience of the text. Esther cannot have been written any earlier than Xerxes' reign, ending in 465 BCE.[27] As Bush notes, 1:1, 13–14, 19, 4:11, et al., indicate some degree of elapsed time:[28] while the text itself seems familiar with many

---

26. Edelman, 'Ethnicity and Early Israel', 25ff. However, she also points out that archaeological evidence in this period likewise falls short (54).

27. Ahasuerus is simply the Hebrew equivalent of Persian, Xšayāršā. See Frederic Bush, *Ruth/Esther*, WBC 9 (Nashville: Thomas Nelson, 1996), 345.

28. Bush, *Ruth/Esther*, 295.

Persian customs,[29] it often assumes that its readers are not.[30] Therefore, a composition at a time near to the setting seems unlikely. Moreover, there are historical difficulties, which also might imply distance from the time period, like the known absence of Xerxes on campaign during key events of the book.[31] Some version of Esther was known to Josephus in the first century CE.[32] Likewise, the story is known to Clement, in a similar time period, and he expects the story to be known to the recipients of his letter, a Christian audience in Corinth.[33] It is safe to assume, then, that it was widespread by this point. The translation of the Septuagint and other versions provides a possible, earlier *terminus ante quem*:[34] the colophon, if trustworthy, dates the translation to the first century BCE at the latest.[35] It is true that 2 Macc 15:36 refers to the day of Mordechai,[36] but Moore is correct that this does not necessitate the existence of the book of Esther.[37] On the basis of all of this, the text of Esther appears to have been written either in the late Persian or Hellenistic period.[38]

---

29. Cf. Carey Moore, *Esther*, AB 7B (New Haven: Yale University Press, 1971), xli; Shemaryahu Talmon, '"Wisdom" in the Book of Esther', *VT* 13 (1963): 419–55 (422).

30. E.g. Esth 1:13; 3:7; 4:11.

31. Moore, *Esther*, xlv–xlvi.

32. Josephus, *Antiquities* XI 6.

33. 1 Clem 55:6.

34. Thus, Elias Bickerman, 'The Colophon of the Greek Book of Esther', *JBL* 63 (1944): 339–62; Karen Jobes, *The Alpha-Text of Esther: Its Character and Relationship to the Masoretic Text*, SBLDS 153 (Atlanta: Scholars Press, 1996), 171–72, 226ff.; Kristin de Troyer, *The End of the Alpha Text: Translation and Narrative Technique in MT 8:1–17, LXX 8:1–17, and AT 7:14–41*, Septuagint and Cognate Studies 48 (Atlanta: SBL, 2000), 398; Moore, *Esther*, lviii.

35. Ibid., 112–13.

36. Cf. Hans Bardtke, 'Esther', in Hans Bardtke and Hans Hertzberg, *Der Prediger. Das Buch Esther*, KAT (Berlin: Evangelische Verlagsanstalt Berlin, 1972), 239–408 (253).

37. Moore, *Esther*, lxiii.

38. Some have tried to be more precise. Levenson suggests that the book is likely written before the Seleucid persecution and the Hasmonaean rebellion, because, he suggests, it presents a relatively positive view of the king. However, more negative views of the king are also possible, that he is a comically incompetent ruler, given to too much wine and easily swayed by his advisers. We would also need to explain why a negative view of a Greek king would require the text to look unfavourably on a Persian king from the past, rather than with nostalgia. Jon Levenson, *Esther*, OTL (Louisville: Westminster John Knox, 1997), 23–27, especially 26.

As for the audience's characteristics, we can presume that they understood Hebrew. Moreover, the text seems to assume a basic familiarity with other biblical literature: for example, parallels with the Joseph story are plain and necessary to understand Esther properly.[39] Other potentially obscure references are to Agag, the king of the Amalekites, and to Mordecai and Esther's own ancestors, Shimei and Kish, who are all known from 1 Samuel.[40] Therefore it is fair to presume that the audience of the book is Jewish, with some minimal knowledge, at least, of the narrative that the Hebrew Bible ascribes to their history. Nonetheless, the text is not given to particular religiosity – as is well-known, there is no mention of God in the Masoretic version of the book, nor is there any praying or reference to biblical law. On the other hand, certain cultural practices are certainly present in the narrative: fasting and the use of sackcloth are both used as means of mourning, with little explanation of their purpose. Rather, the audience is supposed to understand. Therefore, while the text presumes a particular ethnic or national background and familiarity with important Hebrew literature, it may not necessarily presume adherence to a form of Hebrew religion.

Since the book dates to either the Persian or Hellenistic period, its audience is one that lives as one nation among many under a single empire. The text's concern for the status of its audience among so many nations is clear, foremost, in that the book's main crisis is the threat of other nations destroying the Jews. In this way, the text involves its audience in the text, depicting them as directly involved (Esth 3:6, 13; 4:3, 16, et al.). As such, the text directly comments on the interests of its audience, by using the Jews in the story as a proxy for them: a primary concern, then, of the audience is survival in the context of empire.

*3.2.3. Audience – Daniel*

It is agreed by most commentators that the final form of Daniel belongs to the second century BCE.[41] Even for those of the minority view, the book

---

39. Cf. Gillis Gerleman, *Esther*, BKAT (Neukirchen-Vluyn: Neukirchener Verlag, 1979), 11–23; Ludwig Rosenthal, 'Die Josephsgeschichte, mit den Büchern Ester und Daniel verglichen', *ZAW* 15 (1895): 278–84.

40. Yitzhak Berger, 'Esther and Benjaminite Royalty: A Study in Inner-Biblical Allusion', *JBL* 129 (2010): 625–44; Bush, *Ruth/Esther*, 362.

41. Dieter Bauer, *Das Buch Daniel*, Neuer Stuttgarter Kommentar Altes Testament (Stuttgart: Katholisches Bibelwerk, 1996), 27–29; Collins, *Daniel*, 38; Goldingay, *Daniel*, 328–29; Hartman and Di Lella, *Daniel*, 42; Newsom, *Daniel*, 215; Otto Plöger, *Das Buch Daniel*, KAT (Gütersloh: Gütersloher Verlagshaus Gerd Mohn, 1965), 28–30.

in its final form is particularly aimed towards those in Jerusalem who would live through the Antiochene crisis of 167–164 BCE,[42] and so this is our starting point for discussing the audience. The picture painted by the books of Maccabees suggests a Judaean population, oppressed.[43] Some of the population has accepted, or even promoted, the religious interventions of Antiochus IV.[44] However there is also a segment of the population that resists their imperial overlords.[45] Josephus presents the same basic picture of multiple attitudes among the populace towards their overlords.[46] Some scholars have connected the writers of Daniel with the anti-Antiochus party, the *ḥăsîdîm*, sometimes connecting them also with the *maśkîlîm* of Daniel (Dan 1:4; [1:17]; [7:8]; [9:13, 22, 25]; 11:33, 35; 12:3, 10).[47]

It can be, by no means, certain that the *ḥăsîdîm* and the *maśkîlîm* are the same: although Maccabees presents the populace as falling into just two categories, that may just be a simplification. It would not be surprising if the *maśkîlîm* represented a third position, unrelated to the *ḥăsîdîm*, and more pacifist.[48] Of this group, we could still observe several things. Firstly, they seem to be a subset of conservative Jews.[49] Secondly, as Gardner argues, they may be described with priestly and royal overtones.[50] At the least, it is justified to observe that the *maśkîlîm* fulfil both leading (royal) and teaching (priestly) functions in Daniel. Moreover, the designation *maśkîlîm* implies that they are educated, which in turn implies high social status.[51]

42. Lucas, *Daniel*, 312.
43. 1 Macc 1:20–61.
44. 1 Macc 2:23; 2 Macc 4:7–15.
45. 1 Macc 1:62–63; 2:1–22, 42–48.
46. Josephus, *Antiquities* XII 3–9; *War* I 1.
47. Bauer, *Daniel*, 214; Collins, *Daniel*, 137, 385; Goldingay, *Daniel*, 279, 302–304; Hartman and Di Lella, *Daniel*, 43–45; Martin Hengel, *Judaism and Hellenism: Studies in their Encounter in Palestine during the Early Hellenistic Period* (Eugene: Wipf & Stock, 1974), 175–80; Newsom, *Daniel*, 22–23, 351–53; Otto Plöger, *Theocracy and Eschatology*, trans. S. Rudman (Oxford: Blackwell, 1968), 17–18. For a careful consideration of the precise referents of the term *maśkîlîm*, see Anne Gardner, 'שׂכל in the Hebrew Bible: Key to the Identity and Function of the Maskilim in Daniel', *RB* 118 (2008): 496–514.
48. John Collins, *The Apocalyptic Imagination: An Introduction to Jewish Apocalyptic Literature*, 3rd ed. (Grand Rapids: Eerdmans, 2016), 139; Philip Davies, 'Ḥasidim in the Maccabean Period', *JJS* 28 (1977): 127–40, especially 130–31.
49. Goldingay, *Daniel*, 279.
50. Gardner, 'שׂכל in the Hebrew Bible', 507–14.
51. Cf. Collins, *Daniel*, 69–70; Lucas, *Daniel*, 287.

In Daniel, alongside the *maśkîlîm*, we can also find the group, the *rabbîm*, the 'many' (Dan 9:27; chs. 11 and 12, *passim*; perhaps also 7:10).[52] However, the relationship between the *maśkîlîm* and the *rabbîm* differs from that between the two groups of people presented by the books of Maccabees: whereas the relationship between the *ḥăsîdîm* and the rest was an adversarial one in Maccabees, the *rabbîm* are presented more positively, as those faithful lay Jews who are led and taught by the *maśkîlîm*.[53] If we glimpse the final shapers of Daniel in the *maśkîlîm*, then it stands to reason that we see the intended audience of the final form of the text in the *rabbîm*.[54] As Goldingay suggests, the designation *rabbîm*, itself, implies a widespread following for the *maśkîlîm*.[55] The text assumes its audience is large.

However, while the relevance of the *maśkîlîm–rabbîm* distinction is clear for the visions of the second half of the book, it poses some difficulties for the stories of the first half, with which we will be mostly concerned. It is often agreed that these stories derive from an earlier time.[56] However, we must still come to an understanding of why these stories were included in a book collated for a second-century audience of faithful lay Jews and what they might mean to such an audience. Unlike in the visions, where direct references to the *rabbîm* occur, there is no obvious set of characters, which corresponds to the lay population of the Jews: Daniel and his colleagues are presented as exceptional cases, who do *not* live in a community of Jews. However – although it is no longer taken for granted that these stories are optimistic about life under empire, as we shall explore below – the situation presented by the stories is perhaps less hostile than the one experienced by its audience.

Nonetheless, there are similarities to be found in the situation of the Antiochene crisis and what is described in Dan 1–6. The books of Maccabees and also Josephus, likely drawing on them, depict the resistance to imperial orders to defile oneself religiously as the central point of conflict around which the crisis grew.[57] Conflicts of this kind occur in Dan 1, 3 and 6. It appears that Daniel and his colleagues function

---

52. Cf. Hartman and Di Lella, *Daniel*, 271, 299–300.

53. Ibid., 271, 305.

54. Perhaps it might be possible to suggest that the *maśkîlîm* are writing for themselves. However, the analogy of teacher–student relationship to author–audience make the *rabbîm* a better candidate for the audience.

55. Goldingay, *Daniel*, 303.

56. Collins, *Daniel*, 38; Goldingay, *Daniel*, 328; Lucas, *Daniel*, 313; Newsom, *Daniel*, 9.

57. Josephus, *Antiquities* XII 4; 1 Macc 2:1–22.

as exemplars in these stories, rejecting defilement just like the *ḥăsîdîm*. In this way, Daniel and his colleagues represent both the *maśkîlîm* and the *rabbîm* in the first six chapters: they are the *maśkîlîm*, identified as such in Dan 1:4, who stand for religious integrity. However, they are also characters that the *rabbîm* are to emulate.

We can also, perhaps, relate the first six chapters to the visions as a kind of statement of qualifications:[58] Daniel, who is presented as the origin of the visions, is shown to be qualified to comment on the Antiochene situation, because he successfully negotiated comparable situations in chs. 1, 3 and 6 and because he proves himself an able interpreter of visions, the recipient of insight from God.

In summary, the audience of Daniel should be considered a group of Jews under imperial dominance. Like in Esther, there is a threat to these people from elements within the empire. However, unlike Esther, Daniel specifically directs itself towards those it considers faithful Jews.

### 3.2.4. Loanwords in Esther and Daniel

#### 3.2.4.1. Setting – דָּת, 'law', a case study

Although we will see that the loanwords do more than just establish the setting, it is clear that the setting is a key component of their purpose. In Esther, apart from any pattern to the distribution of the loanwords within different parts of the book, the starkest feature of their use is the comparative prevalence of words that are Persian in origin. The prevalence of these words is unsurprising given the setting of the text. Another feature of particular note among the loanwords in Esther is the prominence of דָּת, 'law', in the text. This word provides us with an appropriate case study for the way in which the text is able to use loanwords to depict a particular setting.

The use of the loanword דָּת in Esther is to the exclusion of the more common Hebrew, תּוֹרָה. It is, however, not the only word of this semantic domain found in Esther: מִצְוָה, דָּבָר, מַאֲמַר and פִּתְגָם.[59] Nevertheless, דָּת is the most frequent. It covers a wide semantic range, including the king's

---

58. Cf. Matthias Henze, 'The Narrative Frame of Daniel: A Literary Assessment', *JSJ* 32 (2001): 6–24 (6).

59. In Esther the words are found as follows: מִצְוָה in 3:3; דָּבָר in 1:12, 19; 2:8; 3:15; 4:3; 8:14, 17 and 9:1; מַאֲמַר in 1:15; 2:20; 9:32; and פִּתְגָם in 1:20. The word דָּת has a wide semantic range, as we shall see. However, each meaning can be met by an appropriate substitute. The definition of a verbal command is paralleled by מַאֲמַר (e.g. Esth 1:15). The abstract sense of the law can be covered by מִצְוָה – Koehler and Baumgartner offer as one of its definitions that it refers to a '(set of all the) commandments' (e.g. Deut 4:40; Ps 119:115; Ezra 7:11). Physical copies of a law

command (e.g. 2:8); a more abstract sense of law (e.g. 1:15); and perhaps even a physical copy of a law (8:17). In general, דָּת, which is also attested once in Ezra 8:36, refers to Persian law, but not exclusively so:

> Then Haman said to King Ahasuerus, 'There is a certain people scattered and separated among the peoples in all the provinces of your kingdom; their laws (דָּתֵיהֶם) are different from those of every other people and they do not keep the king's laws, so that it is not appropriate for the king to tolerate them'. (Esth 3:8)

Fountain understands this case as Haman slighting the Jews.[60] However, the exception could perhaps be better explained by understanding that Haman is levelling a charge of insurrection against the Jews – דָּת is administered by the Persian king alone and so if the Jews have another source of דָּת it is an expression of rebellion against the Persian administration. In Biblical Aramaic, however, the word is regularly used to refer to both Persian law and God's law.[61] In wider Aramaic, too, the word has a broad range of meaning, even including senses of the word beyond its normal legal associations – faith, limit.[62] In Esther, then there is no reason to assume that the word is necessarily limited to just Persian law.

On the other hand, the sense of the word suggested by the Hebrew witnesses is borne out in examination of the Old Persian prototype of דָּת, *dāta*: it can stand as a metonym for the king's rule,[63] or also of the divine law of Ahuramazda.[64] It is not clear in these cases whether law is meant in an abstract or concrete sense and the poor attestation of Old Persian does not allow us to speculate further. However, as far as the word is attested in Old Persian, *dāta*, is strongly associated with the (divinely authorized) rule of the king. While it is true that divinely authorized kingship is a major theme of the Achaemenid inscriptions – so there is some degree of selection bias here – it nonetheless demonstrates the conceptual connection between דָּת and the king's rule.

Therefore, we are faced with a choice in how to evaluate the Hebrew evidence. On the one hand it is possible that the Hebrew evidence is in fact

---

could be covered by פַּתְשֶׁגֶן (e.g. Esth 3:14) or מִשְׁנֶה (e.g. Deut 17:18). *HALOT*, s.vv. 'פַּתְשֶׁגֶן', 'מִשְׁנֶה', 'מִצְוָה', 'מַאֲמַר'.

60. A. Kay Fountain, *Literary and Empirical Readings of the Book of Esther*, Studies in Biblical Literature 43 (New York: Lang, 2002), 140.
61. E.g. Ezra 7:12; Dan 6:5.
62. *Comprehensive Aramaic Lexicon*, s.v. 'dt'.
63. DNa 21, DB 1.23, DSe 20, 37, XPh 18.
64. XPh 49, 52.

representative of the word's use in Hebrew at one stage of the language. If this is the case, there may have been semantic narrowing on the word's entry to Hebrew, explaining why it is used predominately to refer to Persian law. However, the case of Esth 3:8 would remain unexplained. Therefore, and further on the basis of the Aramaic evidence, it is more probable that the Hebrew evidence attests to a non-representative subsection of the word's use. It is thus better to assume that the Hebrew word דָּת could be used more broadly than just for Persian laws. The apparent preference to use the word to refer to Persian law is simply a reflection of the fact that Esther rarely refers to laws other than Persian laws. In that case, then, we must still explain the prevalence of דָּת to mean law instead of other native options.

The text is not compelled to use the word דָּת. As we have pointed out, there is a wide range of words that could be used in its place and at times are.[65] Nor, despite first appearances, does it have particular denotative force that must be considered. Rather it is the connotative, pragmatic value that is unique about the word, when compared to the other options – the word is unique among the possible words for law because it is a word of Persian origin, which therefore carries with it the connotative value of that setting. In that way also, the prevalence of other Persian words in sections of Esther works to depict a particular setting.

### 3.2.4.2. Distribution of loanwords in Esther

However, we can say more about the loanwords in Esther than just that they reflect the setting of the text. In order to consider the effect of loanwords on the text, we have examined their distribution across different sections of the text, using the divisions found in Bush's commentary.[66] Other divisions could slightly affect the results, if one loanword were shifted from one section to another or if sections differ drastically in the level of homogeneity. However, as an indication of trends in the text, rather than absolutes, such differences are of less importance – in the case of Esther, we are not concerned with particular sections being totally devoid of loanwords but rather we are interested in the general trends of greater or lesser prevalence.[67]

---

65. As discussed previously: פִּתְשֶׁגֶן, מִצְוָה, מַאֲמָר or מִשְׁנֶה cover the different senses of the word. *HALOT*, s.vv. 'מַאֲמַר', 'מִצְוָה', 'מִשְׁנֶה' and 'פַּתְשֶׁגֶן'.

66. Bush, *Ruth/Esther*, 336–37.

67. This will be different in other texts we examine. For example, in Exodus' description of the tabernacle we are interested in the way the text describes individual objects. As such, there is a more concrete way to divide the text, such that sections with no loanwords are significant.

In looking at the distribution, it is clear that the setting is an insufficient explanation for the use of loanwords in Esther – while the whole of Esther is set in Persia, the distribution of Iranian loanwords is uneven and Akkadian loanwords are just as common. On the other hand, that insufficiency does not imply that the setting is not a central part of the explanation. Rather, it is the setting alongside other factors.

For the sake of counting the distribution, I have excluded some words, on the grounds that they are borrowed early or show evidence of high nativization. These words are כִּסֵּא, יַיִן, חֹתָם and סוּס. I have also excluded יְקָר,[68] כְּתָב,[69] and דָּר,[70] due to the level of uncertainty over their origin.

68. Kautzsch and Wagner suggest that יְקָר is a loan from Aramaic based on its vocalic pattern. Kautzsch, *Die Aramaismen*, 38–39; Wagner, *Die Aramaismen*, 62–63. However, this is a less reliable criterion than phonetic equivalences. There is a basic point to be made, which is that the rarity of a vocalic pattern in Hebrew need not imply that that vocalic pattern is not genuinely Hebrew. On the other hand, it is true that this pattern cannot be constructed out of known Semitic morphological patterns and that Proto-Semitic *qatāl* must be represented in Hebrew as *qātōl*, following the regular rules. Hans Bauer and Pontus Leander, *Historische Grammatik der Herbräischen Sprache des Alten Testaments* (Halle a. S.: Max Niemeyer, 1922), 469–70; Fox, *Semitic Noun Patterns*, 183–85. Nonetheless, the same principle applies: the rarity of the pattern does not need to imply that it is not genuine. Moreover, we must contend with another possibility, which is that words of this pattern, while more recently invented in Hebrew, are not necessarily derived from another language. Kautzsch suggests that there is a possibility that this word, along with שְׁאָר, 'remainder', both go back to a genuinely Hebrew noun-form. Kautzsch, *Die Aramaismen*, 38. Along similar lines, we might consider the possibility that this word-form could be dialectal, rather than a strict loanword from Aramaic. Alternatively, Wagner suggests that Hebrew borrowed the noun-form from Aramaic, as a productive noun-form. Wagner, *Die Aramaismen*, 122. He suggests that it is borrowed from Aramaic. It is also possible that it has been formed of analogy from the forms *$q^etīl$ and *$q^etūl$, which appear to contain native Hebrew words (for $q^etīl$ see Fox, *Semitic Noun Patterns*, 193–94. For $q^etūl$, cf. גְּבוּל, 'boundary' or יְבוּל, 'produce' and others). If that is the case, words of such a form could easily be formed natively within the Hebrew system at any point after it borrowed the vocalic pattern. Such forms would not necessarily be felt as foreign, on comparison with native words like גְּדוּד, 'troop', which share a similar syllabic structure. That יְקָר is a loan from Aramaic is certainly possible. However, it is also plausible that it is a native form.

69. Kautzsch and Wagner suggest that כְּתָב is an Aramaism on the same grounds as יְקָר, namely its apparently Aramaic vocalization. Kautzsch, *Die Aramaismen*, 45; Wagner, *Die Aramaismen*, 69. As such, the same details for the discussion apply and the same degree of doubt.

70. For details, see 2.3, 'The loanwords in Esther'.

## 3. Text Analysis

**Table 1** The Distribution of the Loanwords in the Book of Esther

| Division of Text (Bush) | Title[71] | Loanwords | Loanwords/ Words [Iranian][72] (Akkadian)[73] | Percentage [Iranian] (Akkadian) | Foreign Proper Nouns/Words (percentage) | Proper nouns and Loanwords/Words (percentage) |
|---|---|---|---|---|---|---|
| 1:1–22 | Deposal of Vashti | Many, varied origin | 19/371 [9/371] (7/371) | 5.12 [2.43] (1.89) | 44/371 (11.86) | 63/371 (16.98) |
| 2:1–18 | Esther Becomes Queen | Some, varied origin | 13/369 [3/369] (7/369) | 3.52 [0.81] (1.90) | 29/369 (7.86) | 42/369 (11.38) |
| 2:19–23 | Mordecai uncovers a plot | One, Akkadian | 1/69 [0/69] (1/69) | 1.45 [0] (1.45) | 13/69 (18.84) | 14/69 (20.29) |
| 3:1–6 | Haman decides to annihilate the Jews | None | 0/107 [0/107] (0/107) | 0 [0] (0) | 17/107 (15.89) | 17/107 (15.89) |
| 3:7–15 | Haman sets his plot in motion | Many, varied origin | 15/196 [7/196] (6/196) | 7.65 [3.57] (3.06) | 13/196 (6.63) | 28/196 (14.29) |
| 4:1–3 | The Jews lament | Some, varied origin | 3/52 [1/52] (2/52) | 5.76 [1.92] (3.85) | 2/52 (3.85) | 5/52 (9.62) |
| 4:4–17 | Esther agrees to appeal to the king | Some, mostly Persian | 8/233 [5/233] (3/233) | 3.43 [2.15] (1.29) | 26/233 (11.16) | 34/233 (14.59) |
| 5:1–5a | Esther sets up her first banquet | Some, Akkadian | 2/86 [0/86] (2/86) | 2.33 [0] (2.33) | 8/86 (9.30) | 10/86 (11.63) |
| 5:5b–8 | Esther sets up the second banquet | None | 0/55 [0/55] (0/55) | 0 [0] (0) | 5/55 (9.09) | 5/55 (9.09) |

71. Adapted from Bush, *Ruth/Esther*, 336–37.
72. I have counted פִּלֶגֶשׁ as a loan but not Iranian, because its precise origin is unknown.
73. For this count, I have considered אֲבַדָּן as a loan from Aramaic rather than Akkadian.

| | | | | | | |
|---|---|---|---|---|---|---|
| 5:9–14 | Haman is persuaded to hang Mordecai | None | 0/124 [0/124] (0/124) | 0 [0] (0) | 14/124 (11.29) | 14/124 (11.29) |
| 6:1–11 | Haman made to honour Mordecai | Some, varied origin | 3/206 [2/206] (1/206) | 1.46 [0.97] (0.49) | 15/206 (7.28) | 18/206 (8.74) |
| 6:12–14 | Haman's wife and friends predict his downfall | One, Akkadian | 1/57 [0/57] (1/57) | 1.75 [0] (1.75) | 8/57 (14.04) | 9/57 (15.79) |
| 7:1–10 | Esther pleads with the king | Few, Akkadian | 3/187 [0/187] (3/187) | 1.60 [0] (1.60) | 21/187 (11.23) | 24/187 (12.83) |
| 8:1–8 | Esther and Mordecai win authority to counteract Haman's edict | Few, varied origin | 5/162 [0/162] (1/162) | 3.09 [0] (0.06) | 23/162 (14.20) | 28/162 (17.28) |
| 8:9–17 | Mordecai issues a counterdecree | Many, half of which are Persian | 15/181 [8/181] (5/181) | 8.29 [4.42] (2.76) | 8/181 (4.42) | 23/181 (12.71) |
| 9:1–5 | The Jews put their enemies to the sword | Some, varied origin | 5/94 [2/94] (2/94) | 5.32 [2.13] (2.13) | 4/94 (4.26) | 9/94 (9.57) |
| 9:6–19 | The aetiology of Purim | Some, mostly Akkadian | 8/209 [2/209] (6/209) | 3.83 [0.96] (2.87) | 25/209 (11.96) | 33/209 (15.79) |
| 9:20–32 | The festival of Purim is set up | Some, mostly Akkadian | 12/242 [2/242] (10/242) | 4.96 [0.83] (4.13) | 12/242 (4.96) | 24/242 (9.92) |
| 10:1–3 | Epilogue | None | 0/46 [0/46] (0/46) | 0 [0] (0) | 7/46 (15.22) | 7/46 (15.22) |
| Total | | | 113/3046 [41/3046] (57/3046) | 3.71 [1.35] (1.87) | 294/3046 (9.65) | 407/3046 (13.36) |

In considering the distribution we first notice that the vast majority of loanwords are from either Iranian or Akkadian sources. In particular, the degree to which Iranian words are found here is much higher than elsewhere in the Bible.[74] The first chapter has a high proportion of loan-

---

74. Although precise statistics are difficult to find, if we consider the words identified in works that identify Persian loanwords, few are found outside of Esther,

words from a variety of sources. The other sections that contain high numbers of loanwords are 3:7–15 and 8:9–17. These sections contain a high proportion of Iranian loanwords and are similar to one another in vocabulary and topic – both involve sending letters through the Persian empire. Several scholars identify a concentric structure in Esther, in which the first half of the text sets up events that are reversed in the second half.[75] In such a scheme, these two episodes correspond to one another such that their use of similar vocabulary is unsurprising.

In addition we note three lists of minor characters, whose names – while not loanwords in the strict sense – nonetheless create a similar effect; the lists are found in Esth 1:10 (7 names), 1:14 (7 names) and 9:7–9 (10 names).[76] If we take these into account, we find that ch. 1 and the aetiology of Purim in 9:6–19, which are already relatively rich in loanwords, become more so to the point that they are just as full of foreign terminology as 3:7–15 and 8:9–17. To some extent, it is possible to explain these names as part of the setting, especially those that appear in ch. 1. However, it is more difficult to explain the names in Esth 9 in this way: the setting is well-established at that point; returning to foreign names at this point (having left them behind through the course of the book with no change in the setting) would require more explanation. On the other hand, it is possible to see this correspondence as part of the aforementioned concentric structure: the appearance of a list of Persian nobles at the end of Esther puts the reader in mind of the nobles from ch. 1.

When, however, we consider the full extent of the foreign proper nouns in Esther, we notice that these foreign proper nouns are far more common than loanwords in Esther. Largely this is owing to the fact that every character in the narrative is primarily referred to by foreign names. In particular, 2:19–23 and 8:1–8 stand out as of high concentration. It is especially interesting to notice that in several sections in which the loanwords are most predominant, the foreign names are much less concentrated. One wonders whether this occurs because loanwords and foreign names are used for similar purposes: as one takes more of the role, the other is less necessary. However – with the exception of Esther, who

---

Daniel or Ezra–Nehemiah. Cf. Ellenbogen, *Foreign Words*; Hinz, *Altiranisches Sprachgut*; Scheftelowitz, *Arisches im Alten Testament*; Tavernier, *Iranica in the Achaemenid Period*.

75. E.g. Joyce Baldwin, *Esther*, Tyndale Old Testament Commentaries (Leicester: Inter-Varsity, 1984), 29–33; David Clines, *The Esther Scroll*, JSOTSup 30 (Sheffield: JSOT Press, 1984), 26–30; Michael Fox, *Character and Ideology in the Book of Esther* (Eugene: Wipf & Stock, 2010), 156–57; Levenson, *Esther*, 5–12.

76. Cf. Gehman, 'Notes on the Persian Words'.

has an alternative Hebrew name, Xerxes, who can be referred to as 'the king' – there are generally no alternatives to these names, because they belong to characters that belong to their setting. If that is the case it is more difficult to make a case that these names represent genuine choices of the text. In terms of the overall inundation of the reader in foreign vocabulary they are clearly quite relevant: one in eight words is either a loanword or a foreign name. Although each occurrence of these names is not necessarily optional for the text, they still flow from the text's choice of setting. In addition, the use of foreign names in lists implies a degree of choice: for example, the list in 1:10 could have equally been represented as הַסָּרִיסִים.

In addition to the above observations, we still must explain why Akkadian loanwords are used as much as Persian throughout. While the Persian loanwords contribute to the setting, it is not immediately clear what purpose the Akkadian words might serve. We should note that with respect to the setting, the use of loanwords resembles Esther and Mordecai's use of foreign names in public. In Esther, despite the Persian setting, not only do the Jewish protagonists have apparently Babylonian names, Mordecai and Esther, the Babylonian name, Esther, is used in place of the Hebrew name Hadassah, apparently as a public name in Persian society (Esth 2:7). The incongruity of the Babylonian names with the Persian setting may be secondary for our concerns; rather, the main effect may be to develop a contrast between (internal) Jewish ethnic identity and the otherness of the society which these characters (externally) inhabit. In the same way then, we could note that the major effect of the loanwords is to communicate a difference between the Jewish protagonists and their foreign rivals, without always being concerned with which foreign nationality it is.[77]

---

77. Another approach could be diachronic – there is a stream of scholarship that has viewed Esther as a historicized Babylonian myth, based on the triumph of Marduk and Ishtar over the Elamite deities, Humban and Mashti (see the summary in Moore, *Esther*, xlvi–xlix.) If the text had origins in the Akkadosphere, the presence of Akkadian loanwords would be unsurprising. Nevertheless, the lack of any concrete Babylonian prototype for the book of Esther as we have it makes it difficult to evaluate the claim that any of Esther's vocabulary might derive from such a hypothetical text. Moreover, such hypotheses would function poorly in Daniel, where there is a mix of Persian, Akkadian and Greek loanwords but no suggestion that the text was first written in those languages. Our first suggestion, then, that the effect of the text is to distinguish between Jewish and other, is so far a better conclusion. As we analyze Daniel, then, and afterwards return to Esther, we shall pay attention to other effects that unite Esther and Daniel in their use of loanwords.

### 3.2.4.3. *Distribution of loanwords in Daniel*

As it was for Esther, again it is necessary to make some divisions to analyze the distribution of the loanwords in Daniel. I have essentially followed the chapter divisions, since in the case of Daniel the chapters correspond to narrative units. Only in the case of ch. 9 have I separated the chapter, due to the different content of the two halves of the chapter.

As I have suggested above, הֵיכָל, חָתַם, יַיִן, כָּרְסֵא, קֶרֶן and תּוֹר are early loans, nativized to the extent that we cannot assume that they had any significant rhetorical effect. In the case of יַיִן this has little effect, since it only occurs four times in Daniel. Similarly, כָּרְסֵא is only used three times and so also תּוֹר. הֵיכָל appears more frequently. Its seven mentions occur across the first six chapters and do not greatly change the overall distribution of loanwords. חָתַם occurs five times and several of them are in sections which otherwise contain few or no loanwords. Nonetheless, it is not a large enough change to make a very significant difference. However, in the case of קֶרֶן it does make a significant difference because it is very common in chs. 7 and 8: it occurs ten times in ch. 7 and nine in ch. 8. In ch. 8 it is the only loanword in the chapter and in ch. 7 it vastly changes the concentration of the loanwords, though there are still some left.

In addition, there are several words which have been discounted, which others have believed to be loanwords:

בַּדִּים,[78]
כְּתָב,[79]
כֶּתֶם,[80]

---

78. Although Grintz suggested that this word might relate to Egyptian *bḏ ꜣ*, 'linen splint, mast', Noonan is right that the semantics of *bḏ ꜣ* connect much better to בַּדִּים, 'poles', a homonym of our current lexeme. More recently, however, Noonan suggests that *bḏ ꜣ* is the source of both homonyms, agreeing with Grintz that the word is used also to refer to linen. However, in the cited forms it is unclear that the word means linens: in the Edwin Smith Surgical Papyrus, 5.13, 5.20, 8.21, *bḏ ꜣ* is qualified by nj ḥbs, 'of linen', suggesting that the word itself means a splint and can be specified to be one of linen, if necessary; in the cited cases in the Coffin Texts, 'mast' is appropriate. (cf. Raymond Faulkner, *The Ancient Egyptian Coffin Texts*, 3 vols. [Warminster: Aris & Phillips, 1977], 2:111, 121.) Therefore, since it is unlikely that *bḏ ꜣ* meant 'linen' by itself, it is implausible that it could be the source of a Hebrew word meaning linen. Grintz, 'Archaic Terminology', 13–15; Noonan, 'Foreign Loanwords', 109–10; Noonan, *Non-Semitic Loanwords*, 72–73.

79. As we have discussed at 3.2.4.2, 'Distribution of Loanwords in Esther', it is doubtful whether or not this word is to be considered a loanword.

80. Many scholars derive כֶּתֶם from Akkadian *kutimmu*, 'goldsmith', and prior from Sumerian *lu kugdim*, 'goldsmith'. Landesdorfer, *Sumerisches Sprachgut*, 47;

מוּם,⁸¹
נְדָנֶה.⁸²

With these words excluded, the distribution is as follows.

Lipiński, 'Emprunts Suméro-akkadiens', 68; Rabin, 'Foreign Words', 1073; Zimmern, *Akkadische Fremdwörter*, 27. Because of Egyptian *ktm*, 'a kind of gold', Ellenbogen and Noonan hypothesize an African source. Ellenbogen, *Foreign Words*, 95; Noonan, 'Foreign Loanwords', 60–62. For the Egyptian word, see *CDD* 20, s.v. 'ktm'; Erichsen, *Demotisches Glossar*, s.v. 'ktm'; Erman and Grapow, *Wörterbuch*, s.v. 'ktm.t'; *Thesaurus Linguae Aegyptiae*, s.v. 'ktm.t'. Similarly, Rubin and Mankowski suggest the following: Sumerian > Akkadian > Egyptian > Hebrew. Mankowski, *Akkadian Loanwords*, 76–77; Rubin, 'Sumerian Loanwords', 665. Indeed, as Hoch points out the Egyptian is most likely a loan, since it is written in group writing. Naturally, this could indicate a loan from an African source or from Akkadian. However, given the widespread Semitic forms, as detailed by Hoch, including Phoenician and Old South Arabic, the simplest explanation is that this word derives from a Semitic root, KTM, pertaining to goldsmithing (producing words for both 'goldsmith' and the type of gold they produce) from where it was loaned into both Egyptian and Sumerian. James Hoch, *Semitic Words in Egyptian Texts of the New Kingdom and Third Intermediate Period* (Princeton: Princeton University, 1994), 10, 338.

81. Vernes and Brown both note the similarity of Hebrew מוּם or מאוּם to Greek μῶμος, 'fault'. Brown, *Israel and Hellas*, 1:232; Vernes, *Les Emprunts de la Bible*, 84–85. Brown, however, is not optimistic that the word is in fact a loan, merely noticing the possibility. While Vernes attributed the word to a Greek loan, Brown considers it a 'Mediterranean' word, a word belonging to a substrate language in the Mediterranean. See also Collins, *Daniel*, 127, who notices that the Greek translates מאוּם as μῶμος, suggesting that it 'plays on the sound'. The loan is possible, since the correspondence is good phonetically and semantically. Moreover, the Hebrew word מוּם is unusual insofar as, if it were considered a native word, it would appear to derive from a root structure that is atypical – the first and third consonant are identical. Cf. Greenberg, 'The Patterning of Root Morphemes in Semitic', 162–81. Nevertheless, the alternative spelling מאוּם suggests that it is possible to reconstruct the root as *מוא, which then produced a reduplicated root, *מואמוא. Assuming the loss of the final vowels, this root would produce a noun with the consonants מאם. The remnant of the *waw* continues in the *šureq*. With this reconstruction, then, we can draw parallels to other Semitic forms, like Akkadian *mā'um*, 'excrement', and the Syriac root, ܡܐܡܝ, *mwmy*, 'to be reviled', which attests to the reduplicated form more clearly. *CAD* 10, s.v. 'mā'u'; *Comprehensive Aramaic Lexicon*, s.v. 'mwmy'.

82. The word נָדָן, 'sheath', as it is found in 1 Chr 21:27, and also נְדָנֶה, recognized by some as a version of the same word, here in Daniel, is thought to be a Persian loanword by several scholars, on the basis of Avestan, *nidāna*, 'sheath'. Scheftelowitz, 'Zur Kritik, IV', 310–11; Tisdall, 'The Āryan Words, III', 367–68; Wagner, *Die Aramaismen*, 81; Wilson, 'Foreign Words', 215; Wilson-Wright, 'From Persepolis to Jerusalem', 156. While it is plausible that נָדָן is a loanword, the meaning 'sheath' barely

**Table 2** The Distribution of the Loanwords in the Book of Daniel

| Division of Text | Title | Setting | Language | Loanwords/Total words [Iranian][83] (Akkadian) | Percentage [Iranian] (Akkadian) | Foreign Proper Nouns | Proper nouns and Loanwords/Words (percentage) |
|---|---|---|---|---|---|---|---|
| Dan 1 | Court Tale 1: The royal food | Babylonian Empire | Hebrew | 19/306 [6/306] (10/306) | 6.21 [1.96] (3.27) | 10 | 29/306 (9.48) |
| Dan 2 | Court Tale 2: The king's dream | Babylonian Empire | Mostly Aramaic[84] | 38/843 [16/843] (4/843) | 4.51[85] [1.90] (0.47) | 24 | 62/843 (7.35) |

fits the context here in Daniel. It is better, then, to either treat the words as separate homophonous entities or follow the emendation, בְּגוֹן דְּנָה, 'on account of this'. Cf. *HALOT*, s.v. 'נִדְנֶה'. Several commentaries point out that an equivalent phrase to what is found here in Dan 7:15 is used in 1QApGen 2.10 and argue on that basis that if the phrase is attested outside of Daniel, it should not be considered in need of emendation. Goldingay, *Daniel*, 146; Lucas, *Daniel*, 162; Newsom, *Daniel*, 214. Nonetheless, Collins disagrees, because of the Old Greek, which reads ἐν τούτοις, which speaks in favour of the above emendations. Collins, *Daniel*, 275. Moreover, 1QApGen is thought to borrow imagery and language from Daniel, such that it is unsurprising that it should borrow the phrase from the Masoretic text, making it a poor witness to the phrase's existence independent of Masoretic Daniel. Fitzmyer suggests that the phrase is directly modelled after Daniel. Joseph Fitzmyer, *The Genesis Apocryphon of Qumran Cave 1 (1Q20): A Commentary*, 3rd ed. (Rome: Editrice Pontificio Istituto Biblico, 2004), 131. Cf. Daniel Machiela, *The Dead Sea Genesis Apocryphon: A New Text and Translation with Introduction and Special Treatment of Columns 13–17* (Leiden: Brill, 2009), 94. It is better, therefore, to follow the emendation, such that the word is excluded from the count of loanwords in the Masoretic text.

83. For the purposes of this count, I have included כָּרוֹז and תִּפְתָּיֵ as loans from Persian, although I admit some level of debt over their origin, as discussed above.

84. The Aramaic begins in v. 4. There are two loanwords in the Hebrew section which is 40 words in length. The percentage in the Hebrew section of ch. 2 is 5.00% and in the Aramaic section it is 4.54%.

85. It should be noted that 14 of these instances are counts of פַּרְזֶל, which has no obvious native alternative. Without these instances, the percentage is considerably lower, 1.90%.

| | | | | | | | |
|---|---|---|---|---|---|---|---|
| Dan 3 | Court Tale 3: The furnace | Babylonian Empire | Aramaic | 46/632 [24/632] (7/632) | 7.28 [3.80] (1.11) | 59 | 105/632 (16.61) |
| Dan 4 | Court Tale 4: The king's insanity | Babylonian Empire | Aramaic | 12/599 [4/599] (4/599) | 2.00 [0.67] (0.67) | 17 | 29/599 (4.84) |
| Dan 5 | Court Tale 5: The writing on the wall | Babylonian Empire | Aramaic | 21/524[86] [5/524] (12/524) | 4.01 [0.95] (2.29) | 16 | 37/524 (7.06) |
| Dan 6 | Court Tale 6: The lion's den | 'Median' Empire | Aramaic | 21/551 [18/551] (3/551) | 3.81 [3.27] (0.54) | 15 | 36/551 (6.53) |
| Dan 7 | The vision of the beasts and the man | Babylonian Empire | Aramaic | 6/492 [4/492] (0/492) | 1.22 [0.81] (0) | 2 | 8/492 (1.63) |
| Dan 8 | The second vision of the ram and the goat | Elam, Babylonian Empire | Hebrew | 1/383 [0/383] (1/383) | 0.26 [0] (0.26) | 8 | 9/383 (2.35) |
| Dan 9:1–20 | Daniel's prayer | 'Median' Empire | Hebrew | 1/336 [0/336] (1/336) | 0.30 [0] (0.30) | 4 | 5/336 (1.49) |
| Dan 9:21–27 | The 70 weeks | 'Median' Empire | Hebrew | 0/126 [0/126] (0/126) | 0 [0] (0) | 0 | 0/126 (0) |
| Dan 10 | Vision of the angels | Persian Empire | Hebrew | 2/342[87] [0/342] (0/342) | 0.58 [0] (0) | 9 | 11/342 (3.22) |
| Dan 11–12 | The angel's message | Persian Empire | Hebrew | 4/788 [2/788] (1/788) | 0.51 [0.25] (0.13) | 10 | 14/788 (1.78) |
| Dan 1–6 | | | | 157/3455 [73/3455] (40/3455) | 4.54 [2.11] (1.16) | 141 | 298/3455 (8.63) |

86. I have not counted here חרטמיא, as found in 4QDan[a]. Cf. Also, Syrohexaplar and Ms. 88, φαρμάκοι. However, it is absent from Papyrus 967. Collins, *Daniel*, 3; Lucas, *Daniel*, 121.

87. I have counted here תַּרְשִׁישׁ, even though there may be few – if any – native alternatives, it does not change the effect of an unusual, foreign word appearing in the text. Nonetheless, the concentration of loanwords in this section of the text is fairly minimal – with or without תַּרְשִׁישׁ.

| | | | | | | | |
|---|---|---|---|---|---|---|---|
| Dan 7–12 | | | | 14/2467 [6/2467] (3/2467) | 0.57 [0.24] (0.12) | 33 | 47/2467 (1.91) |
| Total | | | | 171/5922 [79/5922] (43/5922) | 2.89 [1.33] (0.73) | 174 | 345/5922 (5.83) |

Immediately the most obvious observation to be made is the near absence of loanwords in chs. 8–12. At first this is suggestive, because it coincides with the transition from Aramaic to Hebrew. However, this distinction does not function across the whole book, because ch. 1 is both Hebrew and one of the chapters richest in loanwords. Moreover, while ch. 7 contains more loanwords than the chapters that follow, it still contains many fewer than the chapters that precede it. Rather, while there is some degree of overlap between the use of Aramaic and the loanwords, it provides a poor explanation, overall, for the way the words are used in the book.[88] Nor does the setting of each chapter succeed in explaining the use of loanwords. While ch. 6, set in the Persian period, has a comparatively high number of Iranian words it does not have so high a concentration as ch. 3, which is set in the Babylonian period. Moreover, chs. 9–12, though set in the Persian period, have almost no loanwords from Iranian languages.

However, there is one criterion which explains the distribution of loanwords well, which is whether the text is in the form of a court tale or not.[89] Chapter 7 is the only chapter not containing court tales that contains a significant quantity of loanwords. However, it has fewer loanwords than every single court tale. Nonetheless, it remains, then, to be explained why ch. 7 contains more loanwords than chs. 8–12, and in particular ch. 8 with which it shares so much content. To answer this, we conclude that the distribution of loanwords in Daniel is explained by a combination of the language of writing and genre: thus ch. 7 contains some loanwords because it is in Aramaic, chs. 2–6 because they are Aramaic court tales and ch. 1 because it is a court tale.[90] In addition,

---

88. Even if, as Collins thinks, Dan 1 originated in Aramaic and was translated back to Hebrew, that does not account for the present state of the text, nor the absence of loanwords in Dan 7. Collins, *Daniel*, 38.

89. We will discuss the genre of court tales below.

90. There are other potential explanations, especially considering that Dan 8–12 appears to be the most recent section. Given how important the presence of Aramaic in Daniel is to theories of its redaction, it is unsurprising that there should be some overlap here. Nonetheless, I find this explanation the most economical.

we might speculate that, just as in Esther, ch. 1 is presented with an especially high concentration of loanwords because of its role in setting the tone for the whole book.[91]

In addition, we note that the Iranian loanwords are particularly associated with tales of conflict, rather than tales of contest: both tales of conflict, chs. 3 and 6, have more than 3% Iranian loanwords, whereas the chapter with the next highest percentage has 1.96%.[92] In addition, we note that Esther, which also contains a high percentage of Iranian loanwords, likewise can be classified as a tale of conflict. In the case of Esther, we recall that the loanwords were especially concentrated around a particular moment in the narrative's circular construction, namely the reversal of fate on which the tale of conflict is based.

### 3.2.4.4. *Court tales in the ancient Near East*

The fact that the loanwords in Daniel are limited to the court tales implies that this genre is a relevant factor for studying the literary use of loanwords. This is especially so when we consider that Esther too can be classified as a court tale.

There is a recognition among scholars of a text type of 'Court Tales' that is present in a range of biblical and other ancient texts, including the stories of Joseph, Daniel and Esther; 4Q550 and 4Q242; 3 Esdr 3–4, Tobit and Judith; Ahiqar, a wisdom text first attested in Aramaic from Elephantine in the fifth century; a variety of Egyptian works, including the Middle Bronze Age Egyptian Tale of Sinuhe; and Greek sources, such as Herodotus.[93] Notwithstanding certain objections to the idea that the court tales represent a text-type,[94] the genre is identifiable as a more general categorization by a family of narrative features, including:[95]

---

91. Cf., for example, Newsom, *Daniel*, 38–39.

92. In particular, the list of officials contributes to this as many of them are designated by loanwords. However, as we shall explore further, these lists are typical of the tales of conflict.

93. Collins, *Daniel*, 42; Goldingay, *Daniel*, 6; Holm, *Of Courtiers and Kings*, 195–97; Lucas, *Daniel*, 24; Newsom, *Daniel*, 12–15; Lawrence Wills, *The Jew in the Court of the Foreign King*, HDR 26 (Minneapolis: Fortress, 1990), 39–74.

94. Susan Niditch and Robert Doran, 'The Success Story of the Wise Courtier: A Formal Approach', *JBL* 92 (1977): 179–93 (179).

95. Cf. John Collins, 'The Court Tales in Daniel and the Development of Apocalyptic', *JBL* 94 (1975): 218–34; Collins, *Daniel*, 45–47; Holm, *Of Courtiers and Kings*, 196–201; Lucas, *Daniel*, 25.

a. An initial state of prosperity; the hero is a member of the court;
b. Danger to the hero at the hands of an enemy or conspiracy;
c. Problem posed to the king, such as a dream or a riddle;
d. The hero alone can solve the problem;
e. Confinement or death sentence;
f. Failure of the hero's rivals;
g. Rescue and restoration or reward of the hero;
h. An emphasis on the skill or wisdom of the hero;
i. The final state of the heroes is more exalted than their initial status;
j. A 'ruled ethnic perspective'.[96]

Both Esther and each of the first six chapters of Daniel conform to this pattern.[97] Within this group, the stories have been divided into the subtypes of 'tales of contest' – tales involving the solving of a riddle – and 'tales of conflict' – tales about conflict between courtiers.[98] Thus, for example, in Daniel we can identify chs. 2, 4 and 5 as tales of contest, in which Daniel interprets dreams or visions that other courtiers are unable to explain. In chs. 3 and 6 we can identify tales of conflict in which Daniel or his friends are imperilled by hostile courtiers.[99] Moreover, while ch. 1 does not fall into either category obviously – Humphreys identifies it as an introduction to the book, rather than a tale of conflict or contest[100] – it

---

96. Wills, *The Jew in the Court*, 150–52.
97. As we have already noted above, Esther is routinely identified as a court tale. However, since much of the literature on Court Tales deals primarily with Daniel, let us justify that Esther too can be considered in this group. In Esther, both Mordecai and Esther can be read as heroes of the court genre. Mordecai is threatened by Haman's conspiracy because he refuses to bow down to him, resulting in a death sentence (Esth 3:16). Ultimately, he is exalted to a higher station than where he began (Esth 6; 10:2–3). Esther too fulfils the role of court hero. She becomes queen and thus a member of the court (Esth 2:15–18). At the end of the narrative her position is of greater influence (e.g. Esth 8:7; 9:29). Like Mordecai, Esther also sits under the threat of death from Haman. Daniel could be classed as a 'story-collection' similar to the Greek Ἡοῖαι, 'Catalogue of Women', or the Egyptian 'Tales from King Cheops' Court'. Holm, *Of Courtiers and Kings*, especially 186–201.
98. Cf. W. Lee Humphreys, 'A Life-Style for Diaspora: A Study of the Tales of Esther and Daniel', *JBL* 92 (1973): 211–23, especially 219–20; Newsom, *Daniel*, 13.
99. Collins, *Daniel*, 45; Goldingay, *Daniel*, 67, 122; Lucas, *Daniel*, 26; Newsom, *Daniel*, 13.
100. Humphreys, 'A Life-Style for Diaspora', 219.

does contain some of the distinguishing features, such that it is routinely identified as part of the grouping.[101]

We are concerned with the court tales in Esther and Daniel, because of the prevalence of loanwords in them; as we have seen above, the court tales in Daniel are rich with loanwords, whereas other kinds of literature in the book lack them. In particular, in the case of conflict stories, we note that there is a tendency to use Persian loanwords.

If we consider, then, how the loanwords are used in conflict tales, it becomes apparent that they frequently appear in lists. Coxon has recognized lists as a characteristic feature of the court tales in Daniel, falling into several categories: secular officials, cultic personnel, musical instruments, metals, items of clothing, persons in the king's entourage and nationalities.[102]

**Table 3** Lists in Daniel

| Category | List reference (Daniel, MT versification) | Loanwords/ Items in list |
|---|---|---|
| Secular officials | 3:2 | 7/8 |
| | 3:3 | 7/8 |
| | 3:27 | 4/4 |
| | 4:33 | 1/2 |
| | 6:4 | 2/2 |
| | 6:5 | 2/2 |
| | 6:7 | 2/2 |
| | 6:8 | 5/5 |

101. Collins, *Daniel*, 38–52; Goldingay, *Daniel*, 6; Hartman and Di Lella, *Daniel*, 55; Newsom, *Daniel*, 12–18, 39; Michael Segal, *Dreams, Riddles, and Visions: Textual, Contextual, and Intertextual Approaches to the Book of Daniel* (Berlin: de Gruyter, 2016), 22–26. Segal further suggests that the first chapter can be separated out into a frame narrative about the training of the courtiers and a second narrative about the choice of pure food. His suggestion is that the frame narrative could be rightly characterized as a tale of conflict. As we have said, it does contain some of the motifs of a tale of conflict, but also lacks key elements, such as the initial state of prosperity: Daniel and his friends are not yet members of the court (Dan 1:5). Moreover, while we can imagine rivals for Daniel and his friends, they do not play a prominent role in the story as it presently stands – the threat comes, so it seems, directly from the king, rather than competing courtiers.

102. Peter Coxon, 'The "List" Genre and Narrative Style in the Court Tales of Daniel', *JSOT* 35 (1986): 95–121.

| | | |
|---|---|---|
| Cultic personnel | 2:2 | 3/4[103] |
| | 2:10 | 3/3 |
| | 2:27 | 2/4 |
| | 4:4 | 3/4 |
| | 5:7 | 2/3 |
| | 5:11 | 3/4 |
| Musical Instruments | 3:5 | 4/7[104] |
| | 3:7 | 3/6 |
| | 3:10 | 4/7 |
| | 3:15 | 4/7 |
| Metals and other materials | 2:35 | 1/5 |
| | 2:45 | 1/5 |
| | 5:4 | 1/6 |
| | 5:23 | 1/6 |
| Items of Clothing | 3:21 | 2/4 |
| Persons in the king's entourage | 5:2 | 2/3 |
| | 5:3 | 2/3 |
| | 5:23 | 2/3 |
| Nationalities | 3:4 | 0/3 |
| | 3:7 | 0/3 |
| | 3:29 | 0/3 |
| | 3:31 | 0/3 |
| | 5:19 | 0/3 |
| | 6:26 | 0/3 |
| | 7:14 | 0/3 |
| Foreign Names | 1:7 | 4/8 |
| | 2:49 | 3/3 |
| | 3:12 | 3/3 |
| | 3:13 | 3/3 |
| | 3:14 | 3/3 |
| | 3:16 | 3/3 |
| | 3:19 | 3/3 |
| | 3:20 | 3/3 |
| | 3:22 | 3/3 |
| | 3:23 | 3/3 |
| | 3:26 | 3/3 |
| | 3:26 | 3/3 |
| | 3:28 | 3/3 |
| | 3:29 | 3/3 |
| | 3:30 | 3/3 |

103. Although not discussed above, the ethnonym, כַּשְׂדִּים presumably derives from foreign source.

104. For the same reasons discussed above, I have not included קַרְנָא as a loanword.

As is plain, four of the kinds of lists are strongly associated with the use of loanwords: the secular officials, the cultic personnel, the musical instruments and the items of clothing. These three lists with their repetitions account for 62 of the loanwords, despite making up only 85 words in total. The lists are found at key points of each court tale. In ch. 2, the list of cultic personnel is found initially when the problem is introduced, that the king needs them to solve the dream (2:2). It is then repeated when the cultic personnel are unable to solve the dream (2:10) and when Daniel succeeds (2:27). In ch. 3 the secular officials are identified in a list in the tale's exposition (3:2, 3). They are reintroduced in 3:27 at the resolution of the tale. The list of musical instruments (3:5, 7, 10, 15) functions as the means of conflict and recurs at key points of the crisis, where Daniel's friends resist or are punished. In ch. 4, lists of loanwords occur at the exposition (4:4) and at the conclusion (4:33). In ch. 5, the queen, שֵׁגָל, and other members of the king's entourage are likewise introduced at exposition (5:2, 3) and conclusion (5:23). A list of cultic personnel, unable to interpret the writing, are the impetus for Daniel's summoning. Finally, in ch. 6, a list of officials is introduced and repeated in the exposition (6:4, 5, 7, 8). These lists of loanwords, however, do not occur in the visions or dreams, in discussion between characters or in the descriptions of the consequences for disobedience (such as in the description of Daniel's time in the lion den). Rather, the lists are limited to reference to actual narrative events and so are intimately connected to the common narrative structure of the court tale.[105]

The same can be done for Esther, though the lists of nouns are less frequent.

**Table 4** Lists in Esther

| Category | List reference (Esther) | Loanwords/[106]Items in list/Words in list |
|---|---|---|
| Officials | 1:3 | 1/3/7 |
|  | 3:12 | 2/2/5 |
|  | 8:9 | 2/3/4 |
|  | 9:3 | 2/4/7 |

105. Although we are concerned with the Hebrew text of Daniel, we do note that these lists are much rarer in the Old Greek, which differs significantly in chs. 4–6 from the other versions.

106. For this table I have included foreign names in the count. See the discussion above, under 3.2.4.2, 'The Distribution of Loanwords in Esther'.

| Luxury goods | 1:6 | 6/12/21 |
| --- | --- | --- |
| | 8:15 | 2/3/10 |
| Names | 1:10 | 7/7/7 |
| | 1:14 | 7/7/7 |
| | 9:7–9 | 10/10/20 |
| Nationalities | 1:22 | 0/3/12 |
| | 3:12 | 0/3/8 |
| | 8:9 | 0/3/6 |

The effect in Esther is not as strong as in Daniel. Nonetheless, there appears to be some degree of similarity in the approach to the lists of officials, for which both books share a preference for the words, אֲחַשְׁדַּרְפָּן and פֶּחָה. The vocabulary used for the different nationalities is also similar, though in both cases loanwords are not employed. Similar to the pattern in Daniel, these lists are concentrated around the exposition and conclusion of the story. Likewise, as we have seen, other loanwords are also concentrated around a key point of reversal, when Haman and Mordecai send their letters.

To some extent it is clear from the content of the lists that they and the loanwords function together to present a particular setting. As we have already seen, in Esther, despite the presence of Akkadian loanwords, the use of Iranian loanwords is appropriate to depict the Persian court. Other (non-Iranian) loanwords likewise denote the trappings of the Persian court or its courtiers. Among the Iranian loanwords in Esther, there is an emphasis on words which depict the law and administration of the Persian empire. In Daniel, the source language of the loanwords is not indicative: while the stories are set in the Babylonian and Persian courts – and many of the loanwords do derive from either Iranian languages or Akkadian – the distribution of the words does not correspond to the setting of each story. Moreover, there is a set of loanwords which find their origin in Greek, which fits neither narrative setting. Similarly, in Esther, there are many Akkadian loanwords, though the setting is Persia. Nevertheless, just as in Esther the loanwords belong to the semantic areas of law, administration and luxury goods. In the case of Dan 1–6, it is the setting in the court – rather than in Babylon or Persia – that provides the reason for the use of the loanwords, as well as the genre-related factors discussed above.

The fact that Daniel and Esther share this technique of using loanwords raises the question of whether this is a feature of these two texts specifically or of the court tale genre more broadly. In 4Q550, there are only two potential loanwords I can identify. The first, and only partially reconstructed, is [ארג]ונא (4Q550ᶜ line 5) which is identified as such on the basis of the likelihood that a court tale might involve dressing someone in purple.[107] To some extent, then, the logic that reconstructs ארגון relies on the assumption that that word fits in a court tale: the line is almost entirely lost, with only נה ארג remaining. On the other hand, it does still seem the most plausible option. The second, אוש׳, is thought by some to be a loanword from a theoretical Persian *āwāč-.[108] However, although the proposals are plausible, there does not appear to be sufficient evidence for us to claim that 4Q550 might have contained a high proportion of loanwords.

Although the court tale preserved in 3 Esdras is only known in Greek, it appears probable that a Hebrew or Aramaic *Vorlage* would contain loanwords in a pattern similar to that found in Daniel.[109] The court tales identified in Judith and Tobit,[110] on the other hand, do not give any obvious indication that a hypothetical Hebrew *Vorlage* would work with the same vocabulary, although it is impossible to know with certainty – nor do the Hebrew and Aramaic sections of Tobit preserved from Qumran.[111] Quite likely this is related to the lesser importance of the court setting in

---

107. 'Presumably, the herald proclaims that the son of Patireza be clothed in purple'. John Collins and Deborah Green, 'The Tales from the Persian Court (4Q550ᵃ⁻ᵉ)', in *Antikes Judentum und Frühes Christentum*, ed. Bernd Kollman et al. (Berlin: de Gruyter, 1999), 39–50 (43). In this Collins follows Milik, who explicitly bases the reconstruction on Dan 5:7. József Milik, 'Les Modèles Araméens du Livre d'Esther dans la Grotte 4 de Qumràn', *RevQ* 15 (1992): 321–406 (336). Cf. Émile Puech, *Qumran Grotte 4 XXVII: Textes Araméens Deuxieme Partie*, DJD 37 (Oxford: Clarendon, 2009).

108. Cook, *Dictionary of Qumran Aramaic*, 4; Sokoloff, *DJBA*, 86.

109. Cf. 3 Esd 3:2: καὶ πᾶσιν τοῖς σατράπαις καὶ στρατηγοῖς καὶ τοπάρχαις τοῖς ὑπ' αὐτὸν ἀπὸ τῆς ἰνδικῆς μέχρι τῆς αἰθιοπίας ἐν ταῖς ἑκατὸν εἴκοσι ἑπτὰ σατραπείαις, 'and to all the satraps and generals and governors who were under him from India to Ethiopia in the 127 Satrapies'.

Likewise, 3 Esd 3:6: καὶ πορφύραν περιβαλέσθαι καὶ ἐν χρυσώμασιν πίνειν καὶ ἐπὶ χρυσῷ καθεύδειν καὶ ἅρμα χρυσοχάλινον καὶ κίδαριν βυσσίνην καὶ μανιάκην περὶ τὸν τράχηλον, 'and to be dressed in purple and to drink from gold vessels and to sleep on gold and a gold-bridled chariot and a linen diadem and a necklace around the neck'. Notice that the Greek uses words (κίδαριν and μανιάκην) borrowed from the same Iranian words that Daniel and Esther have borrowed.

Likewise, 3 Esd 4:47: τότε ἀναστὰς δαρεῖος ὁ βασιλεὺς κατεφίλησεν αὐτὸν καὶ ἔγραψεν αὐτῷ τὰς ἐπιστολὰς πρὸς πάντας τοὺς οἰκονόμους καὶ τοπάρχας καὶ στρατηγοὺς καὶ σατράπας, 'Then, Darius got up and kissed him and wrote letters to all the stewards and governors and generals and satraps' (all translations mine).

110. Newsom, *Daniel*, 12.

111. There are nonetheless, some present, such as רבשקה, an Akkadian loanword (4Q196 2.7 = Tob 1:22).

Judith and Tobit. While in Ahiqar there are a few loanwords – סָרִיס, for example[112] – they are not as prevalent as in Esther or Daniel. In the stories of Joseph, similarly, while not to the same extent found in Daniel and Esther, some loanwords are nonetheless present.[113]

In Sinuhe, however, there is a pattern of using Semitic loanwords to represent Asiatic peoples.[114] While this is obviously parallel in some respects – though with a lower concentration of loanwords – to what is found in Daniel and Esther, it is also opposite: it is the non-prestige group that is identified by loanwords, while the prestigious group associated with the administration provides the dominant language of the text. Whereas in Daniel and Esther, it is the ruling class that is marked out, in Sinuhe it is the foreign underclass.

Therefore, the case appears to be that among court tales, it is Daniel, Esther and plausibly 3 Esd 3–4 – if we are right to suspect loanwords in the Hebrew *Vorlage* on the basis of similar phraseology – that share in a particular approach to using loanwords. It is, therefore, not an essential component of the court tale, but one that applies to a significant subset. So then, if a feature of biblical court tales is that they should contain loanwords from a variety of languages, especially Akkadian and Persian, that accounts for their presence in both books, despite not fitting the context.

### 3.2.4.5. *Lists, satire, criticism*

As we have seen, the lists of loanwords in Daniel, and to some extent in Esther, occur at critical moments of the narrative. As we have likewise seen, the lists contain a high proportion of loanwords.

To understand the consequences of these two facts we must also recognize that the lists are superfluous, because the category could easily stand for the list elements: 'officials' for 'satraps, governors, etc.'.[115] From this, we can either conclude that mentioning each element of the list might function denotatively or that the lists function connotatively; that is, the lists raise the question of whether this is a kind of exaggeration or if the

---

112. Ahiqar 3.38, 4.63.
113. E.g. סָרִיס in Gen 40:7 and חַרְטֹם in Gen 41:8.
114. Benjamin Hinson, 'Sinuhe's Life Abroad: Ethnoarcheological and Philological Reconsiderations', in *Current Research in Egyptology 14 (2013)*, ed. Kelly Acetta et al. (Oxford: Oxbow Books, 2014), 81–93.
115. In fact, the Old Greek does just this at Dan 3:3: 'and the aforementioned stood in front of the image' (NETS), compared with 'So the satraps, the prefects, and the governors, the counselors, the treasurers, the justices, the magistrates, and all the officials of the provinces, assembled for the dedication of the statue' (NRSV).

reader is to assume that all of the list items – for example, the officials in Dan 6:7 – are 'intended' to be understood as truly present.

To understand the probable effect of these lists we must consider the stance of the text and the audience towards their use. As we have seen, the lists are associated with the narrative's setting, namely, the foreign court. The text often reports the events from an outsider perspective, the narrative focalized through Daniel.[116] As we have suggested above, in the context of the Antiochene crisis, Daniel is presented here as a figure to be emulated by the 'many', as he represents the ideals of the anti-Antiochene party.[117] The characterization of Daniel in the first six chapters, as we shall examine further, below, implies a stance against the empire, as Daniel refuses to participate in various practices expected of an imperial courtier.[118] Therefore, there would be merit in seeing the listing as part of a criticism of the imperial rulers; the king's largesse is in fact his excess and the lists are hyperbole to draw attention to that fact. The administration's officials are listed to indicate the extent of the bureaucracy rather than as a depiction of power. Such an interpretation would sit well with the line of scholarly thought which identifies satirical and other humorous

---

116. Thus, for example, in the first chapter the narrative only provides us with the details known to Daniel, such as decisions that he makes (1:8). Nonetheless this is not constant throughout chs. 1–6, as the narrator often adopts an external perspective when Daniel is not present in the court. Cf. Bill Arnold, 'The Use of Aramaic in the Bible: Another Look at Bilingualism in Ezra and Daniel', *JNSL* 22 (1996): 1–16; Joshua Berman, 'The Narratological Purpose of Aramaic in Ezra 4:8–6:18', *Aramaic Studies* 5 (2007): 165–91.

117. See 3.2.3, 'Audience – Daniel'.

118. While in the past scholars tended to understand Daniel as basically optimistic towards the place of the Jews under imperial powers, there has been a move towards a more pessimistic view. For the earlier view, see Humphreys, 'A Life-Style for Diaspora'. For the later view: Shane Kirkpatrick, *Competing for Honor: A Social-Scientific Reading of Daniel 1–6*, BibInt 76 (Leiden: Brill, 2005); Amy Willis, *Dissonance and the Drama of Divine Sovereignty in the Book of Daniel*, LHBOTS 520 (New York: T&T Clark, 2010), especially Chapter 2, 'The Shape of Sovereignty in Nebuchadnezzar's Dream (Daniel 2:31–45)'; Anathea Portier-Young, *Apocalypse Against Empire: Theologies of Resistance in Early Judaism* (Grand Rapids: Eerdmans, 2011); Daniel Smith-Christopher, 'Gandhi on Daniel 6: A Case of Cultural Exegesis', *BibInt* 1 (1993): 321–28; David Valeta, *Lions and Ovens and Visions: A Satirical Reading of Daniel 1–6*, Hebrew Bible Monographs 12 (Sheffield: Sheffield Phoenix, 2008). For a summary of recent opinions, see Newsom, *Daniel*, 14–18. More recently still, Newsom has also expressed pessimism over the potential for success by resistance in court tales. Carol Newsom, 'Resistance is Futile! The Ironies of Danielic Resistance to Empire', *Int* 71 (2017): 167–77.

elements in the court tales found in Daniel.[119] Moreover, identifying satirical elements in Dan 1–6 is not contrary to identifying the stories as court tales.[120]

However, whether the effect is humorous or not, this criticism of the court is an attitude which is unusual among court tales. While, for example, Ahiqar is endangered there is no implication that Sennacherib is blameworthy. The court, as the setting of the court tale, is often perceived as neutral.[121] However, in the case of Daniel – and also Esther – the genre has been adapted as a means of criticism. The loanwords are particularly useful for this purpose, because in using them as a means to criticize the foreign king, the text safeguards the Hebrew protagonists.

Nonetheless, we must recognize a tension: Daniel is a member of the foreign court and a recipient of its riches, yet it would be difficult to claim

---

119. Hector Avalos, 'The Comedic Function of the Enumerations of Officials and Instruments in Daniel 3', *CBQ* 53 (1991): 580–88; Lucas, *Daniel*, 87.

120. While some scholarship (e.g. Valeta's earlier position) has seen a sharp distinction in genre between Menippean satire on the one hand, and court tales on the other, it is not necessarily so. When we speak of the court tale as a genre, as discussed above, it is not so much a strict genre, which texts were written to fit, but rather a set of narrative elements that are commonly strung together. As such there is no necessary incompatibility between Menippean satire and the court tale (cf. Valeta's revised position). For the sake of comparison, Valeta's dissertation ('Lions and Ovens and Visions, Oh My! A Satirical Analysis of Daniel 1–6' [PhD diss., The University of Denver, 2004], 4) proposed: 'While the narratives of Daniel 1–6 have characteristics that invite scholars to classify them as court tales, didactic wisdom tales, folklore, and the like, *they are, in fact*, in the nature of political satires with an aim to resist the forces of empire' (emphasis mine). This earlier position was also represented in his article 'Court or Jester Tales? Resistance and Social Reality in Daniel 1–6', *Perspectives in Religious Studies* 32 (2005): 309: 'These identifications [of Dan 1–6 as court tales] perpetuate a fundamental incongruity of Daniel studies, namely, that the narratives of Dan 1–6 depict a more positive view of imperial rule than the negative portrayals of the apocalyptic visions of Dan 7–12'. In the published version of his dissertation (*Lions and Ovens and Visions*, 4) the statement stands amended: 'While the narratives of Daniel 1–6 have characteristics that invite scholars to classify them as court tales, didactic wisdom tales, folklore, and the like, *they also contain elements* in the nature of political satires with an aim to resist the forces of empire' (emphasis mine).

121. Indeed, Newsom believes this is also largely the case in the Danielic court tales (although she does recognize the addition of ethnic and religious tensions to these tales) since ultimately the rule of the foreign kings, like Nebuchadnezzar, is not removed by God, except for the (late) dream in Dan 2. Newsom, 'Resistance is Futile!', 171–74.

that the text censures him for that involvement.[122] More to the point, for an audience in the Antiochene period, Daniel's accommodation seems to run counter to the spirit of opposition to Antiochus: it would, rather, suggest the plausibility of a mix of accommodation and resistance.

However, if we consider the role of the loanwords for the audience, we can cast light on this problem: the loanwords establish a sense of difference between Jewish ethnic identity and foreign ethnicities. The reason that the audience identifies with Daniel is not because of his role or lack of a role in the Babylonian and Persian courts, but rather his Jewish ethnic identity, which they share. Since it is possible for Daniel and his friends to attain high station in the court, with all the rewards that that entails, without losing the text's favour, we must conclude that the imperial court itself is not the issue. Rather, the competing interests of different ethnicities within the court are what matter to the text. Thus, it is acceptable to the audience for Daniel or his friends to accept the benefits of the court because doing so does not compromise the means by which the audience identifies with them, namely their ethnic identity. All of this suggests that the text aims to teach its audience that ethnic identity is important and that it should not be compromised in negotiating life under empire.

Moreover, concern over the audience's ethnic identity is related to the text's choice of genre, the court tale, which is characterized by a ruled ethnic perspective.[123] Ultimately it is this desire to explore ethnic identity through that genre that also results in the text's choice to use loanwords. Thus, loanwords become a secondary characteristic of court tales because they aid in the goal of raising ethnic identity, through ethno-linguistic difference.

### 3.2.4.6. *Daniel 1, unresolved tensions and the characterization of Daniel*

Due to the above – understanding the text as satire and understanding the division it proposes between Jews and foreigners – we are able to address some of the questions that the book poses. For example, this understanding of the text better informs our reading of the text's opening.

---

122. This tension is played out especially in ch. 5. Thus, for example, in Dan 5:17, Daniel rejects the king's rewards. Moreover, the rewards in question are listed in 5:17 using predominately loanwords. At first it would appear that the attitude shown here is a clear rejection of the benefits of the court. However, ultimately, he receives the rewards without objection (Dan 5:29). A similar tension can be found in Dan 2:46, in which Daniel receives the king's prostration, an offering and incense, apparently without objecting to this quasi-worship.

123. See above under 3.2.4.4, 'Court Tales in the Ancient Near East'.

The introductory nature of ch. 1 of Daniel is well understood.[124] The setting of Dan 1 is established within Dan 1:1–5 as 'the king's palace', which continues as the setting of the court tales – the visions are set elsewhere. The summary treatment of the exile in the first two verses raises the theological questions associated with exile – the new status of the Judahites, the status of the temple apparatus – but does not address them: it would have been entirely possible to begin Daniel without any specific reference given to the exile, but by including this information the text prompts the reader to believe that it is relevant context for understanding what follows. It is the nature of those questions that they are tied to the setting of the book, the place to which the Judahites and temple apparatus have been brought. Therefore, the setting in the king's palace becomes representative of the theological questions posed by the book of Daniel. Moreover, the setting is maintained active in the mind of the audience – without repeating the location verbally – by the persistence of the loanwords, which draw attention to the administration, the luxury and the otherness of the king's court. The tension, then, provides a lens through which Daniel's actions are to be understood and evaluated. Thus, his choices to avoid partaking of the king's food, denoted by a loanword, פַּתְ־בַּג (Dan 1:8), also connote a rejection of the court and foreign identity.

This choice is the first decision Daniel makes in the course of the book as it stands in its final form and so it is crucial for understanding his characterization.[125] Moreover, it is a decision that will be echoed throughout the book as he and his friends refuse to commit idolatry in chs. 3 and 6. However, scholars have puzzled over the cause of Daniel's fear of defilement:[126] it is not obvious why the decision to reject the king's food is so important to Daniel and the text. Their suggestions include several ways that the food might be considered impure or unclean.[127] It may be the case that there was some material cause, although it is not obvious what the problem with imbibing the king's wine should be.[128] Moreover, the פַּתְ־בַּג does not contain meat and should not be prohibited under legal

---

124. Collins, *Daniel*, 129; Lucas, *Daniel*, 49–50; Choon-Leong Seow, *Daniel*, Westminster Bible Companion (Louisville: Westminster John Knox, 2003), 9.

125. So also, Plöger, *Das Buch Daniel*, 40. Similarly, Goldingay notes that the choice forms the central moment of a chiastic structure in the story of ch. 1. Further, even if we do not accept the chiasm, it is nonetheless clear that the decision is the climactic point of the story arc. Goldingay, *Daniel*, 8.

126. Goldingay, *Daniel*, 18–19; Hartman and Di Lella, *Daniel*, 133; Lucas, *Daniel*, 54; Newsom, *Daniel*, 47–8.

127. Ibid.

128. Seow, *Daniel*, 25.

grounds.¹²⁹ Another possibility, which Koch entertains, is that the use of the king's rations would allow Daniel's successes to be attributed to it, rather than to God.¹³⁰ Similarly, Bauer suggests that accepting the rations would mark Daniel as someone close to the king.¹³¹

However, as Lucas and Newsom note, there is another approach, which is to understand the פַּתְ־בַּג as a marker of identity or ownership.¹³² By accepting the king's rations, Daniel would accept allegiance to the king. These scholars notice that when the word reappears in Dan 11:25–26, the text makes a similar assumption about the connection between identity and eating the פַּתְ־בַּג. However, they do not explain how the text expects the reader to make this connection – after all, the association made between identity and eating the פַּתְ־בַּג in Dan 11 does not necessarily imply that the reader should retroject this meaning to ch. 1. However, when we read Dan 1 with attention paid to the loanwords, we notice that the Iranian loanword פַּתְ־בַּג is an obvious choice to signal imperial identity, due to the association between the court and loanwords that we have explored above. The choice of word is a clear deviation from ordinary Hebrew vocabulary and so prompts the reader to consider the reason for the deviation. The difference between פַּתְ־בַּג and other more generic words for food is its status as a loanword from an imperial nation and its specific association with the king. To choose this word, then, triggers those associations for the readers of the text and helps them to form their judgments about the characters.

There are other cases, too, where we see the imperial identity and Judahite identity juxtaposed by employing foreign vocabulary: the renaming of Daniel and his compatriots in 1:7 with foreign(-sounding) names;¹³³ similarly in ch. 3, the musical instruments that accompany idolatry, and in ch. 6, the decree which cannot be changed, which is the source of Daniel's predicament, are all denoted by loanwords.¹³⁴ In all three of these tales in Daniel, whatever it is that must be resisted is denoted in terms – loanwords – that reinforce the foreign atmosphere; in doing so the text maintains the division between Judahite and imperial

129. Collins, *Daniel*, 141–42; Koch, *Daniel*, 59.
130. Koch, *Daniel*, 61.
131. Bauer, *Daniel*, 74.
132. Lucas, *Daniel*, 54–55; Newsom, *Daniel*, 48.
133. Lucas, *Daniel*, 53; Newsom, *Daniel*, 47.
134. While some might object that the musical instruments are not replaceable by equivalent native words, there are nonetheless more generic terms that could be used in their place: e.g. נְגִינוֹת, 'stringed instruments'. Cf. *Comprehensive Aramaic Lexicon*, s.v. 'ngynh'.

identity. Therefore, we can see that what the text is concerned with in Dan 1 is not primarily a question of piety, but rather one of ethnic (religious) identity.

### 3.2.4.7. *Characterization of Esther*

Previously, we examined the characterization of Daniel, in light of how court tales use loanwords to propose a distinction between Jews and foreigners. Similarly, one of the questions in the book of Esther that the loanwords can help us answer is over the morality of Esther's actions. One stream of interpretation has seen her actions as basically justifiable or praiseworthy, given the circumstances.[135] Others are more inclined to doubt Esther's heroic status or at least recognize that her character is not entirely praiseworthy; in particular, she is often charged with passivity.[136] Approaching this question from a rhetorical standpoint, we consider how the character of Esther is developed throughout the text by its use of loanwords and how the audience responds to those developments.

We have already noted that the loanwords help bring Esther into line with other court tales, like those in Daniel. In terms of character, this promotes comparison between Esther and the typical hero of the court in the court tale. One characteristic of the court tale is that there is an emphasis on the skill of the hero. While this is true of Daniel, it is not obviously true of Esther or Mordecai. Therefore, we must begin to question what kind of hero Esther may be. The way the loanwords portray Esther helps us to do so.

One of the key factors for the audience's perception of Esther is the fact that she belongs to the same ethnic group as them.[137] In addition to

---

135. This is an interpretation that goes back at least as far as Clement of Alexandria. Van Wijk-Bos is a modern commentator who is basically positive in her presentation of Esther. See 1 Clem 55, and Johanna van Wijk-Bos, *Ezra, Nehemiah, and Esther*, Westminster Bible Companion (Louisville: Westminster John Knox, 1998), 106–7.

136. Linda Day, *Esther*, Abingdon Old Testament Commentaries (Nashville: Abingdon, 2005), 6; Fox, *Character and Ideology*, 197ff.; Esther Fuchs, 'Status and Role of Female Heroines in the Biblical Narrative', in *Women in the Hebrew Bible: A Reader*, ed. Alice Bach (New York: Routledge, 2013), 77–84 (80–81); Jonathan Grossman, *Esther: The Outer Narrative and the Hidden Reading*, Siphrut 6 (Winona Lake: Eisenbrauns, 2011), 65; Barry Webb, *Five Festal Garments*, Horizons in Biblical Theology (Downers Grove: Intervarsity, 2000), 120.

137. In this I differ in approach somewhat to Wetter, whose work I find nonetheless worth referring to at this point. Wetter claims that in her stay in the harem, Esther undergoes a *rite-de-passage*, by which she is stripped of her ethnic and religious

genre, the loanwords help establish setting for the book of Esther and, in particular, they prompt the audience to consider the characters in terms of ethno-linguistic identity: because the loanwords set the story in a foreign court and persist throughout the narrative, the audience is constantly reminded of the foreign setting (and the foreignness they too would feel, were they to be present in that same setting). Thus, the actions and interactions of each character are cast in terms of their ethno-linguistic identity relative to the audience. All of this is to arrive at the conclusion that the presumed audience of this Hebrew text will identify most naturally with Mordecai and Esther and the other Jews. However, although the audience identifies with these characters, we must not assume that they necessarily endorse their actions. Rather, a strong identification with a character prompts the audience to have a greater interest in determining whether or not they approve of the character's actions. As Esther takes different decisions over the course of the narrative, the audience's understanding of her character gradually develops.

In particular, Esther – and the audience, taking her side – is cast against the mechanisms of the state: one of the officials, Haman, intends to use the laws of the Persians, and their immutability, to enforce the destruction of the Jews. He intends to make this possible by leveraging the administrative power of the Persian empire, its mail system and so on. As we have already seen, the law, דָּת, is represented with a Persian loanword. So also, the various aspects of the administration, which Haman leverages, are represented by loanwords.

The moment at which Haman puts his plan into motion is Esth 3:10–15. In this section, the proportion of loanwords out of all the words is relatively high (7.2%).[138] All of the loanwords relate in some way to the power of the Persian empire, and so at this moment of crisis in the book of Esther, the audience is reminded of the extent of the threat, not just against Esther herself, but against all the Jews throughout the empire. At this moment, the text raises the stakes of the crisis, extending it throughout the empire. This is true, even without noticing the effect of the loanwords. However, the presence of the loanwords underscores that the full weight of Persian law and administrative power stands against the Jewish people.

---

identity, to which she is summoned back by Mordecai in ch. 4. It appears difficult to support this thesis in the light of 2:10, which appears to suggest that Esther's ethnic identity was very much still intact, if hidden – she cannot hide it if she does not believe it exists. Anne-Mareike Wetter, 'In Unexpected Places: Ritual and Religious Belonging in the Book of Esther', *JSOT* 36 (2012): 321–32 (326–27).

138. See 'Appendix Two: Lists and Distribution of Loanwords in Esther'.

In fact, symbols of Persian power, denoted by loanwords, are found in several key moments of Esther's character development. For example, at the moment of her coronation, 2:17, she receives the diadem, כֶּתֶר, an Iranian loanword. The diadem is a symbol of Persian power and in Esther, in particular, one of royal station.[139] When she succeeds in approaching the king, in 5:2, he extends the sceptre, שַׁרְבִיט, an Akkadian loanword.

In the denouement of Esther, these loanwords are revisited as Esther and Mordecai take control of the administration in order to save the Jews. In this way, in Esth 8:9–17, much of the same vocabulary is revisited as well as additional words.[140]

Therefore, ultimately Esther and Mordecai gain control of the Persian administration in order to save the Jews in a reversal of the crisis set in motion by Haman. However, in the meantime, there is a tension between Esther's position of power and her failure to use this power. The experience of Esther is punctuated by loanwords reminding the audience of Persian power, and in particular her receipt of that power. This raises a problem for how Esther is portrayed, because on the one hand, it is Persian power that is being marshalled against her and the Jews. On the other hand, she herself has the potential to use this power. This tension, which is the ultimate source of suspense in the book, is one that is employed potentially at the expense of the way the audience perceives Esther, because she delays in her use of power.

Commentators have taken a variety of views on Esther's delay, in part because although there are many speculative possibilities, the text gives no explicit explanation for it.[141] However, it is Esther's hesitant character that best explains her reluctance to act. There are several approaches people have taken to paint Esther in a better light. Gerleman considers Esther's actions as bold, when she decides to approach the king.[142] However, as Moore points out, the danger is exaggerated.[143] On the other hand, Bush suggests that Esther is clever to trick the king into publicly agreeing to a *carte blanche* and that she asks for a second request as part of a strategy to arouse the king's interest.[144] Nonetheless, this interpretation seems

---

139. In Esth 1:11, it is associated with the then queen, Vashti. In Esth 6:8, it is one of a list of kingly gifts, all of which have been used by the king. Cf. Bush, *Ruth/Esther*, 349–50.

140. See 'Appendix Two: Lists and Distribution of Loanwords in Esther'.

141. Cf. Day, *Esther*, 99–100.

142. Gerleman, *Esther*, 109.

143. Moore, *Esther*, 52, 57.

144. Bush, *Ruth/Esther*, 320–21, 405–408. So also, Fox, *Character and Ideology*, 73.

improbable, since there is no reason for the reader to believe that Esther did not have victory assured from 5:3.[145] It is true, as Day points out, that the text may be playing on the opposite approaches taken by Vashti and Esther.[146] However, it is far from clear that the text condemns Vashti's approach. Ultimately, Gerleman may be correct to say that 'it is obvious that the delay is a stylistic artifice':[147] there are obvious reasons, like suspense, for the text to delay and no obvious reason for Esther to do the same. And yet, if we dispense with the notion that Esther must act in a praiseworthy manner, then the solution is simple: Esther made a mistake. In truth, this is the most economical solution, since the text does not require perfection of its characters. We have already seen Esther's great reluctance on display on ch. 4. It is no surprise that it should resurface at this point.[148]

In the interim between Esth 3:10–15 and 8:9–17, the time in which the suspense of Haman's plot is maintained, at several points the audience receives timely reminders of Esther's potential to save the Jewish people. The obvious example is when Esther is twice offered a gift up to half of the kingdom, and yet demurs from saving the Jews (Esth 5:3 and 5:6). Another clear example is Esther's claim in 4:11 that she would be unable to approach the king, when in 2:22 she was able to do so without problem. Even in ch. 6 – which on the surface appears to be an interruption of Mordecai's plot into Esther's plot, just as Esther's plot was about to reach its climax – there are also points which remind the audience of the tension surrounding Esther. Mordecai is the recipient of royal honours in a way that is reminiscent of Esther's accession to the throne in Esth 2: for example, just as Esther was the recipient of the royal diadem, כֶּתֶר, in 2:17, so is Mordecai in 6:8. This Persian loanword not only prompts comparison between Mordecai and Esther, but does so in the context of their status in the Persian empire and their ability to leverage the Persian

---

145. Gerleman, *Esther*, 110.

146. Day, *Esther*, 101.

147. 'Daß die Retardierung ein stilistischer Kunstgriff ist, liegt auf der Hand'. Translation mine. Gerleman, *Esther*, 109.

148. A modern reader might be tempted to excuse the reluctance as not especially detrimental. However, this is to lose track of the audience of the text. As we have noted already, the text goes to considerable effort to include its audience in the potential dire consequences of Haman's plot. For an audience so tied up in the success of Esther's mission, her reluctance to act is perilous. It is only the modern reader with suitable distance from the text that has the luxury of dismissing Esther's reluctance as basically inconsequential.

administration. Thus, while the text maintains the suspense of Esther's failure to act on her power in 5:3 and 5:6, it continues to prompt the audience to remember her status within the Persian empire, including by deploying loanwords carefully.

Therefore, as the text progresses, questions are raised about Esther's decisions – or lack thereof – and the text achieves this in part by its use of loanwords to establish the Persian administration as an outside threat to the Jewish people, but one which Esther is uniquely positioned to influence. In postponing Esther's decisions, the text achieves suspense but does so at the expense of her integrity. Ultimately, Esther does succeed in leveraging her influence to save the Jewish people, but the audience is left with a flawed hero.

### 3.2.5. Conclusion: how is ethnic identity presented by the loanwords in Esther and Daniel?

Overall, the loanwords in Daniel and Esther follow a similar pattern of use. Although there is a clear relationship between the setting of the books and the loanwords that appear in them, that alone is insufficient to account for the use of Babylonian and Greek loanwords in Persian settings or, indeed, Iranian loanwords in a Babylonian setting. To some extent this can be explained as a generalized sense of otherness in the imperial court. However, we must seek other patterns to their use, which can be found with respect to the genre of court tales and the function of lists therein. By using loanwords, the text sets up a distinction between the Jewish protagonists and their imperial rulers.

Loanwords are used in Esther and Daniel to explore the relationship between the audience, the characters and the setting. Because the characters and the audience belong to the same ethnic and linguistic group, the loanwords help to pit them together against the foreign setting of the text. The loanwords create an opposition between Esther, Daniel and their compatriots, on the one hand – who all share a linguistic community – and the foreign court, on the other – whose language is represented by the loanwords. That is, because the reader identifies with the Jewish protagonists, the imperial rulers are cast as other to the audience. This step of making distinctions is crucial to the process of satirization, because the imperial rulers cannot be effectively criticized if the audience identifies with them. By adopting a critical face towards the other, the texts then strengthen the sense of unity that there is between the Jewish, Hebrew-speaking, protagonists and the likewise Hebrew-speaking audience.

However, the use of the genre as a means of criticizing the court also complicates matters for the protagonists, who are also members of the court,[149] even though they share the ethnic characteristics of the audience. As such, the text invites a level of criticism of the protagonists. Even though they are members of the same group as the audience, they are also members of the foreign court. Because the text does not automatically approve of characters, just based on their ethnic background, it also comments on how members of the ethnic group should ideally behave. Thus, for example, the text promotes proactivity in securing the safety of the group by criticizing the reluctance of Esther to act to save the Jews. In this way, the text constructs the group identity, if idealistically, so as to require prioritizing the group over the individual.

What each of these concerns would mean to any given member of the audience is less certain. For an audience member who agrees with the text's position of pro-activity in securing the ethnic group's safety, we can imagine that the impact of texts like Daniel and Esther would be one of encouragement: just as Daniel and Esther prosper, so might such an audience also hope to prosper in their imperial surrounds. However, it is far from clear that all recipients of the text would have felt this way. As an example, if a reader of the text favoured accommodation to the imperial rulers, they might be persuaded by the ultimate success of Esther (who moves from passivity, her ethnic identity hidden, to a more active role) to pursue a more activist role or to identify more strongly with their ethno-linguistic identity.

### 3.3. *Depicting empire, defining the group*

#### 3.3.1. *Loanwords: a literary tool for commenting on the audience's relationship to other nations*

So far, we have discussed how loanwords are used to define the outside nations; that is, they allow texts to reinforce boundaries between their audience and other peoples on the basis of shared linguistic experience. In the case of Daniel and Esther, the loanwords shape the audience's perception of the protagonists and other characters. In Ezra, however, the loanwords are used to draw attention to the shared traits of the narrator with their audience. In the first seven chapters of Ezra, the use of loanwords is tied closely to the use of Aramaic intertwined with Hebrew. The text takes advantage of the two as a means to promote solidarity between the reader and the narrator by means of their shared linguistic competencies.

---

149. Daniel is even labelled with foreign vocabulary, such as חַרְטֹם – the Egyptian word for a court magician.

## 3.3.2. Audience – Ezra–Nehemiah

In Ezra we are relatively fortunate in locating the audience. If we accept the unity of Ezra and Nehemiah,[150] there can be no doubt that the primary audience for Ezra lived in a time after both Ezra and Nehemiah's journeys to Jerusalem. In addition, there does not appear to be any evidence of knowledge of the later Hellenistic era or the fate of the temple under the Hellenistic rulers. Therefore, the likeliest audience for Ezra is a Jewish population living under the Persian empire or perhaps the early Hellenistic era.[151] Yet, we can improve on this if we consider the details of the lists of people that are interspersed throughout Ezra–Nehemiah. Thus, for example, in Neh 12:10–11 we are given a list of the descendants of Jeshua, son of Jozadak, who returned to Jerusalem with Zerubbabel.[152] Jeshua is presented by Ezra–Nehemiah as returning in the first year of Cyrus.[153] He, therefore, corresponds to the man referred to by Josephus as Jesus, son of Josedek the high priest.[154]

Now, Neh 12:10–11 traces the descendants of Jeshua thus: Jeshua, Joiakim, Eliashib, Joiada, Jonathan,[155] and Jaddua. Following Josephus, we find that he refers to the son of Jesus, Joakeim, high priest in the time of Xerxes I.[156] The son of Joakeim, Eliasib, succeeds him as high priest.[157] The descendants continue thus: Jodas, son of Eliasib,[158] John son of Jodas, high priest during the time of Artaxerxes III and his general Bagoses,[159] and finally Jaddous, son of John, who became high priest under Darius III, who reigned from 336 until 330 BCE.[160] The correspondence between the names in Nehemiah and Josephus is exceptionally close, such that there should be no problem with recognizing that Jaddous is Josephus'

---

150. Blenkinsopp, *Ezra–Nehemiah*, 38–39; Fensham, *The Books of Ezra and Nehemiah*, 1–4; Williamson, *Ezra, Nehemiah*, xxi–xxiii.

151. The *terminus post quem* is subject to whether Artaxerxes II appears in the text as well as Artaxerxes I. Cf. Richard Saley, 'The Date of Nehemiah Reconsidered', in *Biblical and Near Eastern Essays*, ed. Gary Tuttle (Grand Rapids: Eerdmans, 1978), 151–65; Blenkinsopp, *Ezra–Nehemiah*, 140–41; Edwin Yamauchi, 'The Reverse Order of Ezra/Nehemiah Reconsidered', *Themelios* 5 (1980): 7–13.

152. Ezra 3:2; Neh 12:1, Haggai passim.

153. Ezra 1:1; 3:1, 8.

154. Josephus, *Antiquities* 11.3.10 (11.73).

155. Jonathan is apparently an error or alternative for Johanan. Cf. Neh 12:22.

156. Josephus, *Antiquities* 11.5.1 (11.121).

157. Josephus, *Antiquities* 11.5.5 (11.158).

158. Josephus, *Antiquities* 11.7.1 (11.297).

159. Josephus, *Antiquities* 11.7.1 (11.297).

160. Josephus, *Antiquities* 11.7.2 (11.302). Ehsan Yarshater, ed., *Encyclopedia Iranica* (London: Routledge & Kegan Paul, 1982–), s.v. 'DARIUS v. Darius III'.

Hellenization of Jaddua.[161] Since the list does not continue to Onias, the subsequent high priest, it seems most probable that Ezra–Nehemiah was finished during the life of Jaddua.[162] It is likelier still that it was completed while Jaddua was high priest, which is largely in the early Hellenistic period.[163]

Therefore, the book of Ezra–Nehemiah in its final form can be seen as a retrospective from the beginning of the Hellenistic period, looking back on the whole Achaemenid period and the fate of the Judaeans during that time. Even if it was completed in the Jaddua's brief time under Darius III, it is not improbable that it ceased to be updated after that point as the end of the Achaemenid period forms an obvious and natural endpoint to the narrative of Ezra–Nehemiah.[164] Additionally, the text's concern with Jerusalem and the Jews who prioritized returning imply that its primary audience is Jerusalemite Jews in the early Hellenistic period.

The concerns of this audience are addressed throughout Ezra–Nehemiah, particularly how the returnees should relate to the nations around them under the hegemony of an empire.[165] As we will see, when the text turns to the returnees' relationship with other nations in the

---

161. Blenkinsopp raises another issue, namely the historicity (or otherwise) of Josephus' reconstruction: perhaps Josephus has merely constructed what he says based off the biblical account. However, if this were so, one would assume that Josephus would identify 'Darius the Persian' (Neh 12:22) as Darius II rather than Darius III, to make the lengths of time served by each high priest more plausible. Together with Blenkinsopp, I am inclined to accept Josephus' claim that Jaddua was high priest at the time of Darius III and Alexander, but reject his presentation of direct father–son relationships between each of these high priests. Cf. Blenkinsopp, *Ezra–Nehemiah*, 336–41.

162. However, see also Williamson, *Ezra, Nehemiah*, 361, who claims the period of Jaddua likely the work of only a glossator and that most of ch. 12 dates to the period of Johanan.

163. Cf. Fried, *Ezra*, 4–5.

164. Similarly, we could imagine that Ezra–Nehemiah only reached its final form much later in the Hellenistic period and that it ended at Jaddua because he coincides with the end of the Achaemenid period. Nonetheless, I find this unlikely because of the optimism that Ezra–Nehemiah appears to have about the fate of the temple. It is not impossible that this represents nothing but nostalgia. However, I find an early Hellenistic date the more probable option.

165. See, for example, A. Philip Brown II, *Hope Amidst Ruin: A Literary and Theological Analysis of Ezra* (Greenville: Bob Jones University Press, 2009), 146–79; Mark Throntveit, *Ezra–Nehemiah*, IBC (Louisville: John Knox, 1992), 25–26, 78–80; van Wijk-Bos, *Ezra, Nehemiah, and Esther*, 10–11.

empire and the attempts of those nations to hinder their goals to rebuild the city or the temple, it adopts Aramaic and loanword-dense prose as evidence of competence for participation on an equal footing in those situations. Therefore, the text has an optimistic view for the potential of the returnees, or Jews in general, to engage in the internal politics of the empire. This differs from what we observed in Daniel, above, which has a more ambivalent attitude towards the potential of Jews to succeed in the court. However, it accords well with the positive view of Nehemiah's use of his position in the Persian court and governance structure.[166]

For an audience that lives under empire, such as one of the Hellenistic kingdoms, the ability to interact with other national groups on an equal footing is important for the self-conception of their nation and its viability. The optimism of the text towards the viability of the Jewish community in the Achaemenid empire encourages readers in the early Hellenistic period to be optimistic for their future under the Hellenistic kings.

### 3.3.3. *Ezra 1–7*
#### 3.3.3.1. *Distribution of the loanwords in Ezra 1–7*

A high proportion of the loanwords in Ezra 1–7 derives from an Iranian language, as is appropriate for its setting and composition.

As with the previous tables, there are some words which we have discounted. As in earlier chapters, we have discounted הֵיכָל, 'temple', סוּס, 'horse', and תּוֹר, 'bull', because they are so early. As discussed above,[167] we have not counted בְּלוֹ or הֲלָךְ, on the grounds that they are calques, rather than full loans. We have also excluded כְּפוֹר, although some have considered it a loanword, due to the degree of uncertainty.[168]

---

166. Tamara Eskenazi, *In an Age of Prose: A Literary Approach to Ezra–Nehemiah*, SBLMS 36 (Atlanta: Scholars Press, 1988), 144–45; Fensham, *Ezra and Nehemiah*, 149–64 *passim*; Throntveit, *Ezra–Nehemiah*, 58–70. While Eskenazi's reading of Nehemiah's character is less positive, overall she recognizes that he is portrayed as pious in his initial appearance in the king's court.

167. See under מִדָּה, in 2.5, 'Loanwords in Ezra 1–7'.

168. Some scholars count כְּפוֹר, 'bowl', a loan from Akkadian, *kaparu*. Blenkinsopp, *Ezra–Nehemiah*, 79; Zimmern, *Akkadische Fremdwörter*, 34. However, the correspondence of the vowels is very poor. If there is a loan, it must be very early – prior to the Canaanite shift. This may be, but a simpler explanation is that these words are Semitic cognates.

**Table 5** The Distribution of the Loanwords in Ezra 1–7

| Division of Text | | Title | Loanwords/Words [Iranian] (Akkadian or Sumerian) | Percentage [Iranian] (Akkadian or Sumerian) | Language | Proper Nouns of Foreign Derivation[169] | Loanwords and Proper Nouns/Words | Loanwords and Proper Nouns (percentage) |
|---|---|---|---|---|---|---|---|---|
| Ezra 1:1–2a | | Introduction | 0/24 [0/24] (0/24) | 0.00 [0.00] (0.00) | Hebrew | 6 | 6/24 | 25.00 |
| Ezra 1:2b–4 | | Cyrus' letter | 0/64 [0/64] (0/64) | 0.00 [0.00] (0.00) | Hebrew | 0 | 0/64 | 0.00 |
| Ezra 1:5–11 | | Preparation for the return | 3/98 [3/98] (0/98) | 3.06 [3.06] (0.00) | Hebrew | 8 | 11/98 | 11.22 |
| | Ezra 1:9–11 | Inventory | 2/39 [2/39] (0/39) | 5.13 [5.13] (0.00) | Hebrew | 2 | 4/39 | 10.26 |
| Ezra 2:1–70 | | The return | 4/542 [1/542] (2/542) | 0.74 [0.18] (0.37) | Hebrew | 15 | 19/542 | 3.51 |
| Ezra 3:1–13 | | Rebuilding commences | 0/250 [0/250] (0/250) | 0.00 [0.00] (0.00) | Hebrew | 4 | 4/250 | 1.60 |
| Ezra 4:1–7 | | Initial opposition | 2/117 [1/117] (1/117) | 1.71 [0.85] (0.85) | Hebrew | 13 | 15/117 | 12.82 |
| Ezra 4:8–16 | | Rehum's response and letter | 7/164 [4/164] (3/164) | 4.27 [2.47] (1.83) | Aramaic | 3 | 10/164 | 6.10 |
| | Ezra 4:9–16 | Rehum's letter | 5/151 [3/151] (2/151) | 3.31 [1.99] (1.32) | Aramaic | 3 | 8/151 | 5.30 |
| Ezra 4:17–22 | | Artaxerxes' reply | 2/83 [1/83] (1/83) | 2.41 [1.20] (1.20) | Aramaic | 0 | 2/83 | 2.41 |
| Ezra 4:23–24 | | The work stops | 2/39 [2/39] (0/39) | 5.13 [5.13] (0.00) | Aramaic | 2 | 4/39 | 10.26 |

169. For a list of those names considered foreign for the purposes of this table see 'Appendix Four: Lists and Distribution of Loanwords in Ezra 1–7'.

## 3. Text Analysis

| Passage | Sub-passage | Description | | | Language | | | |
|---|---|---|---|---|---|---|---|---|
| Ezra 5:1–5 | | Prophets and Zerubbabel recommence work | 4/90 [3/90] (1/90) | 4.44 [3.33] (1.11) | Aramaic | 3 | 7/90 | 7.78 |
| Ezra 5:6–17 | | Tattenai's letter | 10/239 [7/239] (3/239) | 4.18 [2.93] (1.26) | Aramaic | 18 | 28/239 | 11.72 |
| | Ezra 5:11–17 | The Jew's summary of Cyrus' letter | 3/160 [2/160] (1/160) | 1.88 [1.25] (0.63) | Aramaic | 15 | 18/160 | 11.25 |
| Ezra 6:1–12 | | Darius' reaction and reply | 12/231 [5/231] (7/231) | 5.19 [2.16] (3.03) | Aramaic | 10 | 22/231 | 9.52 |
| | Ezra 6:3–12 | Darius' reply | 10/206 [4/206] (6/206) | 4.85 [1.94] (2.91) | Aramaic | 6 | 16/206 | 7.77 |
| Ezra 6:13 | | The officials' reaction | 2/16 [1/16] (1/16) | 12.5 [6.25] (6.25) | Aramaic | 2 | 4/16 | 25.00 |
| Ezra 6:14–16 | | Completion of the temple | 1/50 [0/50] (1/50) | 2.00 [0.00] (0.00) | Aramaic | 4 | 5/50 | 10.00 |
| Ezra 6:16–18 | | Dedication | 0/36 [0/36] (0/36) | 0.00 [0.00] (0.00) | Aramaic | 0 | 0/36 | 0.00 |
| Ezra 6:19–22 | | Passover | 0/60 [0/60] (0/60) | 0.00 [0.00] (0.00) | Hebrew | 1 | 1/60 | 1.67 |
| Ezra 7:1–10 | | Ezra's arrival | 0/119 [0/119] (0/119) | 0.00 [0.00] (0.00) | Hebrew | 6 | 6/119 | 5.04 |
| Ezra 7:11–26 | | Artaxerxes' letter to Ezra | 17/281 [15/281] (2/281) | 6.05 [5.34] (0.71) | Aramaic | 2 | 19/281 | 6.76 |
| Ezra 7:27–28 | | Doxology | 0/36 [0/36] (0/36) | 0.00 [0.00] (0.00) | Hebrew | 0 | 0/36 | 0.00 |
| Hebrew sections | | | 9/1310 [5/1310] (3/1310) | 0.69 [0.38] (0.23) | Hebrew | 53 | 62/1310 | 4.73 |
| Aramaic sections | | | 57/1229 [38/1229] (19/1229) | 4.64 [3.09] (1.55) | Aramaic | 44 | 101/1229 | 8.22 |
| Total | | | 66/2539 [43/2539] (22/2539) | 2.60 [1.69] (0.87) | | 97 | 163/2539 | 6.42 |

The distribution of the loanwords is correlated to the use of Aramaic. This is true when only the loanwords are considered, but also when foreign names are likewise included.

### 3.3.3.2. *The correspondence of the loanwords to the use of Aramaic*

Because of this correlation, the question of the use of loanwords and foreign names in Ezra needs to be considered in the light of Ezra's use of Aramaic. Not only are the loanwords more common in the Aramaic sections, but the presence of Aramaic itself in the book is a contact phenomenon; the loanwords and the use of multiple languages are both phenomena that belong to the same group of interactions between languages. As we shall explore further, below, some approaches to the presence of Aramaic have centred on the composition history of Ezra and Nehemiah;[170] other scholars approach the Aramaic in both Ezra and Daniel from a literary perspective.[171]

The question that is relevant for our purposes is what kind of relationship exists between the use of Aramaic and the use of loanwords. One possibility would be that the loanwords are simply the artefact of the use of Aramaic. Several of the loanwords that appear in the Aramaic sections of Ezra are not known to have been used in Hebrew. If this is the case, then the discussion of the use of loanwords in Ezra is just one part of the discussion of the use of Aramaic. Another possibility would be that the loanwords simply coincide with the use of Aramaic; that is, Aramaic and loanwords are used for similar purposes in Ezra and so are used in the same places.

Fortunately, we have the Aramaic of Daniel as a test point. As we have seen, the loanwords in Daniel do not align neatly with its use of Aramaic. The rate of loanwords in Dan 7, for example, is much lower when compared to the rate of loanwords in Ezra: therefore, we conclude that the Aramaic of Daniel does not necessitate the use of loanwords; similarly, then, we should not assume that the use of loanwords in the Aramaic sections of Ezra is simply because those sections happen to be in Aramaic.

Moreover, the use of loanwords in the Ezran correspondence has a gratuitous character. Not only do almost all the words have a native Aramaic equivalent,[172] several of them are in a sense superfluous in

---

170. E.g. H. G. M. Williamson, 'The Aramaic Documents in Ezra Revisited', *JTS* NS 59 (2008): 41–62.

171. For example, but among others that we will discuss below, Berman, 'The Narratological Purpose of Aramaic'.

172. For detail, see the synonyms supplied under 2.5, 'Loanwords in Ezra 1–7'. The only exception is the verb תְּרְגֻּם, 'to translate'.

context: either they occur alongside synonyms or they are adverbial, adding circumstantial information or character. That is to say, there are poor grounds to assume that the loanwords and foreign names are used only because of the shift to Aramaic. Instead, the better approach is to consider that both the Aramaic and the loanwords are used for similar purposes.

### 3.3.3.3. *The Aramaic of Ezra*

It is necessary, therefore, to consider the purpose to which Aramaic is used in Ezra (and Daniel). Ultimately, we will suggest that Aramaic and Hebrew are used together as part of the text's construction of the identity of its audience.

Early approaches to the problem of Aramaic in Ezra focused on redactional and translational explanations. So, for example, Clines speaks of an 'Aramaic chronicle' as a documentary source for the composers of Ezra and Nehemiah.[173] Blenkinsopp identifies multiple documentary Aramaic sources.[174] More recently, Fried, Williamson and Steiner have also defended the idea that the Aramaic sections derive from actual Aramaic documents, if not necessarily in their precise current form.[175] There is, however, a problem with such explanations, because they do not explain the persistence of the two languages in the book – they do not address the question of why an editor who combined Hebrew and Aramaic (or was responsible for translating part of the book) would permit the two languages to continue side by side. Nor do they address the impact that such a choice has on the audience.

Thus, a variety of solutions have been proposed that rely on a consideration of what effect the presence of both languages has for the reader. In this way, Snell suggests that the Aramaic is used in both Ezra and Daniel to give the appearance of authenticity.[176] That is, Aramaic is used to portray the speech or writing of Aramaic speakers. There does seem to be some degree of merit to this suggestion – in the case of Daniel the Aramaic is introduced in 2:4 when the officials of the court begin to speak. However, the explanation is deficient in several respects, because it explains neither why Cyrus' letter should be presented in Hebrew, nor

---

173. Clines, *Ezra, Nehemiah, Esther*, 8–9.
174. Blenkinsopp, *Ezra–Nehemiah*, 42.
175. Fried, *Ezra*, 223–29, 253–55, 263–64, 275–76, 331; Richard Steiner, 'Bishlam's Archival Search Report in Nehemiah's Archive: Multiple Introductions and Reverse Chronological Order as Clues to the Origin of the Aramaic Letters in Ezra 4–6', *JBL* 125 (2006): 641–85; Williamson, 'The Aramaic Documents'.
176. Daniel Snell, 'Why is There Aramaic in the Bible?', *JSOT* 18 (1980): 32–51.

why the narrative sections of Ezra 4:8–6:18 are in Aramaic. Rather, an approach that considers both the onset of Aramaic and its continuance is necessary.

Arnold and Berman suggest that in the case of Ezra the purpose of the Aramaic is to suggest a shift of perspective or some other affective change in the stance of the narrator towards the text.[177] Thus, sections of the text that are given in Aramaic, the *lingua franca* of the empire, are presented from an internationalist perspective – that is, presented by a narrator who is external to the narrative. On the other hand, Hebrew sections are presented from a parochial Judahite perspective. It is an attractive thesis. However, it is also difficult to verify: the narrator's stance towards the text is not so clear at every point that we can verify the perspective in each section of Aramaic. In fact, Steinmann takes issue with Berman's thesis because of pro-Judaean stances that can be detected in some parts of the Aramaic sections and because of the triple introduction to the Aramaic section in 4:7–10.[178] Although the triple introduction does not necessarily need to be explained by redaction,[179] his evidence of pro-Judaean stances is convincing. For example, Steinmann points to a difference in perspective between the letters and the narrative sections in 4:21 and 24: whereas Artaxerxes' letter only refers to the rebuilding of the city, the narrative in 4:24 refers to the 'work on the house of God in Jerusalem'. The reference to the 'house of God' betrays both priorities and language characteristic of a Jewish perspective.[180] Steinmann, however, does recognize that, regardless of the origin, the effect of the Aramaic is to bring readers to an internationalist perspective.[181] On the other hand, it is hard to justify that the letters are presented from the perspective of an external narrator – rather, each letter is narrated mostly from the perspective of its (foreign) author.

---

177. Arnold, 'The Use of Aramaic in the Bible'; Berman, 'The Narratological Purpose of Aramaic'. This approach is also adopted by Fried to explain the narrative sections of Aramaic. Fried also explains some sections through redactional processes: she views, for example, 4:24 as a resumptive repetition of 4:5, and as such justifies the use of Aramaic in that section on the basis of a redactional unit (4:6–24). Fried, *Ezra*, 209, 221, 234–35.

178. Andrew Steinmann, 'Letters of Kings about Votive Offerings, the God of Israel and the Aramaic Document in Ezra 4:8–6:18', *JHS* 8 (2008): 1–14 (2).

179. For example, it is also possible that the introductions are for appearance's sake, to give the impression that the letters derive from a source, in the line of Snell's explanation of the Aramaic. Snell, 'Why is There Aramaic in the Bible?'

180. Steinmann, 'Letters of Kings', 11.

181. Ibid., 14.

Here, scholars like Arnold are discussing perspective in a way that does not involve focalization to a particular character, but rather they speak of the perception of the reader being coloured.[182] Thus the narrative is presented either from an international 'perspective' or from a pro-Judaean 'perspective'. In both cases, however, we are speaking of an external, unfocalized narrator. In reality, what has been termed perspective is in truth a question of the traits that are cast on the external narrator, namely whether the narrator is neutral or pro-Judaean. At times the external narrator reveals this pro-Judaean bias, whereas at other times the narrator takes – at least overtly – a neutral stance.

Hogue has recently approached this question from the perspective of triglossia and code-switching.[183] He suggests that the Aramaic found in Ezra must be distinguished between a vernacular form in the narrative and an official form in the letters.[184] Alongside Hebrew they would form a triglossic text: the Official Aramaic offers an international perspective, the narrative, 'Vernacular' Aramaic offers a local perspective, and the Hebrew connotes the return to their native land.[185] The difference between these forms of Aramaic is tied to word order: SOV word-order is reflective of Official Aramaic and SVO of vernacular Western Aramaic.[186] This approach is promising, because it helps us to explain why narrative sections as well as epistolary sections should be written in Aramaic. However, in order to explain why the text would not just use vernacular Hebrew, Hogue suggests that the vernacular Aramaic represents a voice that disagrees with the ideology of the Hebrew sections, even identifying it as the 'Ashdodite' denounced by Neh 13:24.[187] These three registers are then used to explain each point of language shift. However, Hogue's explanation of the functions of the three languages does not provide a good explanation of Ezra 6:13–22. Hogue claims that the Hebrew returns, 'when ritual recommences in the temple in v. 19'.[188] However, if we are to maintain with Hogue that Hebrew represents the return to the old state of things, the more natural resumption point would be for the dedication

---

182. E.g. Arnold, 'The Use of Aramaic', 3; Berman, 'The Narratological Purpose of Aramaic', 168.

183. Timothy Hogue, 'Return from Exile: Diglossia and Literary Code-Switching in Ezra 1–7', *ZAW* 130 (2018): 54–68.

184. Ibid., 58–60.

185. Ibid.

186. Ibid., 63.

187. Ibid., 59–60.

188. Ibid., 66.

of the temple in v. 16, which also involves the recommencement of ritual sacrifice in the temple.

Nonetheless, the analogy to code-switching and the attention to the points at which the language changes is helpful. However, in order apply the concept of code-switching to the presence of Aramaic in the Bible, we must take into account the literature on this topic.

### 3.3.3.4. *Contact linguistic phenomena*

Code-switching and nonce borrowing are two contact-linguistic phenomena that are closely related to loanwords or perhaps categories that overlap with loanwords. Code-switching, in particular, has been suggested to be the first stage of borrowing; it is not universally accepted to be so.[189] A third, related phenomenon is termed 'style-switching'. While code-switching is limited to just a few books of the Hebrew Bible, style-switching is a broader and more common type of influence, often involving loanwords or pieces of atypical morphology, that give a sense of another language or dialect, without actually changing languages.

Code-switching, in the normal sense, is an oral phenomenon in which two bilingual speakers will change between languages, in the course of a single conversation.[190] It occurs between speakers competent in both languages; that is, the switch from one language to another does not occur due to the inability of one speaker to express the material in the first language – or at least it does not occur necessarily for that reason.[191] Rather, it is suggested, it occurs for stylistic reasons: as 'either (i) a comment on the speaker's perception of self or (ii) it can be a comment on his/her perception of the tenor of the ongoing interaction, its participants, its topics, etc.'.[192] Further, it can seek to change the terms of the conver-

---

189. Shana Poplack and Nathalie Dion, 'Myths and Facts about Loanword Development', *Language Variation and Change* 24 (2012): 279–315.

190. See, for example, Carol Myers-Scotton, *Contact Linguistics: Bilingual Encounters and Grammatical Outcomes* (Oxford Scholarship Online, 2002), 44: 'Codeswitching can take many forms, but it can be defined most generally as the use of two or more varieties in the same conversation'. Code-switching is defined in terms of the same *conversation*. Similarly, ibid., 110: 'This [i.e. "classic codeswitching"] is defined as switching between *speakers* who have sufficient proficiency in one of the participating languages to use it as the sole source of the morphosyntactic frame of bilingual CPs' (emphasis mine).

191. See, e.g., Kay McCormick, 'Code-Switching: Overview', in Mesthrie, ed., *Concise Encyclopedia of Sociolinguistics*, 447–54 (453).

192. Myers-Scotton, *Contact Linguistics*, 44.

sation or to associate with identities linked to a particular language.[193] Thus it can also be used to achieve such ends as self-effacement, interaction with notions of national identity and solidarity, avoidance of undesired ethno-linguistic identities, creating new identities and claiming desirable identities.[194] Further, one could add that code-switching is used more frequently when the speaker reports speech, wishes to change the group of people being addressed, to provide parenthetical comment, or to reiterate, when the speaker changes activity or role, changes topic or for wordplay or topicalization.[195] This list should be regarded as an open one, since it is based on observation.

Code-switching is hypothesized to operate under rigid principles: for example, the morpheme-order principle and the system-morpheme principle.[196] The morpheme-order principle is that the code-switched morphemes as a group obey the normal order of the 'matrix language' (the language into which code-switched material is embedded). The system-morpheme principle is that system morphemes (grammatical morphemes) that refer grammatically to content outside of their head constituent will come from the matrix language. Myers-Scotton further hypothesizes that single content morphemes from the embedded language must only replace content morphemes from the matrix language.[197] If this rule is disobeyed, the sentence will be continued in the embedded language. The more peripheral information is to the sentence, she also hypothesizes, the more likely it is to be conveyed in the embedded language. Finally, the more formulaic an expression in the embedded language, the more likely it is to be embedded.[198]

Because it is primarily an oral phenomenon, it cannot strictly speaking occur in written texts: the spontaneity of code-switching in conversation cannot be reproduced in a written text. In this sense there can be no code switches in the Hebrew Bible.

---

193. Myers-Scotton, *Contact Linguistics*, 45. See also Carol Myers-Scotton, *Social Motivations for Codeswitching: Evidence from Africa* (Oxford: Clarendon, 1993).

194. Carol Myers-Scotton, *Multiple Voices: An Introduction to Bilingualism* (Hoboken: Wiley-Blackwell, 2008), 158–69.

195. See, e.g., Peter Auer, 'Code-Switching: Discourse Models', in Mesthrie, ed., *Concise Encyclopedia of Sociolinguistics*, 443–46 (444).

196. Myers-Scotton, *Multiple Voices*, 244–50.

197. Ibid.

198. Carol Myers-Scotton, 'Comparing Code-switching and Borrowing', *Journal of Multilingual and Multicultural Development* 13 (1992): 19–39.

Nevertheless, there is a broader sense in which the idea of code-switching may be applied to written texts: when a written text changes between languages, it is sometimes referred to as 'written code-switching'; this phenomenon follows a similar, yet distinct, set of rules. Thus, for example, Onysko argues that an Anglo-American context promotes the use of intra-sentential code switches in German newspapers.[199] In particular, the use of loanwords in the immediate context can be a factor.[200] Inter-sentential written code-switching, he finds, is predominately due to quotation.[201] Montes-Alcalá's work examining English embedded in Spanish, however, demonstrates the distinction we must make between this written code-switching and oral code-switching. Montes-Alcalá explains her data in mostly socio-pragmatic and stylistic terms and finds that these explanations are more or less equivalent to the socio-pragmatic and stylistic motivations for oral code-switching.[202] Nevertheless there is no equivalent to theoretical principles of code-switching.

This broader sense of code-switching, written code-switching, can be applied to the Hebrew Bible, when the text changes between Hebrew and Aramaic.[203] Although editorial, recensional or redactional activity must be considered, there is a person (or persons) who chose to preserve the two languages side by side. The choice to preserve two languages, rather than translate, is equivalent for our purposes to a single author establishing the use of two languages. Although it might appear to be less spontaneous than ordinary 'written code-switching', written code switches are themselves not spontaneous: every act of writing involves a degree of removal from spontaneity. Thus, for example, the single verse of Aramaic in Jer 10:11 amidst an otherwise Hebrew text might be explained, as for example by Holladay,[204] as an emphatic summarizing comment on what precedes it.[205]

---

199. Alexander Onysko, *Anglicisms in German: Borrowing, Lexical Productivity and Written Codeswitching* (Berlin: de Gruyter, 2007), 290.

200. Ibid., 293.

201. Ibid., 305.

202. Thus, for example, Montes-Alcalá, 'Two Languages, One Pen', 72: 'All in all, it has been shown that bilingual individuals do code-switch when writing to other bilinguals, possess sufficient linguistic and cultural knowledge of the nuances of both Spanish and English when code-switching, and that rather than being arbitrary, this mode of writing fulfils specific socio-pragmatic and stylistic functions similar to those attested in oral code-switching'.

203. Gen 31:47; Ezra 4:8–6:18; 7:12–26; Jer 10:11; Dan 2–7.

204. William Holladay, *Jeremiah 1*, Hermeneia (Minneapolis: Fortress, 1986), 324–25.

205. Cf. Onysko, *Anglicisms in German*, 308.

Nonce borrowing, in contrast to code-switching, is a term popularized by Poplack[206] to denote a word borrowed in a singular instance to fit a speaker's need. Such words, despite the name, are a different phenomenon to ordinary loans because they do not have any currency beyond the particular conversation. The term is itself a ground for controversy; it is not agreed whether nonce borrowings are their own category[207] or merely a species of code-switching.[208] However, it is logical that any instance we could discover in a written document must be excluded from the category of nonce borrowing: the process of writing any word down guarantees its currency beyond that moment. Therefore, even *hapax legomena* in the Hebrew Bible are not to be considered nonce borrowings, in the strict sense.

In the same way, however, that we can conceive of a broader sense of code-switching, it is possible to conceive of a broader sense of 'pseudo'-nonce borrowing. In cases like John 19:17, the text presents a Greek place name, Κρανίου Τόπον ('place of the skull') accompanied by an equivalent 'Hebrew' name, Γολγοθα (Golgotha).[209] Although the word is in one sense 'borrowed' into Greek and ultimately into English, the fact that it is accompanied by a native Greek version of the name means that there is no reason for the word to have any true currency beyond that text. On the other hand, the fact that the word has entered into English, even if only ever used in reference to John 19 and similar accounts, stands as evidence that the word did gain currency beyond that one text. Therefore, despite certain analogies between this pseudo-nonce-borrowing and nonce borrowing, it is best to treat such cases as *Fremdwörter* with a very low level of nativization.

A third related phenomenon, which has been noted in the Hebrew Bible, is 'style-switching'. Style-switching is a technique by which a biblical text changes to a style that contains linguistic features associated with another language. It has been noted by scholars such as Kaufman,[210]

---

206. Shana Poplack, David Sankoff and Christopher Miller, 'The Social Correlates and Linguistic Processes of Lexical Borrowing and Assimilation', *Linguistics* 26 (1988): 47–104.

207. Shana Poplack, 'What Does the Nonce Borrowing Hypothesis Hypothesize?', *Bilingualism – Language and Cognition* 15 (2012): 644–48.

208. Margaret Deuchar and Jonathan Stammers, 'What is the "Nonce Borrowing Hypothesis" Anyway?', *Bilingualism – Language and Cognition* 15 (2012): 649–50.

209. Granted, Golgotha is a place name and is a different category of borrowing to most loanwords or nonce-borrowings, but it is still foreign lexical material in Greek.

210. Stephen Kaufman, 'The Classification of the North West Semitic Dialects of the Biblical Period and Some Implications Thereof', in *Proceedings of the Ninth*

Rendsburg[211] and Young.[212] It is to be distinguished from code-switching between dialects in that it does not necessarily entail real competence in both languages/dialects and is not prone to extended islands of the embedded language or dialect; rather, the writer refers to another dialect or language based on their own, potentially limited, knowledge of that language. In fact, style-switching is more comparable to the Anglo-American context, noted by Onysko and considered above, that facilitates the use of Anglicisms.

### 3.3.3.5. *Code-switching and the Aramaic of Ezra*

If we understand the intertwining of Hebrew and Aramaic as a written form of code-switching, we can fully explain the presence of both Hebrew and Aramaic in Ezra. In particular, it becomes unnecessary to explain why the text does not revert to Hebrew where we might expect it to: as we have seen in our discussion of code-switching, it is common for discourse to continue in the switched language even after the triggering factor is past or no longer relevant. Because code-switches are not compulsory, the changes in language do not need to occur at each point when the topic shifts. Therefore, we explain the four changes in language thus:

The first change, in Ezra 4:8, might be adequately explained by Snell's approach: the most obvious assumption for the reader is that there is a change in language because of the presentation of a new text, whether as a result of a change in source document or simply because the text is attempting to give the appearance of authenticity. However, at this point we agree with Hogue that the social status of Aramaic and Aramaic-speakers is raised as a possible cause for the change.

When in 6:19 the text returns to Hebrew, there is no new letter or other explicit motivation given by the text. The change coincides with a move to discuss the celebration of Passover by the returnees, which provides a plausible motive for a return to Hebrew.[213] The text delays the change in language from 6:16 to 6:19 because Passover is, for it, the more important

---

*World Congress of Jewish Studies, Jerusalem, 4–12 August, 1985: Panel Sessions, Hebrew and Aramaic*, ed. Moshe Goshen-Gottstein (Jerusalem: Magnes, 1988), 41–57 (54–56).

211. See, for example, Gary Rendsburg, 'Style-Switching', in *EHLL*, 3:633–36; Rendsburg, 'Aramaic-like Features'; Rendsburg, 'What We Can Learn?'

212. Ian Young, 'The Diphthong *\*ay* in Edomite', *JSS* 37 (1992): 27–30; Ian Young, 'Evidence of Diversity in Pre-Exilic Judahite Hebrew', *HS* 38 (1997): 7–20.

213. Arnold attributes the change to the end of the themes of building and opposition. However, if this were the case we should expect the change earlier, in Ezra 6:16. Snell agrees that it is likely to do with the book of Moses and Passover. Arnold, 'The Use of Aramaic', 7; Snell, 'Why is There Aramaic in the Bible?', 34.

event. Whereas the switch to Aramaic in 4:8 was about the ability of the community to participate and succeed in international diplomacy, the switch to Hebrew in 6:19 is about the uniqueness of Passover.

The same motives found in Ezra 4:8 also explain the return to Aramaic in 7:12. As the narrator turns back to international diplomacy, it resumes the use of Aramaic, as we expect now, having already encountered the change in Ezra 4:8. Returning to Hebrew, in 7:27 coincides with a change of addressee. The shift to addressing God is accompanied by a change to Hebrew because prayer to the God of the Hebrew-speaking Jews, a prayer in which the Hebrew-speaking audience participates, should exclude the international Aramaic community.[214]

However, the analogy to code-switching achieves more than just explaining each instance of language shift. Unlike style-switching, linguistic code-switching requires two people with competence in every language involved. Similarly, the presence of Aramaic and Hebrew together does not just presume the linguistic characteristics of the producers of the text, but more importantly of the recipients of the text. The text desires for its audience to be able to navigate Aramaic, with its use in international diplomacy, and Hebrew, with its use in parochial religious matters.

*Aside: an account of the Aramaic and Hebrew in Daniel*

It is similarly possible to give an account of the presence of Hebrew and Aramaic together in Daniel. The initial change from Hebrew to Aramaic is simple to explain: it is occasioned by the text reporting the speech of the Chaldaeans (in Dan 2:4). As the text stands, it presents as though the Chaldaeans originally spoke these words in Aramaic – even though from a redactional standpoint it may be that אֲרָמִית is a later addition, to apologize for the change in language. As was the case in Ezra, the failure to change back after the speech of the Chaldaeans is a natural part of code-switching.[215]

The change back from Aramaic to Hebrew in 8:1 is not so straightforward to explain. It occurs at a structural boundary, which might give occasion to the change. However, there have been other structural

---

214. My approach in this accords well with Sérandour's observation that the choice of language in Ezra often corresponds to the difference between profane and sacred topics. In his reckoning, there is a change of language here because of the decisive change in topic. This is consistent with how code-switching works. However, as with other approaches, it fails to account for all the detail. Ezra 6:16–18 deals plainly with the sacred domain, and yet is presented in Aramaic. Arnaud Sérandour, 'Hébreu et Araméen dans la Bible', *REJ* 159 (2000): 345–55, especially 347.

215. See above, 3.3.3.4., 'Code-Switching and Nonce Borrowing'.

boundaries and 7:1 seems a more obvious candidate to trigger the writing to switch back to Hebrew. Portier-Young argues that this moment of change represents a 'reorientation to covenant alone', after a focus on the world of empires in the previous chapters, including ch. 7.[216] For Portier-Young, these changes represent different situations, in which different expectations apply to the audience: 'The authors of Daniel now [i.e. in ch. 8] ask their readers to dis-identify with the earlier claims of the empire and make the unexpected – and difficult – identification with a people bound in covenant to God alone'.[217] According to Portier-Young's approach, the Aramaic sections underscore the conflict between temporal and divine kingdoms, whereas the final sections of the book in Hebrew communicate that the time for negotiation between imperial and divine powers has passed. Aramaic was the appropriate language in the past, but the new circumstances demand Hebrew. However, pitting the Hebrew and Aramaic sections of this book against one another is mistaken: as with Ezra–Nehemiah, the final shapers of Daniel demonstrate their own competence in both languages and assume the competence of their audience in both languages. It is difficult to claim that the book of Daniel represents a move away from the language of empire (Aramaic) towards the language of covenant (Hebrew), because the final book still requires its audience to be competent in both. Therefore, rather than representing a transition from Aramaic to Hebrew, we must consider the use of Aramaic and Hebrew *together*. For this reason, we must also reject – at least in the final form of the book – the views of Rouillard-Bonraisin who ties the use of Aramaic and Hebrew to *different* audiences: the vernacular (Aramaic) intended for broad consumption and the religious tongue (Hebrew) intended for a narrower audience.[218] Still, Rouillard-Bonraisin's insight is helpful in that it clarifies that the audience of the whole book is narrow: it is limited to those who are competent in both the vernacular Aramaic and also the esoteric Hebrew.

Plöger's view that these languages represent different spheres is superior, because it allows for a single audience operating across both spheres: the Aramaic represents the foreign sphere and the Hebrew represents the native sphere.[219] Somewhat similarly, Valeta argues that Aramaic

---

216. Anathea Portier-Young, 'Languages of Identity and Obligation: Daniel as a Bilingual Book', *VT* 60 (2010): 98–115 (113–15).

217. Ibid., 113.

218. Hedwige Rouillard-Bonraisin, 'Problemes du bilinguisme en *Daniel*', in *Mosaïque de langues, mosaïque culturelle. Le bilinguisme dans le Proche-Orient ancient*, ed. Françoise Briquel-Chatonnet (Paris: Jean Maisonneuve, 1996), 145–70.

219. Plöger, *Das Buch Daniel*, 26–27.

is used to satirize the empire;[220] this sits well with our conclusions about the use of loanwords in the text and also makes sense with a text that assumes an audience competent in both languages. However, it is difficult to find satire in ch. 7. Furthermore, Valeta's explanation that the language of chs. 1 and 7 is mismatched in order to draw attention to the shift in language seems unlikely, because a shift in language would have been striking no matter where it occurred.[221] Therefore, the use of Aramaic as a means of satire is an incomplete explanation.

As we have seen above, one of the reasons that code-switches may take place in spoken language is that the speaker wishes to portray themselves in a different role.[222] It is, therefore, striking that at the beginning of ch. 8, the narrator of the frame narrative changes for the first time, unambiguously, to the voice of Daniel. Although much of ch. 7 is related in the first person, this is part of an embedded narrative that commences when Daniel wrote down the dream. The frame narrative, which appears in 7:1, is still written in the third person; the rest of ch. 7, however, belongs to the embedded narrative. It is not until 8:1 that the introductory date formula signals that we have resumed the frame narrative. However, in this verse the frame narrative changes from its customary third person to the first person. This unusual change coincides with the change from Aramaic back to Hebrew.[223]

Therefore, we may give an account for the presence of both Hebrew and Aramaic in Daniel like this: both languages are present because, by the use of both, the text specifies its 'authors' and its audience as people competent in both the vernacular (Aramaic) and the religious language (Hebrew). The use of Aramaic also supports the text's satirization of empire in chs. 2–6. The first change between languages is due to the text quoting Aramaic speech in 2:4. The text continues in Aramaic, because code-switches are not obligatory and do not necessarily need to revert back. Finally, the text reverts to Hebrew in 8:1 to mark the change of narrator, from third person to first person, wherein the text associates itself more strongly with the new narrator, Daniel.

---

220. David Valeta, 'Polyglossia and Parody: Language in Daniel 1–6', in *Bakhtin and Genre Theory in Biblical Studies*, ed. Roland Boer (Atlanta: SBL, 2007), 91–108, especially 104–5.

221. Valeta, 'Polyglossia and Parody', 106.

222. See above, 3.3.3.4, 'Code-Switching and Nonce Borrowing'.

223. This observation coincides with Arnold's explanation of Daniel's Aramaic. However, whereas Arnold tried to explain all of the use of Aramaic by perspective, we only need to explain the moment of change. Arnold, 'The Use of Aramaic', 13.

### 3.3.3.6. *The effect of the loanwords in light of the effect of the Aramaic*

As we noted above, the use of Aramaic is strongly correlated to the use of loanwords in Ezra 1–7. If then, we accept that the use of Aramaic is a means for the narrator and its audience to claim competence in Aramaic, and thereby membership in the international community which uses Aramaic, we then conclude that the loanwords serve a similar purpose. Just as the Aramaic uses the shared linguistic competency between the narrator and the reader to suggest the diplomatic competency of their community, so do the loanwords and the foreign names.

However, whereas the code-switches between languages act on the moment of change and at times persist beyond what triggered the change, there is no reason for the loanwords and foreign names to persist. In fact, this is what we observe. Therefore, in 6:14, where the focus of the narrative moves decisively away from international correspondence – but the change in language is postponed until there is a reason to prefer Hebrew – the loanwords decrease in frequency drastically, in accordance with the change. The only loanword found between 6:14 and the return to Hebrew in 6:19 is the name of the month Adar. Therefore, although the code-switching marks particular moments of change, the loanwords offer the text a more fine-grained tool.

As further evidence of the way the Aramaic and loanwords are functioning, we also note that the letter in Ezra 1:2–4, or at least its substance,[224] is repeated in Ezra 6:3–5, now in Aramaic and with loanwords and foreign names.[225]

The same content has been delivered in both Hebrew, without loanwords, and in Aramaic, with loanwords. The second time this content is delivered it is in the context of the Judaeans' diplomacy with the nations around them, whereas in the first chapter, it is presented as a matter for the returning Jews alone, with no suggestion of the opposition of the surrounding nations. Therefore, in ch. 1 there is no need for the narrator or the text's readers to justify their competence in international diplomacy and accordingly there is no need for the text to change to loanword-rich Aramaic prose at this point.

---

224. This is not to suggest that there is necessarily any genetic connection between the texts. Rather, the same information is conveyed using different stylistic choices, as informed by the differing perspectives in each case.

225. See 'Appendix Four: Lists and Distribution of Loanwords in Ezra 1–7'.

## 3.3.4. *Conclusion: the loanwords create a sense of linguistic identity as a part of the group identity*

The use of the Aramaic and loanwords is part of the narrator's strategy to engage its reader as a part of the same linguistic community. One of the consequences of this is that the factors that define this community – its ability to use both Aramaic and Hebrew, to use loanword-dense or loanword-sparse prose – appear as a unifier of the community of the narrator and its readers. Moreover, it excludes others from this community, who can only speak one or neither of these languages. This helps cast light on the complicated picture of whom Ezra–Nehemiah considers part of its audience's community. Whereas it is clear that the 'people of the land' are not a part of the community, as their help is rejected and intermarriage forbidden, many scholars have interpreted this in religious terms.[226] Some, like Eskenazi and Christopher-Smith, have approached these actions through the lens of identity-construction and have noted other factors, like the control of the land and ethnic difference.[227] However, the linguistic component of ethnic identity and its role in the text of Ezra–Nehemiah has gone unremarked.[228] Hebrew in some form remains accessible in the early Hellenistic period to the Judaean population and Aramaic is common among the Judaeans' neighbours and overlords. It is also accessible to some segments of the Judaean population, at least. There is some evidence – the Bar Kochba letters – for the existence of spoken Hebrew even into the second century CE.[229] Nonetheless, it is likely that Aramaic was also prevalent, especially among the literate

---

226. E.g. Blenkinsopp, *Ezra–Nehemiah*, 107; Fensham, *Ezra and Nehemiah*, 125; Throntveit, *Ezra–Nehemiah*, 25–26; van Wijk Bos, *Ezra, Nehemiah, and Esther*, 41.

227. Eskenazi, 'Imagining the Other', 230–56; Daniel Smith-Christopher, 'Between Ezra and Isaiah: Exclusion, Transformation, and Inclusion of the "Foreigner" in Post-Exilic Biblical Theology', in Brett, ed., *Ethnicity and the Bible*, 117–42.

228. That there was a speech community is, perhaps, obvious. Thus, scholars like Polak, will analyze the characteristics of the vernacular that they see preserved in Ezra–Nehemiah. However, it is the role that this shared trait plays in the construction of identity that seems to have gone unnoticed. Cf. Frank Polak, 'Sociolinguistics and the Judean Speech Community', in Lipschitz and Oeming, eds., *Judah and the Judeans in the Persian Period*, 589–628.

229. Cf. P. Kyle McCarter, 'Hebrew', in Woodard, ed., *The Cambridge Encyclopedia of the World's Ancient Languages*, 319–64 (320–21); Richard Steiner, 'Ancient Hebrew', in Hetzron, ed., *The Semitic Languages*, 145–73 (146).

population.[230] However, rather than the use of one language it is the combination of the two which most defines the text's audience: the use of Hebrew excludes a foreign audience; the use of Aramaic excludes those Hebrew-speakers who cannot understand Aramaic. The use of these two languages together implies that the text approves of a situation in which its audience is competent in the use of both.

Just as in Daniel and Esther, Ezra 1–7 makes use of loanwords to create a means of defining the other and the relationship of the reader to that other. However, whereas Daniel and Esther focus on the court and the interactions of individuals, Ezra's use of loanwords engages the reader more directly as a part of the community, by drawing on their ability to understand the loanword-dense Aramaic with which it paints international diplomacy. Whereas in Daniel and Esther, the narrator stands apart from both the audience and the characters, in Ezra, the audience is encouraged to identify with the narrator. Another point of difference is that the targets of otherization in Ezra 1–7 are not individual members of the court, but rather other people who likewise inhabit the Persian and/or Hellenistic provinces. Unlike Daniel and Esther, in Ezra 1–7 we perceive some of the grounds on which the boundaries of the group are drawn: while in Daniel and Esther, the other is presented as the target of satire, the focus on individuals means that the question of who is part of which group is less pertinent. In Ezra 1–7, however, linguistic identity is a clear component of the group's identity.

### 3.4. Depicting the past, defining the group

#### 3.4.1. Loanwords: a literary tool for defining the group's shared past

As we turn now to Exodus and the effect of the loanwords in the accounts of the building of the tabernacle, we turn to a text in which there are no clear foreign rivals. Unlike in Ezra, Esther and Daniel there is no division of characters along national or linguistic lines. Nonetheless, the text uses loanwords in its depiction of the tabernacle in a way that defines the shared experience of its audience, as a single nation in the definitive narrative of exodus from a foreign power.

---

230. Holger Gzella, *A Cultural History of Aramaic: From the Beginnings to the Advent of Islam* (Leiden: Brill, 2015), 226–29; Catherine Hezser, *Jewish Literacy in Roman Palestine*, Texte und Studien zum antiken Judentum (Tübingen: Mohr Siebeck, 2001), 229; Seth Schwartz, 'Language, Power and Identity in Ancient Palestine', *Past & Present* 148 (1995): 12–31.

## 3.4.2. *Audience – Exodus*

So far, we have made attempts at understanding the audience of each text and in part that has been assisted by the relatively uncontroversial dates that these texts can be assigned. Whether for final forms or for individual strata, the dating of Exodus is more controversial. However, the observations that we will make about the text are sufficiently general that they function for a wide range of possibilities. In addition to looking at the dates of composition, we can consider clues in the text about what sort of audience the text might be written for.

The most obvious point to make is that this audience considers the tabernacle of very great significance, as signalled by the volume of text dedicated to it.[231] Likewise, as we shall explore further below, the text utilizes ideas of covenant membership. Therefore, it seems reasonable that it is directed at people who conceive of themselves as members of that covenant, which is to say that they perceive some degree of continuity between themselves and the Israelites depicted in the text. The requisite features of the audience of this text, then, are broad enough to work equally within any of the time-frames that scholars have suggested,[232] either for the completion of Exodus or for its individual strata.

---

231. Hamilton, *Exodus*, 449–50.

232. The section in which we find most of the loanwords is typically assigned to the Priestly source, P. P has been dated both 'early' (i.e. Monarchic) and 'late' (i.e. post-Deuteronomistic). It is also no longer taken for granted that all of P was written at the same time. The following is a short summary of what is a very extensive bibliography. Michael Coogan, *The Old Testament: A Historical and Literary Introduction to the Hebrew Scriptures*, 2nd ed. (Oxford: Oxford University Press, 2011), 402–403; Dozeman, *Exodus*, 31–35; Avi Hurvitz, 'The Usage of שש and בוץ in the Bible and its Implication for the Dating of P', *HTR* 60 (1967): 117–21; Hurvitz, 'The Evidence of Language in Dating the Priestly Code: A Linguistic Study in Technical Idioms and Terminology', *RB* 81 (1974): 24–56; Hurvitz, 'לשונו של המקור הכהני ורקעה ההיסטורי' [The Language of the Priestly Source and its Historical Setting – the Case for an Early Date], *Proceedings of the World Congress of Jewish Studies* 8 (1981): 83–94; Hurvitz, 'Dating the Priestly Source in Light of the Historical Study of Biblical Hebrew: A Century after Wellhausen', *ZAW* 100 (1988): 88–100; Hurvitz, 'Once Again: The Linguistic Profile of the Priestly Material in the Pentateuch and its Historical Age. A Response to J. Blenkinsopp', *ZAW* 112 (2000): 180–91; Jacob Milgrom, *Leviticus 1–16*, AB 3 (New York: Doubleday, 1991), 3–7; Propp, *Exodus 19–40*, 730–32; Young, Rezetko and Ehrensvärd, *Linguistic Dating of Biblical Texts*, especially 2:12–17.

### 3.4.3. *Exodus 25–40*

#### 3.4.3.1. *The tabernacle according to the book of Exodus*

The description of the tabernacle in the book of Exodus uses a high proportion of loanwords – moreover, loanwords from predominantly a single source language. The tabernacle is first commissioned in detailed instructions in Exod 25–31 and then built in Exod 35–40, reusing the same wording. The two accounts together account for a large section of Exodus and provide its conclusion. Among the topics that attract attention in this section of Exodus are, the purpose of the account's precision and repetition (both between commissioning and construction and the repetitive style used in the instructions[233]), the parallels between this account and the first creation account,[234] the relationship between these two descriptions and the golden calf incident which is told in the interim,[235] and the function of the tabernacle as it relates to ancient Near Eastern temples and cosmic mountains.[236] Some attention is also given to the question of why so much effort is given over to these instructions, which strain the attention of many modern readers.[237] While the loanwords in this section of Exodus have been noticed, there has been no attempt to explain their effect in the narrative or how that affects the broader themes of Exodus.

Within the narrative there are many loanwords, coming predominantly from Egyptian. We saw in the case of Daniel and Esther that loanwords have been used in such a way that the audience identifies with one ethno-linguistic group of people portrayed in the narrative but not with others, namely their imperial rulers. In the case of the tabernacle narratives, however, there is only one identifiable ethno-linguistic group of people in the narrative: the Israelites building the tabernacle.

#### 3.4.3.2. *The tabernacle and the covenant: an introduction to Exodus 25–40*

As we will see, the distribution of the loanwords is highly concentrated in the sections that deal with the tabernacle. As such, it is necessary to discuss what the role of the tabernacle is in the Book of the Covenant and the book of Exodus as a whole.

---

233. Propp, *Exodus 19–40*, 710–20.

234. Terence Fretheim, *Exodus*, IBC (Louisville: John Knox, 1991), 268–72; Sarna, *Exodus*, 156.

235. Fretheim, *Exodus*, 267.

236. Dozeman, *Exodus*, 569–75; J. Gerald Janzen, *Exodus*, Westminster Bible Companion (Louisville: Westminster John Knox, 1997), 193.

237. Fretheim, *Exodus*, 263–68.

The Sinaitic covenant is outlined in Exod 19:3–6, consisting of four elements: a condition of obedience, a requirement of divine ownership – that is, Israel's fulfilment of the role of priests and a holy nation – a promise of divine presence and the history of God's actions for Israel. The Book of the Covenant precedes the tabernacle and associated narratives. Fischer and Markl argue that the construction of the tabernacle should be read in light of the covenant;[238] in particular, they conceive of the tabernacle as a 'symbolic manifestation of the covenant'.[239] Their evidence for this claim is based on correspondences between the language of the covenant and aspects of the tabernacle's construction: as Israel is to be God's kingdom, so the tabernacle is like a palace; just as Israel is to be a holy nation per the covenant, so the tabernacle's construction frequently refers to holiness; just as Israel is to be God's jewel[240] in Exod 19:5, so are the names of the tribes inscribed on jewels in Exod 28.[241] More evidence of this can be found throughout the tabernacle accounts.

The way the covenant is proposed, the divine presence is based on Israel's obedience and fulfilment, which is justified on the basis of God's actions for Israel. The consequence of the covenant is God's presence among Israel. These elements of the covenant are manifested to some extent in the material form of the tabernacle but also in the language used for the tabernacle's description, especially in the way the loanwords are used.

The most obvious of the elements of the covenant in the tabernacle accounts is that of divine presence. The stated purpose of the tabernacle is as a means for God to dwell with Israel (Exod 25:8; 29:43–46). Moreover, the tabernacle accounts end with the arrival of God's presence in the tabernacle (Exod 40:34–38). As the holiness of the tabernacle was prefigured by the geography of Sinai,[242] God's presence in the tabernacle

---

238. Georg Fischer and Dominik Markl, *Das Buch Exodus*, Neuer Stuttgarter Kommentar – Altes Testament (Stuttgart: Verlag Katholisches Bibelwerk, 2009), 277–79; cf. Sarna, *Exodus*, 159: 'It is the Ark and its contents, the symbol of the covenant between God and Israel, that give meaning to the Tabernacle, for the religio-moral imperatives of the Decalogue constitute the foundation of Israelite society'.

239. My translation. Fischer and Markl, *Das Buch Exodus*, 278: 'Symbolische Verwirklichung des Bundes'. Cf. Barry Webb, 'Heaven on Earth: The Significance of the Tabernacle in its Literary and Theological Context', in *Exploring Exodus*, ed. Brian Rosner and Paul Williamson (Nottingham: Apollos, 2008), 154–76 (157).

240. What the NRSV translates as 'treasured possession' would be translated by Fischer and Markl as 'jewel'. Fischer and Markl, *Das Buch Exodus*, 278.

241. Ibid., 278–79.

242. We will discuss this further in the following paragraphs.

is also prefigured by his presence on Sinai. God's presence is, likewise, a key concern of the narratives that intervene in Exod 32–34.[243]

God's ownership of Israel, according to the covenant, is expressed in Israel's status as a kingdom of priests and a holy nation (Exod 19:5–6). This concern for holiness and priestly status is manifested in the physical spaces within the tabernacle. However, it is not just that the tabernacle's description incidentally involves holiness due to its function. Rather, the narrative is structured in such a way as to draw attention to this particular characteristic.

In this respect, the spaces within the Sinai narrative are a helpful entry point into the narrative. Not only is the location of Sinai particularly significant within the Pentateuch as a whole, but the more immediate narrative is also constructed around the locations on and around the mountain. It has been noticed that the locations on the mountain parallel the parts of the tabernacle and later the temple.[244] The peak of the mountain where Moses meets with God is analogous to the holy of holies, the lower parts to the outer parts of the tabernacle. Likewise, the vision Moses and the elders share of God enthroned in the heavens in Exod 24:10 ties the Sinai landscape to a heavenly prototype of the temple. The narrative presents these spatial divisions on Sinai prior to its explanation of the tabernacle. The events of the narrative – or rather the spaces of the narrative – then, control how the reader understands the instructions for the tabernacle that follow. Thus, it is not simply that the tabernacle reproduces certain elements of the narrative in which it is embedded, but that the narrative informs us of the meaning of the tabernacle's design.

Further, the spatial parallels between the narrative and the tabernacle are not the only connections to be made; the parallels between the tabernacle

---

243. Cf. Daniel Timmer, 'Creation, Tabernacle and Sabbath: The Function of the Sabbath Frame in Exodus 31:12–17; 35:1–3' (PhD diss., Trinity Evangelical Divinity School, 2006), 210–19.

244. Dozeman, *Exodus*, 569–71; Propp, *Exodus 19–40*, 300–301, 688. Both have a tripartite division, with descending grades of holiness. Whereas only the High Priest can enter the Holy of Holies, so only Moses meets God directly at the peak. Partway up the mountain, a smaller group is allowed (Exod 24:1), as the Holy Place is for priests alone. Finally, all the people are allowed at the foot of the mountain and, likewise, the outer court of the tabernacle. More broadly, mountains, like the tabernacle, are conceived as locations of divine presence. These mountains include the Temple Mount, but also Mount Paran (Hab 3:3; Deut 33:2) or Bashan (Ps 68:15). This motif is also familiar from Canaanite religion (Zaphon, cf. *KTU* 1.41) and the Greeks (Ida [cf. *Iliad* III 276], Olympus [cf. *Odyssey* VI 42] and others).

apparatus and elements of the Sinai narrative are also particularly striking. The Sinai mountain is described only sparsely in the narrative; no details of the mountain itself are given. The image that is painted by the narrator is constructed wholly around the elements of God's appearance, namely the lightning, the earthquake and the trumpet blasts (Exod 19:20–25; 20:18–20; 24:12–18). We note that in the description of the tabernacle the fire of the lampstand and the incense are reminiscent of the smoke, fire and lightning at Sinai.[245] Because the imagery of the mountain is restricted to these particular elements, the parallels are all the more striking when reading the instructions for the tabernacle.

Just as holiness plays a role in the geography of Sinai, so it is also materialized in the structure of the tabernacle. In each case there is a series of locations each with different grades of holiness and different people permitted to be present.[246] Haran argues, further, that the gradated holiness is also reflected in the materials used for the construction of the tabernacle and its furniture.[247] Thus concern for holiness and God's ownership of Israel are represented in both the geography and components of the tabernacle.

The covenant's element of obedience is reflected in word-order and figures of repetition in the accounts of the tabernacle's commissioning and construction. Throughout the instructions for the building of the tabernacle the sentence-initial position is occupied repeatedly by second-person singular verbs. This is typical of 'predicate-focused sentences', which answer an implied question about what the subject is doing[248] – in this case answering the implied question, 'what is Moses to do?' In the building account, the sentence-initial verbs are third-person, answering the

---

245. Cf. Durham, *Exodus*, 364–65, 407–408. Fire and cloud/smoke are very strongly associated with the divine presence in Exodus (Exod 3:2; 13:21–22; 14:19–24; 16:10; 19:9, 16–18; 24:14–17; 33:9).

246. Cf. Menahem Haran, *Temples and Temple-Service in Ancient Israel* (Oxford: Clarendon, 1978), 175–88; Sunhee Kim, 'The Concepts of Sacred Space in the Hebrew Bible: Meanings, Significance, and Functions' (PhD diss., Boston University, 2014), 197.

247. Haran, *Temples and Temple-Service*, 158–65.

248. Jean-Marc Heimerdinger, *Topic, Focus and Foreground in Ancient Hebrew Narratives* (Sheffield: Sheffield Academic Press, 1999); Robert Holmstedt, 'Word Order and Information Structure in Ruth and Jonah: A Generative-Typological Analysis', *JSS* 54 (2009): 111–39; Holmstedt, 'The Typological Classification of the Hebrew of Genesis: Subject–Verb or Verb–Subject?', *JHS* 11 (2001): 1–39; Nicholas Lunn, *Word-order Variation in Biblical Hebrew Poetry: Differentiating Pragmatics and Poetics* (Milton Keynes: Paternoster, 2006), 94–120.

implied question, 'what did Bezalel do?' The repetition of this sentence structure functions in such a way as to emphasize the obedience of Moses and Bezalel to the instructions that have been given. To the narrative audience of the commissioning, which is to say Moses and secondarily the Israelites when Moses reports back, it is the repetition of the verbs alone that suggest a call to obedience. For the reader, however, who sees the commissioning and the building together, it is the correspondence of the instructions to the outcome that stresses the obedience.

Given that the tabernacle accounts follow the covenant code directly, it is unsurprising that aspects of those accounts should reflect that context. Moreover, the strength of Fischer and Markl's explanation of the tabernacle – that it is the physical manifestation of the covenant – is that it allows the second half of Exodus to be read as a unity, by explaining the links between the lengthy descriptions of the tabernacle, the covenant code and the golden calf incident; all three speak to the single theme of covenant. It is not, however, without weakness insofar as the thematic echoes of the covenant in the tabernacle do not necessarily require that the covenant is the overriding concern of the tabernacle literature.[249] Nevertheless, the use of loanwords in the tabernacle accounts, as we will see, draw attention to the same elements of the covenant that are outlined above. Moreover, they provide a sense of narrative to the tabernacle that is otherwise missing by drawing attention to an additional element of the covenant, namely God's actions on the behalf of Israel in the exodus.

### 3.4.3.3. *The distribution of loanwords in Exodus 25–40*

To understand how the loanwords of Exod 25–40 contribute to the way the elements of the covenant pervade that text, it is necessary to analyze the patterns of those loanwords' use.

Although there is a high proportion of loanwords in the sections attributed to Priestly sources, which is to say in the commissioning of the tabernacle (Exod 25–31) – and also in the parallel completion of the tabernacle (Exod 35–39) – the distribution of those loanwords is uneven. In addition, the only potential loanwords in the section Exod 32–34 are

---

249. Holiness would be another good candidate for a unifying theme. The majority of Propp's discussion of the tabernacle, for example, is centred around holiness. Hamilton prefaces orients his discussion around worship and the divine presence. Thus, too, Dozeman. Dozeman, *Exodus*, 569; Hamilton, *Exodus* 449; Propp, *Exodus 19–40*, 682-94.

the verb קרן (if it is correctly derived from the loanword קֶרֶן) and שׁוֹר. If so, nonetheless, both words appear nativized to the extent that their status as a loanword is unlikely to result in any particular rhetorical effect.

Returning to the commissioning of the tabernacle, however, if we follow a modified version of Durham's division of the text,[250] certain sections contain very few loanwords while other sections have a high concentration.

For the purposes of this distribution, we have excluded several words. In the case of יַיִן, חוֹתָם, רִמּוֹן and קֶרֶן it is because, although they are loanwords, they are too early to be treated as such. However, there are also some other words, which some have considered possible loanwords, for which we have found insufficient evidence:

בַּד[251]
זֵר[252]
חוֹשֵׁב, חֵשֶׁב[253]


250. Durham, *Exodus*, ix–x.
251. We refer here to the sense of the word 'linen', rather than 'pole'. As we have discussed at 3.2.4.3, 'Distribution of Loanwords in Daniel', this word is not to be considered a loanword, following Noonan's reasoning. Noonan, 'Foreign Loanwords', 109–10.
252. Grintz considered זֵר a loan from Egyptian *ḏr*, 'side, limit, boundary'. Grintz, 'Archaic Terminology', 17–18; Erman and Grapow, *Wörterbuch*, s.v. 'ḏrw'; *Thesaurus Linguae Aegyptiae*, s.v. 'ḏr.w'. If this is the case it would have to be an early loan to explain the equivalence of *ḏ* with *zayin*, since *ḏ* was realized as /ṭ/ after the end of the second millennium BCE. Cf. Loprieno, 'Ancient Egyptian', 170. Zimmern and Landesdorfer, on the other hand, considered it a loanword from Akkadian, *zirru*, 'cornice, wreath', Landesdorfer further suggesting Sumerian SUR, as a point of origin, 'to bound in'. Landesdorfer, *Sumerisches Sprachgut*, 69; Zimmern, *Akkadische Fremdwörter*, 31, 38. The *Chicago Assyrian Dictionary*, however, gives the meaning as 'reed fence'. *CAD* 21, s.v. 'zirru A'. Without any better evidence, it is too speculative to suggest that this word is a loan.
253. Driver and Grintz both suggested an Egyptian origin, either *ḥśb*, 'cross band' (Driver), or *ḥbš*, 'garment' (Grintz). Godfrey Driver, 'Technical Terms in the Pentateuch', *WO* 2 (1956): 254–63 (258); Grintz, 'Archaic Terminology', 18. Driver suggests it is related to *ḥśb*, 'cross band'. Grintz connects it to *ḥbš*, 'garment'. Cf. also, *CDD* 14, s.v. 'ḥbs'; Erichsen, *Demotisches Glossar*, s.v. 'ḥbs'; Erman and Grapow, *Wörterbuch*, s.vv. 'ḥsb', 'ḥbs'; *Thesaurus Linguae Aegyptiae*, s.vv. 'ḥsb', 'ḥbs'. However, it is simpler, as Dillman did, to connect these both to the root, חבש, 'to surround', by way of metathesis. Augustus Dillman, *Die Bücher Exodus und Leviticus* (Leipzig: Hirzel, 1897), 334. He cites Syriac ܚܒܫ, 'to close in', and

כַּפֹּרֶת[254]
כְּרוּב[255]

Arabic, *ḥasaba*, 'to confine, restrict'. Propp suggests this may have happened due to confusion with the root חשׁב, 'to reckon', that is common in this part of Exodus. Propp, *Exodus 19–40*, 436. The development would happen thus: the root *\*ḥ-b-š*, 'to bind' > the noun, *\*ḥibš*, 'belt' > the noun *\*ḥišb*, segholated to *ḥēšeb*, 'belt' > the additional sense of the verb *ḥ-š-b*, 'to weave'.

254. Görg, Hamilton and Milgrom raise the possibility that this word might derive from the Egyptian *kp(n)rdwy*, 'sole of the foot'. Manfred Görg, 'Eine neue Deutung für *kăpporæt*', *ZAW* 89 (1977): 115–18; Hamilton, *Exodus*, 460; Milgrom, *Leviticus 1–16*, 1014. However, the etymology based on the Hebrew verb כִּפֶּר, 'to make atonement', and the noun כֹּפֶר, 'bribe, ransom', is more convincing. Noonan agrees, bringing as evidence Arabic, *kapara*, 'to cover' and Akkadian, *kapāru*, 'to clean, make atonement'. Noonan, 'Foreign Loanwords', 172–74. Moreover, the equivalence of the consonants is not good, since in Egyptian *d* was realized as an ejective. Similarly, Grintz's hypothesis that it derives from Egyptian *k ʒp.t*, 'roof', is less convincing than that the word is simply Semitic, since the equivalence between *ʒ* and ר is poor after phonetic changes in the second millennium BCE (*ʒ* changes from /R/ to the glottal stop /ʔ/) and we would need to explain the metathesis of the *ʒ* and *p*. Grintz, 'Archaic Terminology 2', 163–68; Loprieno, 'Ancient Egyptian', 172.

255. Propp suggests that the word כְּרוּב, 'cherub', frequent in this section, may be 'related' to Akkadian *karābu*, 'to bless', and the tutelary *kurību* statues, although it is unclear whether he believes that relationship is one of borrowing or of cognates. Propp, *Exodus 19–40*, 386–87; Cf. *CAD* 8, s.vv. 'karābu', 'kāribu', 'kurību'. Wilson, Rabin and Zimmern suggested the relationship may be borrowing. Rabin, 'Foreign Words', 1074; Wilson, 'Foreign Words', 211; Zimmern, *Akkadische Fremdwörter*, 69. Vernes, on the other hand, suggested that the Hebrew word derived from Greek γρύψ, 'griffin'. Vernes, *Les emprunts*, 72–76. The word, however, appears to be genuinely Semitic: in addition to Akkadian and Greek evidence, we should also consider the Aramaic כְּרַב, 'to plough', and כָּרוֹב (in the Peshitta of 1 Cor 9:10), 'plougher' or perhaps 'ox'. *Comprehensive Aramaic Lexicon* s.vv. 'krb', 'krwb'. If Ezek 1:10 and Ezek 10:14 are to be read together, there is a simple solution: in Ezek 1:10 the living creatures have the faces of a human, a lion, an eagle and an ox (שׁוֹר) and Ezek 10:14 the living creatures have the same faces, except that in place of an ox there is a 'cherub', כְּרוּב. If these two passages are to be read together, there is a straightforward identification between כְּרוּב and שׁוֹר. Thus, it is also unsurprising that the 'cherubs' of Ezek 1 have calves' legs (Ezek 1:7). There is no reason to propose a loan when all the evidence may be accounted for by a Northwest Semitic verb for ploughing, which has then generated a *nomen agentis*, meaning 'ox', which has then been applied to ox-like heavenly beings. If the Akkadian is truly connected, the Akkadian verb, 'to bless', then either

פָּרֹכֶת[256]
שְׁחֵלֶת[257]
and שֹׁהַם.[258]

would have semantically developed denominally from ox-like tutelary statues, such as the *lamassu* or – less likely – in a fashion similar to Latin, *colo*, 'to till (the land), to revere, worship', whence English derives both 'cult' and 'cultivate'. Cf. Lewis and Short, s.v. 'colo'.

256. The word פָּרֹכֶת is thought by Propp to relate to Akkadian, *paruktu*, 'wooden sail', and by Hamilton and Rabin to *parakku*, 'deity's shrine', which in turn goes back to Sumerian *barag*, 'dais'. Hamilton, *Exodus*, 472; Propp, *Exodus 19–40*, 418; Rabin, 'Foreign Words', 1074. Cf. *ePSD*, s.v. 'barag [dais]'. Still, the Hebrew פָּרֹכֶת is constructed from fabric (Exod 26:31), such that the meaning, 'curtain', is much preferable to 'shrine'. Therefore, there is no reason to suspect anything other than a *qattālat* noun formed from the Semitic root, PRK, 'to cover' – attested in Akkadian, *parāku*, 'to cover', as Koehler and Baumgartner suggest. *HALOT*, s.v. 'פָּרֹכֶת'.

257. Propp speculates that שְׁחֵלֶת might be a loanword. Propp, *Exodus 19–40*, 484–85. He compares the word to a variety of Semitic forms: Neo-Babylonian, *suḫullatu*, a plant; Old Akkadian and Babylonian, *saḫlu*, Rabbinic Hebrew, שְׁהָלִים, Aramaic, תַחְלֵי, (Old Aramaic, שחלין), all 'cress'; Ugaritic, *šḥlt*, 'cress seeds'; and Hittite *zaḫḫeli-*, a plant. There is also Arabic, *suḥālat*, 'barley husks'. Lane, *Arabic–English Lexicon*, s.v. سُحَالة. However, the primary meaning of this word appears to be 'filings, shavings', applied also to metals and so perhaps it should be considered unrelated. As Propp points out, while the correspondence of שׁ in Hebrew to Aramaic ת imply Proto-Northwest-Semitic *ṯ, this would not produce Akkadian *s* and Akkadian *ḫ* should not correspond to Ugaritic *ḥ*. All of this speaks in favour of an early culture word, which would also explain the presence of the word in Hittite. However, the correspondence of שׁ in Hebrew to Aramaic ת implies that if there is a borrowing, it probably happened before the split of Proto-Northwest-Semitic *ṯ into Hebrew שׁ and Aramaic ת. As such, in Hebrew it is to be considered a part of the inherited lexicon from Proto-Northwest-Semitic, rather than a loanword.

258. Propp suggests that this word is likewise a trade word, because of inconsistencies in the correspondence of sibilants. Propp, *Exodus 19–40*, 375. He points to Akkadian *sāmtu*, 'carnelian', and *siāmu*, 'to be red', Ugaritic *šmt*, a mineral and Ge'ez *sōm*, *sāwm*, a gemstone. The difficulty is that, if this is an original Semitic word, Akkadian *s* should not correspond to Ugaritic or Hebrew *š*. One possibility would be that these are, as Propp suggests, words borrowed alongside trade, with no obvious point of origin. However, it is not clear that the Hebrew שֹׁהַם does in fact relate to these other words, due to the lack of the *he* in the other forms. The word's etymology is unclear and there is no compelling reason for a loan hypothesis. Therefore, for the purposes of this analysis we have not treated it as borrowed.

**Table 6** The Distribution of the Loanwords in Exodus 25–40

| Durham's division | Modified division | Subject Matter | Loanwords | Loanwords/Words [Egyptian] | Percentage [Egyptian] | Parallel Passage (in Exod. 35–39) |
|---|---|---|---|---|---|---|
| 25:1–9 | | Call for Materials | Many, varied origin | 7/74 [4/74] | 9.46 [5.41] | 35:4–9, 20–29 |
| 25:10–22 | 25:10–16 | Ark | Many, Egyptian | 10/77 [10/77] | 12.99 [12.99] | 37:1–5 |
| | 25:17–22 | Ark Cover | None[259] | 0/91 [0/91] | 0 [0] | 37:6–9 |
| 25:23–30 | | Table | Many, Egyptian | 7/84 [7/84] | 8.33 [8.33] | 37:10–16 |
| 25:31–40 | | Lampstand | Some, Egyptian | 4/114 [4/114] | 3.51 [3.51] | 37:17–24 |
| 26:1–37 | 26:1–6 | Fine Curtains | Some, varied origin | 4/92 [1/92] | 4.35 [1.09] | 36:8–13 |
| | 26:7–14 | Goat-hair Curtains | One, Egyptian | 1/109 [1/109][260] | 0.92 [0.92] | 36:14–19 |
| | 26:15–30 | Supports and Framework | Few, Egyptian | 4/179 [4/179] | 2.23 [2.23] | 36:20–34 |
| | 26:31–35 | Veil | Some, varied origin | 4/73 [2/73] | 5.48 [2.74] | 36:35–36 |
| | 26:36–37 | Screen | Many, varied origin | 4/27 [2/27] | 14.81 [7.41] | 36:37–38 |
| 27:1–8 | | Altar | Many, Egyptian | 8/96 [8/96] | 8.33 [8.33] | 38:1–7 |
| 27:9–19 | | Courtyard | Some, varied origin | 5/129 [3/129] | 3.88 [2.33] | 38:9–20 |
| 27:20–21 | | Light of the Lampstand | None | 0/37 [0/37] | 0 [0] | None[261] |

259. Were we to count כַּפֹּרֶת or כְּרוּב as loanwords, there would be 14 loanwords in this section (15.38%). This would significantly alter the argument that follows.

260. However, note the use of words homophonous with Egyptian loanwords in 26:9: compare שֵׁשׁ, 'six', with שֵׁשׁ, 'linen', or לְבָד, 'alone', with לְבַד, 'to the linen roll'. Although Egyptian loanwords are not actually present in the verse they are evoked nonetheless.

261. There is no parallel material in Exod 35–39, but there is a parallel text in Lev 24:1–3.

| | | | | | | |
|---|---|---|---|---|---|---|
| 28:1–43 | 28:1–5 | Priestly Clothing | Many, varied origin | 6/77 [3/77] | 7.79 [3.90] | 39:1 |
| | 28:6–14 | Ephod | Many, varied origin | 9/115 [5/115] | 7.83 [4.35] | 39:2–7 |
| | 28:15–28 | Breastplate | Many, predominantly Egyptian | 29/178 [21/178] | 16.29 [10.67] | 39:8–21 |
| | 28:29–30 | Instructions for use of Breastplate | None | 0/43 [0/43] | 0 [0] | None[262] |
| | 28:31–35 | Robe | Many, varied origin | 5/61 [2/61] | 8.20 [3.28] | 39:22–26 |
| | 28:36–38 | Flower | One, Akkadian | 1/47 [0/47] | 2.13 [0] | 39:30–31 |
| | 28:39–43 | Other clothing | Many, predominantly Egyptian | 6/74 [4/74] | 8.11 [5.41] | 39:27–29 |
| 29:1–46 | | Commissioning of the Priests | Few, predominantly Egyptian | 9/649 [7/649] | 1.39 [1.08] | None[263] |
| | 29:5–9 | Clothing of the Priests | Many, predominantly Egyptian | 7/61 [5/61] | 11.48 [8.20] | None |
| 30:1–10 | | Altar of Incense | Many, mostly Egyptian | 6/131 [5/131] | 4.58 [3.82] | 37:25–28 |
| 30:11–16 | | Tabernacle Levy | None | 0/90 [0/90] | 0 [0] | None |
| 30:17–21 | | Basin | Few, Akkadian | 1/57 [0/57] | 1.75 [0] | 38:8 |
| 30:22–38 | | Anointing Oil and Incense | Some, varied origin | 5/190 [1/190] | 2.63 [0.53] | 37:29 |
| 31:1–11 | | Commissioning of the Artisans | Few, Akkadian | 2/119 [0/119] | 1.68 [0] | 35:30–36:1 |
| 31:12–18 | | Sabbath Regulations | None | 0/94 [0/94] | 0 [0] | 35:1–3 |
| Total | | | | 137/3107 [94/3107] | 4.41 [3.03] | |

262. There is no parallel material in Exod 35–39, but there are parallel texts in Exod 29:5–9 and Lev 8:5–9.

263. There is no parallel material in Exod 35–39, but there is a parallel text in Lev 8.

From the distribution in Exod 25–31 there are a few things that should be noticed. Firstly, the Egyptian loanwords are only found in the description of the materials used in its construction; thus 27:20–21 contains no Egyptian loanwords because it deals with instructions given for the use of the lampstand rather than the instructions for its construction from the materials. The same can be said of the instructions for the use of the breastplate, the tabernacle levy and the whole of ch. 31, which also lack Egyptian loanwords. The notable absences, then, are that there are no Egyptian loanwords used in the description of the ark cover, the fine curtains, the basin or the anointing oil. Secondly, the Egyptian words are absent after ch. 30 until the parallel material resumes in ch. 35. Fourthly, the Egyptian loanwords are used more in the description of the furniture of the tabernacle and the priestly garments and only moderately in the description of the tent and courtyard. This can be partially explained by the preoccupation of these sections with precise measurements. Therefore, insofar as the materials are mentioned, there are still Egyptian loanwords (שֵׁשׁ and תְּחָשִׁים occur in 26:31 and 26:14, respectively, for example). However, the predominance of measurements in the sections overshadow other concerns in the sections. With all of these observations, it is the ark cover that is most anomalous.

The sections, although repeated in Exod 35–39, appear in a different order. Several of the sections which lack Egyptian loanwords are absent in this section, notably the instructions for the light of the lampstand, for the tabernacle levy and the instructions for the use of the breastplate. In addition, the description of the basin and anointing oil and incense is severely reduced. The effect of these three changes is that, instead of being interspersed with sections of fewer or no Egyptian loanwords, the building account gathers the Egyptian loanwords in a single section from Exod 36:8–39:21, uninterrupted except for once in 38:21–31.[264]

### 3.4.3.4. *The rhetorical effect of the loanwords*

Considering that the loanwords are distributed in this way, it is necessary to examine the commissioning and construction accounts to

---

264. Also of note, the LXX of this section is likewise significantly shortened and rearranged. Cf. Anneli Aejmelaeus, 'Septuagintal Translation Techniques: A Solution to the Problem of the Tabernacle Account?', in *On the Trail of the Septuagint Translators: Collected Essays* (Leuven: Peeters, 2007), 107–22, especially 109; David Gooding, *The Account of the Tabernacle: Translation and Textual Problems of the Greek Exodus* (Cambridge: Cambridge University Press, 1959); Martha Wade, *Consistency of Translation Techniques in the Tabernacle Accounts of Exodus in the Old Greek* (Leiden: Brill, 2003), 228–32.

determine what effect we could expect those loanwords to have had. The rhetorical effect of the loanwords in this section of Exodus will, as we have already indicated, situate the tabernacle in the context of the covenant by echoing its key elements. Specifically, the use of Egyptian loanwords contributes to this effect and such loanwords are found throughout the entire passage.

The materials for the construction of the tabernacle are initially presented in a list in Exod 25:3–7. The list is organized into groups of materials; first, precious metals, then fabrics, animal hides, wood, materials for burning and gemstones for the ephod. Most of the materials are loanwords: תְּכֵלֶת, אַרְגָּמָן, שֵׁשׁ, תְּחָשִׁים, שִׁטִּים, סַמִּים and אֵפֹד. It is possible that some of the other words may also be loanwords without our knowledge; Zimmern suggests, for example, that שֹׁהַם derives from Akkadian *sāmtu, sāndu*.[265] While it is difficult to accept his particular etymology, it is difficult to rule out that the Hebrew word may be a loanword from somewhere else. Nevertheless, at minimum it seems unlikely that זָהָב, כֶּסֶף or שֶׁמֶן could be loanwords.[266] While it is a less obvious case, נְחֹשֶׁת too seems to be native, with cognates in Aramaic and Arabic.[267] Thus, there appear to be no loanwords among the precious metals. From v. 4 onwards, however, the loanwords are fairly evenly distributed among the various categories of material. A slight majority of these words are of Egyptian provenance, the exceptions being סַמִּים and תְּכֵלֶת, which have Mesopotamian origins and the culture word, אַרְגָּמָן. Except for the part that lists the precious metals, every section of the list has at least one Egyptian loanword. The prominent use of these Egyptian words at the outset of the section creates

---

265. Zimmern, *Akkadische Fremdwörter*, 59.

266. Identifying a word as native with certainty is just as problem-filled as identifying a word as a loan with certainty. In cases where there are cognates to be found in genetically related languages, we presume that the word is native, unless there is clear evidence of borrowing. In some cases, it is possible to have more certainty if it can be demonstrated that two cognate forms in related languages could not have been borrowed from each other. Nevertheless, in some cases, there are neither cognates to be found nor plausible loan hypotheses. In such cases it is better to assume the word is native, unless there is a compelling reason otherwise. For כֶּסֶף compare Akkadian *kaspu*, Aramaic כספא, Ugaritic *ksp*. For זָהָב compare Aramaic דהבא; if the word was borrowed, it was borrowed prior to the differentiation between the Hebrew and Aramaic reflexes of Proto-Semitic *ḏ*. For שֶׁמֶן, see Alexander Militarev and Leonid Kogan, *Anatomy of Man and Animals*, vol. 1 of *Semitic Etymological Dictionary* (Münster: Ugarit-Verlag, 2000), 218–19.

267. Biblical Aramaic, נְחָשׁ, Dan 2:32, 35, etc.; Arabic *nuḥās*. Cf. *HALOT*, s.vv. 'נְחֹשֶׁת' (Hebrew), 'נְחָשׁ' (Aramaic).

an atmosphere evocative of Egypt. The effect is especially noticeable, since the words are not entirely nativized. This does, however, raise some questions over the audience, namely, to whom the effect could be noticeable. Noonan does, for example, suggest that the loanwords in the exodus and wilderness narratives could not belong to a late – which is to say, Priestly – writer, because such a writer would not recognize the terms as Egyptian, much less a later audience:

> The vast majority of Egyptian loanwords in the exodus and wilderness narratives relate to particular aspects of material culture, including terms for specific pieces of clothing (תְּחָרָא, שֵׁשׁ, פְּאֵר, אַבְנֵט), minerals (אַחְלָמָה, פִּטְדָה, נוֹפֶךְ, לֶשֶׁם), and plants (שִׁטָּה, סוּף, גֹּמֶא). Such technical vocabulary presumably would be hard to come by without research, assuming that resources for such research was [sic] even available. In any case, why would a late writer go through the effort of researching such mundane details, trying to make his account look authentic, especially when his audience probably would not even know the difference?[268]

The argument relies on the recognizability of the loanwords as such and at what stages they would be recognizable. However, the belief that the words are not recognizable to a late writer or late audience meets two obstacles. The first obstacle is that the words are identifiable as loanwords to us because of their non-conformity to regular Hebrew words; this evidence ought to have been more apparent to native speakers of Hebrew – late or otherwise – than it is at present, when our knowledge of the vocabulary of Hebrew is limited. Moreover, the identification of common vocabulary between Hebrew and Egyptian would have been much easier in a time in which both languages were spoken.[269] The second obstacle is that the passage of time does not guarantee that the words lose the denotative or connotative force that derived from their status as loanwords. Rather, it is quite possible for words to maintain their foreign connotation over a long period of time: for example, the English word 'marquis' is still in the twenty-first century quite recognizable as a word of French origin, due to its pronunciation, despite being borrowed in the fourteenth century.[270] From this example it seems plausible that Egyptian words, particularly those which in some way did not conform to Hebrew

---

268. Noonan, 'Egyptian Loanwords', 67.
269. It is difficult to be sure of how prevalent Egyptian language was in the Iron Age in the Levant. However, evidence of trade, as well as diplomatic and military relations imply that it was plausible. Cf. Mumford, 'Egypt and the Levant', 69–89.
270. *OED*, s.v. 'marquis'.

norms, such as that of the triliteral root, or those which are associated with items of Egyptian material culture, could be recognized as such or have some connotative effect even to a late audience. Similarly, words that are tied to physical items can maintain some of the denotation they derive from being loanwords – even when their status as loanwords ceases to be obvious – because of their semantic opposition to the original native words. Thus, for example, English 'marmalade', borrowed in the fifteenth century from Portuguese *marmelada*, 'quince jam', maintains its opposition to the more common 'jam', even if the precise fruit used for the conserve has changed over time.[271] Thus, even if a word does not overtly maintain its foreign connotation, it is possible for it to maintain a distinction from the native term on a denotative level, without necessarily triggering conscious connotations. Therefore, it seems plausible that some words – that may have at an earlier stage carried obvious connotations – could still carry some level of distinction – certainly in a denotative sense, but perhaps also in register – derived from the opposition of the real objects referred to by the borrowed and native terms (while marmalade and jam both belong to the same category, they are not the same).

Thus, in the same way, the Egyptian loanwords used in Exodus typically coexist with a native alternative, either a simple synonym or some other means of expressing the same thing. If all of the words were to belong to a 'high' register, it is conceivable that the loanwords could be used for that purpose, rather than specifically for an Egyptian connotation. If that should be the only consideration in Exod 25–40, however, we should expect just as many loans from other high-prestige languages as Egyptian loans. Since, however, the words are predominantly Egyptian and are atypical of Hebrew, the better explanation is that the loanwords carry the connotation of Egypt.[272] Moreover, one notes that while the presence of Egyptian *realia* in the Levant may have originated in the Chalcolithic and peaked in Iron Age 1A, goods from Egypt, including jewellery, bronze implements, weights, jewellery, seals and architecture are found as recently as the Persian period.[273] Since the material distinction between the objects being denoted was apparently retained, it is a reasonable assumption that later writers or audiences had the means to distinguish between the words that referred to those real objects. Nevertheless, it is also plausible that the priestly writings drew from earlier sources with

---

271. Ibid., s.v. 'marmalade'.
272. In addition, as we have argued above and continue to so here, the distance of time is not necessarily an obstacle to the audience recognizing a loanword as foreign.
273. Mumford, 'Egypt and the Levant', 69–89, especially 69, 79, 85.

likewise earlier writers and earlier audiences; that is, even if Noonan is right that the loanwords could have only entered the text in a period soon after their borrowing, that does not preclude their use for literary purposes (at that earlier point) or lessen their literary effect across both earlier sources and later editions – although one expects that Egypt must have still been a relevant cultural or political force at the time of their use.

Taking the position, then, that for multiple audiences the loanwords would have had an effect, it needs to still be noted that in addition to the Egyptian loans there are also several Mesopotamian words in the list. Nevertheless, it is the distribution of the Egyptian words throughout the whole list that causes the effect; the repetition of the trait of 'Egyptian loanword' throughout the list creates the atmosphere by continuing to reinforce the connotation of that trait with each instance. The same does not apply to the Mesopotamian words which are limited to particular parts of the list. It might be argued, all the same, that the Mesopotamian words and Egyptian words together contribute to a sense of non-specific foreignness or high register that complements the Egyptian atmosphere.

As the instructions for the tabernacle unfold, however, there are patterns to the use of loanwords that suggest concerns beyond just promoting an Egyptian atmosphere. The key terms that are initially laid forth in the list are resumed in the description. It is a figure of equivalence – as the text employs the same strategy repeatedly; it is a figure of addition – insofar as the text adds new loanwords to the ones found in the initial list; and it is a figure of permutation – as the text is employing lexical choices that deviate from the norm of native *vocabula*. As was also the case in the list, the words that are introduced later in the narrative are also largely of Egyptian origin. Again, there are a number of loanwords of other origins too. Of particular interest is that, while the loanwords are too frequently used in this section to be accidental, the word order of the sentences betrays no attempt to draw attention to the words.

The descriptions of the ark, table, lampstand, altar and ephod and other priestly garments all involve Egyptian loanwords. The ark is described in Exod 25:10–16:

¹⁰וְעָשׂוּ אֲרוֹן עֲצֵי שִׁטִּים אַמָּתַיִם וָחֵצִי אָרְכּוֹ וְאַמָּה וָחֵצִי רָחְבּוֹ וְאַמָּה וָחֵצִי קֹמָתוֹ:
¹¹וְצִפִּיתָ אֹתוֹ זָהָב טָהוֹר מִבַּיִת
וּמִחוּץ תְּצַפֶּנּוּ
וְעָשִׂיתָ עָלָיו זֵר זָהָב סָבִיב:
¹²וְיָצַקְתָּ לּוֹ אַרְבַּע טַבְּעֹת זָהָב
וְנָתַתָּה עַל אַרְבַּע פַּעֲמֹתָיו וּשְׁתֵּי טַבָּעֹת עַל־צַלְעוֹ הָאֶחָת וּשְׁתֵּי טַבָּעֹת עַל־צַלְעוֹ הַשֵּׁנִית:
¹³וְעָשִׂיתָ בַדֵּי עֲצֵי שִׁטִּים
וְצִפִּיתָ אֹתָם זָהָב:

¹⁴וְהֵבֵאתָ אֶת־הַבַּדִּים בַּטַּבָּעֹת עַל צַלְעֹת הָאָרֹן
לָשֵׂאת אֶת־הָאָרֹן בָּהֶם:
¹⁵בְּטַבְּעֹת הָאָרֹן יִהְיוּ הַבַּדִּים
לֹא יָסֻרוּ מִמֶּנּוּ:
¹⁶וְנָתַתָּ אֶל־הָאָרֹן אֵת הָעֵדֻת
אֲשֶׁר אֶתֵּן אֵלֶיךָ:

The loanwords that are found in the description are שִׁטִּים in vv. 10 and 13, טַבַּעַת in vv. 12, 14 and 15 and בַּדִּים in vv. 13, 14 and 15. Except for בְּטַבְּעֹת in v. 15 the loanwords all occur in post-verbal positions. Since the sentences in vv. 10–14 are null-subject statements, there is no question of whether the subject or verb should take first place in the sentence, but the loanwords are in unmarked positions. The loanwords in vv. 10–14 are, therefore, not to be understood as the topic, new referents or marked for focus. The topic is the ark and the words are active referents because they have been introduced in the initial list in 25:3–7. The word order of the sentences conforms to the structure associated with predicate focus; each of these sentences (vv. 10–14) conveys an answer to the implicit question, 'what are you [i.e. Moses] to do?'²⁷⁴ Nevertheless, the words are lexically marked. As discussed, these words have native equivalents. Thus, it is a fair inference that because טַבַּעַת is an atypical term it does not refer to a typical ring but an Egyptian ring. All of this suggests the choice of the text is, on the one hand, to allude to Egyptian *realia* through its lexical choices and yet not to draw attention to those lexical choices, allowing them to occur in unmarked locations. The sentence in v. 15, as we have mentioned, deviates from the pattern, in which the loanword appears as the first element of the sentence. Though somewhat unexpected, the word order is adequately explained by an argument focus, with the goal of explaining the role that the rings are to play.²⁷⁵ Nevertheless, the overall strategy of the passage is to allude to Egypt, without drawing attention to that purpose.

In this opening, a pattern is established – alluding to Egypt without drawing attention to that allusion – that continues throughout the commissioning account and then repeated in the building account. It can be observed in the same manner as above, nearly without exception in the cases of the table, lampstand and altar.

---

274. For a fuller explanation of focus and word order, see Heimerdinger, *Topic, Focus and Foreground*; Holmstedt, 'Word Order and Information Structure'; Holmstedt, 'Typological Classification'; Lunn, *Word-order Variation*, 41–47.

275. Heimerdinger, *Topic, Focus and Foreground*, 169.

Slightly more complicated is the lengthy description of the priestly garments in Exodus 28, in which there are once again many loanwords to be found.[276] Once again, the majority of these words are Egyptian and recognizably so. Again, the words' placement in the sentence conforms to the pattern observed in other cases, that the loanwords are generally placed in syntactically unmarked positions. The only true exception to this is אַבְנֵט in v. 39.[277]

The commissioning of the altar of incense in Exod 30:1–10 is also a more complicated case:

¹וְעָשִׂיתָ מִזְבֵּחַ מִקְטַר קְטֹרֶת
עֲצֵי שִׁטִּים תַּעֲשֶׂה אֹתוֹ:
²אַמָּה אָרְכּוֹ וְאַמָּה רָחְבּוֹ רָבוּעַ יִהְיֶה
וְאַמָּתַיִם קֹמָתוֹ מִמֶּנּוּ קַרְנֹתָיו:
³וְצִפִּיתָ אֹתוֹ זָהָב טָהוֹר אֶת־גַּגּוֹ וְאֶת־קִירֹתָיו סָבִיב וְאֶת־קַרְנֹתָיו
וְעָשִׂיתָ לּוֹ זֵר זָהָב סָבִיב:
⁴וּשְׁתֵּי טַבְּעֹת זָהָב תַּעֲשֶׂה־לּוֹ מִתַּחַת לְזֵרוֹ עַל שְׁתֵּי צַלְעֹתָיו
תַּעֲשֶׂה עַל־שְׁנֵי צִדָּיו
וְהָיָה לְבָתִּים לְבַדִּים
לָשֵׂאת אֹתוֹ בָּהֵמָּה:
⁵וְעָשִׂיתָ אֶת־הַבַּדִּים עֲצֵי שִׁטִּים
וְצִפִּיתָ אֹתָם זָהָב:
לַיהוָה: פ

In vv. 1 and 4 Egyptian loanwords, שִׁטִּים and טַבְּעֹת, occur in pre-verbal situations. Therefore, the pattern is not followed here.[278] Nevertheless,

---

276. Since the passage is so lengthy, we are better served by pointing to the lists in 'Appendix Five: Lists of Loanwords in Exodus 25–40'.

277. Other potential exceptions (אֲפֻדָּת in v. 8, חֹתָם in v. 11, אֵפֹד in v. 15, חוֹתָם in v. 21 and תַּחְרָא in v. 32) are either highly nativized, one of several pre-verbal elements or the second element of a construct chain.

278. Note that in the parallel building text, שִׁטִּים does not appear pre-verbally, but טַבְּעֹת does so. In the case of שִׁטִּים in v. 1, then, it is possible to explain the fronting of the loanword from the differences between the commissioning and building accounts: as discussed above, in the commissioning account the altar of incense is described after an interlude in Exod 29, in which none of the materials mentioned in Exod 25–28. Therefore, when introducing the words again in Exod 30, because they are no longer active referents, it is necessary to treat them as such, bringing them into pragmatically marked positions. For טַבְּעֹת in v. 4 it could be possible to read the sentences punctuated differently, so that שְׁתֵּי טַבְּעֹת זָהָב in the beginning of v. 4 was the object of עָשִׂיתָ in v. 3 rather than in v. 4. Nevertheless, in

that some loanwords should be emphasized at some point does not detract from the observation that in most cases the loanwords are not emphasized.

In summary, throughout the commissioning account loanwords are used according to a particular pattern. The result of that pattern is that an Egyptian atmosphere is established in the audience's mind by the use of Egyptian loanwords in Exod 25–40. In general, this is achieved without drawing particular attention to the words themselves, though at times the loanwords appear in marked positions.

In both accounts, however, the effect is disrupted in the description of the ark cover by the complete absence of loanwords, only for them to reappear in the description of the table.[279] Whatever the origin of the differences, the effect draws attention to the ark cover and the cherubim: the switch in register as the reader progresses from the presence of Egyptian loanwords to their absence suggests difference between the objects being described. It has been suggested that the ark cover and the cherubim are the place most associated with the divine presence,[280] which may explain why they are singled out. Moreover, there are clear connections between the ark and the covenant.[281] In that case, the deviation draws attention to both the covenant and the divine presence.[282] However,

---

the text as it stands, the focus of the sentence commencing v. 4 is on the object, שְׁתֵּי טַבְּעֹת זָהָב. As it stands, then, the first sentence of v. 4 functions as an explanation of the preceding sentence, the object relocated to the beginning so as to give it an expanding focus (Heimerdinger, *Topic, Focus and Foreground*, 169); thus, the instruction for building the two rings under the moulding should be understood as an explanation of the function of the moulding – to allow the altar to be carried on poles – which is otherwise unclear.

279. There are also no Egyptian loanwords in the description of the incense. However, the commissioning of the incense is found in Exod 30 (and thus surrounded by sections which have few loanwords). The 'building' of the incense is reduced to a single verse and so is far less important in the building account. Thus, the effect of the absence is neither as great nor as significant.

280. Durham, *Exodus*, 359–60; Daegeuk Nam, 'The "Throne of God" Motif in the Hebrew Bible' (PhD diss., Andrews University, 1989), 1–5; Propp, *Exodus 19–40*, 515–21. Cf. Also, Num 7:89. Heb 9:5 may also reflect a similar understanding of the function of the cherubim in the tabernacle.

281. Cf. Sarna, *Exodus*, 159.

282. Moreover, as noted above, the cherubim prefigure the golden calf; that is, there is further reason to draw attention to the cherubim, so that they can serve as contrast with the golden calf – an authorized location of divine presence contrasted

the presence of the Egyptian loanwords, in the tabernacle accounts, which are so concerned with the covenant, points to another element of the covenant: the covenant is based on God's rescue of Israel from Egypt, as is clear from its initial expression in Exod 19:1–6.

### 3.4.3.5. *Representing the exodus in the tabernacle*

The effect of the constant allusion to Egypt throughout the accounts of the tabernacle's commissioning and construction is that a strong connection between the tabernacle's construction and the exodus from Egypt is established. Although interpreting the tabernacle's construction as a reminder of the exodus is novel, it is plausible.

Firstly, the materials that are used for the tabernacle's construction could be understood as the riches brought out of Egypt. Even on the basis of the local context, this is a reasonable conclusion. The only explicit explanation for the origin of the materials given in the immediate context is that it is produced from among the Israelites;[283] the question of where the Israelites derived the wealth is not specifically addressed in the immediate context. Nevertheless, even if the origin is not made explicit, that does not rule out that it may reveal the origin implicitly: the logic of the narrative does lend itself to the suggestion that the wealth derived from Egypt, because deriving the wealth from elsewhere requires us to imagine far less likely situations. Moreover, when the tabernacle accounts are placed in their narrative context, the reader has been informed that the Israelites plundered the Egyptians (Exod 12:35–36). Thus, the simplest solution is to assume that is the source of the tabernacle's materials is Egypt, the solution proposed by Propp.[284] If the materials denoted by the Egyptian loanwords find their origin in the exodus, it is not unreasonable that those materials should act as a reminder of the exodus. If these Egyptian materials act as a reminder, it is not unreasonable that they are denoted by Egyptian loanwords for the same purpose.

Moreover, in many Hebrew writings there is a prominent connection between the exodus and the covenant, not just in the statement of the Sinaitic covenant in Exod 19. In covenant renewals, for example, the exodus is remembered ceremonially: Joshua's covenant renewals make

---

with the illegitimate. As has been suggested above, the recurrence of Egyptian loanwords is secondary to the emphasis that is placed on obedience to the instructions. Therefore, while the text's use of loanwords does highlight the divine presence and covenant, it does so in the context of requiring obedience.

283. Exod 25:2–9; 35:4–9, 20–29.
284. Propp, *Exodus 19–40*, 370.

explicit reference to Egypt (Josh 24:14–17); Josiah's covenant renewal is accompanied by Passover celebrations (2 Kgs 23; 2 Chr 34–35). The Deuteronomic literature frequently cites God's actions in bringing Israel out of Egypt as grounds for covenant obedience.[285] Therefore, if the tabernacle is understood as an expression of the covenant, it is unsurprising that the exodus should be represented in the tabernacle. To some extent this connection is borne out in other narratives about the tabernacle and the temple. Movements of the ark, the core of the tabernacle, for example, are often likewise associated with exodus themes.[286] Likewise, when Solomon dedicates the temple, he does so with specific reference to the Exodus and to Israel's time at Sinai.[287] Therefore, it would be unsurprising that Exodus would contain references to Egypt, when it discusses the construction of the tabernacle, as symbol of the covenant.

Not only is this interpretation of the tabernacle plausible, but it illuminates aspects of its imagery that we would expect to find in it but are otherwise obscure: as Smith notes, the practice of temples in the ancient Near East is to encode a narrative associated with the God of the temple and to do so through their furnishings.[288] Thus the first temple recapitulates God's creation of the world, with garden and cosmological motifs.[289] The imagery of the tabernacle, however, appears somewhat more obscure. While there are motifs of creation and the cosmos that can be found in the tabernacle, similar to those of the first temple, such as the cherubim, these motifs explain only a limited degree of the furnishings of the tabernacle; it would be difficult to claim that creation provided the narrative behind the tabernacle in the way it does for the temple. The tabernacle account, however, constantly alludes to the narrative of exodus from Egypt, whenever it uses materials denoted by Egyptian loanwords. This

---

285. Moshe Weinfeld, 'Deuteronomic Phraseology', in *Deuteronomy and the Deuteronomic School* (Oxford: Clarendon, 1972), 326–30.

286. Thus, for example, the recovery of the ark from the Philistines in 1 Sam 5–6 parallels the plagues of Egypt and the exodus. Cf. Walter Brueggemann, *First and Second Samuel*, IBC (Louisville: John Knox, 1990), 34–42, passim; Robert Gordon, *1 & 2 Samuel: A Commentary* (Exeter: Paternoster, 1986), 95–100, passim. Similarly, the passage of the ark through the Jordan might be treated as a recapitulation the passage of Israel through the Red Sea.

287. 1 Kgs 7:9, 16, 21 *et al.*

288. Mark Smith, 'Like Deities, Like Temples (Like People)', in *Temple and Worship in Biblical Israel*, ed. John Day (London: T&T Clark, 2005), 3–27 (6–10).

289. Mark Smith and Elizabeth Bloch-Smith, *The Pilgrimage Pattern in Exodus*, JSOTSup 239 (Sheffield: Sheffield Academic Press, 1997), 81–100.

suggests that whereas the first temple was primarily associated with the imagery of the narrative of creation, the tabernacle was associated by Exodus primarily with imagery of the narrative of God's rescue of his people from Egypt.

### 3.4.4. *Conclusion: the loanwords highlight the group's shared history in foreign lands*

As we noted at the start, there are only a few details we can secure about the audience of Exodus. However, we can observe that unlike in Daniel or Esther, the loanwords are not creating distinctions between different groups of characters in the text, with which the audience may or may not identify: there is no group of 'others' in the description of the tabernacle who is rejected. Rather, as the immediate function of the loanwords is to bring the exodus to mind, they also have a uniting force on an audience composed of people who maintain a sense of connection to the exodus. In this way, then, the loanwords function in Exod 25–40 as a means of identification with the Israelite nation, just as they did in Daniel and Esther. It does so with an opposite approach: whereas Daniel and Esther used the foreign connotation of the loanwords as a marker for an identity to reject, Exodus uses the foreign connotation of its loanwords as a reminder of (perceived) common experience in foreign lands.

As we noted at the outset, the audience of Exodus likely views itself as in continuity with the Israelites who make the covenant in Exodus. Therefore, the book of Exodus presents the experience of Exodus as a uniting force for the members of the covenant, who use the tabernacle, and thereby for the audience. The text achieves this by maintaining allusions to Egypt throughout the commissioning and construction of the tabernacle, by deploying a high concentration of Egyptian loanwords.

## Conclusions

Biblical texts, including Esther, Daniel, Ezra and Exodus, use loanwords as a means of drawing ethnic boundaries along the lines of linguistic divisions.

As a rhetorical tool, loanwords have shared characteristics that lend themselves towards particular goals; loanwords deviate from other words in Hebrew because they carry the potential to be used in a way that activates their etymology. When loanwords from a particular language are used in high concentrations, the effect is that the common features of those loanwords become more and more salient to the reader. In particular, the ability of these words to be associated with their point of origin allows them to be used to connote that place of origin.

The loanwords are used throughout the texts we have examined in a variety of ways. Esther and Daniel, Ezra and Exodus each have their individual concerns. In Esther and Daniel, loanwords are used to explore the relationship of the protagonists to their setting. In Ezra, loanwords are used together with Aramaic as a means for including linguistic identity as a part of the group's identity. In Exodus, loanwords are used as a means for portraying the exodus in the construction of the tabernacle. In addition, there are other texts which will use loanwords for purposes other than those we have documented here – Song of Songs, for example, uses the vocabulary of foreign goods, arguably, as a depiction of wealth or for exoticism (not to exclude that there may be other motives too). Another purpose, which we have noticed at some points of the texts we have studied here, is the avoidance of loanwords to describe particularly religious experiences: the focal point of the divine presence, the ark cover, in the tabernacle in Exod 25:17–22; the dedication of the temple and celebration of the Passover in Ezra 6:16–22; Daniel's prayer in Dan 9:1–20. In fact, this tendency may be an effect of the association of loanwords with foreign nations, if worship with YHWH is conceived as a particularly native concern.

In the example texts that we have studied, we have looked at one way that biblical texts can leverage high concentrations of loanwords to connote their foreign place of origin – as a means by which the narrator can introduce concepts of nationality into the text. By manipulating references to other cultures, the texts shape the way the audience perceives those other cultures and their own. In Esther and Daniel, loanwords are used as a means of making the distinction between the foreign court and the Jewish protagonists that inhabit it. In particular, these texts allow their audience to evaluate the right way to act in the foreign court for a member of this ethno-linguistic community. In Ezra 1–7, the shared linguistic competencies of the narrator and the audience highlight linguistic identity as a component of the group identity. In Exod 25–40, the text uses loanwords as a way to represent a (perceived) common exit from a foreign land.

These are different texts with audiences in different times. However, there is a common thread between them, namely that the use of loanwords allows texts to define communities according to their experience of foreign cultures. These texts construct identity for their audiences in contrast to foreign cultures by using loanwords. The Israelite identity as it is constructed in these texts is tied to a linguistic community. The different texts we have looked at do not necessarily present the same view of ethnicity: on the one hand, they raise some angles that are obvious – such as, the enduring relevance of the exodus as a point of assumed shared history, even much later. On the other hand, there are elements of ethnic identity, which perhaps should be obvious, but have nevertheless remained obscure – such as language: obscure perhaps for the lack of an obvious way to gauge the importance of language to the community. It may be surprising that it is not necessarily the Hebrew language that acts as an ethnic identifier, because in Ezra it is the combination of Aramaic with Hebrew that creates the linguistic community in which the text operates. Loanwords are also used in several texts to characterize people or settings as foreign or other and so set the boundaries of the ethnicity, likewise linguistically. Characters such as Daniel or Esther are able to retain their membership of the ethnic group – despite their involvement in foreign courts – in part because the constant use of loanwords reinforce the idea that the boundaries of the group are drawn along linguistic and ethnic lines.

There are, of course, other considerations in plotting ethnicity in the Hebrew Bible, not least, archaeological considerations. However, archaeological considerations are likely to miss the role of language, since it is only preserved in texts. By studying texts and their use of foreign vocabulary in the form of loanwords, we amend the situation and find that for these selected biblical texts loanwords are an important way of defining who is a member of the community of the audience of those texts.

# Appendix One:
# Root Constraints and the Shared Vocabulary of Aramaic and Hebrew

As will be outlined in Appendix Six, if we are blind to the constraints that are applied to the consonants of Semitic roots, we should expect to be able to distinguish about 38% of Aramaic and Hebrew roots, based on the differences in their inherited consonantal inventories. If, however, we wish to account for some of the constraints that are suggested to exist on Semitic roots, the calculation is more involved. The constraints subtract from the maximum number of possible roots and from the maximum possible roots without one of the four consonants that are distinguishable. The first constraint is that there are no roots consisting of three of the same consonant. The second constraint is that there triliteral verbal roots containing the same consonant in the first and third position are rare.[1] In addition, stop consonants that are pronounced in the same location mostly do not occur at the same time in first and third position. The third constraint is that there are no roots with the same consonant in the first and second position. Similarly, to the second constraint, stop consonants pronounced in the same location mostly do not occur at the same time in first and second position. Further, the sonorants $n$, $l$ and $r$ do not occur together in first and second position. The fourth constraint is that if a dental consonant is in the first position, there is never a sibilant or interdental consonant in the second position.[2]

It is possible to calculate the total number of roots, considering the constraints, if we divide the question into several cases, based on the class of consonant found in the first position.

Thus, for example, in the case of the labial consonants, we would find that the total number of possible roots is given by $3 \times 24 \times 24 = 1728$: there are 3 labial consonants ($b$, $p$ and $m$). By the second and third constraints,

---

1. There are exceptions, such as נָתַן, שָׁרַשׁ or שָׁלַל. The verb שָׁלַשׁ appears to be denominative.
2. Cf. Greenberg, 'The Patterning of Root Morphemes'.

if there is a labial in first position there generally will not be one in second or third. These constraints contain the first constraint implied within them. The fourth constraint does not apply in this case, since the root begins with a labial and not a dental. Thus, there are three options for the first consonant – the three labials – and 24 options for the second and third – every non-labial consonant.

The calculation of the roots that can be distinguished follows similar logic. We must break the problem into three cases, based on whether the distinguishable consonant is found in the second position, the third position or both. Because there are three labial consonants, four distinguishable consonants and 20 other consonants the total number is given by $3\times4\times20+3\times20\times4+3\times4\times4=528$.

We can verify this result by independently calculating the number of indistinguishable roots and subtracting that number from the total number of roots. The number of indistinguishable roots is given by $3\times20\times20=1200$. The calculation is the same as that for the total number of roots except that the four distinguishable consonants are excluded from the second and third positions. Thus, for I-labial roots, the indistinguishable roots (1200) and the distinguishable roots (528) together produce the total number of roots (1728).

Similar calculations, with suitable variations according to the constraints, can be made for all the possible first consonants, resulting thus:

Table 7 Inherited Semitic Roots that are Distinguishable in Hebrew and Aramaic

|  | Distinguishable | Indistinguishable | Total |
|---|---|---|---|
| I-labial ($b, p, m$) | $3\times4\times20+3\times20\times4+3\times4\times4=528$ | $3\times20\times20=1200$ | $3\times24\times24=1728$ |
| I-velar ($g, k, q$) | $3\times4\times20+3\times20\times4+3\times4\times4=528$ | $3\times20\times20=1200$ | $3\times24\times24=1728$ |
| I-guttural (ʔ, h, ḥ, ʕ) | $4\times4\times19+4\times19\times4+4\times4\times4=672$ | $4\times19\times19=1444$ | $4\times23\times23=2116$ |
| I-dental ($d, t, ṭ$) | $3\times0\times20+3\times15\times3+3\times0\times3=135$ | $3\times15\times20=900$ | $3\times15\times23=1035$ |
| I-ḏ | $1\times15\times23=345$ | 0 | $1\times15\times23=345$ |
| I-sonorant ($n, l, r$) | $3\times4\times20+3\times22\times4+3\times4\times4=552$ | $3\times22\times20=1320$ | $3\times26\times24=1872$ |
| I-interdental ($ṯ, ḏ, ṱ$) | $3\times26\times26=2028$ | 0 | $3\times26\times26=2028$ |

| | | | |
|---|---|---|---|
| I-sibilant ($s, ś, š, ṣ, z$) | 5×4×22+5×22×4+5×4×4=960 | 5×22×22=2420 | 5×26×26=3380 |
| I-semi-vowel ($y, w$) | 2×4×22+2×22×4+2×4×4=384 | 2×22×22=968 | 2×26×26=1352 |
| **Total** | 6132 | 9452 | 15584 |
| **Percentage** | 39.35 | 60.65 | 100 |

Although it is somewhat counter-intuitive, in percentage terms there is not a very significant difference whether or not the constraints are introduced; this is because there is only a small degree to which the constraints affect the distinguishable consonants differently from the indistinguishable.

# Appendix Two:
# Lists and Distribution of Loanwords and Foreign Names in Esther

## *Loanwords in Esther*

**Table 8** Loanwords in Esther

| Chapter | Number of loanwords (number of unique lemmata) | Loanwords (verse) (bold = Akkadian, italics = Iranian, underlined = early, uncertain or thoroughly nativized) |
|---|---|---|
| Chapter 1 | 23 (15) | *בִּירָה* (5); *בִּיתָן* (5); פַּרְתְּמִים (3); **כַּסֵּא** (2); *בִּירָה* (2); אַרְגָּמָן (6, twice); דַּר (6); כַּרְפַּס (6); סֹחָרֶת (6); שֵׁשׁ (6); תְּכֵלֶת (6); יַיִן (7); *דָּת* (8); יַיִן (10); *סָרִיס* (10); *סָרִיס* (15); *דָּת* (15); *דָּת* (13); *סָרִיס* (12); *כֶּתֶר* (11); פִּתְגָם (20); *דָּת* (19) |
| Chapter 2 | 14 (7) | *בִּירָה* (3); *סָרִיס* (3); *בִּירָה* (5); *דָּת* (8); *דָּת* (8); פִּלֶגֶשׁ (14); *סָרִיס* (14); שֵׁשׁ (12); שֵׁשׁ (12); *סָרִיס* (21); *כֶּתֶר* (17); טֶבֶת (16); *סָרִיס* (15) |
| Chapter 3 | 17 (12) | *דָּת* (8); *דָּת* (8); *פּוּר* (7); *נִיסָן* (7); *אֲדָר* (7); **כַּסֵּא** (1); גֶּנֶז (9); *אֲחַשְׁדַּרְפָּן* (12); חָתַם (12); טַבַּעַת (10); *פֶּחָה* (12); *אֲדָר* (13); *דָּת* (14); פַּתְשֶׁגֶן (14); *בִּירָה* (15); *דָּת* (15) |
| Chapter 4 | 11 (6) | גֶּנֶז (11); *סָרִיס* (5); *סָרִיס* (4); *דָּת* (3); *אֵפֶר* (3); **אֵפֶר** (1); *דָּת* (7); *שַׁרְבִיט* (11); *דָּת* (8); פַּתְשֶׁגֶן (8); *דָּת* (11); (16) |
| Chapter 5 | 4 (3) | **כַּסֵּא** (1); *שַׁרְבִיט* (2); *שַׁרְבִיט* (2); יַיִן (6) |
| Chapter 6 | 9 (4) | פַּרְתְּמִים (9); סוּס (11); סוּס (10); סוּס (9); *סָרִיס* (14); *כֶּתֶר* (8); סוּס (8); סוּס (9, twice); *סָרִיס* (2) |
| Chapter 7 | 6 (3) | יַיִן (2); *בִּיתָן* (7); יַיִן (7); יַיִן (8); *בִּיתָן* (8); *סָרִיס* (9) |

| Chapter 8 | 24 (15) | טַבַּעַת (2); **שַׁרְבִיט** (4); אִבְדָן (6); חָתַם (8, twice); **פָּחָה** (9); **סִין** (9); **אֲחַשְׁדַּרְפָּן** (9); טַבַּעַת (8, twice); רֶמֶךְ (10); סוּס (10); טַבַּעַת (10); חָתַם (10); אֲחַשְׁתְּרָן (10); **אֲחַשְׁתְּרָן** (14); **אֲדָר** (12); דָּת (13); פִּתְשֶׁגֶן (13); (10); דָּת (17); **תְּכֵלֶת** (15); אַרְגָּמָן (15); דָּת (14); בִּירָה (14) |
| Chapter 9 | 25 (9) | אִבְדָן (5); **פָּחָה** (3); אֲחַשְׁדַּרְפָּן (3); דָּת (1); **אֲדָר** (1); דָּת (14); דָּת (13); בִּירָה (12); בִּירָה (11); בִּירָה (6); פּוּר (24); אֲדָר (21); אֲדָר (19); אֲדָר (17); אֲדָר (15); **אִגֶּרֶת** (26); פּוּר (26, twice); זְמָן (27); פּוּר (28); **אִגֶּרֶת** (29); פּוּר (29); זְמָן (31); פּוּר (31); פּוּר (32) |
| Chapter 10 | 0 | - |

Akkadian loanwords: אִגֶּרֶת אֲדָר אֵפֶר בִּירָה בִּיתָן טֵבֵת כִּסֵּא נִיסָן סִיוָן סָרִיס פּוּר פֶּחָה שַׁרְבִיט תְּכֵלֶת

Iranian loanwords: אֲחַשְׁדַּרְפָּן אֲחַשְׁתְּרָן גֶּנֶז דָּת זְמָן כַּרְפַּס כֶּתֶר סֹחֶרֶת פַּרְתְּמִים פִּתְגָם פִּתְשֶׁגֶן רֶמֶךְ

Others: אִבְדָן (Aramaic); אַרְגָּמָן (Anatolian); דַּר (uncertain); חָתַם (Egyptian); טַבַּעַת (Egyptian); יַיִן (Indo-European); סוּס (Indo-European); פִּלֶגֶשׁ (Indo-European); שֵׁשׁ (Egyptian)

## Foreign names in Esther

Both here and in the lists of foreign names in other books, there is room for discussion. I have used the principle that place names or personal names with no obvious native etymology should be treated as foreign. I readily agree that in several cases there is room for disagreement. Nonetheless, such disagreements are unlikely to be over sufficient names to cause a great difference to the overall effect of these foreign names. Since we only discuss the cumulative effect of all the names together, the import of a few errant cases is minimal. In general, Koehler and Baumgartner's lexicon and the commentaries have been of use in this section.

**Table 9** Foreign Names in Esther

| English Name | Hebrew Name | Chapter 1 | Chapter 2 | Chapter 3 | Chapter 4 | Chapter 5 |
|---|---|---|---|---|---|---|
| Abagtha | אֲבַגְתָא | 10 | | | | |
| Adalia | אֲדַלְיָא | | | | | |
| Admatha | אַדְמָתָא | 14 | | | | |

|  |  | | | | | |
|---|---|---|---|---|---|---|
| Agagite | אֲגָגִי | | | 1, 10 | | |
| Aridai | אֲרִדַי | | | | | |
| Aridatha | אֲרִידָתָא | | | | | |
| Arisai | אֲרִיסַי | | | | | |
| Aspatha | אַסְפָּתָא | | | | | |
| Babylon | בָּבֶל | | 6 | | | |
| Bigtha | בִּגְתָא | 10 | | | | |
| Bigthan | בִּגְתָן | | | 21 | | |
| Bigthana | בִּגְתָנָא | | | | | |
| Biztha | בִּזְתָא | 10 | | | | |
| Carkas | כַּרְכַּס | 10 | | | | |
| Carshena | כַּרְשְׁנָא | 14 | | | | |
| Cush | כּוּשׁ | 1 | | | | |
| Dalphon | דַּלְפוֹן | | | | | |
| Esther | אֶסְתֵּר | | 7, 8, 10, 11, 15, 15, 16, 17, 18, 20, 20, 22, 22 | 4, 5, 8, 9, 10, 12, 13, 15, 17 | | 1, 2, 2, 3, 4, 5, 5, 6, 7, 12 |
| Haman | הָמָן | | | 1, 2, 4, 5, 5, 6, 7, 8, 10, 11, 12, 15 | 7 | 4, 5, 5, 8, 9, 9, 9, 10, 11, 12, 14 |
| Hammedatha | הַמְּדָתָא | | | 1, 10 | | |
| Harbona | חַרְבוֹנָא | 10 | | | | |
| Hathach | הֲתָךְ | | | | 5, 6, 9, 10 | |
| Hegai | הֵגַי | | 8, 8, 15 | | | |
| India | הֹדּוּ | 1 | | | | |
| Marsena | מַרְסְנָא | 14 | | | | |
| Medes | מָדַי | 3, 14, 18, 19 | | | | |
| Mehuman | מְהוּמָן | 10 | | | | |
| Memucan | מְמוּכָן | 14, 16, 21 | | | | |
| Meres | מֶרֶס | 14 | | | | |
| Mordecai | מָרְדֳּכַי | | 5, 7, 10, 11, 15, 19, 20, 20, 21, 22, 22 | 2, 3, 4, 5, 6, 6, 6 | 1, 1, 4, 5, 6, 7, 9, 10, 12, 13, 15, 17 | 9, 9, 13, 14 |

## Appendix Two

| English Name | Hebrew Name | Chapter 1 | Chapter 2 | Chapter 3 | Chapter 4 | Chapter 5 |
|---|---|---|---|---|---|---|
| Nebuchadnezzar | נְבוּכַדְנֶאצַּר | | 6 | | | |
| Parmashta | פַּרְמַשְׁתָּא | | | | | |
| Parshandatha | פַּרְשַׁנְדָּתָא | | | | | |
| Persia | פָּרַס | 3, 14, 18, 19 | | | | |
| Poratha | פּוֹרָתָא | | | | | |
| Shaashgaz | שַׁעֲשְׁגַז | | 14 | | | |
| Shethar | שֵׁתָר | 14 | | | | |
| Susa | שׁוּשַׁן | 2, 5 | 3, 5, 8 | | 15, 15 | 8, 16 |
| Tarshish | תַּרְשִׁישׁ | 14 | | | | |
| Teresh | תֶּרֶשׁ | | 21 | | | |
| Vaizatha | וַיְזָתָא | | | | | |
| Vashti | וַשְׁתִּי | 9, 11, 12, 15, 16, 17, 19 | 1, 4, 17 | | | |
| Xerxes | אֲחַשְׁוֵרוֹשׁ | 1, 1, 2, 9, 10, 15, 16, 17, 19 | 1, 12, 16, 21 | 1, 6, 7, 8, 12 | | |
| Zeresh | זֶרֶשׁ | | | | | 10, 14 |
| Zethar | זֵתָר | 10 | | | | |

| English Name | Hebrew Name | Chapter 6 | Chapter 7 | Chapter 8 | Chapter 9 | Chapter 10 |
|---|---|---|---|---|---|---|
| Abagtha | אֲבַגְתָא | | | | | |
| Adalia | אֲדַלְיָא | | | | 8 | |
| Admatha | אַדְמָתָא | | | | | |
| Agagite | אֲגָגִי | | | 3, 5 | 24 | |
| Aridai | אֲרִדַי | | | | 9 | |
| Aridatha | אֲרִידָתָא | | | | 8 | |
| Arisai | אֲרִיסַי | | | | 9 | |
| Aspatha | אַסְפָּתָא | | | | 7 | |
| Babylon | בָּבֶל | | | | | |
| Bigtha | בִּגְתָא | | | | | |
| Bigthan | בִּגְתָן | | | | | |
| Bigthana | בִּגְתָנָא | 2 | | | | |
| Biztha | בִּזְתָא | | | | | |
| Carkas | כַּרְכַּס | | | | | |

| | | | | | | |
|---|---|---|---|---|---|---|
| Carshena | כַּרְשְׁנָא | | | | | |
| Cush | כּוּשׁ | | | 9 | | |
| Dalphon | דַּלְפוֹן | | | | 7 | |
| Esther | אֶסְתֵּר | 14 | 1, 2, 2, 3, 5, 6, 7, 8 | 1, 1, 2, 3, 4, 4, 7, 7 | 12, 13, 29, 31, 32 | |
| Haman | הָמָן | 4, 5, 6, 6, 7, 10, 11, 12, 13, 14 | 1, 6, 6, 7, 8, 8, 9, 9, 10 | 1, 2, 2, 3, 5, 7 | 10, 12, 13, 14, 24 | |
| Hammedatha | הַמְּדָתָא | | | 5 | 10, 24 | |
| Harbona | חַרְבוֹנָא | | 9 | | | |
| Hathach | הֲתָךְ | | | | | |
| Hegai | הֵגַי | | | | | |
| India | הֹדּוּ | | | 9 | | |
| Marsena | מַרְסְנָא | | | | | |
| Medes | מָדַי | | | | | 2 |
| Mehuman | מְהוּמָן | | | | | |
| Memucan | מְמוּכָן | | | | | |
| Meres | מֶרֶס | | | | | |
| Mordecai | מָרְדֳּכַי | 2, 3, 4, 10, 11, 12, 13 | 9, 10 | 1, 2, 2, 7, 9, 15 | 3, 4, 4, 20, 23, 29, 31 | 2, 3 |
| Nebuchad-nezzar | נְבוּכַדְרֶאצַּר | | | | | |
| Parmashta | פַּרְמַשְׁתָּא | | | | 9 | |
| Parshandatha | פַּרְשַׁנְדָּתָא | | | | 7 | |
| Persia | פָּרַס | | | | | 2 |
| Poratha | פּוֹרָתָא | | | | 8 | |
| Shaashgaz | שַׁעֲשְׁגַז | | | | | |
| Shethar | שֵׁתָר | | | | | |
| Susa | שׁוּשַׁן | | | 14, 15 | 6, 11, 12, 13, 14, 15, 15, 18 | |
| Tarshish | תַּרְשִׁישׁ | | | | | |
| Teresh | תֶּרֶשׁ | 2 | | | | |
| Vaizatha | וַיְזָתָא | | | | 9 | |
| Vashti | וַשְׁתִּי | | | | | |
| Xerxes | אֲחַשְׁוֵרוֹשׁ | 2 | 5 | 1, 7, 10, 12 | 2, 20, 30 | 1, 1, 3 |
| Zeresh | זֶרֶשׁ | 13, 13 | | | | |
| Zethar | זֵתַר | | | | | |

# Appendix Three:
# Lists and Distribution of Loanwords in Daniel

## *Loanwords in Daniel*

**Table 10** Loanwords in Daniel

| Chapter | Number of loanwords (number of unique lemmata) | Loanwords (verse) (bold = Akkadian, italics = Iranian, underlined = early, uncertain or thoroughly nativized) |
|---|---|---|
| Chapter 1 | 23 (9) | יַיִן (4); מַדָּע (4); הֵיכָל (4); פַּרְתְּמִים (3); **סָרִיס** (3); פַּתְבַּג (5); יַיִן (5); *סָרִיס* (7); יַיִן (8); **סָרִיס** (8); בַּג (8); *סָרִיס* (9); *מֶלְצָר* (10); **סָרִיס** (11); פַּתְבַּג (13); פַּתְבַּג (15); יַיִן (16); פַּתְבַּג (11); **אַשָּׁף** (18); *סָרִיס* (17); מַדָּע (16); *מֶלְצָר* (16); חַרְטֹם (20); (20) |
| Chapter 2 | 38 (10) | נִבְזְבָּה (5); הַדָּם (5); אַזְדָּא (5); חַרְטֹם (2); **אַשָּׁף** (2); חַרְטֹם (10); **אַשָּׁף** (10); דָּת (9); אַזְדָּא (8); (6); *דָּת* (13); *דָּת* (15); *זְמָן* (16); *רָז* (18); *רָז* (19); *זְמָן* (21); **אַשָּׁף** (27); חַרְטֹם (27); *רָז* (27); *רָז* (28); *רָז* (29); *רָז* (30); פַּרְזֶל (33, twice); פַּרְזֶל (34); פַּרְזֶל (35); פַּרְזֶל (40, three times); פַּרְזֶל (41, three times); פַּרְזֶל (42); פַּרְזֶל (43, twice); פַּרְזֶל (45); *רָז* (47, twice); **סְגַן** (48) |
| Chapter 3 | 50 (20) | דְּתָבַר (2); אֲחַשְׁדַּרְפַּן (2); גְּדָבַר (2); אֲדַרְגָּזַר (3); תִּפְתָּי (2); פֶּחָה (2); **סְגַן** (2); **סְגַן** (3); דְּתָבַר (3); אֲחַשְׁדַּרְפַּן (3); סַבְּכָא (5); כָּרוֹז (4); זַן (5); תִּפְתָּי (3); **פֶּחָה** (3); קֶרֶן (5); קַתְרוֹס (5); פְּסַנְתֵּרִין (5); סוּמְפֹּנְיָה (5); פְּסַנְטֵרִין (7); סַבְּכָא (7); זַן (7); *זְמָן* (7); סַבְּכָא (7); קֶרֶן (7); *זְמָן* (8); זַן (10); קַתְרוֹס (7); קַתְרוֹס (10); פְּסַנְתֵּרִין (10); סוּמְפֹּנְיָה (10); סוּמְפֹּנְיָה (10); קֶרֶן (10); זַן (15); סַבְּכָא (15); קֶרֶן (15); פְּסַנְתֵּרִין (15); קַתְרוֹס (15); קֶרֶן (15); הַדָּבָר (24); סַרְבַּל (21); **פַּרְבַּל** (21); פִּתְגָם (16); סַרְבַּל (27); **סְגַן** (27); הַדָּבָר (27); אֲחַשְׁדַּרְפַּן (27); **פֶּחָה** (27); הַדָּם (29) |

| Chapter 4 | 17 (11) | רָז (6); חַרְטֹם (4); חַרְטֹם (4); **אַשָּׁף** (1); הֵיכָל (14); פִּתְגָם (12); פַּרְזֶל (11); **אֲנַב** (9); **אֲנַב** (6); תּוֹר (26); הֵיכָל (22); תּוֹר (20); פַּרְזֶל (18); **אֲנַב** (33); הַדְּבָר (33); זְמָן (30); תּוֹר (29); |
| --- | --- | --- |
| Chapter 5 | 26 (13) | לְחֵנָה (3); הֵיכָל (2); לְחֵנָה (2); שֵׁגָל (2); הֵיכָל (5); נִבְרְשָׁא (3); פַּרְזֶל (4); הֵיכָל (5); שֵׁגָל (3); **אַשָּׁף** (11); הַמְנִיךְ (7); **אַרְגְּוָן** (7); (16); הַמְנִיךְ (16); **אַרְגְּוָן** (15); **אַשָּׁף** (11); חַרְטֹם (21); תּוֹר (20); **אַרְגְּוָן** (17); **כָּרְסֵא** (21); נִבְזְבָּה (29); הַמְנִיךְ (23); שֵׁגָל (23); פַּרְזֶל (23); לְחֵנָה (29); כְּרַז |
| Chapter 6 | 23 (10) | אֲחַשְׁדַּרְפַּן (1); אֲחַשְׁדַּרְפַּן (2); (3); (5); סְרַךְ (4); סְרַךְ (4); אֲחַשְׁדַּרְפַּן (3); סְרַךְ (7); אֲחַשְׁדַּרְפַּן (6); דָּת (6); סְרַךְ (7); (9); דָּת (8); סְרַךְ (8); **פֶּחָה** (8); סָגַן (8); הַדְּבָר חָתַם (16); זְמָן (14); דָּת (13); דָּת (11); זְמָן (18); הֵיכָל (19); **זָכוּ** (23) |
| Chapter 7 | 18 (5) | קֶרֶן (7); פַּרְזֶל (7); קֶרֶן (8, four times); **כָּרְסֵא** קֶרֶן (19); פַּרְזֶל (11); זְמָן (12); קֶרֶן (9, twice); דָּת (24); קֶרֶן (21); זְמָן (22); קֶרֶן (20, twice); זְמָן (25); (25) |
| Chapter 8 | 10 (2) | בִּירָה (2); קֶרֶן (3, twice); קֶרֶן (5); קֶרֶן (6); קֶרֶן (21); קֶרֶן (20); קֶרֶן (9); קֶרֶן (8); קֶרֶן (7); |
| Chapter 9 | 3 (2) | חָתַם (24); חָתַם (24); **אֵפֶר** (3) |
| Chapter 10 | 3 (3) | תַּרְשִׁישׁ (6); לַפִּיד (6); יַיִן (3) |
| Chapter 11 | 4 (4) | **אַפֶּדֶן** (45); **מְחִיר** (39); צִי (30); פַּתְבַּג (26) |
| Chapter 12 | 2 (1) | חָתַם (9); חָתַם (4) |

Akkadian loanwords: אֲנַב אֵפֶר אַרְגְּוָן אַשָּׁף בִּירָה הֵיכָל זָכוּ כַּרְבֵּל כָּרְסֵא לְחֵנָה מְחִיר מֶלְצַר סָגַן סָרִיס פֶּחָה שֵׁגָל

Iranian loanwords: אֲדַרְגָּזַר אֲזְדָּא אֲחַשְׁדַּרְפַּן אַפֶּדֶן גְּדָבַר דָּת דְּתָבַר הַדְּבָר הַדָּם הַמְנִיךְ זְמָן זַן כָּרוֹז כְּרַז נִבְרְשָׁה סַרְבָּל סְרַךְ פַּרְתְּמִים פַּתְבַּג פִּתְגָם רָז תִּפְתָּי

Others: יַיִן (Indo-European, early); חָתַם (Egyptian, early); חַרְטֹם (Egyptian); לַפִּיד (Greek or Luwian); מַדָּע (Aramaic); נִבְזְבָּה (Greek); סַבְּכָא (Greek); סוּמְפּוֹנְיָה (Greek); פְּסַנְתֵּרִין (Greek); פַּרְזֶל (Luwian); צִי (Egyptian); קַתְרוֹס (Greek); קֶרֶן (Indo-European, early); תּוֹר (Indo-European?, early) תַּרְשִׁישׁ (uncertain, perhaps Phoenician or Tartessian)

## Foreign names in Daniel

See also, the comments on the foreign names in Esther.

**Table 11** Foreign Names in Daniel

| English Name | Hebrew Name | Chapter 1 | Chapter 2 | Chapter 3 | Chapter 4 | Chapter 5 | Chapter 6 |
|---|---|---|---|---|---|---|---|
| Abednego | עֲבֵד נְגוֹ | 7 | 49 | 12, 13, 14, 16, 19, 20, 22, 23, 26, 26, 28, 29, 30 | | | |
| Arioch | אַרְיוֹךְ | | 14, 15, 15, 24, 25 | | | | |
| Ashpenaz | אַשְׁפְּנַז | 3 | | | | | |
| Babylon | בָּבֶל | 1 | 12, 14, 18, 24, 24, 48, 48, 49 | 1, 12, 30 | 3, 26, 27 | 7 | |
| Belshazzar | בֵּלְשַׁאצַּר | | | | | 1, 2, 9, 22, 29, 30 | |
| Belteshazzar | בֵּלְטְשַׁאצַּר | 7 | 26 | | 5, 6, 15, 16, 16, 16 | 12 | |
| Chaldeans | כַּשְׂדִּי | | 5, 10, 10 | 8 | 4 | 7, 11, 30 | |
| Cyrus | כּוֹרֶשׁ | 21 | | | | | 29 |
| Darius | דָּרְיָוֶשׁ | | | | | | 1, 2, 7, 10, 26, 29 |
| Egypt | מִצְרַיִם | | | | | | |
| Elam | עֵילָם | | | | | | |

| | | | | | | | |
|---|---|---|---|---|---|---|---|
| Ethiopians | כּוּשִׁי | | | | | | |
| Greece | יָוָן | | | | | | |
| Kittim | כִּתִּיִּים | | | | | | |
| Libyans | לוּב | | | | | | |
| Media | מָדַי | | | | | 28 | 1, 9, 13, 16 |
| Meshach | מֵישַׁךְ | 7 | 49 | 12, 13, 14, 16, 19, 20, 22, 23, 26, 26, 28, 29, 30 | | | |
| Nebuchad-nezzar | נְבוּכַדְנֶצַּר | 1, 18 | 1, 1, 28, 46 | 1, 2, 2, 3, 3, 5, 7, 9, 13, 14, 16, 19, 24, 26, 28, 31 | 1, 15, 25, 28, 30, 31, 34 | 2, 11, 18 | |
| Persia | פָּרַס | | | | | 28 | 9, 13, 16, 29 |
| Shadrach | שַׁדְרַךְ | 7 | 49 | 12, 13, 14, 16, 19, 20, 22, 23, 26, 26, 28, 29, 30 | | | |
| Shinar | שִׁנְעָר | 2 | | | | | |
| Susa | שׁוּשַׁן | | | | | | |
| Tigris | חִדֶּקֶל | | | | | | |
| Ulai | אוּלַי | | | | | | |
| Uphaz | אוּפָז | | | | | | |
| Xerxes | אֲחַשְׁוֵרוֹשׁ | | | | | | |

# Appendix Three

| English Name | Hebrew Name | Chapter 7 | Chapter 8 | Chapter 9 | Chapter 10 | Chapter 11 | Chapter 12 |
|---|---|---|---|---|---|---|---|
| Abednego | עֲבֵד נְגוֹ | | | | | | |
| Arioch | אַרְיוֹךְ | | | | | | |
| Ashpenaz | אַשְׁפְּנַז | | | | | | |
| Babylon | בָּבֶל | 1 | | | | | |
| Belshazzar | בֵּלְשַׁאצַּר | 1 | 1 | | | | |
| Belteshazzar | בֵּלְטְשַׁאצַּר | | | | 1 | | |
| Chaldeans | כַּשְׂדִּי | | | | | | |
| Cyrus | כּוֹרֶשׁ | | | | 1 | | |
| Darius | דָּרְיָוֶשׁ | | | 1 | | 1 | |
| Egypt | מִצְרַיִם | | | 15 | | 8, 42, 43 | |
| Elam | עֵילָם | | 2 | | | | |
| Ethiopians | כּוּשִׁי | | | | | 43 | |
| Greece | יָוֵן | | 21 | | 20 | 2 | |
| Kittim | כִּתִּיִּים | | | | | 30 | |
| Libyans | לוּב | | | | | 43 | |
| Media | מָדַי | | 20 | 1 | | 1 | |
| Meshach | מֵישַׁךְ | | | | | | |
| Nebuchad-nezzar | נְבוּכַדְנֶצַּר | | | | | | |
| Persia | פָּרַס | | 20 | | 1, 13, 13, 20 | 2 | |
| Shadrach | שַׁדְרַךְ | | | | | | |
| Shinar | שִׁנְעָר | | | | | | |
| Susa | שׁוּשַׁן | | 2 | | | | |
| Tigris | חִדֶּקֶל | | | | 4 | | |
| Ulai | אוּלַי | | 2, 16 | | | | |
| Uphaz | אוּפָז | | | | 5 | | |
| Xerxes | אֲחַשְׁוֵרוֹשׁ | | | 1 | | | |

# Appendix Four:
# Lists and Distribution of Loanwords in Ezra 1–7

*Loanwords in Ezra 1–7*

**Table 12** Loanwords in Ezra 1–7

| Chapter | Number of loanwords (number of unique lemmata) | Loanwords (verse) (bold = Akkadian, italics = Iranian, underlined = early, uncertain or thoroughly nativized) |
|---|---|---|
| Chapter 1 | 3 (2) | *אֲגַרְטָל* (9, twice); **גִּזְבָּר** (8) |
| Chapter 2 | 5 (5) | דַּרְכְּמוֹנִים (69); **סוּס** (66); *תִּרְשָׁתָא* (63); *פֶּחָה* (69); **כֻּתֹּנֶת** (69) |
| Chapter 3 | 2 (1) | הֵיכָל (10); הֵיכָל (6) |
| Chapter 4 | 15 (9) | *אִגְּרָה* (8); *נִשְׁתְּוָן* (7); *תִּרְגַּם* (7); הֵיכָל (1); *פַּרְשֶׁגֶן* (11); *אִגְּרָה* (9); *אֲפַרְסַתְכָיֵא* (8); *נִשְׁתְּוָן* (11); *אִפְּתֹם* (13); *מִנְדָּה* (13); הֵיכָל (14); *פִּתְגָם* (23); *נִשְׁתְּוָן* (23); *פַּרְשֶׁגֶן* (23); *מִדָּה* (20); *נִשְׁתְּוָן* (17) |
| Chapter 5 | 18 (11) | *אִגְּרָה* (5); *נִשְׁתְּוָן* (3); *זְמָן* (3); *פֶּחָה* (3); *אֲשַׁרְנָא* (3); *פִּתְגָם* (6); *פַּרְשֶׁגֶן* (6); *פֶּחָה* (6); *אֲפַרְסְכָיֵא* (6); הֵיכָל (7); *אֲשַׁרְנָא* (9); *אָסְפַּרְנָא* (8); *פִּתְגָם* (11); הֵיכָל (15); *גִּנֵּז* (14, three times); *פֶּחָה* (14); (17) |
| Chapter 6 | 19 (12) | *גִּנֵּז* (1); *בִּירָה* (2); **נִדְבָּךְ** (4, twice); הֵיכָל (5, twice); *פֶּחָה* (6); *אֲפַרְסְכָיֵא* (6); *פֶּחָה* (7); *פִּתְגָם* (9); **תּוֹר** (8); **נְכַס** (8); *מִדָּה* (8); *אָסְפַּרְנָא* (8); *פֶּחָה* (13); *אָסְפַּרְנָא* (12); *אָסְפַּרְנָא* (13); **תּוֹר** (17); *אִדָּר* (15) |
| Chapter 7 | 18 (11) | *נִשְׁתְּוָן* (11); *פַּרְשֶׁגֶן* (11); *דָּת* (12); *דָּת* (14); *אָסְפַּרְנָא* (17); **תּוֹר** (17); *גִּנֵּז* (20); *אָסְפַּרְנָא* (21); *אֲדַרְגָּזַר* (23); *מִנְדָּה* (21); *דָּת* (21); **גִּזְבָּר** (21); *דָּת* (24); *דָּת* (25); *אָסְפַּרְנָא* (26); *דָּת* (26, twice); שְׁרֹשִׁי (26); **נְכַס** (26) |

Akkadian loanwords: אִגְּרָה אַדָּר בִּירָה הֵיכָל כֻּתֹּנֶת מִדָּה מִנְדָּה נִדְבָּךְ נְכַס פֶּחָה תִּרְגֵּם

Iranian loanwords: אֲגַרְטָל אֲדַרְזְדָּא אַסְפַּרְנָא אֲפַרְסְכָיֵא אֲפַרְסַתְכָיֵא אַפֶּתֹם אֲשַׁרְנָא גִּזְבָּר גֶּנֶז דָּת זְמָן נִשְׁתְּוָן פַּרְשֶׁגֶן פִּתְגָם שָׁרֹשׁוּ תִּרְשָׁתָא

Others: דַּרְכְּמוֹנִים (Greek); סוּס (Indo-European, early); תֹּר (Indo-European?, early)

## Foreign names in Ezra 1–7

See also the comments on the foreign names in Esther. In addition, Clines and Fried both comment on many of the names in their commentaries.[1]

**Table 13** Foreign Names in Ezra 1–7

| English name | Hebrew name | Chapter 1 | Chapter 2 | Chapter 3 | Chapter 4 | Chapter 5 | Chapter 6 | Chapter 7 |
|---|---|---|---|---|---|---|---|---|
| Artaxerxes | אַרְתַּחְשַׁסְתְּא | | | | 7, 7 | | | 1, 7, 11 |
| Asenah | אַסְנָה | | 50 | | | | | |
| Ashurbanipal | אָסְנַפַּר | | | | 10 | | | |
| Assyria | אַשּׁוּר | | | | 2 | | 22 | |
| Babylon | בָּבֶל | 11 | 1, 1 | | | 12, 12, 13, 14, 14, 17 | 1, 5 | 6, 9, 16 |
| Barkos | בַּרְקוֹס | | 53 | | | | | |
| Bigvai | בִּגְוַי | | 2, 14 | | | | | |
| Chaldean | כַּשְׂדִּי | | | | | 12 | | |
| Cyrus | כּוֹרֶשׁ | 1, 1, 2, 7, 8 | | 7 | 3, 5 | 13, 13, 14, 17 | 3, 3, 14 | |
| Darius | דָּרְיָוֶשׁ | | | | 5, 24 | 5, 6, 7 | 1, 12, 13, 14, 15 | |

1. Clines, *Ezra, Nehemiah, Esther*; Fried, *Ezra*, especially 92–130.

| | | | | | | | | |
|---|---|---|---|---|---|---|---|---|
| Ecbatana | אַחְמְתָא | | | | | 2 | | |
| Elam | עֵילָם | | 7, 31 | | | | | |
| Elamites | עֵלְמָי | | | 9 | | | | |
| Esarhaddon | אֵסַר־חַדֹּן | | | 2 | | | | |
| Media | מָדַי | | | | | 2 | | |
| Mithredath | מִתְרְדָת | 8 | | 7 | | | | |
| Mordecai | מָרְדֳּכַי | | 7 | | | | | |
| Nebuchad-nezzar | נְבוּכַדְנֶצַּר | 7 | 1, 1 | | | 12, 14 | 5 | |
| Persia | פָּרַס | 1, 1, 2, 8 | | 7 | 3, 5, 5, 7, 24 | | 14 | 1 |
| Phinehas | פִּינְחָס | | | | | | 5 | |
| Sheshbazzar | שֵׁשְׁבַּצַּר | 8, 11 | | | 14, 16 | | | |
| Shethar-Bozenai | שְׁתַר בּוֹזְנַי | | | | 3, 6 | 6, 13 | | |
| Sisera | סִיסְרָא | | 53 | | | | | |
| Susanite | שׁוּשַׁנְכָי | | | 9 | | | | |
| Tarpalite? | טַרְפְּלָי | | | 9 | | | | |
| Urukite | אַרְכְּוָי | | | 9 | | | | |
| Xerxes | אֲחַשְׁוֵרוֹשׁ | | | 6 | | | | |
| Zattu | זַתּוּא | | 8 | | | | | |
| Zerubbabel | זְרֻבָּבֶל | | 2 | 2, 8 | 2, 3 | 2 | | |
| Ziha | צִיחָא | | 43 | | | | | |

# Appendix Five:
# Lists and Distribution of Loanwords in Exodus 25–40

**Table 14** Loanwords in Exodus 25–40

| Chapter | Number of loanwords (number of unique lemmata) | Loanwords (verse) (bold = Egyptian, italics = Akkadian, underlined = early, uncertain or thoroughly nativized) |
|---|---|---|
| Chapter 25 | 28 (10) | תַּחַשׁ (5); שֵׁשׁ (4); *תְּכֵלֶת* (4); אַרְגָּמָן (4); *סַמִּים* (5); אֵפֹד (7); שִׁטָּה (10); טַבַּעַת (12); שִׁטָּה (13); בַּדִּים (13); טַבַּעַת (12); שִׁטָּה (14); טַבַּעַת (14); בַּדִּים (15); טַבַּעַת (15); בַּדִּים (14); שִׁטָּה (23); טַבַּעַת (26); בַּדִּים (27); טַבַּעַת (27); בַּדִּים (28); שִׁטָּה (28); גָּבִיעַ (31); גָּבִיעַ (33); גָּבִיעַ (33); גָּבִיעַ (34) |
| Chapter 26 | 17 (6) | תַּחַשׁ (4); *תְּכֵלֶת* (1); שֵׁשׁ (1); אַרְגָּמָן (1); טַבַּעַת (14); שִׁטָּה (15); טַבַּעַת (26); שִׁטָּה (29); אַרְגָּמָן (31); שֵׁשׁ (31); *תְּכֵלֶת* (31); שִׁטָּה (32); אַרְגָּמָן (36); שֵׁשׁ (36); *תְּכֵלֶת* (36); שִׁטָּה (37) |
| Chapter 27 | 15 (8) | שִׁטָּה (1); קֶרֶן (2); קֶרֶן (2); יָעִים (3); טַבַּעַת (4); טַבַּעַת (7); בַּדִּים (6); שִׁטָּה (6); בַּדִּים (6); *תְּכֵלֶת* (16); שֵׁשׁ (16); אַרְגָּמָן (16); שֵׁשׁ (9); אַרְגָּמָן (7); שֵׁשׁ (18) |
| Chapter 28 | 62 (20) | שֵׁשׁ (5); אַרְגָּמָן (4); כֻּתֹּנֶת (4); אֵפֹד (4); אַבְנֵט (5); אֵפֹד (6); אַרְגָּמָן (6); שֵׁשׁ (6); *תְּכֵלֶת* (5); *תְּכֵלֶת* (6); אֲפֻדָּה (8); אַרְגָּמָן (8); שֵׁשׁ (8); אַרְגָּמָן (15); אֵפֹד (12); אֵפֹד (15); חֹתָם (11); בָּרֶקֶת (16); זֶרֶת (16); *תְּכֵלֶת* (15); שֵׁשׁ (15); אַחְלָמָה (18); נֹפֶךְ (18); סַפִּיר (18); פִּטְדָה (17); חֹתָם (20); תַּרְשִׁישׁ (19); שְׁבוֹ (19); יָשְׁפֵה (20); אֵפֹד (24); טַבַּעַת (23); טַבַּעַת (23); אֵפֹד (21); אֵפֹד (26); טַבַּעַת (26); אֵפֹד (27); אֵפֹד (25); אֵפֹד (28); אֵפֹד (27); טַבַּעַת (27); אֵפֹד (28); טַבַּעַת (28); *תְּכֵלֶת* (28); רִמּוֹן (33); אַרְגָּמָן (32); תַּחְרָא (31); *תְּכֵלֶת* (31); *תְּכֵלֶת* (33); רִמּוֹן (34); רִמּוֹן (34); חֹתָם (33); *תְּכֵלֶת* (37); אַבְנֵט (39); כֻּתֹּנֶת (39); שֵׁשׁ (39); *תְּכֵלֶת* (36); אַבְנֵט (40); כֻּתֹּנֶת (40); שֵׁשׁ (39) |

| Chapter 29 | 11 (7) | כֻּתֹּנֶת (5); אֵפֹד (5); אֵפֹד (5); אֵפֹד (5); אֵפֹד (5); אַבְנֵט (8); כֻּתֹּנֶת (9); קֶרֶן (12); הִין (40); הִין (40); יַיִן (40) |
| Chapter 30 | 15 (8) | טַבַּעַת (4); בַּדִּים (4); קֶרֶן (2); קֶרֶן (3); שִׁטָּה (1); כִּיּוֹר (10); קֶרֶן (7); סַמִּים (5); שִׁטָּה (5); בַּדִּים (34); חֶלְבְּנָה (34); כִּיּוֹר (28); הִין (24); סַמִּים (18); סַמִּים (34) |
| Chapter 31 | 2 (2) | סַמִּים (11); כִּיּוֹר (9) |
| Chapter 32 | 1 (1) | חָרוּת (16) |
| Chapter 33 | 0 (0) | |
| Chapter 34 | 1 (1) | שׁוֹר (19) |
| Chapter 35 | 23 (9) | תַּחַשׁ (7); שִׁטָּה (6); תְּכֵלֶת (6); שֵׁשׁ (6); אַרְגָּמָן (6); כִּיּוֹר (16); סַמִּים (15); אֵפֹד (9); סַמִּים (8); כִּיּוֹר (7); תַּחַשׁ (23); שֵׁשׁ (23); אַרְגָּמָן (22); טַבַּעַת (23); שֵׁשׁ (25); אַרְגָּמָן (25); שִׁטָּה (24); תְּכֵלֶת (23); אַרְגָּמָן (35); סַמִּים (28); אֵפֹד (27); תְּכֵלֶת (25); שֵׁשׁ (35); תְּכֵלֶת (35) |
| Chapter 36 | 16 (6) | תַּחַשׁ (11); תְּכֵלֶת (8); שֵׁשׁ (8); אַרְגָּמָן (8); טַבַּעַת (31); שִׁטָּה (20); טַבַּעַת (29); שִׁטָּה (19); תְּכֵלֶת (35); שֵׁשׁ (35); אַרְגָּמָן (34); תְּכֵלֶת (37); שֵׁשׁ (37); אַרְגָּמָן (36) |
| Chapter 37 | 27 (6) | שִׁטָּה (1); טַבַּעַת (3); טַבַּעַת (3); בַּדִּים (3); שִׁטָּה (4); בַּדִּים (5); טַבַּעַת (5); שִׁטָּה (4); טַבַּעַת (10); בַּדִּים (14); טַבַּעַת (13); בַּדִּים (15); גָּבִיעַ (17); גָּבִיעַ (19); בַּדִּים (26); קֶרֶן (25); שִׁטָּה (25); קֶרֶן (20); גָּבִיעַ (19); בַּדִּים (28); טַבַּעַת (27); בַּדִּים (27); שִׁטָּה (28); סַמִּים (29) |
| Chapter 38 | 19 (9) | בַּדִּים (5); יָעִים (3); קֶרֶן (2); קֶרֶן (2); שִׁטָּה (1); טַבַּעַת (7); בַּדִּים (6); שִׁטָּה (6); בַּדִּים (5); טַבַּעַת (7); כִּיּוֹר (8); שֵׁשׁ (9); שֵׁשׁ (16); אַרְגָּמָן (18); שֵׁשׁ (18); תְּכֵלֶת (18); אַרְגָּמָן (23); שֵׁשׁ (23); תְּכֵלֶת (23) |
| Chapter 39 | 72 (25) | שֵׁשׁ (2); אַרְגָּמָן (2); אֵפֹד (1); תְּכֵלֶת (1); אַרְגָּמָן (2); תְּכֵלֶת (2); אַרְגָּמָן (3); שֵׁשׁ (3); פַּח (3); תְּכֵלֶת (3); תְּכֵלֶת (5); שֵׁשׁ (5); אַרְגָּמָן (5); אֲפֻדָּה (3); שֵׁשׁ (8); אַרְגָּמָן (8); אֵפֹד (8); אֵפֹד (7); חֹתָם (6); פִּטְדָה (10); בָּרֶקֶת (9); זֶרֶת (9); תְּכֵלֶת (8); שְׁבוֹ (12); אַחְלָמָה (11); סַפִּיר (11); נֹפֶךְ (10); כֻּתֹּנֶת (14); חֹתָם (13); תַּרְשִׁישׁ (13); יָשְׁפֵה (12); אֵפֹד (17); טַבַּעַת (16); טַבַּעַת (16); טַבַּעַת (14); אֵפֹד (18); אֵפֹד (19); טַבַּעַת (19); אֵפֹד (20); טַבַּעַת (20); אֵפֹד (21); אֵפֹד (21); |

*Appendix Five* 249

| | | |
|---|---|---|
| | | (21) תְּכֵלֶת; (21) טַבַּעַת; (21) טַבַּעַת; **אֵפֹד** (21); (24) אַרְגָּמָן; (23) תַחְרָא; (22) תְּכֵלֶת; **אֵפֹד** (22); (25) רִמּוֹן; (25) רִמּוֹן; (24) תְּכֵלֶת; (24) רִמּוֹן (26) רִמּוֹן; (26) כְּתֹנֶת; (27) **שֵׁשׁ**; **פְּאֵר** (28); (29) אַרְגָּמָן; (28) **אַבְנֵט**; (28) שֵׁשׁ; (28) שֵׁשׁ; (29) תְּכֵלֶת; (29) תְּכֵלֶת; **חֹתָם** (30); **שֵׁשׁ** (29); (31) תַּחַשׁ; (34) סַמִּים; (38) כִּיּוֹר (39) |
| Chapter 40 | 5 (3) | (27) כִּיּוֹר; (20) בַּדִּים; (11) כִּיּוֹר; (7) כִּיּוֹר (30) |

Egyptian loanwords: אַבְנֵט אַחְלָמָה אֵפֹד אָפַד אֲפֻדָּה בַּדִּים בָּרֶקֶת גָּבִיעַ הִין זֶרֶת חֹתָם טַבַּעַת יָעִים נֹפֶךְ פְּאֵר פַּח שִׁטָּה שֵׁשׁ תַחְרָא תַּחַשׁ
Akkadian loanwords: כִּיּוֹר כְּתֹנֶת סַמִּים שְׁבוֹ תְּכֵלֶת
Others: אַרְגָּמָן (Anatolian); חֶלְבְּנָה (Culture Word); חָרוּת (Aramaic); יַיִן (Indo-European) יְשֻׁפֵה (Hurrian); סַפִּיר (Unknown Semitic Source); פִּטְדָה (Unknown); קֶרֶן (Indo-European); רִמּוֹן (Culture Word); שׁוֹר (Indo-European?, early); תַּרְשִׁישׁ (Phoenician or 'Tartessian')

# Appendix Six:
# An Outline of Linguistic Change
# in Aramaic and Akkadian

*An outline of linguistic change in Aramaic*

The Aramaic language underwent a series of changes from its Northwest Semitic stock such that it is possible to recognize borrowings that occurred after those changes from what Aramaic and Hebrew share due to inheritance. As has already been discussed, there will have been borrowings that are not necessarily detectable by these means.

*Early phonetic changes (prior to c. 500 BCE)*
In this period Hebrew undergoes the Canaanite shift, in which /ā/ > /ō/, while Aramaic does not. Based on the shifted forms in the Amarna letters, this has happened by the end of the fourteenth century.[1]

At some point between the attested Old Aramaic and Imperial Aramaic,[2] the Semitic interdentals merged with the dentals. In Hebrew, however, the interdentals merged with the sibilants.[3] Likewise another Semitic sound merged with ע in Aramaic[4] but צ in Hebrew. While the interdentals seem

---

1. Holger Gzella, 'Northwest Semitic in General', in *The Semitic Languages: An International Handbook*, ed. Stefan Weninger et al., Handbücher zur Sprach- und Kommunikations-wissenschaft 36 (Berlin: de Gruyter, 2011), 425–51 (428).

2. The change in spelling from ז to ד in words that inherited the hypothetical voiced interdental is first attested in 483 BCE. See Takamitsu Muraoka and Bezalel Porten, *A Grammar of Egyptian Aramaic*, 2nd ed., Handbooks of Oriental Studies 1. The Near and Middle East 32 (Leiden: Brill, 1997), 4.

3. Leonid Kogan, 'Proto-Semitic Phonetics and Phonology', in *The Semitic Languages: An International Handbook*, ed. Stefan Weninger et al., Handbücher zur Sprach- und Kommunikations-wissenschaft 36 (Berlin: de Gruyter, 2011), 54–150 (55).

4. Margaretha Folmer, 'Old and Imperial Aramaic', in *Languages from the World of the Bible*, ed. Holger Gzella (Berlin: de Gruyter, 2012), 128–59 (134).

to be preserved in Old Aramaic, phonologically if not orthographically,[5] it is possible that this latter sound change had already happened in Old Aramaic, which would explain the choice of ק to represent the sound.[6] It is possible, therefore, to form a series of correspondences:

Table 15 Northwest Semitic Consonants in Hebrew and Aramaic

| Proto-Northwest Semitic | Old Aramaic Orthography[7] | Later Aramaic | Hebrew |
| --- | --- | --- | --- |
| š | שׁ | שׁ | שׁ |
| ṯ | שׁ | ת | שׁ |
| t | ת | ת | ת |
| z | ז | ז | ז |
| ḏ | ז | ד | ז |
| d | ד | ד | ד |
| ṣ | צ | צ | צ |
| ṱ | צ | ט | צ |
| ṭ | ט | ט | ט |
| ḍ | ק | ע | צ |
| ʿ | ע | ע | ע |

Thus, for example, a root ארע in Aramaic (ארק in the Old Aramaic orthography) is a reflex of the same Northwest Semitic root as ארץ in Hebrew.

One further change that took place before the Achaemenid period was the dissimilation of emphatic consonants such that ק becomes כ in the presence of צ or ט.[8] However, in light of changes in the opposite direction in Imperial Aramaic[9] – ט becomes ת in the presence of ק – it is possible to explain these changes as phonotactic variations, similar to the metathesis of sibilants, rather than historical developments.

---

5. Ibid., 133.
6. Ibid., 134.
7. Stephen Kaufman, 'Aramaic', in *The Semitic Languages*, ed. Robert Hetzron (London: Routledge, 1997), 114–31 (119).
8. Folmer, 'Old and Imperial Aramaic', 135.
9. Stuart Creason, 'Aramaic' in *The Cambridge Encyclopedia of the World's Ancient Languages*, ed. Roger Woodard (Cambridge: Cambridge University Press, 2004), 391–426 (401).

*Imperial Aramaic (c. 500 BCE–c. 200 BCE)*
A further change that took place, in the Achaemenid period as far as attestation suggests, is nasalization of vowels before (originally) geminated consonants.[10] Whether this initially represented the actual articulation or not cannot be absolutely decided, but without evidence to the contrary that appears to be the best explanation.[11]

*Post-imperial Aramaic (c. 200 BCE–)*
The consonants שׂ and ס merged. At an earlier date there appears to have been confusion between the phonemes but not full convergence.[12] While this may not always apply directly to hypothesized loans in Hebrew, it is important for evaluating lexical evidence from Syriac.

*Vocalization*
In vocalized Aramaic and Tiberian Hebrew it is possible to contrast the vocalizations of a variety of Hebrew and Aramaic nouns. By means of comparative historical linguistics, it is possible to hypothesize a Proto-Semitic form based on the reflexes found in Aramaic, Hebrew and other Semitic languages.[13] Theoretically, then, it should be possible to determine whether a particular form found in the Hebrew Bible is or is not typical of Hebrew. Thus, a word in the form *qtal* – as opposed to *qetel* – found in Biblical Hebrew might be taken to be an Aramaic borrowing. However, in practice there are two chief difficulties.

The first cause of difficulty is the dating of the changes. Although it is possible to date the Canaanite shift, most vocalic changes are not reflected in the unvocalized texts that can be dated to the period in which these changes are supposed to have happened. The evolution from *\*qatl* to either *qetel* or *qtal*, for example, cannot be detected in unvocalized texts. Therefore, though words of the form *qtal* may appear at first an Aramaic borrowing, we cannot rule out that in the time period in which we have only unvocalized Hebrew that the form *qtal* might have been more common in Hebrew.

The second cause of difficulty is that many of the proposed Semitic vocalization patterns are based on only a few cases, such that there is

---

10. Folmer, 'Old and Imperial Aramaic', 134–35; Kaufman, 'Aramaic', in *The Semitic Languages*, 120; Muraoka and Porten, *Egyptian Aramaic*, 13–16.
11. See also, Muraoka and Porten, *Egyptian Aramaic*, 14–16.
12. Folmer, 'Old and Imperial Aramaic', 135.
13. Fox, *Semitic Noun Patterns*; Kienast, *Historische Semitische Sprachwissenschaft*, 69–128.

disagreement over which patterns are to be reconstructed. Thus Kienast reconstructs *qvtl*, *qatvl*, *qatv̄l*, *qattvl*, *qattv̄l* and *qātil*,[14] whereas Fox reconstructs in addition to those the patterns *qutul*, *qutūl*, *qital*, *qitāl*, *qutāl*, *quttul*, *quttūl*, *qittal*, *qittāl*, *quttal* and *quttāl*.[15] This comes to be a particular difficulty when borrowed forms are taken into account; if a form is perceived as unusual for Hebrew, it is not apparent whether this is a case of a rarely attested form that is nonetheless native to Hebrew or in fact a form that cannot be native to Hebrew.

Due to these difficulties it is impossible to use vocalization as a primary determiner of whether or not a word is borrowed. It is possible, however, that we should expect borrowed words from Aramaic to be more prone to unusual forms.

Although it is true that there are only a few letters for which it will be possible to make phonological judgments regarding borrowing, it follows that in many cases no phonological judgments may be made. In the immediate ancestor of Hebrew and Aramaic, there are 27 consonants that can be distinguished, four of which have different reflexes in Hebrew and Aramaic. However, the proportion of letters (4:23) is, perhaps against intuition, significantly lower than the proportion of words which will contain one of those letters. This is because each word offers as many chances for one of those letters to appear as the word has letters. Thus, for example, a triliteral root, as an indicative measure,[16] has $(27^3 - 23^3) \div 27^3 =$ an approximately 38% chance that it will contain one of the letters that are distinguishable.[17] In reality, the situation is more complex, since there are constraints on which consonants may co-occur.[18]

As an aside, in general, the use of phonological criteria is standard for determining Aramaisms. The apparent reliability of phonological criteria, however, does rely on a number of assumptions. It must be maintained that these criteria are phonemic and not phonetic; they are based on

---

14. Kienast, *Historische Semitische Sprachwissenschaft*, 69–128.
15. Fox, *Semitic Noun Patterns*.
16. This is, of course, an imperfect measure since it does not account for the fact that not every combination of three letters is equally likely.
17. If there are 27 Northwest Semitic consonants, then the total number of possible triliteral roots is $27^3$. The total number of possible triliteral roots that contain none of the four letters is $23^3$, Therefore, the total number of possible triliteral roots that do contain one of the four consonants is $27^3 - 23^3$. The number of roots containing the four consonants divided by the total number of roots gives the percentage chance.
18. See 'Appendix One: Root Constraints and the Shared Vocabulary of Aramaic and Hebrew'.

distinctions that can only be proved at a phonemic level: they are proved through minimal pairs. Thus, for example, שׁ and ת are taken to represent distinct phonemes because of pairs such as תָּם, 'perfect', and שָׁם, 'there'. However, in applying this phonemic distinction to cases beyond the established minimal pair, there is an assumption that the graphemes in question represent only one phoneme. There is a second assumption in applying this to loanwords that the phonetic realizations of the phonemes are such that they not only permit but also require borrowing. Therefore, to consider the case of Hebrew חָרַת, 'to engrave', and חָרַשׁ, 'to engrave, plough, be silent', and Aramaic חרת, 'to engrave, plough', and חרשׁ, 'to be silent', the phonological criteria appear to favour borrowing:[19] we may hypothesize a proto-Semitic root, ḫ-r-ṭ,[20] 'to plough, engrave', which developed as חָרַשׁ in Hebrew and חרת in Aramaic and another Northwest Semitic form, either ḫ-r-š or ḫ-r-š, 'to be silent'. Borrowing from Aramaic into Hebrew would then explain Hebrew חָרַת, 'to engrave'. However, if the Hebrew phoneme that descended from proto-Semitic /ṭ/ maintained, or even developed, both sibilant and non-sibilant realizations internally – whether in dialectal forms, complementary distribution or free variation – it is possible to explain both orthographic forms as resulting from a single morpheme. Despite these concerns, however, it does appear at present that borrowing is a simpler explanation, since it requires less speculation.

## *An outline of linguistic change in Akkadian*

Just as with Aramaic, the Akkadian language underwent a series of changes from proto-Semitic that help identify loanwords. As has already been discussed, there will have been borrowings that are not necessarily detectable by these means.

### *Early changes*
In the time before the earliest recorded Akkadian, it underwent the mergers of inter-dentals and sibilants.[21] Streck argues that in Eblaite the inter-dentals remained distinct.[22] Huehnergard and Woods claim that

---

19. Cf. Wagner, *Die Aramaismen*, 59.
20. Cf. Akkadian, *erēšum*; see *CAD*, s.v. '*erēšu* B.'
21. John Huehnergard, *A Grammar of Akkadian*, HSS 45 (Winona Lake: Eisenbrauns, 2005), 586.
22. Michael Streck, 'Babylonian and Assyrian', in Weninger et al., eds., *The Semitic Languages*, 359–95 (361).

/θ/ remains distinct in Sargonic.²³ Before the time of Old Assyrian and Old Babylonian, before c. 1950 BCE, the gutturals are lost.²⁴ Likewise, proto-Semitic initial or final *y was elided to *aleph* in the same period.²⁵

At this early point, there are also several dissimilations and assimilations: *m* dissimilates to *n* in the presence of labials (Barth's law of dissimilation) and *ṭ* dissimilates to *t* in the presence of other emphatics (Geer's law of dissimilation).²⁶ Assimilation of *dt* and *ṭt* to *tt* and assimilation of *n* to an immediately following consonant also take place.²⁷

The Babylonian vowel harmony is also complete by the time of Old Babylonian, by which, in the presence of /e/, /a/ was assimilated to /e/.²⁸ Likewise the Assyrian vowel harmony has taken place by the time of Old Assyrian, by which /a/ in a syllable that is neither closed nor accented but is assimilated to whatever vowel follows it.²⁹

*Changes during Middle Assyrian and Babylonian (c. 1500–1000 BCE)*
In Middle Assyrian /qt/ assimilates to /qṭ/, in contrast to the earlier dissimilation according to Geer's law.³⁰ In Middle Babylonian, doubled voiced stops dissimilate to nasal and stop: *bb* becomes *mb*, *dd* becomes *nd*, *gg* becomes *ng*.³¹ Likewise in Middle Babylonian and Assyrian etymological *w* begins to be written as *m* intervocalically,³² though comparisons between personal names and their transcriptions in Hebrew suggest that the pronunciation of what was written *m* approximated *w*.³³ In Middle Assyrian, however, intervocalic *w* is in many cases written

---

23. Huehnergard and Woods, 'Akkadian and Eblaite', 235.
24. Huehnergard, *Akkadian*, 586; Streck, 'Babylonian and Assyrian', 361.
25. Huehnergard and Woods, 'Akkadian and Eblaite', 237.
26. Huehnergard, *Akkadian*, 588; Huehnergard and Woods, 'Akkadian and Eblaite', 237.
27. Huehnergard and Woods, 'Akkadian and Eblaite', 238.
28. Ibid., 232.
29. Ibid., 240.
30. Streck, 'Babylonian and Assyrian', 371.
31. Huehnergard and Woods, 'Akkadian and Eblaite', 238; Streck, 'Babylonian and Assyrian', 374.
32. Huehnergard and Woods, 'Akkadian and Eblaite', 239.
33. Mankowski, *Akkadian Loanwords*, 158–59. For example, the Akkadian name *amēl marduk* is represented in Hebrew as Evil Merodach (2 Kgs 25:27). Although in some earlier dialects, the name would have been written *awil marduk*, in Middle Assyrian, Neo-Assyrian and all the Babylonian dialects it was written *amēl* or *amīl*. Cf. *CAD*, s.v. 'amīlu.'

as *aleph*.³⁴ In both Assyrian and Babylonian /št/ and /šṭ/ become /lt/ and /lṭ/, respectively.³⁵ Both also underwent the loss of mimation in this period.³⁶ Also in both Assyrian and Babylonian, *m* assimilated to *n* before dentals and *š*.³⁷

*Later changes*
In Neo-Assyrian several of the developments of the Middle Assyrian period continue to change; thus, for example, etymological *w*, previously written as *m*, came to be represented as *b* in many cases.³⁸ When /lt/ had originated from /št/ it further developed to /ss/.³⁹ In this period, the effects of the Assyrian vowel harmony continued to develop such that it also affected closed syllables.⁴⁰ In Neo-Assyrian, the pronunciation of *š* became /s/ and that of *s* became /š/.⁴¹

---

34. Huehnergard and Woods, 'Akkadian and Eblaite', 237.
35. Streck, 'Babylonian and Assyrian', 371.
36. Ibid., 372, 374.
37. Giorgio Buccellati, *A Structural Grammar of Babylonian* (Wiesbaden: Otto Harrassowitz Verlag, 1996), 38; Huehnergard and Woods, 'Akkadian and Eblaite', 239.
38. Huehnergard and Woods, 'Akkadian and Eblaite', 237.
39. Ibid., 238.
40. Ibid., 240.
41. Mankowski, *Akkadian Loanwords*, 155-57.

# Bibliography

Aartun, Kjell. 'Neue Beiträge zum Ugaritischen Lexikon.' Pages 1–52 in *Ugarit-Forschungen 16*. Edited by Kurt Bergerhof et al. Kevelaer: Butzon & Bercker, 1984.
Aejmelaeus, Anneli. 'Septuagintal Translation Techniques – A Solution to the Problem of the Tabernacle Account?' Pages 107–22 in *On the Trail of the Septuagint Translators: Collected Essays*. Leuven: Peeters, 2007.
Albright, William. 'New Light on the Early History of Phoenician Colonization.' *BASOR* 83 (1941): 14–22.
Albright, William. *Archeology and the Religion of Israel*. 5th ed. Baltimore: The Johns Hopkins University Press, 1968.
Albright, William. 'The Nebuchadnezzar and Neriglissar Chronicles.' *BASOR* 143 (1956): 28–33
Albright, William. Review of *Introduction a la Bible, Tome I*, by André Robert and André Feuillet. *BO* 17 (1960): 241–42.
Alonso Schöckel, Luis. *Diccionario Bíblico Hebreo–Español*. Madrid: Trotta, 2008.
Alter, Robert. *The Art of Biblical Narrative*. New York: Basic Books, 1981.
Anthony, David. 'Horse, Wagon & Chariot: Indo-European Languages and Archaeology.' *Antiquity* 69 (1995): 554–65.
Arnold, Bill. 'The Use of Aramaic in the Bible: Another Look at Bilingualism in Ezra and Daniel.' *JNSL* 22 (1996): 1–16.
Auer, Peter. 'Code-Switching: Discourse Models.' Pages 443–46 in *Concise Encyclopedia of Sociolinguistics*. Edited by Rajend Mesthrie. Oxford: Elsevier, 2001.
Autenrieth, Georg. *Homeric Lexicon*. University of Chicago. http://logeion.uchicago.edu/.
Autran, Charles. 'De quelques vestiges probables, méconnus jusqu'ici, du lexique Méditerranéen dans le sémitique d'Asie Mineure, et, notamment, de Canaan.' *JA* 209 (1926): 1–79.
Avalos, Hector. 'The Comedic Function of the Enumerations of Officials and Instruments in Daniel 3.' *CBQ* 53 (1991): 580–88.
Bailey, Robert, and Ceil Lucas. *Sociolinguistic Variation: Theories, Methods, and Applications*. Cambridge: Cambridge University Press, 2007.
Bal, Mieke. *Death and Dissymmetry*. CSJH. Chicago: Chicago University Press, 1988.
Bal, Mieke. *Narratology: Introduction to the Theory of Narrative*. 3rd ed. Toronto: University of Toronto Press, 2009.
Baldwin, Joyce. *Esther*. Tyndale Old Testament Commentaries. Leicester: Inter-Varsity Press, 1984.
Bardtke, Hans. 'Esther.' In *Der Prediger. Das Buch Esther*, by Hans Bardtke and Hans Hertzberg. KAT. Berlin: Evangelische Verlagsanstalt Berlin, 1972.
Bartholomae, Christian. *Altiranisches Wörterbuch*. Strasbourg: Karl J. Trübner, 1904.

Bauer, Dieter. *Das Buch Daniel*. Neuer Stuttgarter Kommentar Altes Testament. Stuttgart: Verlag Katholisches Bibelwerk, 1996.
Bauer, Hans, and Pontus Leander. *Historische Grammatik der Herbräischen Sprache des Alten Testaments*. Halle a. S.: Max Niemeyer, 1922.
Beekes, Robert. *Etymological Dictionary of Greek*. 2 vols. Leiden: Brill, 2010.
Ben Zvi, Ehud. 'Inclusion in and Exclusion from Israel as Conveyed by the Use of the Term "Israel" in Postmonarchic Biblical Texts.' Pages 95–149 in *The Pitcher is Broken: Memorial Essays for Gösta W. Ahlström*. Edited by Steven Holloway and Lowell Handy. JSOTSup 190. Sheffield: JSOT Press, 1995.
Ben Zvi, Ehud. 'On Social Memory and Identity Formation in Late Persian Yehud: A Historian's Viewpoint with a Focus on Prophetic Literature, Chronicles and the Dtr. Historical Collection.' Pages 95–148 in *Texts, Contexts and Readings in Postexilic Literature Explorations into Historiography and Identity Negotiation in Hebrew Bible and Related Texts*. Edited by Louis Jonker. FAT II 53. Tübingen: Mohr-Siebeck, 2011.
Bennett, Andrew, and Nicholas Royle. *An Introduction to Literature, Criticism and Theory*. 5th ed. Routledge, 2018.
Berger, Yitzhak. 'Esther and Benjaminite Royalty: A Study in Inner-Biblical Allusion.' *JBL* 129 (2010): 625–44.
Berlin, Adele. *Poetics and Interpretation of Biblical Narrative*. Sheffield: Almond Press, 1983.
Berman, Joshua. 'The Narratological Purpose of Aramaic in Ezra 4:8–6:18.' *Aramaic Studies* 5 (2007): 165–91.
Berquist, Jon. 'Constructions of Identity in Postcolonial Yehud.' Pages 55–63 in *Judah and the Judeans in the Persian Period*. Edited by Oded Lipschitz and Manfred Oeming. Winona Lake: Eisenbrauns, 2006.
Bickerman, Elias. 'The Colophon of the Greek Book of Esther.' *JBL* 63 (1944): 339–62.
Black, Jeremy, Andrew George, and Nicholas Postgate. *A Concise Dictionary of Akkadian*. 2nd ed. Wiesbaden, Harrassowitz, 2000.
Blenkinsopp, Joseph. *Ezra–Nehemiah*. OTL. Philadelphia: Westminster Press, 1988.
Bloch-Smith, Elizabeth. 'Israelite Ethnicity in Iron I: Archaeology Preserves What is Remembered and What is Forgotten in Israel's History.' *JBL* 122 (2003): 401–25.
Bompiani, Brian. 'Style-Switching: The Representation of the Speech of Foreigners in the Hebrew Bible.' PhD diss., Hebrew Union College, 2012.
Bonner, Robert. 'The Mutual Intelligibility of Greek Dialects.' *The Classical Journal* 4 (1909): 356–63.
Boyd, Samuel. 'Contact and Context: Studies in Language Contact and Literary Strata in the Hebrew Bible.' PhD diss., The University of Chicago, 2014.
Brown, Francis, Samuel Driver, and Charles Briggs. *A Hebrew and English Lexicon of the Old Testament [BDB]*. Oxford: Clarendon, 1907.
Brown, John. *Israel and Hellas*. 3 vols. Berlin: de Gruyter, 1995–2001.
Brown, A. Philip, II. *Hope Amidst Ruin: A Literary and Theological Analysis of Ezra*. Greenville: Bob Jones University Press, 2009.
Brubaker, Rogers. 'Ethnicity without Groups.' *European Journal of Sociology* 43 (2002): 163–89.
Brubaker, Rogers. *Ethnicity without Groups*. Cambridge, MA: Harvard, 2004.
Brueggemann, Walter. *First and Second Samuel*. IBC. Louisville: John Knox Press, 1990.
Buccellati, Giorgio. *A Structural Grammar of Babylonian*. Wiesbaden: Otto Harrassowitz Verlag, 1996.
Bush, Frederic. *Ruth/Esther*. WBC 9. Nashville: Thomas Nelson, 1996.

Campbell, Lyle. *Historical Linguistics*. 3rd ed. Edinburgh: Edinburgh, 2013.
Chandra, Kanchan. 'Attributes and Categories: A New Conceptual Vocabulary for Thinking about Ethnic Identity.' Pages 97–131 in *Constructivist Theories of Ethnic Politics*. Edited by Kanchan Chandra. Oxford: Oxford University Press, 2012.
Chandra, Kanchan. 'What is Ethnic Identity? A Minimalist Definition.' Pages 51–96 in *Constructivist Theories of Ethnic Politics*. Edited by Kanchan Chandra. Oxford: Oxford University Press, 2012.
Childs, Brevard S. *The Book of Exodus*. 1st paperback ed. OTL. Louisville: Westminster John Knox, 2004.
Ciancaglini, Claudia. *Iranian Loanwords in Syriac*. Beiträge zur Iranistik 28. Wiesbaden: Reichert, 2008.
Clines, David J. A. *The Esther Scroll*. JSOTSup 30. Sheffield: JSOT Press, 1984.
Clines, David J. A. *Ezra, Nehemiah, Esther*. NCBC. Grand Rapids: Wm. B. Eerdmans, 1984.
Collins, John. 'The Court Tales in Daniel and the Development of Apocalyptic.' *JBL* 94 (1975): 218–34.
Collins, John. *Daniel*. Hermeneia. Philadelphia: Fortress, 1993.
Collins, John. *The Apocalyptic Imagination: An Introduction to Jewish Apocalyptic Literature*. 3rd ed. Grand Rapids: Eerdmans, 2016.
Collins, John, and Deborah Green. 'The Tales from the Persian Court (4Q550$^{a-e}$).' Pages 39–50 in *Antikes Judentum und Frühes Christentum*. Edited by Bernd Kollman et al. Berlin: de Gruyter, 1999.
Cook, Edward. *Dictionary of Qumran Aramaic*. Winona Lake: Eisenbrauns, 2015.
Cornelius, Izak. '"A Tale of Two Cities": The Visual Imagery of Yehud and Samaria, and Identity/Self-Understanding in Persian-Period Palestine.' Pages 213–237 in *Texts, Contexts and Readings in Postexilic Literature Explorations into Historiography and Identity Negotiation in Hebrew Bible and Related Texts*. Edited by Louis Jonker. FAT II 53. Tübingen: Mohr-Siebeck, 2011.
Coxon, Peter. 'The "List" Genre and Narrative Style in the Court Tales of Daniel.' *JSOT* 35 (1986): 95–121.
Creason, Stuart. 'Aramaic.' Pages 391–426 in *The Cambridge Encyclopedia of the World's Ancient Languages*. Edited by Roger Woodard. Cambridge: Cambridge University Press, 2004.
Cross, Frank. 'The Priestly Tabernacle in the Light of Recent Research.' Pages 91–105 in *The Temple in Antiquity: Ancient Records and Modern Perspectives, Based on a Symposium Held at Brigham Young University in March 1981*. Edited by Truman Madsen. Provo: Brigham Young University, 1984.
Crowley, Terry, and Claire Bowen. *An Introduction to Historical Linguistics*. 4th ed. Oxford: Oxford University Press, 2010.
Cunchillos, Jesús Luis, Juan Pablo Vita, José Angel Zamora, and Raquel Cervigón. *A Concordance of Ugaritic Words*. Piscataway: Gorgias, 2003.
Cuny, Albert. 'Les Mots du Fonds Préhellénique en Grec, Latin et Sémitique Occidental.' *REA* 12 (1910): 154–64.
Dalley, Stephanie. 'Hebrew *Taḥaš*, Akkadian *Duḫšu*, Faience and Beadwork.' *JSS* 45 (2000): 1–19.
Dalley, Stephanie. Review of *The King's Magnates*, by R. Mattila. *BO* 58 (2001): 197–206.
Dassow, Eva von. 'Freedom in Ancient Near Eastern Societies.' Pages 205–28 in *The Oxford Handbook of Cuneiform Culture*. Edited by Karen Radner and Eleanor Robson. Oxford: Oxford University, 2011.

Davies, Philip. 'Ḥasidim in the Maccabean Period.' *JJS* 28 (1977): 127–40.
Day, Linda. *Esther*. Abingdon Old Testament Commentaries. Nashville: Abingdon, 2005.
Derenbourg, Hartwig. 'Les Mots grecs dans le Livre biblique de Daniel.' Pages 235–44 in *Mélanges Graux*. Edited by Ernest Thorin. Paris: E. Thorin, 1884.
Deuchar, Margaret, and Jonathan Stammers. 'What is the "Nonce Borrowing Hypothesis" Anyway?' *Bilingualism – Language and Cognition* 15 (2012): 649–50.
Dillman, Augustus. *Die Bücher Exodus und Leviticus*. Leipzig: Hirzel, 1897.
Dillman, Augustus. *Lexicon Linguae Aethiopicae Cum Indice Latino*. Leipzig: T. O. Weigel, 1865.
Dinkler, Michal. 'New Testament Rhetorical Narratology: An Invitation toward Integration.' *BibInt* 24 (2016): 203–28.
Donohue, Mark. 'Word Order in Austronesian from North to South and East to West.' *Linguistic Typology* 11 (2007): 349–91.
Dozeman, Thomas. *Exodus*. Eerdmans Critical Commentary. Grand Rapids: Eerdmans, 2009.
Driver, Godfrey. 'Hebrew Poetic Diction.' Pages 26–39 in *Congress Volume: Copenhagen, 1953*. VTSup 1. Leiden: E. J. Brill, 1953.
Driver, Godfrey. 'Technical Terms in the Pentateuch.' *WO* 2 (1956): 254–63.
Driver, Samuel. *An Introduction to the Literature of the Old Testament*. 9th ed. Oxford: Clarendon, 1913.
Durham, John. *Exodus*. WBC 3. Nashville: Thomas Nelson, 1987.
Durkin-Meisterernst, Desmond. *Dictionary of Manichaean Middle Persian and Parthian*. Corpus Fontium Manichaeorum: Subsidia. Turnhout: Brepols, 2004.
Edelman, Diana. 'Ethnicity and Early Israel.' Pages 25–55 in *Ethnicity and the Bible*. Edited by Mark Brett. Leiden: Brill, 1996.
Edelman, Diana. 'YHWH's Othering of Israel.' Pages 41–69 in *Imagining the Other and Constructing Israelite Identity in the Early Second Temple Period*. Edited by Ehud Ben Zvi and Diana Edelman. London: Bloomsbury, 2014.
Eilers, Wilhelm. *Iranische Beamtennamen in der keilschriftlichen Überlieferung*. Abhandlungen für die Kunde des Morgenlandes 25. Leipzig: Deutsche Morgenländische Gesellschaft, 1940.
Ekshult, Mats. 'The Importance of Loanwords for Dating Biblical Hebrew Texts.' Pages 8–23 in *Biblical Hebrew: Studies in Chronology and Typology*. Edited by Ian Young. London: T&T Clark, 2003.
Ellenbogen, Maximillian. *Foreign Words in the Old Testament, their Origin and Etymology*. London: Lowe & Brydone, 1957.
Erichsen, Wolja. *Demotisches Glossar*. Copenhagen: Ejnar Munksgrad, 1954.
Erman, Adolf, and Hermann Grapow. *Wörterbuch der Aegyptischen Sprache*. 6 vols. Berlin: Akademie-Verlag, 1926–61.
Eskenazi, Tamara. *In an Age of Prose: A Literary Approach to Ezra–Nehemiah*. SBLMS 36. Atlanta: Scholars Press, 1988.
Eskenazi, Tamara. 'Imagining the Other in the Construction of Jewish Identity in Ezra–Nehemiah.' Pages 230–56 in *Imagining the Other and Constructing Israelite Identity in the Early Second Temple Period*. Edited by Ehud Ben Zvi and Diana Edelman. London: Bloomsbury, 2014.
Faulkner, Raymond. *The Ancient Egyptian Coffin Texts*. 3 vols. Warminster: Aris & Phillips, 1977.
Fensham, F. Charles. *The Books of Ezra and Nehemiah*. NICOT. Grand Rapids: William B. Eerdmans, 1982.

Fischer, Georg, and Dominik Markl. *Das Buch Exodus*. Neuer Stuttgarter Kommentar – Altes Testament. Stuttgart: Verlag Katholisches Bibelwerk, 2009.
Fitzmyer, Joseph. *The Genesis Apocryphon of Qumran Cave 1 (1Q20): A Commentary*. 3rd ed. Rome: Editrice Pontificio Instituto Biblico, 2004.
Fokkelman, Jan. *Narrative Art in Genesis*. SSN 17. Assen: Van Gorcum, 1975.
Folmer, Margaretha. 'Aramaic as a *Lingua Franca*.' Pages 373–400 in *A Companion to Ancient Near Eastern Languages*. Edited by Rebecca Hasselbach-Andee. Hoboken: John Wiley, 2020.
Folmer, Margaretha. 'Imperial Aramaic as an Administrative Language of the Achaemenid Period.' Pages 587–97 in *Semitic Languages: An International Handbook*. Edited by Stefan Weninger et al. Berlin: de Gruyter, 2011.
Folmer, Margaretha. 'Old and Imperial Aramaic.' Pages 128–59 in *Languages from the World of the Bible*. Edited by Holger Gzella. Berlin: de Gruyter, 2012.
Fountain, A. Kay. *Literary and Empirical Readings of the Book of Esther*. Studies in Biblical Literature 43. New York: Peter Lang Publishing, 2002.
Fox, Joshua. *Semitic Noun Patterns*. HSS 52. Winona Lake: Eisenbrauns, 2003.
Fox, Michael. *Character and Ideology in the Book of Esther*. Eugene: Wipf & Stock, 2010.
Freedman, David Noel, ed. *Anchor Bible Dictionary*. 6 vols. New York: Doubleday, 1992.
Fretheim, Terence. *Exodus*. IBC. Louisville: John Knox Press, 1991.
Fried, Lisbeth. *Ezra: A Commentary*. Critical Commentaries. Sheffield: Sheffield Phoenix, 2015.
Fuchs, Esther. 'Status and Role of Female Heroines in the Biblical Narrative.' Pages 77–84 in *Women in the Hebrew Bible: A Reader*. Edited by Alice Bach. New York: Routledge, 2013.
Galinsky, Hans. 'Stylistic Aspects of Linguistic Borrowing: A Stylistic View of American Elements in Modern German.' Pages 35–72 in *Amerikanismen der deutschen Gegenwartssprache: Entlehnungsvorgänge und ihre stilistischen Aspekte*. Edited by Broder Carstensen and Hans Galinsky. 2nd ed. Heidelberg: C. Winter, 1967.
Garcia Trabazo, and Jose Virgilio. 'Hethitisch *tarkummae-*: ein etymologischer Vorschlag.' Pages 296–307 in *Proceedings of the Eighth International Congress of Hittitology, Warsaw, 5–9 September 2011*. Edited by Piotr Taracha. Warsaw: Agade, 2014.
Gardiner, Alan. *Egyptian Grammar*. 3rd ed. Oxford: Griffith Institute, 1957.
Gardner, Anne. 'שׂכל in the Hebrew Bible: Key to the Identity and Function of the Maskilim in Daniel.' *RB* 118 (2008): 496–514.
Gehman, Henry. 'Notes on the Persian Words in the Book of Esther.' *JBL* 43 (1924): 321–28.
George, A. *Babylonian Topographical Texts*. OLA 40. Leuven: Peeters, 1992.
Gerleman, Gillis. *Esther*. BKAT. Neukirchen-Vluyn: Neukirchener Verlag, 1979.
Gerrig, Richard. *Experiencing Narrative Worlds: On the Psychological Activities of Reading*. New Haven: Yale University Press, 1993.
Gharib, Badr-uz-zaman. *Sogdian Dictionary*. Tehran: Farhangan, 1995.
Gil-White, Francisco. 'How Thick is Blood? The Plot Thickens…: If Ethnic Actors are Primordialists, What Remains of the Circumstantialist/Primordialist Controversy?' *Ethnic and Racial Studies* 22 (1999): 789–820.
Gindin, Thamar. 'Persian Loanwords.' Pages 66–70 in vol. 3 of *Encyclopedia of Hebrew Language and Linguistics*. 4 vols. Edited by Geoffrey Khan. Leiden: Brill, 2012.
Goldingay, John. *Daniel*. WBC 30. Grand Rapids: Zondervan, 1996.
Gooding, David. *The Account of the Tabernacle: Translation and Textual Problems of the Greek Exodus*. Cambridge: Cambrdige University, 1959.

Gordon, Cyrus. *Ugaritic Textbook*. Rev. ed. Rome: Editrice Pontificio Istituto Biblico, 1998.

Gordon, Cyrus. 'The Wine-Dark Sea.' *JNES* 37 (1978): 51–52.

Gordon, Robert. *1 & 2 Samuel: A Commentary*. Exeter: Paternoster, 1986.

Görg, Manfred. 'Eine neue Deutung für kăpporæt.' *ZAW* 89 (1977): 115–18.

Graef, Katrien de. 'The Use of Akkadian in Iran.' Pages 263–82 in *The Oxford Handbook of Ancient Iran*. Edited by Daniel Potts. Oxford: Oxford University Press, 2013.

Greenberg, Joseph. 'The Patterning of Root Morphemes in Semitic.' *Word* 6 (1950): 162–81.

Grillot-Susini, Françoise. *Éléments de Grammaire* Élamite. Études Élamites. Paris: Editions Recherche sur les Civilisations, 1987.

Grintz, Yehoshua. 'מונחים קדומים בתורת כהנים [Archaic Terminology in the Priestly Torah].' *Leš* 39 (1975): 5–20.

Grintz, Yehoshua. '(המשך) מונחים קדומים בתורת כהנים [Archaic Terminology in the Priestly Torah (part two)].' *Leš* 39 (1975): 178–81.

Grossman, Jonathan. *Esther: The Outer Narrative and the Hidden Reading*. Siphrut 6. Winona Lake: Eisenbrauns, 2011.

Gueurnier, Nicole. 'La Pertinence de la Notion d'Écart en Stylistique.' *Langue Française* 3 (1999): 34–45.

Gzella, Holger. *A Cultural History of Aramaic: From the Beginnings to the Advent of Islam*. Leiden: Brill, 2015.

Gzella, Holger. 'Northwest Semitic in General.' Pages 425–51 in *The Semitic Languages: An International Handbook*. Edited by Stefan Weninger et al. Handbücher zur Sprach- und Kommunikations-wissenschaft 36. Berlin: de Gruyter, 2011.

Hamilton, Victor. *Exodus: An Exegetical Commentary*. Grand Rapids: Baker Academic, 2011.

Haran, Menahem. *Temples and Temple-Service in Ancient Israel*. Oxford: Clarendon Press, 1978.

Harrell, James. 'Archeological Geography of the World's First Emerald Mine.' *Geoscience Canada* 31 (2004): 69–76.

Harris, John. *Lexicographical Studies in Ancient Egyptian Minerals*. Berlin: Akademie-Verlag, 1961.

Hartley, John. 'אַרְגָּמָן.' Pages 198–203 in *The Semantics of Ancient Hebrew Colour Lexemes*. Edited by John Hartley. Louvain: Peeters, 2010.

Hartman, Louis, and Alexander di Lella. *The Book of Daniel*. AB 23. Garden City: Doubleday, 1978.

Haruta, Seiro. 'Aramaic, Parthian, and Middle Persian.' Pages 779–94 in *The Oxford Handbook of Ancient Iran*. Edited by Daniel Potts. Oxford: Oxford University Press, 2013.

Haspelmath, Martin. 'Lexical Borrowing: Concepts and Issues.' Pages 35–54 in *Loanwords in the World's Languages: A Comparative Handbook*. Edited by Martin Haspelmath and Uri Tadmor. Berlin: de Gruyter, 2009.

Heijmans, Shai. 'Greek Loanwords.' Pages 148–51 in vol. 2 of *Encyclopedia of Hebrew Language and Linguistics*. 4 vols. Edited by Geoffrey Khan. Leiden: Brill, 2012.

Heimerdinger, Jean-Marc. *Topic, Focus and Foreground in Ancient Hebrew Narratives*. Sheffield: Sheffield Academic Press, 1999.

Henze, Matthias. 'The Narrative Frame of Daniel: A Literary Assessment.' *JSJ* 32 (2001): 6–24.

Hezser, Catherine. *Jewish Literacy in Roman Palestine*. Texte und Studien zum antiken Judentum. Tübingen: Mohr Siebeck, 2001.

Hinson, Benjamin. 'Sinuhe's Life Abroad: Ethnoarcheological and Philological Reconsiderations.' Pages 81–93 in *Current Research in Egyptology 14 (2013)*. Edited by Kelly Acetta et al. Oxford: Oxbow Books, 2014.

Hinz, Walther. *Altiranisches Sprachgut der Neben*überlieferungen. Wiesbaden: Otto Harrassowitz, 1975.

Hinz, Walther, and Heidemarie Koch. *Elamisches Wörterbuch*. 2 vols. Berlin: Dietrich Reimer, 1987.

Hoch, James. *Semitic Words in Egyptian Texts of the New Kingdom and Third Intermediate Period*. Princeton: Princeton University, 1994.

Hoffner, Harry. 'Hittite Equivalents of Old Assyrian *kumrum* and *epattum*.' *Wiener Zeitschrift für die Kunde des Morgenlandes* 86 (1996): 151–156.

Hoffner Harry, and H. Craig Melchert. *A Grammar of the Hittite Language*. Languages of the Ancient Near East 1. Winona Lake: Eisenbrauns, 2008.

Hoftijzer, Jacob, and Karel Jongeling. *Dictionary of North West Semitic Inscriptions* [*DNWSI*]. HO 21. 2 vols. Leiden: Brill, 2003.

Hogan, Jackie. 'The Social Significance of English Usage in Japan.' *Japanese Studies* 23 (2003): 43–58.

Hogue, Timothy. 'Return from Exile: Diglossia and Literary Code-Switching in Ezra 1–7.' *ZAW* 130 (2018): 54–68.

Holladay, William. *Jeremiah 1*. Hermeneia. Minneapolis: Fortress, 1986.

Holm, Tawny. *Of Courtiers and Kings: The Biblical Daniel Narratives and Ancient Story-Collections*. Explorations in Ancient Near Eastern Civilizations 1. Winona Lake: Eisenbrauns, 2013.

Holmstedt, Robert. 'The Typological Classification of the Hebrew of Genesis: Subject–Verb or Verb–Subject?' *JHS* 11 (2001): 1–39.

Holmstedt, Robert. 'Word Order and Information Structure in Ruth and Jonah: A Generative-Typological Analysis.' *JSS* 54 (2009): 111–39.

Holmstedt, Robert, and John Screnock. *Esther: A Handbook on the Hebrew Text*. Baylor Handbook on the Hebrew Bible. Waco: Baylor, 2015.

Hosokawa, Naoko. 'Nationalism and Linguistic Purism in Contemporary Japan: National Sentiment Expressed through Public Attitudes towards Foreignisms.' *Studies in Ethnicity and Nationalism* 15 (2015): 48–65.

Huehnergard, John. *A Grammar of Akkadian*. HSS 45. Winona Lake: Eisenbrauns, 2005.

Huehnergard, John, and Christopher Woods. 'Akkadian and Eblaite.' Pages 218–87 in *The Cambridge Encyclopedia of the World's Ancient Languages*. Edited by Roger Woodard. Cambridge: Cambridge University Press, 2004.

Humphreys, W. Lee. 'A Life-Style for Diaspora: A Study of the Tales of Esther and Daniel.' *JBL* 92 (1973): 211–23.

Hurvitz, Avi. 'The Chronological Significance of Aramaisms in Biblical Hebrew.' *IEJ* 18 (1968): 234–40.

Hurvitz, Avi. 'לשונו של המקור הכהני ורקעה ההיסטורי [The Language of the Priestly Source and its Historical Setting – the Case for an Early Date].' *Proceedings of the World Congress of Jewish Studies* 8 (1981): 83–94.

Hurvitz, Avi. 'Dating the Priestly Source in Light of the Historical Study of Biblical Hebrew. A Century after Wellhausen.' *ZAW* 100 (1988): 88–100.

Hurvitz, Avi. 'The Evidence of Language in Dating the Priestly Code: A Linguistic Study in Technical Idioms and Terminology.' *RB* 81 (1974): 24–56.

Hurvitz, Avi. 'Hebrew and Aramaic in the Biblical Period: The Problem of 'Aramaisms' in Linguistic Research on the Hebrew Bible.' Pages 24–37 in *Biblical Hebrew: Studies in Chronology and Typology*. Edited by Ian Young. London: T&T Clark, 2003.

Hurvitz, Avi. 'Once Again: The Linguistic Profile of the Priestly Material in the Pentateuch and its Historical Age. A Response to J. Blenkinsopp.' *ZAW* 112 (2000): 180–91.

Hurvitz, Avi. 'The Usage of שש and בוץ in the Bible and its Implication for the Dating of P.' *HTR* 60 (1967): 117–21.

Hutchinson, John, and Anthony Smith. 'Introduction.' Pages 1–14 in *Ethnicity*. Edited by John Hutchinson and Anthony Smith. Oxford: Oxford University Press, 1996.

Instituto de Lenguas y Culturas del Mediterráneo y Oriente Próximo. *Diccionario Griego-Español*. http://dge.cchs.csic.es/xdge.

Janzen, J. Gerald. *Exodus*. Westminster Bible Companion. Louisville: Westminster John Knox, 1997.

Jastrow, Marcus. *Dictionary of Targumim, Talmud and Midrashic Literature*. Peabody: Hendrickson, 2006.

Jobes, Karen. *The Alpha-Text of Esther: Its Character and Relationship to the Masoretic Text*. SBLDS 153. Atlanta, Scholars Press, 1996.

Johanson, Lars. 'Written Language Intertwining.' Pages 273–331 in *Contact Languages: A Comprehensive Guide*. Edited by Peter Bakker and Yaron Matras. Language Contact and Bilingualism 6. Berlin: de Gruyter Mouton, 2013.

Johnson, Janet, ed. *The Demotic Dictionary of the Oriental Institute of the University of Chicago* [*CDD*]. 30 vols. Chicago: Oriental Institute, 2001.

Joosten, Jan. 'Biblical Rhetoric as Illustrated by Judah's Speech in Genesis 44.18-34.' *JSOT* 41 (2016): 15–30.

Joüon, Paul, and Takamitsu Muraoka. *A Grammar of Biblical Hebrew*. 2nd ed. SubBi 27. Rome: Editrice Pontificio Instituto Biblico, 2006.

Kaufman, Stephen. *The Akkadian Influences on Aramaic*. AS 19. Chicago: The University of Chicago Press, 1974.

Kaufman, Stephen. 'Aramaic.' Pages 114–31 in *The Semitic Languages*. Edited by Robert Hetzron. London: Routledge, 1997.

Kaufman, Stephen. 'An Assyro-Aramaic *egirtu ša šulmu*.' Pages 119–27 in *Essays on the Ancient Near East in Memory of Jacob Joel Finkelstein*. Edited by Maria Ellis. Hamden: Archon, 1977.

Kaufman, Stephen. 'The Classification of the North West Semitic Dialects of the Biblical Period and Some Implications Thereof.' Pages 41–57 in *Proceedings of the Ninth World Congress of Jewish Studies, Jerusalem, 4–12 August, 1985: Panel Sessions, Hebrew and Aramaic*. Edited by Moshe Goshen-Gottstein. Jerusalem: Magnes, 1988.

Kaufman, Stephen, et al. *Comprehensive Aramaic Lexicon*. Hebrew Union College. http://cal.huc.edu.

Kautzsch, Emil. *Die Aramaismen im Alten Testament: 1. Lexikalischer Teil*. Halle an der Saale: Max Niemeyer, 1902.

Keiser, Stephen. 'Religious Identity and the Perception of Linguistic Difference: The Case of Pennsylvania German.' *Language & Communication* 30 (2014): 1–10.

Kennedy, Graeme. *An Introduction to Corpus Linguistics*. New York: Addison Wesley Longman, 1998.

Kent, Roland. *Old Persian: Grammar, Texts, Lexicon*. New Haven: American Oriental Society, 1950.

Kienast, Burkhart. *Historische Semitische Sprachwissenschaft*. Wiesbaden: Harrassowitz Verlag, 2001.

Kienpointner, Manfred. 'Figures of Speech.' Pages 102–18 in *Discursive Pragmatics*. Edited by Jan Zienkowski et al. Amsterdam: John Benjamins, 2011.

Kim, Sunhee. 'The Concepts of Sacred Space in the Hebrew Bible: Meanings, Significance, and Functions.' PhD diss., Boston University, 2014.

Kirkpatrick, Shane. *Competing for Honor: A Social-Scientific Reading of Daniel 1–6*. BibInt 76. Leiden: Brill, 2005.

Koch, Klaus. *Daniel 1–4*. BKAT. Neukirchen-Vluyn: Neukirchener Verlag, 2005.

Koehler, Ludwig, Walter Baumgartner, and Johann Stamm. *The Hebrew and Aramaic Lexicon of the Old Testament*. Translated and edited by Mervyn Richardson. 2 vols. Leiden: Brill, 2001.

Kogan, Leonid. *Genealogical Classification of Semitic: The Lexical Isoglosses*. Berlin: de Gruyter, 2015.

Kogan, Leonid. 'Proto-Semitic Phonetics and Phonology.' Pages 54–150 in *The Semitic Languages: An International Handbook*. Edited by Stefan Weninger et al. Handbücher zur Sprach- und Kommunikations-wissenschaft 36. Berlin: de Gruyter, 2011.

Kottsieper, Ingo. '"And They Did Not Care to Speak Yehudit": On Linguistic Change in Judah during the Late Persian Era.' Pages 95–124 in *Judah and the Judeans in the Fourth Century B.C.E.* Edited by Oded Lipschits et al. Winona Lake: Eisenbrauns, 2007.

Kövecses, Zoltán. *Metaphor: A Practical Introduction*. 2nd ed. Oxford: Oxford University Press, 2010.

Kurzon, Dennis. 'Indian Loanwords.' Pages 263–64 in vol. 2 of *Encyclopedia of Hebrew Language and Linguistics*. 4 vols. Edited by Geoffrey Khan. Leiden: Brill, 2012.

Lakoff, George, and Mark Johnson. *Metaphors We Live By*. Chicago: University of Chicago Press, 1980.

Lambdin, Thomas. 'Egyptian Loan Words in the Old Testament.' *JAOS* 73 (1953): 145–55.

Landesdorfer, P. *Sumerisches Sprachgut im Alten Testament: eine Biblisch-lexikalische Studie*. Leipzig: J. C. Hinrichs'sche Buchhandlung, 1916.

Landsberger, Benno. 'Akkadisch-hebräische Wortgleichungen.' Pages 176–204 in *Hebräische Wortforschung: Festschrift zum 80. Geburtstag von W. Baumgartner*. Edited by Benedikt Hartman et al. VTSup 16. Leiden: Brill, 1967.

Lane, Edward. *An Arabic–English Lexicon*. London: Williams & Norgate, 1863.

Larcher, Pierre. *Larcher's Notes on Herodotus: Historical and Critical Remarks on the Nine Books of the History of Herodotus*. 2 vols. London: John R. Priestly, 1829.

Lausberg, Heinrich. *Handbook of Literary Rhetoric: A Foundation for Literary Study*. Translated by Matthew Bliss, Annemiek Jansen, and David Orton. Edited by David Orton, R. Dean Anderson. Leiden: Brill, 1998.

Lecoq, Pierre. *Les inscriptions de la Perse achéménide*. Paris: Gallimard, 1997.

Lehmann, Winfred. *Historical Linguistics: An Introduction*. 3rd ed. London: Routledge, 1992.

Leslau, Wolf. *Comparative Dictionary of Ge'ez (Classical Ethiopic)*. Wiesbaden: Otto Harrassowitz, 1987.

Leslau, Wolf. *Ethiopic and South Arabic Contributions to the Hebrew Lexicon*. University of California Publications in Semitic Philology 20. Berkeley: University of California, 1958.

Leslau, Wolf. *Reference Grammar of Amharic*. Wiesbaden: Harrassowitz, 1995.

Levenson, Jon. *Esther*. OTL. Louisville: Westminster John Knox Press, 1997.

Levinson, Stephen. *Presumptive Meanings*. Cambridge: MIT Press, 2000.

Lewis, Charlton, and Charles Short. *A Latin Dictionary [Lewis and Short]*. University of Chicago. http://logeion.uchicago.edu/.
Liddell, Henry, Robert Scott, and Henry Stuart Jones. *A Greek–English Lexicon [Liddell, Scott, and Jones]*. University of Chicago. http://logeion.uchicago.edu/.
Lieblein, J. 'Mots égyptiens dans la Bible.' *Proceedings of the Society of Biblical Archaeology* 20 (1898): 202–10.
Lipiński, Édouard. 'Emprunts Suméro-akkadiens en Hébreu Biblique.' *ZAH* 1 (1988): 61–73.
Lipiński, Édouard. *Semitic Languages: Outline of a Comparative Grammar*. OLA 80. Leuven: Peeters, 2001.
Lo, Alison. *Job 28 as Rhetoric*. VTSup 97. Leiden: Brill, 2003.
López Ruiz, Carolina. 'Tarshish and Tartessos Revisited: Textual Problems and Historical Implications.' Pages 255–80 in *Colonial Encounters in Ancient Iberia: Phoenician, Greek, and Indigenous Relations*. Edited by Michael Dietler and Carolina López Ruiz. Chicago: The University of Chicago Press, 2009.
Loprieno, Antonio. *Ancient Egyptian: A Linguistic Introduction*. Cambridge: Cambridge University Press, 1995.
Loprieno, Antonio. 'Ancient Egyptian and Coptic.' Pages 160–217 in *The Cambridge Encyclopedia of the World's Ancient Languages*. Edited by Roger Woodard. Cambridge: Cambridge University Press, 2004.
Lucas, Ernest. *Daniel*. Apollos Old Testament Commentary 20. Downers Grove: InterVarsity, 2002.
Lugt, Pieter van der. *Rhetorical Criticism and the Poetry of the Book of Job*. OtSt 32. Leiden: Brill, 1995.
Lugt, Pieter van der. *Cantos and Strophes in Biblical Hebrew Poetry*. 3 vols. OtSt 53, 57, 63. Leiden: Brill, 2005, 2010, 2013.
Lunn, Nicholas. *Word-order Variation in Biblical Hebrew Poetry: Differentiating Pragmatics and Poetics*. Milton Keynes: Paternoster, 2006.
Machiela, Daniel. *The Dead Sea Genesis Apocryphon: A New Text and Translation with Introduction and Special Treatment of Columns 13–17*. Leiden: Brill, 2009.
Mackenzie, David. *A Concise Pahlavi Dictionary*. Oxford: Oxford University Press 1971.
Mankowski, Paul. 'Akkadian Loanwords.' Pages 82–84 in vol. 1 of *Encyclopedia of Hebrew Language and Linguistics*. Edited by Geoffrey Khan. Leiden: Brill, 2012.
Mankowski, Paul. *Akkadian Loanwords in Biblical Hebrew*. Winona Lake: Eisenbrauns, 2000.
Marcellino, Marcellinus. 'The Forms and Functions of Western Loanwords in Selected Indonesian Print Media' PhD diss., Georgetown, 1990.
Marks, Herbert. 'Biblical Naming and Poetic Etymology.' *JBL* 114 (1995): 21–42.
Mastjnak, Nathan. 'Hebrew taḥaš and the West Semitic Tent Tradition.' *VT* 67 (2017): 204–12.
Matthews, Peter. *The Concise Oxford Dictionary of Linguistics*. 2nd ed. Oxford: Oxford University Press, 2007.
McCarter, P. Kyle. 'Hebrew.' Pages 319–64 in *The Cambridge Encyclopedia of the World's Ancient Languages*. Edited by Roger Woodard. Cambridge: Cambridge University Press, 2004.
McCormick, Kay. 'Code-Switching: Overview.' Pages 447–54 in *Concise Encyclopedia of Sociolinguistics*. Edited by Rajend Mesthrie. Oxford: Elsevier, 2001.
Meier-Brügger, Michael, Matthias Fritz, and Manfred Mayrhofer. *Indo-European Linguistics*. Berlin: de Gruyter, 2003.

Melchert, H. Craig. *Cuneiform Luvian Lexicon*. Chapel Hill: H. Craig Melchert, 1993.
Milgrom, Jacob. *Leviticus 1–16*. AB 3. New York: Doubleday, 1991.
Milik, Józef. 'Les Modèles Araméens du Livre d'Esther dans la Grotte 4 de Qumràn.' *RevQ* 15 (1992): 321–406.
Militarev, Alexander, and Leonid Kogan. *Anatomy of Man and Animals*, vol. 1 of *Semitic Etymological Dictionary*. Münster: Ugarit-Verlag, 2000.
Millard, Alan. 'The Etymology of Nebrašta', Daniel 5:5.' *Maarav* 4 (1987): 87–92.
Miller, James. 'Ethnicity and the Hebrew Bible: Problems and Prospects.' *Currents in Biblical Research* 6 (2008): 170–213.
Monier-Williams, Monier. *A Sanskrit–English Dictionary*. Oxford: Oxford University, 1899.
Montes-Alcalá, Cecilia. 'Two Languages, One Pen: Socio-Pragmatic Functions in Written Spanish-English Code-Switching.' PhD diss., University of California, 2000.
Montes-Alcalá, Cecilia, and Naomi Shin. 'Las Keys Versus El Key: Feminine Gender Assignment in Mixed-Language Texts.' *Spanish in Context* 8 (2011): 119–43.
Montgomery, James. *A Critical and Exegetical Commentary on the Book of Daniel*. Oxford: Clarendon Press, 1927.
Moore, Carey. *Esther*. AB 7B. New Haven: Yale University Press, 1971.
Moorey, Peter. *Ancient Mesopotamian Materials and Industries: The Archaeological Evidence*. Winona Lake: Eisenbrauns, 1999.
Muchiki, Yoshiyuki. *Egyptian Proper Names and Loanwords in North-West Semitic*. SBLDS 173. Atlanta: Scholars Press, 1999.
Muilenburg, James. 'Form Criticism and Beyond.' *JBL* 88 (1969): 1–18.
Müller, Wilhelm. 'Zwei ägyptische Wörter im Hebräischen.' *OLZ* 3 (1900): 49–51.
Mumford, Gregory. 'Egypt and the Levant.' Pages 72–85 in *The Oxford Handbook of the Archaeology of the Levant: c. 8000–332 BCE*. Edited by Margreet Steiner and Ann Killebrew. Oxford: Oxford University Press, 2014.
Muraoka, Takamitsu, and Bezalel Porten. *A Grammar of Egyptian Aramaic*. 2nd ed. Handbooks of Oriental Studies 1. The Near and Middle East 32. Leiden: Brill, 1997.
Myers-Scotton, Carol. 'Comparing Code-switching and Borrowing.' *Journal of Multilingual and Multicultural Development* 13 (1992): 19–39.
Myers-Scotton, Carol. *Contact Linguistics: Bilingual Encounters and Grammatical Outcomes*. Oxford Scholarship Online, 2002.
Myers-Scotton, Carol. *Multiple Voices: an Introduction to Bilingualism*. Hoboken: Wiley-Blackwell, 2008.
Myers-Scotton, Carol. *Social Motivations for Codeswitching: Evidence from Africa*. Oxford: Clarendon Press, 1993.
Nam, Daegeuk. 'The "Throne of God" Motif in the Hebrew Bible.' PhD diss., Andrews University, 1989.
Nash, Manning. *The Cauldron of Ethnicity in the Modern World*. Chicago: University of Chicago, 1989.
Nate, Richard. 'Catachrēsis.' Pages 88–89 in *Encyclopedia of Rhetoric*. Edited by Thomas Sloane. Oxford: Oxford University Press, 2001.
Nestor, Dermot. 'We Are Family: Deuteronomy 14 and the Boundaries of an Israelite Identity.' *The Bible and Critical Theory* 9 (2013): 38–53.
Newsom, Carol. *Daniel*. OTL. Louisville: Westminster John Knox, 2014.
Newsom, Carol. 'Resistance is Futile! The Ironies of Danielic Resistance to Empire.' *Int* 71 (2017): 167–77.

Niditch, Susan, and Robert Doran. 'The Success Story of the Wise Courtier: A Formal Approach.' *JBL* 92 (1977): 179–93.

Nöldecke, Theodor. 'Kautzsch' Aramaismen im Alten Testament.' Review of *Die Aramaismen im Alten Testament*, by Emil Kautzsch. *ZDMG* 57 (1903): 412–20.

Noonan, Benjamin. 'Foreign Loanwords and *Kulturwörter* in Northwest Semitic (1400–600 B.C.E.): Linguistic and Cultural Contact in Light of Terminology for Realia.' PhD diss., Hebrew Union College, 2012.

Noonan, Benjamin. 'Daniel's Greek Loanwords in Dialectal Perspective.' *BBR* 28 (2018): 575–603.

Noonan, Benjamin. 'Egyptian Loanwords as Evidence for the Authenticity of the Exodus and Wilderness Traditions.' Pages 49–69 in *'Did I not Bring Israel Out of Egypt?': Biblical, Archaeological, and Egyptological Perspectives on the Exodus Narratives*. Edited by James Hoffmeier, Alan Millard, and Gary Rendsburg. BBR Supplement 13. Winona Lake: Eisenbrauns, 2016.

Noonan, Benjamin. 'Hide or Hue? Defining Hebrew תַּחַשׁ.' *Biblica* 93 (2012): 580–89.

Noonan, Benjamin. 'A (New) Old Iranian Etymology for Biblical Aramaic אֲדַרְגָּזֵר.' *Aramaic Studies* 16 (2018): 10–19.

Noonan, Benjamin. *Non-Semitic Loanwords in the Hebrew Bible: A Lexicon of Language Contact*. Linguistic Studies in Ancient West Semitic 14. University Park: Eisenbrauns, 2019.

Nyberg, Henrik. *A Manual of Pahlavi*. 2 vols. Wiesbaden: Harrassowitz, 1974.

O'Connell, Robert. *The Rhetoric of the Book of Judges*. VTSup 63. Leiden: Brill, 1996.

Olmo Lete, Gregorio del, and Joaquín Sanmartín. *A Dictionary of the Ugaritic Language in the Alphabetic Tradition*. HO 112. Leiden: Brill, 2015.

Onysko, Alexander. *Anglicisms in German: Borrowing, Lexical Productivity and Written Codeswitching*. Berlin: de Gruyter, 2007.

Onysko, Alexander, and Esme Winter-Froemel. 'Necessary Loans – Luxury Loans? Exploring the Pragmatic Dimension of Borrowing.' *Journal of Pragmatics* 43 (2011): 1550–67.

Oppenheim, A. Leo. 'A Note on *ša rēši*.' *JANESCU* 5 (1973): 325–34.

Orel, Vladimir, and Olga Stolbova. *Hamito-Semitic Etymological Dictionary*. Leiden: Brill, 1995.

Oxford University Press. *Oxford English Dictionary*. http://www.oed.com/.

Payne, Annick. *Hieroglyphic Luwian: An Introduction with Original Texts*. Wiesbaden: Harrassowitz, 2010.

Payne-Smith, Robert. *A Compendious Syriac Dictionary*. Revised by Jessie Payne-Smith. Oxford: Clarendon Press, 1903.

Peacock, Cory. 'Akkadian Loanwords in the Hebrew Bible: Social and Historical Implications.' PhD diss., New York University, 2013.

Pennsylvania Museum of Anthropology and Archaeology. *Electronic Pennsylvania Sumerian Dictionary* [*ePSD*]. http://psd.museum.upenn.edu/.

Phelan, James. *Experiencing Fiction: Judgments, Progressions, and the Rhetorical Theory of Narrative*. Columbus: Ohio State University Press, 2007.

Phelan, James. *Narrative as Rhetoric: Techniques, Audiences, Ethics, Ideology*. Columbus: Ohio State University Press, 1996.

Phelan, James. *Reading People, Reading Plots: Character, Progression, and the Interpretation of Narrative*. Chicago: The University of Chicago Press, 1989.

Plett, Heinrich. 'Figures of Speech.' Pages 309–14 in *Encyclopedia of Rhetoric*. Edited by Thomas Sloane. Oxford: Oxford University Press, 2001.

Plett, Heinrich. *Literary Rhetoric*. Translated by Myra Scolz and Klaus Klein. Leiden: Brill, 2010.
Plöger, Otto. *Das Buch Daniel*. KAT. Gütersloh: Gütersloher Verlagshaus Gerd Mohn, 1965.
Plöger, Otto. *Theocracy and Eschatology*. Translated by S. Rudman. Oxford: Basil Blackwell, 1968.
Polak, Frank. 'Sociolinguistics and the Judean Speech Community.' Pages 589–628 in *Judah and the Judeans in the Persian Period*. Edited by Oded Lipschitz and Manfred Oeming. Winona Lake: Eisenbrauns, 2006.
Poplack, Shana. 'What Does the Nonce Borrowing Hypothesis Hypothesize?' *Bilingualism – Language and Cognition* 15 (2012): 644–48.
Poplack, Shana, and Nathalie Dion. 'Myths and Facts about Loanword Development.' *Language Variation and Change* 24 (2012): 279–315.
Poplack, Shana, David Sankoff, and Christopher Miller. 'The Social Correlates and Linguistic Processes of Lexical Borrowing and Assimilation.' *Linguistics* 26 (1988): 47–104.
Portier-Young, Anathea. *Apocalypse Against Empire: Theologies of Resistance in Early Judaism*. Grand Rapids: Eerdmans, 2011.
Portier-Young, Anathea. 'Languages of Identity and Obligation: Daniel as a Bilingual Book.' *VT* 60 (2010): 98–115.
Postgate, J. Nicholas. 'The Place of the *Šaknu* in Assyrian Government.' *AnSt* 30 (1980): 67–76.
Powell, Mark. *The Bible and Modern Literary Criticism*. New York: Greenwood, 1992.
Powels, Sylvia. 'Indische Lehnwörter in der Bibel.' *ZAH* 5 (1992): 186–200.
Propp, William. *Exodus 19–40*. AB 2. New York: Doubleday, 2006.
Puech, Émile. *Qumran Grotte 4 XXVII: Textes Araméens Deuxieme Partie*. DJD 37. Oxford: Clarendon, 2009.
Quinn, Arthur. *Figures of Speech: 60 Ways to Turn a Phrase*. Davis, CA: Hermagoras, 1993.
Rabin, Chaim. 'מלים זרות [Foreign Words].' Pages 1070–80 in vol. 4 of אנציקלופדיה מקראית [*Encyclopedia Biblica*]. 9 vols. Jerusalem: Mosad Bialik, 1950–88.
Rabin, Chaim. 'Hittite Words in Hebrew.' *Or (NS)* 32 (1963): 113–39.
Rabin, Chaim. 'The Origin of the Hebrew Word *Pīlegeš*.' *JJS* 25 (1974): 353–64.
Real Academia de Español. *Diccionario panhispánico de dudas*. http://www.rae.es/recursos/diccionarios/dpd/.
Rendsburg, Gary. 'Aramaic-like Features in the Pentateuch.' *HS* 47 (2006): 163–76.
Rendsburg, Gary. 'Biblical Hebrew: Dialects and Linguistic Variation.' Pages 338–41 in vol. 1 of *Encyclopedia of Hebrew Language and Linguistics*. 4 vols. Edited by Geoffrey Khan. Leiden: Brill, 2012.
Rendsburg, Gary. 'A Comprehensive Guide to Israelian Hebrew: Grammar and Lexicon. *Orient* 38 (2003): 5–35.
Rendsburg, Gary. 'Cultural Words: Biblical Hebrew.' Pages 640–42 in vol. 1 of *Encyclopedia of Hebrew Language and Linguistics*. 4 vols. Edited by Geoffrey Khan. Leiden: Brill, 2012.
Rendsburg, Gary. 'Hurvitz Redux: On the Continued Scholarly Inattention to a Simple Principle of Hebrew Philology.' Pages 104–28 in *Biblical Hebrew: Studies in Chronology and Typology*. Edited by Ian Young. London: T&T Clark International, 2003.

Rendsburg, Gary. 'Linguistic Variation and the "Foreign" Factor in the Hebrew Bible.' Pages 177–90 in *Language and Culture in the Near East*. Israel Oriental Studies 15. Edited by Shlomo Izre'el and Rina Drory. Leiden: E. J. Brill, 1995.

Rendsburg, Gary. 'Morphological Evidence for Regional Dialects in Ancient Hebrew.' Pages 65–88 in *Linguistics and Biblical Hebrew*. Edited by Walter Bodine. Winona Lake: Eisenbrauns, 1992.

Rendsburg, Gary. 'Style-Switching.' Pages 633–36 in vol. 3 of *Encyclopedia of Hebrew Language and Linguistics*. 4 vols. Edited by Geoffrey Khan. Leiden: Brill, 2012.

Rendsburg, Gary. 'Style-Switching in Biblical Hebrew.' Pages 65–85 in *Epigraphy, Philology and the Hebrew Bible: Methodological Perspectives on Philological & Comparative Study of the Hebrew Bible in Honor of Jo-Ann Hackett*. Edited by Jeremy Hutton and Aaron Rubin. Atlanta: SBL Press, 2015.

Rendsburg, Gary. 'What We Can Learn about Other Northwest Semitic Dialects from Reading the Bible?' Pages 160–78 in *Discourse, Dialogue, and Debate in the Bible: Essays in Honour of Frank H. Polak*. Edited by Athalya Brenner-Iden. Sheffield: Sheffield Phoenix, 2014.

Renz, Thomas. *The Rhetorical Function of the Book of Ezekiel*. VTSup 76. Leiden: Brill, 1999.

Rezetko, Robert. 'The Spelling of "Damascus" and the Linguistic Dating of Biblical Texts.' *SJOT* 24 (2010): 110–28

Rezetko, Robert, and Ian Young. *Historical Linguistics and Biblical Hebrew: Steps Towards an Integrated Approach*. Ancient Near Eastern Monographs 9. Atlanta: SBL Press, 2014.

Rosenthal, Franz. *A Grammar of Biblical Aramaic*. 6th rev. ed. Wiesbaden: Otto Harrassowitz, 1995.

Rosenthal, Ludwig. 'Die Josephsgeschichte, mit den Büchern Ester und Daniel verglichen.' *ZAW* 15 (1895): 278–84.

Roth, Martha et al., eds. *The Assyrian Dictionary of the Oriental Institute of the University of Chicago* [*CAD*]. 21 vols. Chicago: Oriental Institute, 1956–2010.

Rougement, Georges. 'The Use of Greek in Pre-Sasanian Iran.' Pages 795–801 in *The Oxford Handbook of Ancient Iran*. Edited by Daniel Potts. Oxford: Oxford University Press, 2013.

Rouillard-Bonraisin, Hedwige. 'Problemes du bilinguisme en *Daniel*.' Pages 145–70 in *Mosaïque de langues, mosaïque culturelle. Le bilinguisme dans le Proche-Orient ancient*. Edited by Françoise Briquel-Chatonnet. Paris: Jean Maisonneuve, 1996.

Rubin, Aaron. 'Egyptian Loanwords.' Pages 793–94 in vol. 4 of *Encyclopedia of Hebrew Language and Linguistics*. 4 vols. Edited by Geoffrey Khan. Leiden: Brill, 2012.

Rubin, Aaron. *The Mehri Language of Oman*. Leiden: Brill, 2010.

Rubin, Aaron. 'Sumerian Loanwords.' Pages 665–66 in vol. 3 of *Encyclopedia of Hebrew Language and Linguistics*. 4 vols. Edited by Geoffrey Khan. Leiden: Brill, 2012.

Rubio, Gonzalo. 'Sumerian Temples and Arabian Horses: On Sumerian e2-gal.' Pages 284–99 in *The First Ninety Years: A Sumerian Celebration in Honor of Miguel Civil*. Edited by Lluís Feliu et al. Berlin: de Gruyter, 2017.

Rundgren, Frithiof. 'Aramaica III: An Iranian Loanword in Daniel.' *Orientalia Suecana* 25–26 (1976–77): 45–55.

Rundgren, Frithiof. 'Ein iranischer Beamtenname im Aramäischen.' *Orientalia Suecana* 12 (1963): 89–98.

Rundgren, Frithiof. 'Zur Bedeutung von ŠRŠW – Esra VII 26.' *VT* 7 (1957): 400–4.

Saley, Richard. 'The Date of Nehemiah Reconsidered.' Pages 151–65 in *Biblical and Near Eastern Essays*. Edited by Gary Tuttle. Grand Rapids: Eerdmans, 1978.
Salvesen, Alison. 'כִּסֵּא.' Pages 44–65 in *Semantics of Ancient Hebrew*. Edited by Takamitsu Muraoka. Louvain: Peeters, 1998.
Salvesen, Alison. 'כֶּתֶר.' Pages 67–73 in *Semantics of Ancient Hebrew*. Edited by Takamitsu Muraoka. Louvain: Peeters, 1998.
Salvesen, Alison. 'כֶּתֶר (Esther 1:11; 2:17; 6:8): "Something to Do with a Camel"?' *JSS* 44 (1999): 35–46.
Sánchez Fajardo, José Antonio. 'Anglicisms and Calques in Upper Social Class in Pre-revolutionary Cuba (1930–59): A Sociolinguistic Analysis.' *International Journal of English Studies* 16 (2016): 33–56.
Sarna, Nahum. *Exodus*. JPS Torah Commentary. Philadelphia: Jewish Publication Society, 1991.
Sayce, Archibald. 'Hittite and Mitannian Elements in the Old Testament.' *JTS* 29 (1928): 401–6.
Scheftelowitz, Isidor. *Arisches im Alten Testament: Eine sprachwissenschaftliche und kulturhistorische Untersuchung*. Berlin: S. Calvary & Co., 1901.
Scheftelowitz, Isidor. 'Zur Kritik des griechischen und des massoretischen Buches Esther.' *MGWJ* 47 (1903): 24–37.
Scheftelowitz, Isidor. 'Zur Kritik des griechischen und des massoretischen Buches Esther. (Schluss).' *MGWJ* 47 (1903): 110–20.
Scheftelowitz, Isidor. 'Zur Kritik des griechischen und des massoretischen Buches Esther. (Fortsetzung).' *MGWJ* 47 (1903): 201–13.
Scheftelowitz, Isidor. 'Zur Kritik des griechischen und des massoretischen Buches Esther. (Schluss).' *MGWJ* 47 (1903): 289–313.
Schmid, Wolf. *Elemente der Narratologie*. 3rd ed. Berlin: de Gruyter, 2014.
Schmitt, Rüdiger. 'Apadāna i. Term.' Pages 145–46 in vol. 2 of *Encyclopaedia Iranica*. Edited by Eshan Yarshater. New York: Bibliotheca Persica, 1987.
Schniedewind, William. *A Social History of Hebrew: Its Origins through the Rabbinic Period*. New Haven: Yale University Press, 2013.
Schuh, Russell. *A Grammar of Miya*. Berkeley: University of California Press, 1998.
Schun, Doi. 'The Naturalisation Process of the Japanese Loanwords Found in the Oxford English Dictionary.' *English Studies* 95 (2014): 674–99.
Schwartz, Seth. 'Language, Power and Identity in Ancient Palestine.' *Past & Present* 148 (1995): 12–31.
Seargent, Philip, Caroline Tagg and Wipapan Ngampramuan. 'Language Choice and Addresivity Strategies in Thai–English Social Network Interactions.' *Sociolinguistics* 16 (2012): 510–31.
Sebba Mark, and S. Fligelstone. 'Corpus Linguistics and Sociolinguistics.' Page 767 in *Concise Encyclopedia of Sociolinguistics*. Edited by Rajend Mesthrie. Oxford: Elsevier, 2001.
Segal, Michael. *Dreams, Riddles, and Visions: Textual, Contextual, and Intertextual Approaches to the Book of Daniel*. Berlin: de Gruyter, 2016.
Semino, Elena, and Gerard Steen. 'Metaphor in Literature.' Pages 232–46 in *The Cambridge Handbook of Metaphor and Thought*. Edited by Raymond Gibbs. Cambridge: Cambridge University Press, 2008.
Seow, Choon-Leong. *Daniel*. Westminster Bible Companion. Louisville: Westminster John Knox Press, 2003.
Sérandour, Arnaud. 'Hébreu et Araméen dans la Bible.' *REJ* 159 (2000): 345–55.

Shaffer, Aaron. 'Hurrian *kirezzi*, West-Semitic krz.' *Or (NS)* 34 (1965): 32–34.
Shaw, Ian, and Judith Bunbury. 'A Petrological Study of the Emerald mines in the Egyptian Eastern Desert.' Pages 203–13 in *Lithics at the Millennium*. Edited by Norah Moloney and Michael Shott. London: Archaeopress, 2003.
Shitrit, Talya. 'Aramaic Loanwords and Borrowing.' Pages 165–69 in vol. 1 of *Encyclopedia of Hebrew Language and Linguistics*. 4 vols. Edited by Geoffrey Khan. Leiden: Brill, 2012.
Siddall, Luis. 'A Re-examination of the Title "ša rēši" in the Neo-Assyrian Period.' Pages 225–40 in *Gilgameš and the World of Assyria: Proceedings of the Conference Held at Mandelbaum House, the University of Sydney, 21–23 July, 2004*. Edited by Joseph Azize and Noel Weeks. Leuven: Peeters, 2007.
Silberman, Neil, and David Small, eds. *The Archaeology of Israel: Constructing the Past, Interpreting the Present*. JSOTSup 137. Sheffield: Sheffield Academic Press, 1997.
Singer, Itamar. 'The Hittites and the Bible Revisited.' Pages 723–56 in vol. 2 of *'I Will Speak the Riddles of Ancient Times': Archaeological and Historical Studies in Honor of Amihai Mazar on the Occasion of His Sixtieth Birthday*. Edited by Aren Maeir and Pierre de Miroschedji. 2 vols. Winona Lake: Eisenbrauns, 2006.
Smith, Mark. 'Like Deities, Like Temples (Like People).' Pages 3–27 in *Temple and Worship in Biblical Israel*. Edited by John Day. London: T&T Clark, 2005.
Smith, Mark, and Elizabeth Bloch-Smith. *The Pilgrimage Pattern in Exodus*. JSOTSup 239. Sheffield: Sheffield Academic Press, 1997.
Smith-Christopher, Daniel. 'Between Ezra and Isaiah: Exclusion, Transformation, and Inclusion of the "Foreigner" in Post-Exilic Biblical Theology.' Pages 117–42 in *Ethnicity and the Bible*. Edited by Mark Brett. Leiden: E. J. Brill, 1996.
Smith-Christopher, Daniel. 'Gandhi on Daniel 6: A Case of Cultural Exegesis.' *BibInt* 1 (1993): 321–28.
Snell, Daniel. 'Why is There Aramaic in the Bible?' *JSOT* 18 (1980): 32–51.
Soden, Wolfram von. *Akkadisches Handwörterbuch*. 3 vols. Wiesbaden: Harrassowitz, 1972–85.
Soden, Wolfram von. 'Dolmetscher und Dolmetschen im Alten Orient.' Pages 351–57 in *Aus Sprache, Geschichte und Religion Babyloniens*. Edited by Luigi Cagni and Hans-Peter Müller. Naples: Istituto Universitario Orientale, 1989.
Sokoloff, Michael. *Dictionary of Christian Palestinian Aramaic*. Leuven: Peeters, 2014.
Sokoloff, Michael. *Dictionary of Jewish Babylonian Aramaic of the Talmudic and Geonic Periods*. Publications of the Comprehensive Aramaic Lexicon 3. Ramat Gan: Bar Ilan University, 2002.
Sokoloff, Michael. *Dictionary of Jewish Palestinian Aramaic*. 2nd ed. Publications of the Comprehensive Aramaic Lexicon 2. Ramat Gan: Bar Ilan University, 2002.
Sokoloff, Michael. *A Syriac Lexicon: A Translation from the Latin: Correction, Expansion, and Update of C. Brockelmann's Lexicon Syriacum*. Winona Lake: Eisenbrauns, 2009.
Soldt, Wilfred van. 'Akkadian as a Diplomatic Language.' Pages 405–15 in *Semitic Languages: An International Handbook*. Edited by Stefan Weninger et al. Berlin: de Gruyter, 2011.
Sons, Antje. 'Aneignung des Fremden: Entlehnung aus dem Chinesischen.' *Zeitschrift für Germanistische Linguistik* 26 (1998): 155–76.
Southwood, Katherine. *Ethnicity and the Mixed Marriage Crisis in Ezra 9–10: An Anthropological Approach*. Oxford Theological Monographs. Oxford: Oxford University, 2012.

Sparks, Kenton. *Ethnicity and Identity in Ancient Israel: Prolegomena to the Study of Ethnic Sentiments and Their Expression in the Hebrew Bible*. Winona Lake: Eisenbrauns, 1998.

Stammers, Jonathan, and Margaret Deuchar. 'Testing the Nonce Borrowing Hypothesis: Counter-evidence from English-origin Verbs in Welsh.' *Bilingualism – Language and Cognition* 15 (2012): 630–43.

Starke, Frank. 'Zur Herkunft von akkad. *ta/urgumannu(m)* "Dolmetscher."' *WO* 24 (1993): 20–38.

Steiner, Richard. 'Ancient Hebrew.' Pages 145–73 in *The Semitic Languages*. Edited by Robert Hetzron. London: Routledge, 1997.

Steiner, Richard. 'Bishlam's Archival Search Report in Nehemiah's Archive: Multiple Introductions and Reverse Chronological Order as Clues to the Origin of the Aramaic Letters in Ezra 4–6.' *JBL* 125 (2006): 641–85.

Steinmann, Andrew. 'Letters of Kings about Votive Offerings, the God of Israel and the Aramaic Document in Ezra 4:8–6:18.' *JHS* 8 (2008): 1–14.

Sternberg, Meir. *The Poetics of Biblical Narrative: Ideological Literature and the Drama of Reading*. Indiana Studies in Biblical Literature. Bloomington: Indiana University Press, 1985.

Stevens, Carolyn. 'Translations: "Internationalizing" Language and Music.' Pages 132–55 in *Japanese Popular Music: Culture, Authenticity, Power*. London: Routledge, 2008.

Streck, Michael. 'Babylonian and Assyrian.' Pages 359–95 in *The Semitic Languages: An International Handbook*. Edited by Stefan Weninger et al. Handbücher zur Sprach- und Kommunikations-wissenschaft 36. Berlin: de Gruyter, 2011.

Tadmor, Chaim. '"אַפְּתֹם" in Ezra 4:13.' Pages 143*–45* in *Michael: Historical, Epigraphical and Biblical Studies in Honor of Prof. Michael Heltzer*. Edited by Yitzhak Avishur and Robert Deutsch. Tel Aviv: Archeological Center Publications, 1999.

Tagliamonte, Sali. *Analysing Sociolinguistic Variation*. Key Topics in Sociolinguistics. Cambridge: Cambridge University Press, 2006.

Talmon, Shemaryahu. '"Wisdom" in the Book of Esther.' *VT* 13 (1963): 419–55.

Tavernier, Jan. *Iranica in the Achaemenid Period*. Leuven, Belgium: Peeters, 2007.

Thompson, Dorothy. 'The Multilingual Environment of Persian and Ptolemaic Egypt: Egyptian, Aramaic, and Greek Documentation.' Pages 395–417 in *The Oxford Handbook of Papyrology*. Edited by Roger Bagnall. Oxford: Oxford University, 2011.

Throntveit, Mark. *Ezra–Nehemiah*. IBC. Louisville: John Knox Press, 1992.

Timmer, Daniel. 'Creation, Tabernacle and Sabbath: The Function of the Sabbath Frame in Exodus 31:12–17; 35:1–3.' PhD diss., Trinity Evangelical Divinity School, 2006.

Tisdall, W. St Clair. 'The Āryan Words in the Old Testament: I.' *JQR* 1 (1911): 335–39.

Tisdall, W. St Clair. 'The Āryan Words in the Old Testament: II.' *JQR* 2 (1911): 213–19.

Tisdall, W. St Clair. 'The Āryan Words in the Old Testament: III.' *JQR* 2 (1912): 365–71.

Tisdall, W. St Clair. 'The Book of Daniel: Some Evidence Regarding its Date.' *Journal of the Transactions of the Victoria Institute* 53 (1921): 206–55.

Topoi Excellence Cluster (Freie Universität Berlin and Humboldt-Universität zu Berlin). *Thesaurus Linguae Aegyptiae*. http://aaew.bbaw.de/tla/.

Trismegistos Online Publications. *Trismegistos*. http://www.trismegistos.org/.

Troyer, Kristin de. *The End of the Alpha Text: Translation and Narrative Technique in MT 8:1–17, LXX 8:1–17, and AT 7:14–41*. Septuagint and Cognate Studies 48. Atlanta: SBL, 2000.

Valeta, David. 'Court or Jester Tales? Resistance and Social Reality in Daniel 1–6.' *Perspectives in Religious Studies* 32 (2005): 309–24. [945]

Valeta, David. *Lions and Ovens and Visions: A Satirical Reading of Daniel 1–6*. Hebrew Bible Monographs 12. Sheffield: Sheffield Phoenix Press, 2008.

Valeta, David. 'Lions and Ovens and Visions, Oh My! A Satirical Analysis of Daniel 1–6.' PhD diss., The University of Denver, 2004.

Valeta, David. 'Polyglossia and Parody. Language in Daniel 1–6.' Pages 91–108 in *Bakhtin and Genre Theory in Biblical Studies*. Edited by Roland Boer. Atlanta: SBL, 2007.

Varra, Rachel. 'The Social Correlates of Lexical Borrowing in Spanish in New York City.' PhD diss., City University of New York, 2013.

Vernes, Maurice. *Les Emprunts de la Bible Hébraïque au Grec et au Latin*. Bibliothèque de l'École des Hautes Études: Sciences Religieuses 29. Paris: Ernest Leroux, 1914.

Verreth, Herbert. *A Survey of Toponyms in Egypt in the Graeco-Roman Period*. Trismegistos Online Publications 2. Leuven: Trismegistos Online Publications.

Vita Barra, Juan Pablo. 'Akkadian as a *Lingua Franca*.' Pages 357–72 in *A Companion to Ancient Near Eastern Languages*. Edited by Rebecca Hasselbach-Andee. Hoboken: John Wiley, 2020.

Vogt, Ernst. *A Lexicon of Biblical Aramaic: Clarified by Ancient Documents*. Translated by J. Fitzmyer. SubBi 42. Rome: Gregorian & Biblical Press, 2011.

Wade, Martha. *Consistency of Translation Techniques in the Tabernacle Accounts of Exodus in the Old Greek*. Leiden: Brill, 2003.

Wagner, Guy. *Elephantine XIII: Les papyrus et les ostraca grecs d'Elephantine*. Deutsches Archäologisches Institut Kairo 70. Mainz: Philipp von Zaber, 1998.

Wagner, Max. *Die Lexikalischen und Grammatikalischen Aramaismen im Alttestamentlichen Hebräisch*. Berlin: Alfred Töpelmann, 1966.

Walkins, Calvert. 'Proto-Indo-European: Comparison and Reconstruction.' Pages 25–73 in *The Indo-European Languages*. Edited by Anna Giacalone Ramat and Paolo Ramat. London: Routledge, 1998.

Webb, Barry. *Five Festal Garments*. Horizons in Biblical Theology. Downers Grove: Intervarsity Press, 2000.

Webb, Barry. 'Heaven on Earth: The Significance of the Tabernacle in its Literary and Theological Context.' Pages 154–76 in *Exploring Exodus*. Edited by Brian Rosner and Paul Williamson. Nottingham: Apollos, 2008.

Weinfeld, Moshe. 'Deuteronomic Phraseology.' Pages 326–30 in *Deuteronomy and the Deuteronomic School*. Oxford: Clarendon, 1972.

West, Martin. Review of *Israel and Hellas*, by John Brown, vol. 1. *Classical Review* 47 (1997): 111–12.

Wetter, Anne-Mareike. 'How Jewish is Esther? Or: How is Esther Jewish? Tracing Ethnic and Religious Identity in a Diaspora Narrative.' *ZAW* 123 (2011): 596–603.

Wetter, Anne-Mareike. 'In Unexpected Places: Ritual and Religious Belonging in the Book of Esther.' *JSOT* 36 (2012): 321–32.

Wetter, Anne-Mareike. 'Ruth: A Born-Again Israelite?' Pages 144–62 in *Imagining the Other and Constructing Israelite Identity in the Early Second Temple Period*. Edited by Ehud Ben Zvi and Diana Edelman. London: Bloomsbury, 2014.

Wijk-Bos, Johanna van. *Ezra, Nehemiah, and Esther*. Westminster Bible Companion. Louisville: Westminster John Knox Press, 1998.

Williamson, H. G. M. 'The Aramaic Documents in Ezra Revisited.' *JTS (NS)* 59 (2008): 41–62.

Williamson, H. G. M. 'Eschatology in Chronicles.' *Tyndale Bulletin* 28 (1977): 123–26.

Williamson, H. G. M. *Ezra, Nehemiah*. WBC 16. Waco: Word Books, 1985.
Willis, Amy. *Dissonance and the Drama of Divine Sovereignty in the Book of Daniel*. LHBOTS 520. New York: T&T Clark, 2010.
Wills, Lawrence. *The Jew in the Court of the Foreign King*. HDR 26. Minneapolis: Fortress Press, 1990.
Wilson, Robert. 'Foreign Words in the Old Testament as an Evidence of Historicity.' *The Princeton Theological Review* 26 (1928): 177–247.
Wilson-Wright, Aren. 'From Persepolis to Jerusalem: A Reevaluation of Old Persian–Hebrew Contact in the Achaemenid Period.' *VT* 65 (2015): 152–67.
Wimsatt, William, and Monroe Beardsley. 'The Intentional Fallacy.' Pages 3–18 in *The Verbal Icon: Studies in the Meaning of Poetry*. Edited by William Wimsatt. Lexington: University of Kentucky Press, 1954.
Yahuda, A. 'Hebrew Words of Egyptian Origin.' *JBL* 66 (1947): 83–90.
Yahuda, A. *The Language of the Pentateuch in its Relation to Egyptian*. London: Humphrey Milford, 1933.
Yamauchi, Edwin. 'The Reverse Order of Ezra/Nehemiah Reconsidered.' *Themelios* 5 (1980): 7–13.
Yarshater, Ehsan, ed. *Encyclopedia Iranica*. London: Routledge and Kegan Paul, 1982–.
Young, Ian. 'The Diphthong *ay in Edomite.' *JSS* 37 (1992): 27–30.
Young, Ian. 'Evidence of Diversity in Pre-Exilic Judahite Hebrew.' *HS* 38 (1997): 7–20.
Young, Ian. 'The Greek Loanwords in the Book of Daniel.' Pages 247–68 in *Biblical Greek in Context: Essays in Honour of John A. L. Lee*. Edited by James Aitken and Trevor Evans. Leuven: Peeters, 2015.
Young, Ian. 'The Languages of Ancient Sam'al.' *Maarav* 9 (2002): 93–103.
Young, Ian. 'Late Biblical Hebrew and the Qumran Pesher Habakkuk.' *JHS* 8 (2008): 1–38.
Young, Ian. 'The "Northernisms" of the Israelite Narratives in Kings.' *ZAH* 8 (1995): 65–66.
Young, Ian, Robert Rezetko and Martin Ehrensvärd. *Linguistic Dating of Biblical Texts*. London: Equinox, 2008.
Zadok, Ran. 'Two Terms in Ezra.' *Aramaic Studies* 5 (2007): 260–61.
Zimmern, Heinrich. *Akkadische Fremdwörter als Beweis für Babylonischen Kultureinfluß*. Leipzig: J. C. Hinrichs'sche Buchhandlung, 1917.

# Index of Subjects

Achaemenid
  Kings 29, 156
  Period 135, 151, 188, 189
Akkadian 134
  Loanwords, see Loanwords, Akkadian
Antiochene Crisis 153, 154, 176, 178
Aramaic 134, 135
  in Biblical Texts 192–204
  Loanwords, see Loanwords, Aramaic
Aramaisms, see Loanwords, Aramaic
Assimilation 55, 63, 68, 72, 73, 75, 104, 106, 110, 123, 255, 256
Audience 12, 13, 144, 145, 150–55, 176, 178, 179–89, 193–95, 200–208, 210, 212, 220–22, 225, 226, 228–30
Authorial Intent 13, 19, 139, 143–45, 175, 176

Calendar 27
Calque 11, 87, 103, 189
Canaanite Shift 26, 34, 41, 118, 129, 189, 250, 252
Code-switching 5, 10, 11, 21, 144, 195–204
Comedy, see Satire
Contact Linguistics 1, 10, 11, 196–200
Corpus Linguistics 4, 16–18, 22, 157
  Distribution 4, 12, 18, 19, 34, 85, 86, 137, 142, 144, 145, 155, 157–68, 173, 189–92, 208, 212–18, 222, 234–49
  Relative Concentration 18, 19, 137, 142, 144, 145, 155, 157–68, 174, 175, 182, 189–92, 208, 212–18, 222, 234–49
Court Tales 167–75, 177–79, 181, 185
  Literary Technique
    Lists 170–73
    Loanwords 173–75
    Plot 169
    see also Resistance Literature
    see also Satire
Covenant 2, 202, 207–12, 219, 225–28
Culture Word 24, 42, 43, 44

Deviation
  see Transformation
  see also Rhetoric, Figure of
Dialect 5, 6, 17, 25, 43, 47, 49, 63, 69, 76, 79, 89, 94, 100, 102, 114, 122, 125, 126, 136, 144, 145, 146, 158, 195, 196, 200, 254–56
Dissimilation 43, 44, 54, 60, 72, 73, 76, 92, 106, 111, 124, 251, 255

Egyptian 134
  Group Writing 21, 109, 112, 164
  Loanwords, see Loanwords, Egyptian
Emendation 36–38, 84, 165, 166
Epenthesis 56
Ethnicity 1, 2, 10, 19, 143, 146–50, 152, 162, 169, 177, 178, 180–82, 185–86, 189, 193, 197, 205, 206, 228, 229, 230
  Constructivism 147
  Hybridity 147
  as Rhetoric 148
  Primordialism 148
Ethno-linguistic identity, see ethnicity
Etymology, Folk 14, 22, 50, 112, 126, 144, 145
Exodus Motifs 2, 226–28

*Fremdwort* 20, 21, 199

Genre 17, 167, 168–73, 177, 178, 182, 185,
  see also Court Tales
Greek 134, 135
  Loanwords, see Loanwords, Greek

## Index of Subjects

Pre-Greek Substrate 9, 32
*Hapax Legomenon* 37, 48, 54, 60, 65, 69, 75, 93, 95, 96, 106, 118, 199, 205, 206
ḥăsîdîm 153–55
Hellenistic Period 90, 135, 151, 152, 187–89
Hittite
    Loanwords, see Loanwords, Anatolian
    Imagery 133, 165, 211, 227, 228
    see also, Exodus Motifs

Implicature 15, 18, 136–39, 142, 157
Intertextuality 152, 223, 226–28
Iranian Languages
Loanwords, see Loanwords, Iranian

*Kulturwort*, see Culture Word

Lingua Franca 134, 194
Literary approach 1, 10–19, 136–42, 143–50, 229–30
    Text-centred 12, 13, 150
    see also Narrative Technique
    see also Rhetorical
Loanwords
    Avoidance of 7, 200, 201, 225, 226, 229
    Akkadian and Sumerian 2, 6, 7, 26, 27, 30–34, 43, 44, 49–51, 54–56, 59–61, 64–66, 70, 71, 73, 74, 79, 81, 86, 87, 101–104, 107, 108, 118, 119, 123–26, 129
    Anatolian 9, 10, 31–33, 82
    Aramaic 2, 3–6, 26, 72, 73, 119, 231–33
    Direction of borrowing 23, 24
    Egyptian 7, 8, 40–42, 54, 55, 68, 84, 85, 109–18, 120, 121, 124, 127, 130–33
    Greek 7–10, 72–79, 99, 100
    Hurrian 121, 122, 123
    Identification of (in modern scholarship) 23, 24, 231–33, 250–56
    Indo-European 46, 47, 51, 52, 85, 87, 88
    Iranian 2, 7, 8, 28–30, 35–40, 44–46, 48, 52–54, 57–60, 62, 63, 65–67, 69, 70, 75, 76, 79, 80, 81, 83– 86, 88, 89, 91–98, 104–108

Nativization of 20–23, 41, 44, 46, 47, 56, 77, 84, 85, 88, 100, 105, 107, 119, 120, 128, 130, 141, 142, 158, 163, 199, 213, 220, 224
    Phoenician 89–91
    Recognizability of (for ancient audiences) 144, 145, 220–22
    Sumerian, see Loanwords, Akkadian and Sumerian
Luwian
    Loanwords, see Loanwords, Anatolian

*maśkîlîm* 153–55
Metathesis 37, 92, 213, 214, 251
Monopthongization 34

Narrative Technique 14, 15, 144, 176, 182, 195, 203
    Characterization 144, 148, 150, 162, 176, 178–86, 189, 193, 206, 230
    External Narrator 176, 194, 195, 203
    First Person Narrative 203
    Focalization 169, 176, 178, 194, 195, 204
    Frame Narrative 170, 203, 210
    Narrator 2, 176, 186, 194, 195, 201, 203, 204, 205, 206, 211, 230
    Perspective, see Focalization
    Relationship to Reader 2, 186, 204–206, 230
    Spaces 210
    Setting 2, 5, 138, 144, 150, 151, 155–58, 161, 162, 167, 173, 174, 176, 177, 179, 182, 185, 189, 229, 230
    Suspense 183–85
    Tension 177–79
Narrowing, see Semantic shift
Nativization, see Loanwords, Nativization of
Noun Patterns, see Vowel Patterns

Persian (language) 135
    Loanwords, see Loanwords, Iranian
    Median 47, 48, 57, 58, 67, 86
Phonetics
    Equivalences 25, 48, 49, 55, 68, 84, 85, 90, 92, 132, 158, 213, 214, 231–33
Pragmatics 1, 11, 19, 142, 145, 157, 195, 198, 211, 222–25

Prestige Language 10, 11, 134, 135, 175, 221
Proper Nouns (Foreign) 159, 160, 161, 162, 165, 166, 167, 171, 172, 190–93, 204, 235–38, 241–43, 245–46
Prothesis 58, 92, 97, 109, 110

*rabbîm* 154, 155
Reader, see Audience
Resistance Literature 152, 154, 176, 177, 178, 186
Rhetorical
   Effect 1, 2, 12, 13, 15, 19, 20, 35, 50, 137–39, 142, 143–46, 157, 161, 162, 163, 166, 173, 176, 177, 182, 185, 193, 194, 204, 206, 208, 213, 218–26, 229
   Ethnicity 148, 149
   Figure 10, 15–19, 142, 149, 211, 222
      Catachresis 138, 139, 141, 142
      Code-Switching 144, 195–204
      Hyperbole 29, 175, 176, 183
      Lists 170–73
      Loanwords as 19, 143–50, 229–30
      Repetition 172, 179, 204, 208, 211, 212, 218, 222, 223
      Topic, Focus 211, 212, 222–25
   Final Form 145, 152–54, 179, 188, 202, 207
   Persuasion 13, 15
   Theory 1, 10, 12–19, 181
   see also, Audience
   see also, Transformation

Satire 175–78
Segholation 214
Semantic shift 22, 24, 32
   Broadening 29, 33, 140
   Narrowing 22, 24, 33, 46, 116, 157
Style-switching 5, 144, 199, 200
Sociolinguistics 1, 11, 12, 19
Sumerian 6
   Loanwords, see Loanwords, Sumerian
Synonymy 136–42

Tabernacle 2, 133, 206–13, 218, 219, 222, 225–29
   Analogy with the exodus 226–28
   Analogy with Sinai 210, 211
Transformation 11, 15–19, 136, 141, 142, 145, 162, 178, 180, 193, 198, 222, 223, 225, 229

Variationist linguistics 5, 11, 12, 18, 19
Vowel Patterns 41, 73, 85, 91, 158, 215, 252, 253

Word Order 195, 211, 212, 222, 223

# Index of Biblical Passages

**Hebrew Bible/Old Testament**

*Genesis*

| Ref | Pages | Ref | Pages | Ref | Pages |
|---|---|---|---|---|---|
| 3:21 | 101, 124 | 8:14 | 68 | 25:10–16 | 216, 222, 223 |
| 11:9 | 22 | 8:15 | 68 | 25:10 | 130, 223 |
| 15:17 | 71 | 9:11 | 68 | 25:12 | 119, 223 |
| 18:27 | 30, 60 | 12:35–36 | 226 | 25:13 | 111, 130, 223 |
| 22:24 | 51 | 13:21–22 | 211 | 25:14 | 111, 119, 223 |
| 25:6 | 51 | 14:19–24 | 211 | 25:15 | 111, 119, 223 |
| 30:24 | 145 | 16:10 | 211 | 25:17–22 | 216, 229 |
| 31:47 | 198 | 19 | 226 | 25:23–30 | 216 |
| 35:22 | 51 | 19:1–6 | 226 | 25:26 | 119 |
| 36:12 | 51 | 19:3–6 | 209 | 25:27 | 111, 119 |
| 37:3 | 101, 124 | 19:5–6 | 210 | 25:28 | 111, 130 |
| 37:23 | 101, 124 | 19:5 | 209 | 25:31–40 | 216 |
| 37:31 | 101, 124 | 19:9 | 211 | 25:31 | 115 |
| 37:32 | 101, 124 | 19:16–18 | 211 | 25:33 | 115 |
| 37:33 | 101, 124 | 19:20–25 | 211 | 25:34 | 115 |
| 37:36 | 48, 81 | 20:18–20 | 211 | 26:1–6 | 216 |
| 38:18 | 40, 67, 119 | 20:18 | 71 | 26:1 | 31, 60, 111, 131, 133 |
| 39:1 | 48, 81 | 24:1 | 210 | | |
| 40:2 | 48, 81 | 24:10 | 126, 210 | 26:4 | 133 |
| 40:7 | 48, 81, 175 | 24:12–18 | 211 | 26:7–14 | 216 |
| | | 24:14–17 | 211 | 26:14 | 131, 218 |
| 41:8 | 68, 175 | 25–40 | 2, 10, 41, 54, 55, 109–33, 208–27, 230 | 26:15–30 | 216 |
| 41:42 | 41, 54, 119, 131 | | | 26:15 | 130 |
| | | | | 26:24 | 119 |
| 44:2 | 115 | | 208, 212, 218 | 26:26 | 130 |
| 44:12 | 115 | 25–31 | 224 | 26:29 | 119 |
| 44:16 | 115 | 25–28 | 216, 226 | 26:31–35 | 1216 |
| 44:17 | 115 | 25:1–9 | 219, 223 | 26:31 | 31, 60, 111, 131, 133, 215, 218 |
| | | 25:3–7 | 31, 60, 111, 131, 133 | | |
| *Exodus* | 142, 207 | 25:4 | | | |
| 3:2 | 211 | 25:5 | 130, 131 | | |
| 7:11 | 68 | 25:6 | 124 | 26:32 | 130 |
| 7:22 | 68 | 25:7 | 110 | 26:26–37 | 216 |
| 8:3 | 68 | 25:8 | 209 | | |

| Exodus (cont.) | | 28:20 | 89, 121, 133 | 30:4 | 111, 119, 224 |
|---|---|---|---|---|---|
| 26:36 | 31, 60, 111, 131, 133 | 28:20 (LXX) | 89 | 30:5 | 111, 130 |
| | | 28:20 (Pesh) | 89 | 30:7 | 124 |
| 26:37 | 130 | 28:20 (Vul) | 89 | 30:10 | 128 |
| 27:1–8 | 216 | 28:21 | 40, 67, 119 | 30:11–16 | 217 |
| 27:1 | 130 | | | 30:17–21 | 217 |
| 27:2 | 128 | 28:23 | 119 | 30:18 | 123 |
| 27:3 | 120, 121 | 28:24 | 119 | 30:22–38 | 217 |
| 27:4 | 119 | 28:25 | 110 | 30:24 | 117 |
| 27:6 | 111, 130 | 28:26 | 110, 119 | 30:28 | 123 |
| 27:7 | 111, 119 | 28:27 | 110, 119 | 30:34 | 118, 124 |
| 27:9–19 | 216 | 28:28 | 110, 119, 133 | 31 | 218 |
| 27:9 | 131 | | | 31:1–11 | 217 |
| 27:16 | 31, 60, 111, 131, 133 | 28:29–30 | 217 | 31:9 | 123 |
| | | 28:31–35 | 217 | 31:11 | 124 |
| | | 28:31 | 110, 133 | 31:12–18 | 217 |
| 27:18 | 131 | 28:32 | 131, 224 | 32–34 | 210, 212 |
| 27:20–21 | 216, 218 | 28:33 | 31, 60, 111, 128, 133 | 32 | 119 |
| 28 | 209, 224 | | | 32:16 | 119 |
| 28:1–5 | 217 | | | 33:9 | 211 |
| 28:4 | 101, 109, 110, 124 | 28:36–38 | 217 | 34:19 | 129 |
| | | 28:37 | 133 | 35–40 | 208 |
| 28:5 | 31, 60, 111, 131, 133 | 28:39–43 | 217 | 35–39 | 212, 218 |
| | | 28:39 | 131 | 35 | 218 |
| | | 28:44 | 128 | 35:1–3 | 217 |
| 28:6–14 | 217 | 28:36 | 40, 67, 119 | 35:4–9 | 216, 226 |
| 28:6 | 31, 60, 110, 111, 131, 133 | | | 35:6 | 31, 60, 111, 131, 133 |
| | | 28:39 | 101, 109, 124, 224 | | |
| 28:8 | 31, 60, 110, 111, 131, 133, 224 | 28:40 | 101, 109, 124 | 35:7 | 130, 131 |
| | | | | 35:8 | 124 |
| | | 29 | 217, 224 | 35:9 | 110 |
| | | 29:5–9 | 217 | 35:15 | 124 |
| 28:11 | 40, 67, 119, 224 | 29:5 | 101, 110, 124 | 35:16 | 123 |
| | | | | 35:20–29 | 216, 226 |
| 28:12 | 110 | 29:8 | 101, 124 | 35:22 | 119 |
| 28:15–28 | 217 | 29:9 | 109 | 35:23 | 31, 60, 111, 131, 133 |
| 28:15 | 31, 60, 110, 111, 131, 133, 224 | 29:12 | 128 | | |
| | | 29:40 | 117, 120 | | |
| | | 29:43–46 | 209 | 35:24 | 130 |
| | | 30 | 218, 224, 225 | 35:25 | 31, 60, 111, 131, 133 |
| 28:16 | 117 | | | | |
| 28:17 | 112, 128 | 30:1–10 | 217, 224 | | |
| 28:18 | 124, 126 | 30:1 | 130, 224 | 35:27 | 110 |
| 28:19 | 109, 129 | 30:2 | 128 | 35:30–36:1 | 217 |
| | | 30:3 | 128 | 35:28 | 124 |

| | | | | | | | |
|---|---|---|---|---|---|---|---|
| 35:35 | 31, 60, 111, 131, 133 | 38:3 | 120 | 39:17 | 119 |
| | | 38:5 | 111, 119 | 39:18 | 110 |
| | | 38:6 | 111, 130 | 39:19 | 110, 119 |
| 35:37 | 131 | 38:7 | 111, 119 | 39:20 | 110, 119 |
| 36:8–39:21 | 218 | 38:8 | 123, 217 | 39:21 | 110, 119, 133 |
| 36:8–13 | 216 | 28:9–20 | 216 | | |
| 36:8 | 31, 60, 111, 133 | 38:9 | 131 | 39:22–26 | 217 |
| | | 38:16 | 131 | 39:22 | 110, 133 |
| 36:11 | 133 | 38:18 | 31, 60, 111, 131, 133 | 39:23 | 131 |
| 36:14–19 | 216 | | | 39:24 | 31, 60, 111, 128, 133 |
| 36:19 | 131 | | | | |
| 36:20–34 | 216 | 38:21–31 | | | |
| 36:20 | 130 | 38:23 | 31, 60, 111, 131, 133 | 39:25 | 128 |
| 36:29 | 119 | | | 39:26 | 128 |
| 36:31 | 130 | | | 39:27–29 | 217 |
| 36:34 | 119, 131 | 39:1 | 31, 60, 111, 133, 217 | 39:27 | 101, 124, 131 |
| 36:35–36 | 216 | | | | |
| 36:35 | 31, 60, 111, 133 | 39:2–7 | 217 | 39:28 | 127, 131 |
| | | 39:2 | 31, 60, 110, 111, 131, 133 | 39:29 | 31, 60, 109, 111, 131, 133 |
| 36:36 | 130 | | | | |
| 36:37–38 | 216 | | | | |
| 36:37 | 31, 60, 111, 133 | 39:3 | 31, 60, 111, 127, 131, 133 | 39:30–31 | 217 |
| | | | | 39:30 | 40, 67, 119 |
| 37:1–5 | 216 | | | | |
| 37:1 | 130 | 39:5 | 31, 60, 110, 111, 131, 133 | 39:31 | 133 |
| 37:3 | 119 | | | 39:38 | 124 |
| 37:4 | 111, 130 | | | 39:39 | 123 |
| 37:5 | 111, 119 | 39:6 | 40, 67, 111, 119 | 40:34–38 | 209 |
| 37:6–9 | 216 | | | 40:7 | 123 |
| 37:10–16 | 216 | 39:7 | 110 | 40:11 | 123 |
| 37:10 | 130 | 39:8–21 | 217 | 40:14 | 101, 124 |
| 37:13 | 119 | 39:8 | 31, 60, 110, 111, 131, 133 | 40:20 | 111 |
| 37:14 | 111, 119 | | | 40:27 | 124 |
| 37:15 | 111, 130 | | | 40:30 | 123 |
| 37:17–24 | 216 | 39:9 | 117 | | |
| 37:17 | 115 | 39:10 | 112, 128 | *Leviticus* | |
| 37:19 | 115 | 39:11 | 124, 126 | 4:7 | 124 |
| 37:20 | 115 | 39:12 | 109, 129 | 8 | 217 |
| 37:25–28 | 217 | 39:13 | 89, 121, 133 | 8:5–9 | 217 |
| 37:25 | 128, 130 | | | 8:7 | 101, 109, 124 |
| 37:26 | 128 | | | | |
| 37:27 | 111, 119 | 39:13 (LXX) | 89 | 8:9 (Peshitta) | 70 |
| 37:28 | 111, 130 | 39:13 (Pesh) | 89 | 8:11 | 123 |
| 37:29 | 124, 217 | 39:13 (Vul) | 89 | 8:13 | 101, 109, 124 |
| 38:1–7 | 216 | 39:14 | 40, 67, 119 | | |
| 38:1 | 130 | | | 10:5 | 101, 124 |
| 38:2 | 128 | 39:16 | 119 | 11:35 | 123 |

| *Leviticus* (cont.) | | 23:19 | 73 | 15:32 | 101, 124 |
| 15:3 | 40, 67, 119 | 23:24 | 75 | 16:21 | 51 |
| | | 28:30 | 86, 87 | 16:22 | 51 |
| 16:4 | 101, 109, 124 | 32:34 | 40, 67, 119 | 19:6 | 51 |
| | | | | 20:3 | 51 |
| 16:12 | 134 | 33:2 | 38, 62, 100, 210 | 21:11 | 51 |
| 19:36 | 117 | | | 24:24 | 73 |
| 23:13 | 117 | | | | |
| 24:1–3 | 216 | *Joshua* | | *1 Kings* | |
| | | 2:1 | 130 | 7:9 | 227 |
| *Numbers* | 8 | 3:1 | 130 | 7:16 | 227 |
| 4:6 | 5, 131, 133 | 22:8 | 104 | 7:21 | 227 |
| | | 24:14–17 | 227 | 7:30 | 123 |
| 4:7 | 55, 133 | | | 7:38 | 123 |
| 4:8 | 131 | *Judges* | | 7:40 | 123 |
| 4:9 | 55, 133 | 5 | 5 | 7:43 | 123 |
| 4:10 | 131 | 7:16 | 71 | 7:40 | 120 |
| 4:11 | 55, 131, 133 | 7:20 | 71 | 7:45 | 120 |
| | | 8:26 | 31, 61, 111 | 10:15 | 50, 81, 105 |
| 4:12 | 55, 131, 133 | 8:31 | 51 | | |
| | | 15:4 | 71 | 10:28 | 73 |
| 4:13 | 31, 60, 111 | 15:5 | 71 | 11:3 | 51 |
| 4:14 | 120, 131 | 19:1 | 51 | 20:24 | 50, 81, 105 |
| 4:16 | 124 | 19:24 | 51 | | |
| 4:25 | 131 | 19:25 | 51 | 20:38 | 30, 60 |
| 7:89 | 225 | 19:27 | 51 | 20:41 | 30, 60 |
| 15:4 | 117 | 19:29 | 51 | 21 | 5 |
| 15:5 | 117 | 20:4 | 51 | 21:2 | 73 |
| 15:6 | 117 | 20:5 | 51 | 21:8 | 40, 67, 119 |
| 15:7 | 117 | 20:6 | 51 | | |
| 15:8 | 117 | | | 22:9 | 48, 81 |
| 15:10 | 117 | *Ruth* | 149 | | |
| 15:38 | 55, 133 | | | *2 Kings* | |
| 17:3 | 127 | *1 Samuel* | 152 | 8:6 | 48, 81 |
| 19:9 | 30, 60 | 2:14 | 123 | 9:32 | 48, 81 |
| 19:10 | 30, 60 | 5–6 | 227 | 16:17 | 123 |
| 24:24 | 84 | 8:15 | 48, 81 | 18:17 | 48, 81 |
| 25:1 | 130 | 17:4 | 117 | 18:24 | 50, 81, 105 |
| 28:5 | 117 | 20:25 | 43 | | |
| 28:7 | 117 | | | 20:18 | 48, 81 |
| 28:14 | 117 | *2 Samuel* | | 23 | 227 |
| 31:50 | 41, 119 | 3:7 | 51 | 23:11 | 48, 81 |
| | | 13:18 | 101, 124 | 24:12 | 48, 81 |
| *Deuteronomy* | | 13:19 | 30, 60, 101, 124 | 24:15 | 48, 81 |
| 4:40 | 155 | | | 24:19 | 48, 81 |
| 10:3 | 130 | 5:13 | 51 | 25:14 | 120 |
| 17:18 | 156 | 15:16 | 51 | 25:27 | 255 |

## Index of Biblical Passages

| | | | | | |
|---|---|---|---|---|---|
| *1 Chronicles* | | 27:4 | 33, 98 | 4:14 | 100 |
| 1:32 | 51 | 30:1 | 26, 93 | 4:17–22 | 190 |
| 2:46 | 51 | 30:6 | 26, 93 | 4:17 | 52, 84, |
| 2:48 | 51 | 34–35 | 227 | | 106 |
| 3:9 | 51 | | | 4:18 | 104 |
| 4:11 | 73 | *Ezra* | 91–108, | 4:20 | 102 |
| 7:14 | 51 | | 142, 149 | 4:23–24 | 190 |
| 7:32 | 40, 67, | | 187–89, | 4:23 | 53, 104, |
| | 119 | | 205, 206, | | 106 |
| 8:3 | 27 | | 229 | 5:1–5 | 191 |
| 8:16 | 121 | 1–7 | 2, 10, 186, | 5:3 | 39, 50, 66, |
| 11:44 | 40, 67, | | 189–206, | | 81, 97, 98, |
| | 119 | | 230, 244– | | 101, 105 |
| 15:27 | 70 | | 46 | 5:5 | 104 |
| 21:27 | 164 | 1:1–2a | 190 | 5:6–17 | 191 |
| 28:1 | 48, 81 | 1:1 | 187 | 5:6 | 26, 50, 53, |
| 29:1 | 33, 61, 98, | 1:2b–4 | 190, 204 | | 81, 93, 95, |
| | 140 | 1:5–11 | 190 | | 105, 106 |
| 29:7 | 99 | 1:9–11 | 190 | 5:7 | 52, 84, |
| 29:19 | 33, 61, 98, | 1:8 | 62, 98 | | 106 |
| | 140 | 1:9 | 91 | 5:8 | 94 |
| | | 2 | 190 | 5:9 | 97, 98 |
| *2 Chronicles* | | 2:6 | 105 | 5:11–17 | 191 |
| 1:10 | 72 | 2:63 | 108 | 5:11 | 52, 84, |
| 1:11 | 72, 104 | 2:66 | 105 | | 106 |
| 1:12 | 72, 104 | 2:69 | 99, 101, | 5:14 | 50, 81, |
| 1:16 | 73 | | 124 | | 100, 105 |
| 2:3 | 124 | 3 | 190 | 5:15 | 100 |
| 2:6 | 31, 55, | 3:1 | 187 | 5:16 | 94 |
| | 133 | 3:2 | 187 | 5:17 | 34, 98 |
| 2:13 | 31, 55, 61, | 3:6 | 100 | 6:1–12 | 191 |
| | 111, 133 | 3:8 | 187 | 6:1 | 34, 98 |
| 3:14 | 31, 55, 61, | 3:10 | 100 | 6:2 | 33, 61, 98, |
| | 111, 133 | 4:1–7 | 190 | | 140 |
| 4:6 | 123 | 4:1 | 100 | 6:3–12 | 191 |
| 4:11 | 120 | 4:7 | 104, 107 | 6:3–5 | 204 |
| 4:14 | 123 | 4:8–6:18 | 194, 198, | 6:4 | 103 |
| 4:16 | 120 | | 200, 201, | 6:5 | 100 |
| 6:13 | 123 | | 204 | 6:6 | 50, 81, 95, |
| 9:14 | 50, 81, | 4:8–16 | 190 | | 105 |
| | 105 | 4:8 | 26, 93, | 6:7 | 50, 81, |
| 11:21 | 51 | | 200, 201 | | 105 |
| 13:11 | 124 | 4:9–16 | 190 | 6:8 | 94, 102, |
| 16:14 | 66 | 4:9 | 95 | | 104 |
| 17:12 | 33, 61, 98 | 4:11 | 26, 53, 69, | 6:9 | 107 |
| 17:19 | 141 | | 93, 106 | 6:11 | 52, 84, |
| 18:8 | 48, 81 | 4:13 | 96, 102 | | 106 |

| | | | | | | | |
|---|---|---|---|---|---|---|---|
| *2 Chronicles* (cont.) | | 2:1 | 27 | *Esther* | | 2, 10, 26–56, 142, 149, 150, 151, 155–86, 229, 230, 234–38 |
| 6:12 | 94 | 2:6 | 39, 66, 86, 101 | | |
| 6:13–22 | 195 | | | | |
| 6:13 | 50, 81, 94, 105, 191 | 2:7 | 26, 50, 81, 93, 105 | | |
| 6:14–16 | 191 | 2:8 | 26, 33, 61, 93, 98, 140 | | |
| 6:14 | 204 | | | 1 | 142, 159, 161 |
| 6:15 | 27 | | | | |
| 6:16–22 | 229 | 2:9 | 26, 50, 81, 93, 105 | 1:1 | 150 |
| 6:16–18 | 191, 201 | | | | |
| 6:16 | 196, 200 | 2:16 | 79 | 1:2 | 33, 43, 61, 98 |
| 6:17 | 107 | 3:7 | 50, 81, 105 | 1:3 | 52, 83, 172 |
| 6:19–22 | 191 | | | | |
| 6:19 | 195, 201, 204 | 4:8 | 79 | | |
| | | 4:13 | 79 | 1:5 | 33, 34, 61, 98, 140 |
| 7:1–10 | 191 | 5:4 | 102 | | |
| 7:11–26 | 191 | 5:7 | 79 | 1:6 | 31, 48, 54, 55, 61, 111, 131, 133, 173 |
| 7:11 | 53, 104, 106, 155 | 5:14 | 50, 81, 105 | | |
| 7:12 | 38, 62, 100, 201 | 5:15 | 50, 81, 105 | 1:6 (AT) | 37 |
| 7:14 | 38, 62, 100 | 5:17 | 79 | 1:6 (LXX) | 37, 38 |
| | | 6:5 | 26, 93 | 1:7 | 42 |
| 7:17 | 74, 94, 107 | 6:17 | 26, 93 | 1:8 | 38, 62, 100 |
| | | 6:19 | 26, 93 | | |
| 7:20 | 34, 98 | 7:2 | 33, 61, 98 | 1:10 | 42, 48, 81, 161, 162, 173 |
| 7:21 | 38, 62, 94, 98, 100 | 7:5 | 79 | | |
| | | 7:65 | 108 | | |
| 7:23 | 93 | 7:69 | 99, 101, 108, 124 | 1:11 | 183 |
| 7:24 | 102 | | | 1:12 | 48, 81, 155 |
| 7:25 | 38, 62, 100 | 7:70 | 99 | | |
| | | 7:71 | 99, 101, 124 | 1:13–14 | 150 |
| 7:26 | 38, 62, 94, 100, 104, 106 | | | 1:13 | 38, 62, 100 |
| | | 8:9 | 108 | | |
| | | 10:1 | 40, 67, 119 | 1:14 | 161, 173 |
| 7:27–28 | 191 | | | 1:15 | 38, 48, 62, 81, 100, 155, 156 |
| 7:27 | 201 | 10:2 | 40, 67, 108, 119 | | |
| 8:27 | 99 | | | | |
| 8:36 | 28, 38, 50, 59, 62, 81, 100, 105, 156 | 12 | 188 | 1:19 | 38, 62, 100, 150, 155 |
| | | 12:11 | 187 | | |
| | | 12:10–11 | 187 | | |
| | | 12:22 | 187, 188 | 1:20 | 52, 84, 106, 155 |
| 9:2 | 79 | 12:26 | 50, 81, 105 | | |
| | | | | 1:22 | 173 |
| *Nehemiah* | 149, 187–89 | 12:40 | 79 | 2 | 184 |
| | | 13:11 | 79 | 2:1–18 | 159 |
| 1:1 | 33, 61, 98 | 13:24 | 195 | | |

## Index of Biblical Passages

| | | | | | |
|---|---|---|---|---|---|
| 2:3 | 33, 48, 61, 81, 98, 140 | | 100, 140, 155 | 8:6 | 26 |
| | | | | 8:7 | 169 |
| | | 3:16 | 169 | 8:8 | 40, 41, 67, 119 |
| 2:5 | 33, 61, 98, 140 | 4 | 182, 184 | | |
| | | 4:1–3 | 159 | 8:9–17 | 160, 161, 183 |
| 2:7 | 162 | 4:1 | 30, 60 | | |
| 2:8 | 33, 38, 61, 62, 98, 100, 140, 155, 156 | 4:3 | 30, 38, 60, 62, 100, 152, 155 | 8:9 | 27, 28, 50, 59, 81, 105, 172, 173 |
| | | 4:4–17 | 159 | | |
| 2:9 | 141 | 4:4 | 48, 81 | 8:10 | 29, 40, 41, 46, 54, 67, 119 |
| 2:10 | 182 | 4:5 | 48, 81 | | |
| 2:12 | 38, 54, 62, 100, 131 | 4:7 | 34, 98 | | |
| | | 4:8 | 38, 53, 62, 100, 106 | 8:12 | 27 |
| 2:14 | 48, 51, 81 | | | 8:13 | 38, 53, 62, 100, 106 |
| 2:15–18 | 169 | 4:11 | 38, 54, 62, 100, 150, 184 | | |
| 2:15 | 48, 81 | | | 8:14 | 29, 33, 38, 61, 62, 98, 100, 140, 155 |
| 2:16 | 27 | | | | |
| 2:17 | 183, 184 | 4:16 | 38, 62, 100, 152 | | |
| 2:19–23 | 159, 161 | | | 8:15 | 31, 55, 61, 62, 111, 133, 173 |
| 2:20 | 155 | 5:1–5a | 159 | | |
| 2:21 | 48, 81 | 5:1 | 43 | | |
| 2:22 | 184 | 5:2 | 54, 183 | 8:17 | 38, 62, 100, 155, 156 |
| 3:1–6 | 159 | 5:3 | 184, 185 | | |
| 3:1 | 43 | 5:5b–8 | 159 | | |
| 3:3 | 155 | 5:6 | 42, 184, 185 | 9 | 161 |
| 3:6 | 152 | | | 9:1–5 | 160 |
| 3:7–15 | 159, 161 | 5:9–14 | 160 | 9:1 | 27, 38, 62, 100, 155 |
| 3:7 | 27, 49 | 6 | 169, 184 | | |
| 3:8 | 38, 62, 100, 156, 157 | 6:1–11 | 160 | 9:3 | 28, 50, 59, 81, 105, 172 |
| | | 6:2 | 48, 81 | | |
| | | 6:8 | 46, 183, 184 | | |
| 3:9 | 34, 98 | 6:9 | 46, 52, 83 | 9:5 | 26 |
| 3:10–15 | 182, 184 | 6:10 | 46 | 9:6–19 | 160, 161 |
| 3:10 | 41, 119 | 6:11 | 46 | 9:6 | 33, 61, 98, 140 |
| 3:12 | 28, 40, 41, 50, 59, 67, 81, 105, 119, 172, 173 | 6:12–14 | 160 | | |
| | | 6:14 | 48, 81 | 9:7–9 | 161, 173 |
| | | 7 | 160 | 9:11 | 33, 61, 98, 140 |
| | | 7:2 | 42 | | |
| 3:13 | 27, 152 | 7:7–8 | 140 | 9:12 | 33, 61, 98, 140 |
| 3:14 | 38, 53, 62, 100, 106, 155, 156 | 7:7 | 34, 42 | | |
| | | 7:8 | 34, 42 | 9:13 | 38, 62, 100 |
| | | 7:9 | 48, 81 | | |
| 3:15 | 33, 38, 61, 62, 98, | 8:1–8 | 160, 161 | 9:14 | 38, 62, 100 |
| | | 8:2 | 41, 119 | | |
| | | 8:4 | 54 | 9:15 | 27 |

## Esther (cont.)

| | |
|---|---|
| 9:17 | 27 |
| 9:19 | 27 |
| 9:20–32 | 160 |
| 9:21 | 27 |
| 9:24 | 49 |
| 9:26 | 26, 49, 93 |
| 9:27 | 39, 66, 101 |
| 9:28 | 49 |
| 9:29 | 26, 49, 93, 169 |
| 9:31 | 39, 49, 66, 101 |
| 9:32 | 49, 155 |
| 10 | 160 |
| 10:2–3 | 169 |
| F:11 (LXX) | 151 |

## Job

| | |
|---|---|
| 2:8 | 30, 60 |
| 8:12 | 59 |
| 9:7 | 40, 67, 119 |
| 13:12 | 30, 60 |
| 14:14 | 40, 67, 119 |
| 24:16 | 40, 67, 119 |
| 28 | 15 |
| 28:6 | 126 |
| 28:16 | 126 |
| 28:15 | 73 |
| 28:19 | 128 |
| 30:18 | 101, 124 |
| 30:19 | 30, 60 |
| 33:16 | 40, 67, 119 |
| 37:7 | 40, 67, 119 |
| 38:14 | 40, 67, 119 |
| 41:7 | 40, 67, 119 |
| 41:11 | 71 |
| 42:6 | 30, 60 |

## Psalms

| | |
|---|---|
| 44:13 | 73 |
| 45:10 | 86 |
| 68:15 | 210 |
| 72:9 | 84 |
| 74:14 | 84 |
| 102:10 | 30, 60 |
| 116 | 5 |
| 119:115 | 155 |
| 144:13 | 66 |
| 147:16 | 30, 60 |

## Proverbs

| | |
|---|---|
| 17:16 | 73 |
| 27:26 | 73 |
| 31:22 | 31, 54, 61, 111, 131 |

## Ecclesiastes

| | |
|---|---|
| 3:1 | 39, 66, 101 |
| 5:18 | 104 |
| 6:2 | 104 |
| 8:11 | 52, 84, 106 |
| 10:20 | 72 |

## Song of Songs

| | |
|---|---|
| 3:10 | 31, 61, 111 |
| 4:12 | 40, 67, 111 |
| 5:3 | 101, 124 |
| 5:14 | 89, 90, 126, 133 |
| 5:14 (LXX) | 90 |
| 5:14 (Pesh) | 89 |
| 5:14 (Vul) | 89 |
| 6:8 | 51 |
| 6:9 | 51 |
| 6:11 | 59 |
| 7:6 | 31, 61, 111 |
| 8:6 | 40, 67, 111 |

## Isaiah

| | |
|---|---|
| 3:20 | 127 |
| 3:21 | 41, 119 |
| 8:16 | 40, 67, 119 |
| 13:16 | 86 |
| 13:21 | 84 |
| 20:1 | 79 |
| 22:21 | 101, 109, 124 |
| 23:13 | 84 |
| 24:16 | 85, 86 |
| 28:17 | 120 |
| 29:11 | 40, 67, 119 |
| 33:21 | 84 |
| 34:14 | 84 |
| 36:9 | 50, 81, 195 |
| 39:7 | 49, 81 |
| 40:12 | 117 |
| 41:19 | 130 |
| 41:25 | 79 |
| 44:20 | 30, 60 |
| 45:13 | 73 |
| 54:11 | 126 |
| 50:11 | 71 |
| 55:1 | 73 |
| 56:3 | 49, 81 |
| 56:4 | 49, 81 |
| 58:5 | 30 |
| 61:3 | 30, 127 |
| 61:10 | 127 |
| 62:11 | 71 |

## Jeremiah

| | |
|---|---|
| 3:2 | 86 |
| 6:26 | 30, 60 |
| 10:9 | 31, 55, 61, 111, 133 |
| 10:11 | 198 |
| 15:13 | 73 |
| 22:24 | 40, 67, 119 |
| 29:2 | 49, 81 |
| 32:10 | 40, 67, 119 |
| 32:11 | 40, 67, 119 |
| 32:14 | 40, 67, 119 |

## Index of Biblical Passages

| | | | | | | |
|---|---|---|---|---|---|---|
| *Jeremiah* (cont.) | | 23:6 | 50, 55, 79, 81, 105, 133 | 1 | 154, 155, 165, 167, 169, 178–81, 203 |
| 32:44 | 40, 67, 119 | 23:12 | 50, 79, 81, 105 | 1:1–5 | 179 |
| 34:19 | 49, 81 | 23:20 | 51 | 1:3 | 49, 52, 81, 83 |
| 35:5 | 115 | 23:23 | 50, 79, 81, 105 | 1:4 | 64, 72, 153 |
| 38:7 | 49, 81 | 24:17 | 127 | | |
| 39:3 | 49, 81 | 24:23 | 127 | 1:5 | 69, 83 |
| 39:13 | 49, 81 | 27:7 | 31, 54, 55, 61, 111, 131, 133 | 1:7 | 49, 81, 171, 180 |
| 40:5 | 74 | | | | |
| 41:16 | 49, 81 | | | 1:8 | 49, 69, 81, 83, 176, 179 |
| 50:39 | 84 | 27:16 | 31, 61, 111, 124 | | |
| 51:23 | 50, 79, 81, 105 | 27:24 | 34, 55, 98, 133 | 1:9 | 49, 81 |
| 51:28 | 50, 79, 81, 105 | | | 1:10 | 49, 81 |
| | | 27:30 | 30, 60 | 1:11 | 49, 73, 81 |
| 51:57 | 50, 79, 81, 105 | 28:3 | 133 | 1:13 | 83 |
| | | 28:12 | 40, 67, 119 | 1:15 | 83 |
| 52:18 | 120 | | | 1:16 | 69, 73, 83 |
| 52:25 | 49, 81 | 28:13 | 89, 90, 112, 121, 124, 126, 128 | 1:17 | 72, 153 |
| | | | | 1:18 | 49, 81 |
| *Lamentations* | | | | 1:20 | 61, 68 |
| 3:16 | 30, 60 | | | 2–7 | 198, 201–203 |
| 4:7 | 126 | 28:13 (LXX) | 90 | | |
| 5:4 | 73 | 28:13 (Vul) | 89 | 2–6 | 167, 203 |
| | | 28:18 | 30, 60 | 2 | 165, 169, 172, 177 |
| *Ezekiel* | | 30:9 | 84 | | |
| 1 | 214 | 43:13 | 117 | 2:2 | 61, 68, 171, 172 |
| 1:7 | 214 | 44:18 | 127 | | |
| 1:10 | 214 | 45:24 | 117 | 2:4 | 193, 201, 203 |
| 1:13 | 71 | 46:5 | 117 | | |
| 1:16 | 89, 90, 133 | 46:7 | 117 | 2:5 | 58, 63 |
| | | 46:11 | 117 | 2:5 (Th) | 58 |
| 1:16 (LXX) | 90 | 46:14 | 117 | 2:6 | 74 |
| 1:16 (Pesh) | 89 | | | 2:8 | 58 |
| 1:16 (Vul) | 89 | *Daniel* | 2, 9, 10, 57–91, 142, 152–86, 229, 230, 239–43 | 2:8 (Th) | 58 |
| 1:26 | 126 | | | 2:9 | 38, 62, 84, 100 |
| 4:11 | 117 | | | | |
| 10:1 | 126 | | | 2:10 | 61, 68, 171, 172 |
| 10:9 | 89, 90, 133 | | | | |
| | | | | 2:13 | 38, 62, 100 |
| 10:9 (LXX) | 90 | 1–6 | 154, 155, 166, 169, 173, 176, 177 | | |
| 10:9 (Pesh) | 89 | | | 2:15 | 38, 62, 100 |
| 10:9 (Vul) | 89 | | | | |
| 10:14 | 214 | | | | |
| 16:10 | 54, 131 | | | | |

*Daniel* (cont.)

| Ref | Pages |
|---|---|
| 2:16 | 39, 66, 101 |
| 2:18 | 85 |
| 2:19 | 85 |
| 2:21 | 39, 66, 101 |
| 2:27 | 61, 68, 85, 171, 172 |
| 2:28 | 85 |
| 2:29 | 85 |
| 2:30 | 85 |
| 2:32 | 219 |
| 2:33 | 82 |
| 2:34 | 82 |
| 2:35 | 82, 171, 219 |
| 2:40 | 82 |
| 2:41 | 82 |
| 2:42 | 82 |
| 2:43 | 82 |
| 2:45 | 58, 82, 171 |
| 2:46 | 178 |
| 2:47 | 85 |
| 2:48 | 79 |
| 2:49 | 171 |
| 3 | 154, 155, 166, 167, 169, 172, 179, 180 |
| 3:2 | 28, 50, 57, 59, 62, 79, 81, 88, 98, 105, 170, 172 |
| 3:3 | 28, 50, 57, 59, 62, 79, 81, 88, 98, 105, 170, 172, 175 |
| 3:3 (OG) | 175 |
| 3:4 | 69, 171 |
| 3:5 | 66, 76, 77, 85, 171, 172 |
| 3:7 | 39, 66, 76, 77, 85, 101, 171, 172 |
| 3:8 | 39, 66, 101 |
| 3:10 | 66, 76, 77, 85, 171, 172 |
| 3:12 | 171 |
| 3:13 | 171 |
| 3:14 | 171 |
| 3:15 | 66, 76, 77, 85, 171, 172 |
| 3:16 | 52, 84, 106, 171 |
| 3:19 | 171 |
| 3:20 | 171 |
| 3:21 | 70, 79, 171 |
| 3:22 | 171 |
| 3:23 | 171 |
| 3:24 | 63 |
| 3:26 | 171 |
| 3:27 | 28, 50, 59, 63, 79, 81, 105, 170, 172 |
| 3:28 | 171 |
| 3:29 | 63, 171 |
| 3:30 | 171 |
| 3:31 | 171 |
| 4–6 | 172 |
| 4 | 166, 169, 172 |
| 4:1 | 64 |
| 4:4 | 61, 68, 171, 172 |
| 4:6 | 68 |
| 4:6 | 85 |
| 4:9 | 59 |
| 4:11 | 59 |
| 4:12 | 82 |
| 4:14 | 52, 84, 106 |
| 4:18 | 59 |
| 4:20 | 82 |
| 4:22 | 87 |
| 4:26 | 64 |
| 4:29 | 87 |
| 4:30 | 87 |
| 4:32 | 62, 99 |
| 4:33 | 39, 63, 66, 101, 170, 172 |
| 5 | 166, 169, 172, 178 |
| 5:1 | 57, 95 |
| 5:2 | 64, 71, 86, 87, 171, 172 |
| 5:3 | 64, 71, 86, 171, 172 |
| 5:4 | 82, 171 |
| 5:5 | 64, 75 |
| 5:7 | 31, 60, 61, 65, 111, 171, 174 |
| 5:7 (4QDan<sup>a</sup>) | 68, 166 |
| 5:7 (Ms. 88) | 166 |
| 5:7 (Pap. 967) | 167 |
| 5:7 (Syrohex.) | 166 |
| 5:11 | 61, 68, 171 |
| 5:12 | 85 |
| 5:15 | 61 |
| 5:16 | 31, 60, 111 |
| 5:17 | 74, 178 |
| 5:19 | 171 |
| 5:20 | 71 |
| 5:21 | 87 |
| 5:23 | 71, 82, 86, 171, 172 |
| 5:29 | 31, 60, 69, 111, 178 |
| 6 | 29, 154, 155, 166, 167, 169, 172, 179, 180 |
| 6:1 | 28, 59 |

# Index of Biblical Passages

| | | | | | | |
|---|---|---|---|---|---|---|
| 6:2 | 28, 59 | 7:19 | 82 | 11:39 | 73 | |
| 6:3 | 28, 59, 81 | 7:20 | 85 | 11:45 | 60, 139, | |
| 6:4 | 28, 59, 81, 170, 172 | 7:21 | 40 | | 141 | |
| | | 7:22 | 39, 66, 101 | 12 | 154 | |
| 6:5 | 28, 81, 156, 170, 172 | 7:24 | 85 | 12:3 | 153 | |
| | | 7:25 | 38, 39, 62, 66, 100, 101 | 12:4 | 40, 67, 111 | |
| 6:6 | 38, 59, 62, 100 | | | 12:9 | 40, 67, 111 | |
| | | | | 12:10 | 153 | |
| 6:7 | 28, 59, 81, 170, 172, 176 | 8–12 | 167 | *Joel* | | |
| | | 8 | 163, 166, 167, 202, 203 | 4:18 | 130 | |
| 6:8 | 28, 50, 63, 79, 81, 105, 170, 172 | | | *Jonah* | | |
| | | 8:1 | 201, 203 | 3:6 | 30, 60 | |
| | | 8:2 | 33, 61, 98, 140 | *Micah* | | |
| 6:9 | 38, 62, 100 | 8:3 | 85 | 3:11 | 73 | |
| | | 8:5 | 85 | 6:5 | 130 | |
| 6:11 | 39, 66, 101 | 8:6 | 85 | | | |
| | | 8:7 | 85 | *Nahum* | | |
| 6:13 | 38, 62, 100 | 8:9 | 85 | 2:5 | 71 | |
| | | 8:20 | 85 | | | |
| 6:14 | 39, 66, 101 | 8:21 | 85 | *Habakkuk* | | |
| | | 9–12 | 167 | 3:3 | 210 | |
| 6:16 | 38, 62, 100 | 9 | 163 | | | |
| | | 9:1–20 | 166, 229 | *Haggai* | 187 | |
| 6:18 | 40, 67, 111 | 9:3 | 30, 60 | 1:1 | 50, 81, 105 | |
| 6:19 | 64 | 9:13 | 153 | | | |
| 6:23 | 65, 69 | 9:21–27 | 166 | 1:14 | 50, 81, 105 | |
| 6:26 | 171 | 9:22 | 153 | | | |
| 7–12 | 167 | 9:24 | 40, 67, 111 | 2:2 | 50, 81, 105 | |
| 7 | 163, 166, 167, 192, 202, 203 | 9:25 | 153 | | | |
| | | 9:27 | 154 | 2:21 | 50, 81, 105 | |
| | | 10 | 166 | | | |
| 7:1 | 202, 203 | 10:3 | 69 | 2:23 | 40, 67, 119 | |
| 7:7 | 82, 85 | 10:6 | 71, 89, 90, 111 | | | |
| 7:8 | 85, 153 | | | *Zechariah* | | |
| 7:9 | 72 | 10:6 (LXX) | 90 | 12:6 | 71, 123 | |
| 7:10 | 154 | 10:6 (Vul) | 89 | 14:2 | 86 | |
| 7:11 | 85 | 11–12 | 166 | | | |
| 7:12 | 39, 66, 101 | 11 | 154, 180 | *Malachi* | | |
| | | 11:25–26 | 180 | 1:8 | 50, 81, 105 | |
| 7:14 | 171 | 11:26 | 83 | | | |
| 7:15 | 165 | 11:30 | 84 | 3:21 | 30, 60 | |
| 7:15 (OG) | 165 | 11:33 | 153 | | | |
| | | 11:35 | 153 | | | |

| DEUTEROCANONICAL BOOKS | | 1 Maccabees | 153, 154 | NEW TESTAMENT | |
|---|---|---|---|---|---|
| | | 1:20–61 | 153 | John | |
| Tobit | 168, 174, 175 | 1:62–63 | 153 | 19:17 | 199 |
| | | 2:1–22 | 153, 154 | | |
| 1:22 | 174 | 2:23 | 153 | 1 Corinthians | |
| | | 2:42–48 | 153 | 9:10 (Pesh) | 214 |
| Judith | 168, 174 | | | | |
| | | 2 Maccabees | 153, 154 | Hebrews | |
| Sirach | | 4:7–15 | 153 | 9:5 | 225 |
| 8:18 | 85, 86 | 15:36 | 151 | | |
| 3 Esdras | 174 | | | | |
| 3–4 | 168 | | | | |

# Index of Non-Biblical Ancient Sources

### Hebrew and Aramaic Sources

*1QApGen*
2.10                165

*4Q196*
2.7                 174

*4Q242*             168

*4Q550*             168, 173, 174

*4Q550<sup>c</sup>*
5                   173

*4Q561*
1.4                 63

*4QDan<sup>a</sup>*
5.7                 68, 166

*4QEn<sup>b</sup>*
1.3.2               61

*Ahiqar*            168, 175, 177

Aphrahat
*Demonstrations*
9.184:11            77

*Asshur Ostracon*
17                  57, 62, 84, 95, 100

*Clermont-Ganneau*
42 R.8              59
229 V.2             66, 101

*Elephantine Ostracon*
                    175, 16
R.2                 65

*Idumean Ostracon*
2.81.2              102

*Sefire Treaty Text 1*
222 a29             77

*TAD A4.1*
R.5                 65

*TAD A6.10*
4                   93

*TAD B2.6*
206.R.19            104

*TAD B2.11*
R.13                66, 101

*TAD B4.2*
R.6                 96
R.8                 106

*TAD C1.1 132*      93
3.38                175
4.63                175

*TAD D1.16*
R.2                 93, 94

*TAD D1.17*         59

*TAD D7.29*
7                   81

*TAD D23.1*
Panel 5A.1.9        71

*Tell Shioukh Fawqani*
F 204 I/3.5         74

*Frg. Tg. V*
Exod 27:3           120

*Tg. Esth. II*
5.1-03.2            74

*Tg. J.*
Jer 40:5            74
Ezek 28:13          90

*Tg. Onq.*
Gen 4:21            77
Exod 28:20          90
Exod 28:39          70
Exod 39:13          90

*Tg. Ps.-J.*
Deut 23:24          75

### Egyptian Sources

*Edwin Smith Surgical Papyrus*      112, 163

*Sehel Famine Inscription*
IV.16               112

*The Tale of Sinuhe*
                    168, 175

## GREEK SOURCES

*1 Clement*
55:6     151

Antiphanes
*Fragments*
201     80

Athenaeus
*Deipnosophists*
11.110     84

Herodotus
*Histories*     168
II.44     114
III.41     114
III.89–94     28
III.89     29
VII.90     45

Homer
*Odyssey*
III.139     25
VI.42     210

*Iliad*
III.276     210
VI.621     25

Josephus
*Antiquities* [533, 856, 870, 881, 979, 981, 982, 983, 984, 985]
III.168     89
XI.3.10     187
XI.5.1     187
XI.5.5     187
XI.7.1     187
XI.7.2     187
XI.6     151
XII.3–9     153
XII.4     154

*Wars of the Jews*
I.1     153
V.234     89

Photius
*Lexicon*     46, 80

Pseudo-Xenophon
(the Old Oligarch)
*On the Constitution*
2.8     144

Scholion on Plato's
*Republic*
553c     46

Strabo
*Geography*
XVI 4.6     128

*Suda*     46

Theodoretus
*Interpretatio in Danielem*
81.1324.17     80

Theophrastus
*de Lapidibus*
23–27     113

## LATIN SOURCES

Curtius Rufus
*Historiae Alexandri Magni*
III.13.5     36

Mela
*De Chorographia*
I.55     35

Plautus
*Poenulus*
I.5     144

Quintilian
*Institutio Oratoria*
IX.1.3     16

## PERSIAN SOURCES

$DB$ [127, 129, 130, 887]
1.6     29
1.23     156
3.14     29
2.56     29

$DNa$
15–30
29
21     156

$DSe$
20     156
37     156

$XPh$
14–28
29
18     156
49     156
52     156

$D^2Sa$
1     139

$A^2Hb$
1     139

$A^2Sa$
3–4     139

$A^2Ha$
5     139

# Index of Loanwords in Esther, Daniel, Ezra 1–7 and Exodus 25–40

אֲבַדָּן 26
אַבְנֵט 109, 224
אֲגַרְטָל\* 91, 92
אִגֶּרֶת 26, 27
אֲדָר 27
אֲדַרְגָּזֵר\* 57, 58
אֲדַרְזְדָא 93, 94
אוֹשַׁי 174
אַזְדָּא 58
אַחְלָמָה 109, 110
אֲחַשְׁדַּרְפָּן\* 28, 29, 59
אֲחַשְׁתְּרָן\* 29, 30
אֱנָב\* 59, 60
אַנְרְפַּסְאָ 94, 95
אֵפוֹד 110, 111, 219
אֵפֹד 110, 111
אֲפֻדָּה 110, 111
אַפֶּדֶן\* 60, 139–41
אֵפֶר 30, 31, 60
אֲפַרְסְכָי\* 95, 96
אֲפַרְסַתְכָי\* 95, 96
אַפְּתֹם 96, 97
אַרְגָּוָן 31, 60, 61
אַרְגָּמָן 31–33, 111, 219
אַשָּׁף\* 61
אֶשַּׁרְנָא\* 97, 98

בַּד\* 111, 112, 223
בִּירָה 33, 34, 61, 98, 139, 140
בִּיתָן 34, 139–41
בַּרְזֶל 82
בָּרֶקֶת 112–14

גָּבִיעַ 115, 116
גִּדְבָּר 36, 62
גִּזְבָּר 36, 98
גֶּנֶז\* 34–36, 98

דָּר 36–38
דַּרְכְּמוֹנִים 99, 100
דָּת 38, 39, 62, 100, 155–57, 182
דְּתָבַר\* 62
הַדָּבָר\* 63
הַדָּם\* 63

הֵיכָל 64, 100
הִין 117
הַמַּגִּיד\* 65

וֶרֶד\* 36–38

זְכוּ 65, 66
זְמָן 39, 40, 66, 101
זַן 66, 67
זֶרֶת 117, 118

חֶלְבְּנָה 118, 119
חָרוּת 119
חַרְטֹם 68
חֹתָם 40, 41, 67, 119

טַבַּעַת 41, 42, 119, 223, 224
טֵבֵת 27

יַיִן 42, 43, 69, 120
יָע\* 120, 121
יָשְׁפֵה 121–23

כִּיּוֹר 123, 124
כִּסֵּא 43, 44
כַּרְבֵּל\* 70
כָּרוֹז 69
כְּרֹז\* 69
כָּרְסֵא 43, 44, 71
כַּרְפַּס 44

כֻּתֹּנֶת 101, 102, 124
כֶּתֶר 45, 46, 183

לְחֶנָה 71
לַפִּיד 71, 72

מִדָּה 102, 103
מִנְדָּה 102, 103
מַדָּע 72, 73
מְחִיר 73
מֶלְצַר 73, 74

נֶבְזְבָּה 74
נִבְרְשָׁה 75
נִדְבָּךְ\* 103, 104
נִיסָן 27
נְכַס\* 104
נֹפֶךְ 124
נִשְׁתְּוָן\* 104, 105

סַבְּכָא 76–79
סְגַן\* 79
סוּמְפּוֹנְיָה 76–79
סוּס 46, 47, 105
סֹחֶרֶת 48
סִיוָן 27
סִיפֹנְיָה 76–79
סַם\* 124–26, 219
סַפִּיר 126
סַרְבָּל\* 79, 80
סָרִיס 48, 49, 81
סֶרֶךְ\* 81

פְּאֵר 127
פּוּר 49, 50
פַּח\* 127
פֶּחָה 50, 51, 81, 105
פִּטְדָה 128
פִּלֶגֶשׁ 51, 52

פְּסַנְטֵרִין 77–79
פְּסַנְתֵּרִין 77–79
פַּרְזֶל 82
פַּרְשֶׁגֶן 106
פַּרְתְּמִים 52, 83
פַּת־בַּג 83, 84, 179, 180
פִּתְגָּם 52, 53, 84, 106
פִּתְשֶׁגֶן 53

צִי 84, 85

קִיתָרוֹס 77–79
קֶרֶן 85, 128
קַתְרוֹס 77–79

רָז 85, 86
רִמּוֹן 128, 129
רְמָז* 54

שַׂבְּכָא 76–79
שְׂבוֹ 129
שֵׂגֶל* 86, 87
שׁוֹר 129, 130
שִׂטָּה 130, 131, 219, 223, 224
שַׁרְבִיט 54, 183
שָׁרְשׁוּ 106, 107
שֵׁשׁ 54, 55, 131, 219

תּוֹר 87, 88, 107
תַּחְרָא 131
תַּחַשׁ 131–33, 219
תְּכֵלֶת 55, 56, 133, 219
תִּפְתָּי* 88, 89
תִּרְגֵּם 107, 108
תִּרְשִׁישׁ 89–91, 133
תִּרְשָׁתָא 108

# Index of Words from Ancient Languages

AFRO-ASIATIC
*çibV' 42
*cim 125
*sVm 125

AKKADIAN
alaḫḫinatu 71
-annu 108
-anu 108
appittima 97
aptumu 96
argamannu 31
armannu 129
bāb-ili 22
barāru 76
barraqtu 112
bel pāḫiti 50
biltu 102, 103
birbirrū 76
birtu 34
duḫšu 132
dušû 132
egertu 26
ekallu 64
epattu 110, 11
eperum 30
ḫilabāna 118
ḫilbanītu 118
ḫuluppu 118
ibru 63
igertu 26
ilku 102, 103
inbu 60
īnu 25
iprasakku 95
issi ekalli 87
itbaru 63
kaparu 189
kapāru 214

karābu 214
kāribu 214
karballatu 70
kaspu 219
kitinnu 101
kitu 101
kiu̯ru 124
kurību 214
kussû 43
kutimmu 163
laḫḫinu 71
lamassu 215
lurmû 129
maddattu 103
maḫīru 73
maṣṣaru 73
mā'um 164
*nabraštu 76
nabur šeti 76
nadabākum 103
nadānu 103
natbākum 103
nikkassu 104
nurmû 129
paḫu 127
pāḫutu 50
parakku 215
parāku 215
paruktu 215
parzillu 82
piḫattiḫurunpiki 124
pūru 49
qabûtu 115
ragāmu 107
saḫlu 215
sāmtu 215, 219
sandu 219
samṭu 130
sarbillu 80

*siāmu* 215
*siḫru* 48
*simānu* 39, 40
*sisium* 47
*sīsû* 47
*ša ekalli* 87
*ša rēši* 49
*šabbiṭu* 54
*šaknu* 79
*šammu* 125
*šamṭu* 130
*šarbillu* 80
*šigirtu* 87
*šubû* 129
*suḫullatu* 215
*šurinnu* 97
*šūru* 88
*tabākum* 103
*takiltu* 56
*taklu* 56
*targumannu* 107, 108
*wabru* 34
*(w)āšipu* 61
*(y)ašpu* 121
*zākûtu* 65
*zirru* 213

AMORITE
*Baḫlisapar* 126
*Sapirum* 126

ARABIC
*ʾurgwan* 32
*duḫas* 132
*firzil* 82
*ḥasaba* 214
*ḥatm* 41
*kapara* 214
*safara* 126
*samm* 125
*suḥālat* 215
*šuḥḥar* 48
*tuḥas* 132
*wiʿāʾ* 121
*waʿāy* 121
*yašb* 121
*yašm* 122

ARAMAIC
אבב 60
אבדן 26
אבר 63
אגרה\* 93
אדרגזר\* 57
אדרזדא 93
אוצר 96, 98
אזד 58
אזדא 58
אזל 58
אחידה 85
אחשדרפן 28, 29, 59, 173
אחשמיתא 107
אנב\* 59
אספרנא 94
אעף 106
אפוד 110
אפרסכי\* 95
אפרסתכי\* 95
אפתם 96
ארגון 31, 32, 60, 173
ארתחששתא 69
אשף\* 61
אשרנא\* 97
בירה 33, 98
בית אלהא 64, 100
בית מלכו 64
בלו 102, 103, 189
בקר 88, 107
ברקא 112
גדבר 36, 62, 63
גזבר 98
גנז 35, 36, 62, 98
דהב 219
דין 62
דכי 65
דליק 75
דרמשק 44, 54
דת 38, 62, 100
דתבר\* 62, 63
הדבר\* 63
הדם\* 63
היכל 64, 100, 163, 189
הלך 102, 189
המניך\* 65
זבן 39
זכו 65
זמן 39, 40, 66, 101
זמרא 66

# Index of Words from Ancient Languages

זן 66
חבש 213
חוה 69
חסין 93
חצצרה 77
חרש 61, 68
חרת 254
חרטם 68, 166
חשבן 62, 99
חתם 40, 67, 163
יציב 58
ישפה 121
כל 66
כלוז 69
כנר 77
כסף 74, 219
כרב 214
כרבל* 70, 79
כרוב 214
כרוז 69, 165
כרז 69, 70
כרך 98
כרסא 43, 44, 71, 163
כרפס 44
כתר 45
לחנה 71
מדברן 81
מדה 102, 103
מומי 164
מוריתא 91
מותב 71
מכתב 93
מלה 84
מלך 97
מנדה 102, 103
מצנפא 70
משטוח 103
נבזבה 74
נברשה* 75
נדבך* 103
נדן 164
נדנה 164, 165
נהור 75
נחש 219
נכס* 104
נשתון* 104
ענש 106
סבכא 76, 78, 79
סבל 79
סגן* 79

סומפוניה 76, 78
סוסי 47
סיפניה 76, 79
סמקא 61
סרבל* 79
סרושיתא 107
סריס 175
סרך* 29, 81
עדן 66, 101
ענבא 59
עפר 30
עת 66, 101
פדתא 110
פחה 28, 50, 81, 105, 173
פסנטרין 77, 78
פסנתרין 77
פקוד 57, 59, 62, 63, 79, 81, 88, 95, 100, 104, 105
פרזל 82, 165
פרי 59
פקוד 84, 105
פרשגן 106
פתגם 84, 106
פתשת 131
קובע 115
קיתרוס 77
קנין 104
קרטלא 91
קרן 77, 85
קתרוס 77, 79
רב 57, 59, 63, 79, 81, 88, 95, 105
רז 85
ריש 57, 59, 63, 79, 81, 88, 95, 105
רמן 129
שבכא 76
שגל* 86, 87
שלוח 69
שלטון 81
שלים 93, 94
שפט 62
שפר 126
שרשו 106, 107
שרשי 106
תוכלא 56
תור 87, 107, 163, 189
תחלי 215
תכלתא 55
תמים 93, 94
תפתי* 88, 165
תרגם 107

ARMENIAN
*karoz* 69
*vard* 37

AVESTAN
*aδara-* 57
*asa-perena-* 94
*brāz-* 75
*děrěšta-* 94
*fravi-* 49
*γžar-* 57
*handāman-* 63
*ni-* 75
*nibāzan-* 74
*nidāna-* 164
*ništa-* 105
*nivāzan-* 74
*paθma-* 96
*razah-* 86
*sāra-* 80, 81
*sāra-vāra-* 80
*sraošyā-* 106, 107
*taršta-* 108
*vāra-* 80
*varəδa-* 37
*visarna-* 98
*zrazda-* 94
*zrvan-* 39

EBLAITE
*'ipdum* 110

EGYPTIAN
*bḏ3* 111
*bj3* 82
*bnd* 109
*bndw* 109
*brg.t* 112, 113
*ḏr* 213
*ḏr.t* 117
*ḥbš* 213
*ḥśb* 213
*ḥr-tp* 68
*ḫnmt* 110
*hn.w* 117
*ḫtm* 40
*iʿ* 120
*iʿy* 120, 121
*iʿ.w* 120
*ifd* 110, 111
*k3p.t* 214
*kp(n)rdwy* 214
*ktm* 164
*mfkt* 124
*nšm.t* 122
*p(3)-(n-)t(3)-šd.t* 131
*\*pḏḏ.t* 128
*pḫ3* 127
*pr-ḫtḥrmfk3t* 124
*qbḥ.w* 115
*qbḥy.t* 115
*shrt* 48
*sm.w* 125
*šnḏ* 130
*šnḏ.t* 130
*ssm.t* 47
*śhr.t* 48
*šś* 55
*šś-nšw* 55
*ṯhs* 132
*wnš* 25

ELAMITE
*áš-bar-na* 94
*ba-iz-[zí?]-ik-nu-iš* 53
*bat-ti-z í-ik-nu-še* 53
*ha-za-ir-na* 98
*ha-za-ir-na-qa-ra* 98
*pír-ra-iš-šá-ik-qa* 95
*qa-an-za* 35
*šiši* 47
*tar-qa-sir-ma* 58
*teipti* 89
*ya-aš-pu* 122

GE'EZ
*'afar* 30
*rōmān* 129
*sāwm* 215
*sōm* 215

GREEK
ἄγγαρος 26
ἄγειν 59
ἀργεμώνη 32
ἀργεμώνιον 32
βιβλίον 113
βυβλίον 113
γάζα 35
γένος 66, 67

Γολγοθα 199
γρύψ 214
δαρκμά 100
δαρκνά 100
δαρχμά 100
δραχμή 99, 100
δραχμίον 99
δράσσεσθαι 100
ἔπαρχος 50
ἐπιστολή 104
ἐπίταγμα 52
ἐπιτάσσειν 52
ζαμβύκη 78
ζμάραγδος 113
Ζμάρακτος 113
ζμύρνα 114
ἰαμβύκη 78
ἴασπις 122
ἱεροφάντης 23
ἵππος 47
κάλπασος 44
κάρταλλος 91
κάρπασος 44
κέρας 85
κῆρυξ 69
κηρύσσειν 69
κίθαρις 77, 78
κιθώνη 45
κίταρις 45, 46
Κρανίου Τόπον 199
λάμπας 72
λάμπειν 72
μανιάκης 65
μάραγδος 113
μίκρος 114
μίτρα 45
Μολοσσός 74
μύραινα 114
*μύρνα 114
μῶμος 164
νομίζειν 75
νόμισμα 74
οἶνος 25, 43
οἶνοψ 91
ὀσμή 125
παγίς 127
παλλακή 51
παλλακίς 51
πίνινος 37
ποτιβάζις 83

πρότιμος 52
ῥόδον 37, 38
σαμβύκη 78
σάμβυξ 78
σαράβαρα 79, 80
σατράπης 28, 29
σίφων 78
σκῆπτρον 54
σμάραγδος 113
σμαραγεῖν 113
σμίκρος 114
σμύραινα 114
σμύρνα 114
σῦκ- 23
σῦκον 23
συκοφάντης 23
συμφωνία 77
Ταρτησσός 90
ταῦρος 88
τιάρα 46
τίθεναι 38
φαιν- 23
φαίνειν 23, 38
φάντασμα 23
φαρμάκοι 166
φέρειν 36
φθέγγειν 52
φθέγμα 52
χαλβάνη 118
χάλπασος 44
χιτών 101
χνουβις 68
χνουμις 68
ψάλλειν 78
ψαλτήριον 77, 78
-ωνη 32

HEBREW
אב 59
אבדן 26, 159
אבדון 26
אבנט 109, 224
*אגרטל 91
אדיר 52, 83
אדמה 30, 60
אדר 27
אדרכן 99
אוצר 34
אזור 109
אחלמה 109

אחשדרפן 28, 29, 173
\*אחשתרן 29
אכל 83
אמה 51, 117
אניה 84
אפד 110, 219
אפדה 110
\*אפדן 60, 139, 141
אפר 30, 31, 60
אצבע 42
אציל 52, 83
אקדח 89, 109, 112, 121, 124, 126, 128, 129, 133
ארגון 31, 33
ארגמן 31–33, 111, 219
אֲרָמִית 201
\*אשׁף 61
אש 71
בבל 22
בגד 101, 124, 131
בד 111, 112, 163, 213, 216, 223
בוץ 44, 54, 111, 131
בירה 33, 34, 61, 139, 140
בית 34, 60, 64, 100, 141
ביתן 34, 139, 140, 141
בלל 22
בקר 129
ברזל 82
ברקת 112
בת 117
גבול 158
גביע 115
גדוד 158
גורל 49
גזבר 36, 98
גל 115
\*גנז 34–36
דבר 38, 52, 62, 104, 155
דור 129
דעה 72
דעת 72
דר 36–38, 158
דרכמונים 99
דשא 124
דת 38, 39, 62, 155–57, 182
היכל 64, 100, 163, 189
הין 117
\*ורד 36–38
זבל 34, 60, 64
זהב 219

זיקות 71
זכה 66
זמן 39, 40
זר 213
זרת 117
חבל 26
חבש 213
חושב 213
חח 41, 119
חלבנה 118
חמר 42, 69, 120
חפץ 89, 109, 112, 121, 124, 126, 128, 129, 133
חר 52, 83
חרוש 119
חרות 119
חרש 254
חרטם 68, 175
חשב 213
חתם 40, 41, 67, 119, 158, 163, 213
טבול 127
טבעת 41, 42, 119, 223, 224
טבת 27
יבול 158
ידע 73
ידעני 68
יין 25, 42, 43, 69, 120, 163, 213
ין, see יין
\*יע 120
יקר 158
ירש 91
ישפה 121–23
כוס 115
כיור 123
כלה 26
כסא 43, 158
כסף 219
כפור 189
כפר 214
כפרת 214, 216
כרוב 214, 216
כרפס 44
כשף 68
כתב 158, 163
כתם 163
כתנת 101, 124
כתר 45, 46, 183
לג 117
לט 117
לפיד 71

*Index of Words from Ancient Languages*     301

לשם 122
מאום 164
מאכל 83
מאמר 38, 52, 62, 104, 155
מבצר 33, 61, 141
מדע 72, 73
מום 164
מושב 43
מזח 109
מחיר 73
מטה 54
מטמן 34
מכתב 26
מלך 29, 81, 83
מלכות 29
מלצר 73
מנזר 73
מעוז 33, 61
מצנפת 127
מצוה 38, 52, 62, 104, 155
מקדש 64, 100
מקל 54
מרקח 124
משׂגב 33, 61
משחת 26
משל 28, 50, 105, 108
משנה 53, 106
נוצר 73
נזם 41, 119
נחשת 219
נטף 118
ניסן 27
*נכס 104
נפך 124
נציב 28, 50, 99, 105, 108
נשתון* 104
סדין 101, 131
סוס 29, 46, 47, 105, 158, 189
סחרת 48
סיון 27
*סם 124, 219
ספיר 126
ספל 120, 123
סריס 48, 49, 81, 175
עבד 49, 81
עדי 89, 109, 112, 121, 124, 126, 128, 129, 133
עור 131
אושי 174
עזה 35

ענב 59
עטרה 45
עפר 30, 31, 60
עשׂב 124
עת 39
פאר 127
פור 49
פח* 127
פחה 50, 51, 105, 173
פטדה 89, 128
פלגש 51, 159
פקיד 28, 50, 105, 108
פרכת 215
פרשגן 106
פרתמים 52, 83
פת־בג 83, 84, 179, 180
פתגם 52, 155
פתשגן 53
פשת 44, 54, 111, 131
צבוע 55, 133
צבי 36
צי 84
צנפה 129
קבעת 115
קרן 85, 128, 163, 213
קשר 109
רכש 46, 54, 105
רמך* 54
רמון 128, 129, 213
רקע 127
רשש 90
שאר 158
שבו 129
שכר 73
שׂימה 99
שׂר 28, 50, 108
שבט 54
שהלים 215
שהם 215, 219
שומר 73
שור 87, 88, 129, 213, 214
שושן 36
שחלת 215
שטה 130, 219, 223, 224
שם 254
שמן 219
שפחה 51
שפר 126
שרביט 54, 183
שש 54, 55, 131, 216, 218, 219

תולע 31, 111
תורה 38, 62
תחרא 131
תחש 131, 132, 218, 219
תירוש 91
תכלת 55, 133, 219
תם 254
תרשיש 89, 90, 109, 133, 166
תרשתא 108

HATTIC
*windu* 25

HITTITE
*argaman-* 32
*ipantu-* 110, 111
*kurtal-* 91
*lappiya-* 72
*nurati-* 129
*pul-* 49
*tarkummāi-* 107
*wiyana-* 25
*zaḫḫeli-* 215

HURRIAN
*kiuri 123
*nuranti* 129
*tuḫšiwe* 132

INDO-EUROPEAN
*$b^h$ers-* 82
*$d^h eh_1$-* 38
*$g^h e\underset{\cdot}{u}$-* 107
*$h_1 e\acute{k}wos$* 47
*$keh_2 rug^h$-* 69
*$t\underset{\cdot}{r}g$-* 107

INDO-IRANIAN
*$j^h ar$-* 37
*$raj̑has$* 86

IRANIAN
**apatama(m)-* 96
**ćukra-* 48
**karbaṯla-* 70
**kārūj̄-* 70
**krtar-* 92
**tṛšta-* 108
**vrda-* 37
**xrausa-* 70

LATIN
*aerarium* 35
*argemone* 32
*argemonia* 32
*agrimonia* 32
*athleta* 24
*carbasus* 44
*clepta* 24
*colere* 215
*cornu* 85
**ctunica* 101
*equus* 47
*facere* 38
*ferre* 36
*ferrum* 82
*galbanum* 118
*gaza* 35
*genus* 67
*iaspis* 122
*maragdus* 113
*minister* 74
*nauta* 24
*paelex* 51
*pellex* 51
*pirata* 24
*poeta* 24
*sambuca* 78
*sambucus* 78
*smaragdus* 113
*sycophanta* 23, 24
*taurus* 88
*tunica* 101
*vinum* 25
*zmaragdus* 113

LUWIAN
*arkaman-* 32
*asus-* 47
*azzuš-* 47
**lappit-* 72
**parza-* 82
*parzagulliya-* 82
*parzašša-* 82
**parzilli-* 82

MANICHAEAN MIDDLE PERSIAN
*brāz* 76
*r'z* 86
*s'rw'r* 80

# Index of Words from Ancient Languages

### MANICHAEAN PARTHIAN
'dy'wr  63
ptbg  83
s'rw'r  80

### MEDIAN
aspas-  47
hazār-  57
*razah-  86
suxra-  48
*-zana-  67

### OLD PERSIAN
*āčarna-  98
*āčarnakara-  98
*ādranga-āžara-  58
apadāna-  60, 139
*apara-saraka-  95
*apa-tauma-  96, 97
arštibara-  36
asas-  47
*asprna-  94
*āwāč-  174
*azaiti-  58
*azda-  58, 59
baga-  83
-bara-  36
bātugara-  92
da-  38
dahyāva-  28, 29
*dāra-  37
dāta-  38, 156
*drang-  58
drazdā-  93
*drazhda-  93
fra-  96, 106
*fraištaka-  96
*frasaka-  95
*frastāka-  96
fratama-  52
*ganza-  35, 36
gāzar-  57
hadā-  63
*hadār-  57
*hamyanak-  65
*handarža-kāra-  57
*hazārgāzara-  58
*ǰamāna-  39, 40
-ka-  96
kar-  98

kara-  98
-na-  30
nipištam-  105
nišadaya-  105
ništaya-  105
pari-  106
paruzana-  67
*pati-  83, 89
*patibaga-  83
*patičagna-  53
*patigama-  53
*patiθanhana-  53
pitav-  83
*radah-  86
*rāz-  86
*sāra-ka-  81, 95
stā-  96
tai-  89
takabara-  36
*tāyu-pātā-  89
θuxra-  48
*usprna-  94
Varkazana-  67
*visarna-  98
vispazana-  67
xšaça-  29
xšaçapāvan-  28, 29
*-dana-  67
-zana-  67

### OLD SOUTH ARABIAN
frzn  82
y'y  121

### PAHLAVI
abdom  96
drahm  100
ganǰ  35
handām  63
*nibazw  74
ništavanak  105
ram(ag)  54
rāz  86
Sarakos  81
šalwar  80
srōš  106
zaman(ak)  39
zurwan  39

PHOENICIAN
ברזל 82
זי 25
קבע 115
תרשיש 90

SANSKRIT
ajati 59
aśwas 46
hāra 37
kārpāsá 44
marakata 113
pallavaka 51
pīta 128
rahas 86
śanipriya 126
sthūrus 88

SOGDIAN
yšph 122
ynz 35
rāz 86

SUMERIAN
A.ZAG 66
*A.GAR.TAL 91
BAR 82
BARAG 215
BUR 49
DUḪ.ŠI.A 132
É.GAL 64
GADA 101
$^{GIŠ}$GUZA 43
ḪALUB 118
LU$_2$ KUG.DIM$_2$ 163
NIG$_2$.KA$_9$ 103
NURMA 129
SAL.É.GAL 87
ŠIM 125
ŠUBA 129

UGARITIC
'ib 59
'id 111
'argmn 32
b- 111
bd 111
brḏl 82
ksp 219
ssw 47
šḥlt 215
šmt 215
ṭr 88

URARTIAN
kiri 123

www.ingramcontent.com/pod-product-compliance
Lightning Source LLC
Chambersburg PA
CBHW070749020526
44115CB00032B/1583